As the financial and social costs of the war on drugs become increasingly clear, there has been renewed debate about drug control in American society. Why, for instance, do the current policies lump together more and less dangerous drugs in making possession of any illegal drug a criminal offense? And why does the United States government spend more on law enforcement to repress drug sales than on treatment for individuals who are addicted to drugs?

One alternative to the current prohibitionist policies is decriminalization—a proposal that has drawn both supporters and critics from across the political spectrum. In its most radical form, decriminalization would entail legalizing all drugs; it could, however, also mean ending the prosecution of small-scale offenses, or treating drug use as a medical rather than a criminal problem. In this volume, leading analysts of drug use and drug policy evaluate the prospects for decriminalization as well as its potential impact on public policy, law, medicine, society, and the individual.

Confronting Drug Policy

Published by the Press Syndicate of the University of Cambridge
The Pitt Building, Trumpington Street, Cambridge CB2 1RP
40 West 20th Street, New York, NY 10011-4211, USA
10 Stamford Road, Oakleigh, Melbourne 3166, Australia

First published 1993

Printed in the United States of America

Library of Congress Cataloging-in-Publication Data
Confronting drug policy / edited by Ronald Bayer, Gerald M.
  Oppenheimer.
    p. cm.
    Includes bibliographical references (p.) and index.
    ISBN 0-521-44115-3 (hc.). — ISBN 0-521-44662-7 (pbk.)
    1. Drug abuse — Government policy — United States. 2. Drug
legalization — United States. 3. Narcotics, Control of — United
States. I. Bayer, Ronald. II. Oppenheimer, Gerald M.
HV5825.C634   1993
363.4'5'0973 — dc20   93-19174
                                                           CIP

A catalog record for this book is available from the British
Library.

ISBN 0-521-44115-3 hardback
ISBN 0-521-44662-7 paperback

Confronting Drug Policy

ILLICIT DRUGS IN A FREE SOCIETY

Edited by

RONALD BAYER
GERALD M. OPPENHEIMER

MILBANK MEMORIAL FUND

CAMBRIDGE
UNIVERSITY PRESS

Contents

Foreword

THE MILBANK MEMORIAL FUND, CHARTERED IN 1905 to "improve the physical, mental and moral condition of humanity," has contributed since then to innovation in health and social policy. In its ninth decade the Fund defines its mission as informing public and private decision makers about data and ways of thinking that can improve health policy in two broad areas: the prevention of disease, especially chronic disease, and disability; and the allocation of resources for health care.

Throughout its history the Fund has sponsored publications to communicate the results of research that exemplifies its mission. Since 1923 the Fund has published a journal, The *Milbank Quarterly*, in which most of the articles in this book first appeared.

This book was planned and edited by Ronald Bayer, a member of the editorial board of The *Quarterly*. When Bayer served in 1991 as the interim editor of The *Quarterly*, he asked Gerald Oppenheimer to join him in editing this special issue.

The impetus for the special issue and the book was Ronald Bayer's conviction, as he writes in his introduction, that critical inquiry about drug policy has recently become more vigorous as a result of a renewed public debate about the effectiveness of current law prohibiting the sale and use of narcotic drugs.

The chapters in this collection address many significant issues in contemporary drug policy. Each of the chapters arrays the results of research and analysis. Each author strives for objectivity, in the tradition of the Fund and its publications program.

We hope this book contributes to discussion of new approaches to policy. The consequences of drug addiction afflict everyone in the United States, both directly and indirectly.

Samuel L. Milbank
Chairman

Daniel M. Fox
President

Introduction:
The Great Drug Policy Debate —
What Means This Thing Called
Decriminalization?

RONALD BAYER

Columbia University School of Public Health

A PROFOUND SENSE OF DISSATISFACTION CHARAC-terizes the contemporary American discussion of drug policy. From across the political spectrum a chorus of critical voices is heard, linking those who most typically see each other as ideological antagonists. Their common platform asserts that prohibitionist policies that are given force by the criminal law have failed to prevent the use of drugs, and that efforts to restrict drug use have created a plethora of social evils far worse than the problem of drug use itself. Enormous resources are expended on the effort to interdict the international and domestic commerce in drugs. The courts are clogged with defendants arrested for violating the drug laws and the jails and prisons are filled with inmates convicted of violating those laws, whether by property crimes designed to pay the inflated black-market prices of illicit drugs or by acts of violence spawned by the struggles that pervade the underground economy. The streets of the urban ghettos have become wastelands dominated by the often armed sellers, buyers, and users of drugs. HIV infection spreads among drug injectors under legal conditions that encourage the sharing of syringes and needles. Civil liberties are routinely violated as government agents prosecute the war on drugs. Only a radical change in policy, it is argued, will provide a remedy to this situation. Criminalization is a failure. Decriminalization must then be the answer.

But what means this thing called decriminalization?

Beyond the common commitment to a break with the use of the criminal law as the primary social weapon in the struggle against drug use, there is little agreement. For the minimalists among the advocates of reform, what is necessary is an end to the prosecution of people who have drugs in their possession, or who are engaged in small-scale, street-level trade. For yet others decriminalization implies the need to medicalize the problem, replacing policemen with physicians, punishment with treatment. Finally, increasingly, some have come to believe that only a maximalist conception of decriminalization can meet the challenge created by the disaster that the enforcement of prohibition has produced. Legalization of drugs and creation of a regulated market like that now prevailing for alcohol would be, from this perspective, the only effective remedy to the crisis we are facing. Each of these conceptions of decriminalization entails very different adjustments in the dominant policy perspective, carries with it very different implications for the risks of increased drug use, implies very different standards of tolerance for drug use, suggests very different roles for the functions of medicine and the criminal law.

It is a remarkable feature of the contemporary debate over the future of drug policy that it takes place with only the dimmest recognition of the extended and perspicuous discussion that centered on drug policy in the period following World War II and that all but ended in the mid-1970s. This historical amnesia is the more striking because in virtually all important respects the contemporary debate mimics what occurred in the earlier period. It is my purpose in this introduction to recall the earlier debate in order to place the current discussion into some perspective.

The Rise and Decline of the Decriminalization Debate: Post-World War II Era

For much of this century the United States has sought to confront the challenge of drug use with policies derived from a prohibitionist perspective (Musto 1973). The sale, possession, and use of controlled substances was deemed an appropriate subject of the criminal law. Punishing violators of such restrictive statutes was to serve the ends of both specific and general deterrence. Physicians were restricted from prescribing a broad range of substances that were deemed to have no legitimate clinical purpose. Therapeutic options were virtually unknown, a reflection of both profound pessimism about the ability of medicine to help the drug user and the ideological dominance of those committed to law enforcement. In the face of periodic rises in drug use, public panic ensued. At such moments the severity of the punishment of drug law violators was intensified, the latitude available to judges to impose sentences restricted.

The Liberal Challenge

In the period following World War II, when an increase in heroin addiction provoked great consternation, American liberals took up the challenge of the broad critique of American narcotics policies (Bayer 1975a). Above all else, the liberal position was an exculpatory one, eschewing notions of blameworthiness and guilt that are central to the criminalization of drug use.

The perception of the addict as a victim of blocked opportunity was derived from the sociologists, to whom liberals turned for explanations of troubling behavior and who provided so much of the academic justification for the social policies with which liberalism came to be identified (Cloward and Ohlen 1960). Like the problem of juvenile delinquency to which it was so intimately linked in the public mind, addiction suggested to liberals the need to "finish the work of the New Deal" (*Nation* 1970, 228). This theme ran like a powerful leitmotif through virtually every discussion of heroin use in the journals of liberal opinion during the 1960s and early 1970s. Thus the *Nation* stated: "Society must come to realize that it is a cause—perhaps the major cause—of the affliction that it now observes with such fear and revulsion." Dr. Joel Fort, writing in the *Saturday Review of Literature*, underscored the extent to which addiction was perceived as an indication of social distress by referring to heroin use as a "barometer" of the extent to which society was characterized by "poverty, segregation, slums, psychological immaturity, ignorance and misery" (1962, 30).

Typically, the response provoked by this understanding involved calls for the full range of social programs that would get at the "root causes" of deviancy—programs designed to attack chronic unemployment and the grinding poverty of the underclass. Decrying the resources devoted to interdiction by the Nixon administration, the *Nation* asked: "Why . . . doesn't President Nixon devote more resources to the elimination of the social and economic problems which permit large scale drug abuse to take root?" (1971, 421).

Given the openness of postwar liberalism to deterministic theories of behavior, arguments for the psychopathological theories of heroin use seemed particularly congenial. The influence of mental health professionals — psychiatrists, psychologists, and social workers — on liberalism's perception of drug use cannot be overstated. Not only did they offer to explain discordant behavior in terms that avoided notions of personal guilt, but they also promised a technology of rehabilitation untainted by the brutality of punishment. Thus, the disease concept of addiction provided liberals with a perfect mechanism for achieving the very corrective ends that conservative law enforcement approaches had failed to attain.

With addiction defined as the expression of an underlying psychological disease, liberals could propose a range of treatment alternatives to punitive incarceration. Outpatient clinics providing psychotherapy as well as inpatient, hospital-based treatment were to become, at different moments, the focus of the liberal and reformist approach to drug users. Although clinics might suffice if they could control the heroin user's behavior, quarantine in hospitals for the purpose of treatment might also be necessary to help the addict and to protect the community. Predisposed toward noncoercive solutions, liberalism was by no means unwilling to embrace the imposition of therapeutic solutions. Indeed, no less a figure than Justice William O. Douglas, the exemplar of liberal jurisprudence, wrote in *Robinson v. California*[1] that a state might determine that "the general health and welfare require that [addicts] be dealt with by compulsory treatment involving quarantine, confinement or sequestration."

But within a decade liberals had turned on such confinement as both expensive and ineffective. Writing in 1971, David Bazilon, the noted liberal U.S. Court of Appeals judge, who had done so much to open the legal process to psychiatry and the behavioral sciences, stated: "It certainly sounds more enlightened to treat the drug user than to punish him for his status. But my experience with the civil commitment process suggests that the differences between punishment and compulsory treatment do not justify the extravagant claims made" (Bazilon 1971, 48).

---

[1] *Robinson v. California* 370 U.S. 676 (1962). This case declared that imprisonment of addicts for the status of addiction constituted cruel and unusual punishment.

Medicalization of Drug Addiction

Despite the disenchantment with compulsory closed-ward treatment — a reflection of the due process transformation that was affecting the willingness to tolerate benign confinement of juvenile and mental patients — the hold of the deterministic perspective did not waver (Gostin 1991). The *Robinson* decision had embraced the conception of addiction as a disease and thus had subverted the moral foundations for the use of the criminal law. "It is unlikely that any state at this moment would attempt to make it a criminal offense for a person to be mentally ill, or a leper, or to be afflicted with venereal disease. . . . Even one day in prison would be cruel and unusual punishment for the 'crime' of having a common cold."[2] But the Court had spoken only of the *status* of addiction. Its decision had not extended the exculpatory perspective to the acts associated with that status. For almost a decade, from the mid-1960s onward, legal commentators struggled with this issue and liberal analysts had sought to broaden the meaning of *Robinson* to include those behaviors inextricably linked to the "disease of addiction" (Bayer 1978a), just as they sought to protect alcoholics from imprisonment for acts of public drunkenness. Pharmacological duress was the doctrine employed in the effort to extend *Robinson*. Whereas the Supreme Court had protected the addict as an addict from punishment, the proponents of pharmacological duress sought to extend the protective scope of the court's decision to those whose addiction compelled them to purchase illicit drugs (Lowenstein 1967). "The commission of such offenses is merely an involuntary submission to [a] compulsion" (Goldstein 1973, 153). Some went further and sought to extend the doctrine to property crimes committed to obtain narcotics on the black market (*Georgetown Law Review* 1971). Although ultimately unsuccessful before the courts, the effort to win approval for the doctrine of pharmacological duress underscored its proponents' determination to vanquish the still dominant status of the criminal law in the social response to drug use.

Paralleling the reformist assault on the theoretical and moral justifications for using criminal law in the struggle against drug abuse was a deep concern about how the efforts to incarcerate drug users and those engaged in the small-scale street-level trade in drugs were affecting the

---

[2] *Robinson v. California*, op. cit., 667.

criminal justice system itself. Long a point made by the critics of prohibition, these concerns were ultimately to find expression from individuals whose commitment to the efficient functioning of the agencies of law enforcement drew them to the minimalist conception of decriminalization. "Addicts guilty of no other crime than illegal possession of narcotics are filling the jails, prisons and penitentiaries of our country," declared Judge Morris Ploscowe in an appendix to the joint American Bar Association–American Medical Association (1963) study of the narcotics problem in 1963. Almost ten years later, when the demand for a less punitive response to drug use had begun to have some impact, a state investigation in New York stated: "The Commission could only conclude that the narcotics law enforcement efforts by the police of New York City was [sic] a failure, and a monumental waste of time, of money and manpower. The evidence was clear and compelling that the police effort was directed at the lowest type of street violator, the addict, and that the police work was having no appreciable effect upon narcotics traffic in New York City" (New York State Temporary Commission Investigation 1973, 46).

The most striking feature of the liberal challenge to the prevailing perspective on drug abuse policy was, however, not simply its embrace of the conception of addiction as a disease, and its rejection of the centrality of law enforcement to the effort to limit drug use. Rather, it was the growing belief that efforts to prohibit the use of narcotics in the treatment of the illness of addiction were a profound mistake (Bayer 1975c).

With the untoward social consequences of heroin use perceived as being largely the outgrowth of an unreasonable prohibitionist stance—one that ignored or distorted the history of the American narcotics clinics of the 1920s and the comparative social studies of England (see the article by Oppenheimer in this issue)—and with narcotic drugs seen as having a central role in the treatment of addiction, liberalism was able to launch its attack on enforced abstinence.

The Americanization of Narcotic Maintenance

In 1947 *Opiate Addiction* by Alfred Lindesmith, the sociologist and leading advocate of reform of America's narcotics policies, was published with its powerfully argued call for allowing doctors to prescribe opiates to addicts. Several years later, Rufus King, a leading reform advocate among lawyers published "The Narcotics Bureau and the Harrison Act: Jailing the Healers and the Sick" in the *Yale Law Journal* (1953). On a more popular level, *Harper's Magazine* published a reform proposal under the striking title "Make Dope Legal" (Stevens 1952).

In the period between the late 1950s and the mid-1960s reformers were increasingly vocal in their support for narcotic maintenance. That support found repeated expression in the journals of liberal opinion — *Commonweal, Commentary*, the *Nation*. The *New York Times* also spoke out editorially against the prohibitionist response to addiction. Invariably, the link between crime and drug use, so central to the prohibitionist perspective, was rejected. It was not heroin that produced crime, but rather prohibition that drove the addict to criminality. These arguments were shaped by and helped to shape the proposals of a number of reformist bodies (Berger 1956; New York Academy of Medicine 1955; American Bar Association–American Medical Association 1963).

Whether framed in terms of support for cautiously structured experiments, or in forthright calls for a nationwide network of maintenance clinics, all the proposals aired in this period, which was notable for its increasingly repressive criminal statutes and calls for compulsory closedward treatment by proponents of treatment, had in common certain significant features:

1. Although abstinence from narcotics use was held to be the preferred goal of treatment, these proposals all recognized that for some, if not all, "confirmed" addicts such a goal was unobtainable. For such addicts it was appropriate to provide minimal doses of opiates to prevent the onset of withdrawal distress. The clinical justification for maintenance was based on the assumption that addicts could be medically stabilized on narcotics and that when so stabilized they could function normally. What compelled the addict to seek narcotics was not the desire for euphoria and sedation, but rather a not fully understood psychological "imbalance."

2. None suggested that narcotic maintenance was appropriate for episodic users of heroin, or for the adolescent who had but a brief history of drug involvement. The establishment of clinics was to meet the needs only of the "deeply addicted," or "confirmed addicts." Drug-free treatment was the appropriate response to users who were less severely affected.

3. None urged that maintenance be extended to users dependent on nonnarcotic drugs—cocaine, for example.
4. The threat of diverting narcotics from appropriate clinical purposes to the illicit market was well understood. The exercise of great caution would be necessary when heroin was prescribed to addicts. Thus some proposals would have required the addict to return to the clinic for each of the four or five needed daily doses of heroin. Others would have given registered addicts up to two days of take-home supply.

Heroin maintenance was never to become a viable political option in the United States. A sanitized version of narcotic maintenance, however, was to make striking inroads through the willingness of local, state, and, most important, federal agencies to fund the rapid expansion of methadone maintenance in the early 1970s. Methadone, a synthetic, long-acting narcotic that could be taken orally, met each of the challenges posed by reformers since the end of World War II (Dole 1965). Clinics could stabilize former heroin addicts so that they were no longer driven to seek illicit sources of narcotics; they permitted medical supervision of addicts, who in the past would have been the target of police surveillance; they could undercut the need to engage in crime to purchase heroin. It is not the least of the ironies of the methadone solution that it was given important federal support during the administration of Richard Nixon, who had denounced heroin maintenance as a "concession to weakness and defeat in the drug struggle, a concession which would surely lead to the erosion of our most cherished values for the dignity of man" (quoted in Bayer 1976, 264), and that it was ultimately, if grudgingly, accepted by many black leaders who continued to denounce proposals for heroin maintenance as genocidal.

But the reality of methadone fell far short of the promise that advocates of narcotic maintenance had held out for two decades (Epstein 1974). It soon became clear that many addicts were uninterested in medically supervised care. What they wanted from narcotics was more than the stabilization of their condition. Dr. Robert Newman, director of the New York City Methadone Maintenance Program, drew the only possible conclusion:

When someone wants a heroin treatment program, when methadone maintenance is available that person is saying he or she is unwilling to give up the narcotic effect that heroin will give. If the person no longer wanted to get high, then it would really be strange that he or she would prefer to go four or five or six times a day into a clinic where somebody is going to try to find a vein and inject some heroin. (*Contemporary Drug Problems* 1973, 180).

The Limits of Medicalization

It thus appeared in the early 1970s that the medical conception of decriminalization—at least insofar as heroin was concerned—had reached its limits. It was under these circumstances that liberal Republican Nelson Rockefeller of New York State, an architect in the mid-1960s of New York's compulsory closed-ward treatment approach to drug use and strong supporter in the early 1970s of methadone maintenance, made a radical and sweeping proposal for severe recriminalization of the problem (Bayer 1974). It was also under these circumstances that there first emerged a proposal that represented a radical departure from the reformist thrust of the past six decades. Medicalization had been the centerpiece of the call for decriminalization. Now some began to urge the demedicalization of addiction; but it was demedicalization of a very different kind from what Rockefeller was pressing. Adults who wanted to use drugs, including heroin, should be as free to purchase them as they were free to purchase alcohol.

While liberals and other drug reformers had little difficulty in supporting the legalization of marijuana, which was widely used by middle-class youth and largely viewed as relatively benign, this was not the case for heroin and other "hard drugs." The radical conception of decriminalization posed severe problems for liberals, who had deeply committed themselves to the view that narcotic use reflected the profound inequities of American social life and who believed that legalization would result in a sharp rise in drug use. As a consequence, fissures developed between those committed to the libertarian and to the social welfare traditions of liberalism. Nevertheless the call for legalization did find expression in the journals of liberal opinion (Bayer 1975b).

In a January 1972 editorial, entitled "Society Is Hooked," the editors of the *Nation* called for the "legalization of hard drugs and marijuana." Significantly, however, instead of portraying maintenance as a humane solution to the problems of addiction, as was the case when proposed by reformers like Lindesmith, the editors acknowledged that their program would in all likelihood result in the "epidemic . . . spread[ing] still more rapidly" (*Nation* 1972, 99–100). Gone, too, from the radical challenge to drug policy was the earlier article of liberal faith that addicts given access to heroin would be normal, that enforced abstinence was responsible for their dysfunctional state. Like the proponents of "harm reduction" almost 20 years later, those who pressed for radical change hoped only to contain the damages caused by drug use. But no other option seemed viable. With a pessimistic air, the editors of the *Nation* noted that society as well as the addict were "hooked"; there were no quick "fixes."

The untoward consequences of prohibition for those who did not use drugs were underscored by Peter Drucker in a signed editorial in the *Saturday Review of Literature* where he argued that the "main victims of this monstrous plague" were "the 99 percent of us who are drug free" (Drucker 1972, 26–7). Here was a blunt reversal of the liberal image of the 1960s that portrayed the addict as a victim, as a tragic figure. Only by providing drugs either free or at cost could crime be brought under control. Troubled by the implications of his proposal, Drucker questioned the "morality" of his recommendation, but concluded that the greater immorality was to sustain by law the victimization of the majority by a minority.

Liberal legal theorist Herbert Packer, who had long argued that the "victimless crimes" were an inappropriate target of the criminal law, also endorsed the legalization of all drugs. In "Decriminalizing Heroin," which appeared in the *New Republic*, he wrote: "Enforcing personal morals through the criminal laws is one of this country's principal self-inflicted wounds. We can allow sick people — as we should allow nations to choose their own roads to hell if that is where they want to go — I should have thought that to be the most important lesson of liberalism" (Packer 1972, 11). As with Drucker's essay, making drugs available to those who wanted them was no longer offered as a way of assisting the addict to live a "normal life" but, rather, as a way of giving him the option of traveling the "road to hell."

Nothing more tellingly reveals the difficulty that heroin legalization presented American liberals than the prolonged conflict it engendered within the American Civil Liberties Union. As early as 1970, some within the organization had begun to insist that John Stuart Mill's dictum on the sovereignty of the individual over his or her own self-regarding behavior be applied without modification to all drug use. Thus Jeremiah Guttman, a board member of the New York Civil Liberties

Union, stated in a position paper designed to move the ACLU: "The right *not* to live should be as basic as the right to life. Whether a person chooses to end his life with a bullet through the brain, fifteen years of alcoholic indulgence, or five years of heroin should not be material" (cited in Bayer 1975b). In 1973 a committee of the board of directors of the ACLU that had considered the drug issue concluded that the libertarian commitment of the ACLU left no alternative but to endorse the freedom of adults to use narcotic and nonnarcotic drugs. The evidence it had considered had provided no justification for prohibition because no "direct" harms to others could be traced to drug use. Indeed the harm to others that could be traced to such use was a consequence of the prohibition itself. Only with those under 18 years of age was the physician to play a role as the source of a prescription for narcotics, and then only with parental consent.

This perspective, however, was not so easily accepted by the board of the ACLU, where strong social welfare concerns were raised by members fearful of the extent to which a free market in drugs would have a profound impact on the nation's ghetto poor. Three years later, after considerable debate, when the ACLU board did adopt a new policy on drugs, it was riddled with the contradictions between, on the one hand, a libertarian model of decriminalization within which heroin would be sold under a regulatory regime similar to what prevailed for alcohol, and on the other hand, a medical model, which would require the use of prescriptions. "Nothing in this policy is to be construed as placing the ACLU in opposition to reasonable restraint such as already exists with respect to the production and sale of food, liquor, cigarettes, penicillin, insulin, methadone. . . ." (cited in Bayer 1978b).

The ACLU's tortured effort to confront the problem of narcotic drugs stood in sharp contrast to the ease with which the issue was resolved by two politically conservative libertarians, Milton Friedman, the free-market economist, and Thomas Szasz, the heterodox psychiatrist well known for his claim that mental illness was a myth, who were unencumbered by the social welfare concerns of late twentieth-century American liberals.

At the very moment when the ACLU was struggling with the heroin issue, Friedman wrote in *Newsweek*: "Do we have the right to use force directly or indirectly to prevent a fellow adult from drinking, smoking or using drugs? [The] answer is no" (cited in Friedman and Friedman 1984, 138-9). Beyond his principled position, however, Friedman pointed out that the course of legalization was dictated by pragmatic concerns. Prohibition did not work. It did not prevent drug use; it made the life of both the addict and the nonaddict more miserable. Underscoring a point that would assume great salience two decades later, he concluded: "Legalizing drugs would simultaneously reduce the amount of crime and improve law enforcement. It is hard to conceive of any other single recourse that would accomplish so much to promote law and order."

Like Friedman, Thomas Szasz was not burdened by welfare liberalism's conception of addiction as determined by social deprivation. Thus he was able to articulate a position on drug use derived exclusively from adherence to a radically individualistic perspective.

Although references to the social response to addiction ran throughout Szasz's earlier, often polemical, attacks on the psychiatric establishment, his first fully developed statement on the issue appeared in *Harper's Magazine* in "The Ethics of Addiction" (Szasz 1972). Starting from the premise that individuals are capable of freely choosing among differing behavioral patterns, Szasz noted that drug use and addiction were the results of just such personal decisions. Linking the freedom to use drugs with the right to exchange freely in ideas, he asserted: "In an open society it is none of the government's business what idea a man puts into his head; likewise it should be none of the government's business what drug he puts into his body" (75). For Szasz, then, the social response to addiction was a microcosm of the struggle between collectivist and individualist values. "We can choose to maximize the sphere of action of the state at the expense of the individual or the individual at the expense of the state" (79). The willingness to prohibit the use of drugs as medically unwise, and the role of physicians in enforcing prohibition and in treating drug users against their will, comprised for Szasz a paradigmatic expression of the baleful development of the "therapeutic state."

Two years later these arguments appeared in elaborated form in the book-length polemic, *Ceremonial Chemistry: The Ritual Persecution of Drug Addicts and Pushers*. Using imagery drawn from the history of religion, Szasz argued in typically hyperbolic fashion: "What exists today is nothing less than a worldwide quasi-medical pogrom against opium and the users of opiates" (45). "I regard tolerance with respect to drugs as wholly analogous to tolerance with respect to religion" (53).

It is important not to overstate the extent to which calls for the legalization of drugs had attained explicit support during the 1970s. What gave them resonance, however, was the radical ferment among intellectuals dating from the upheavals of the 1960s, a ferment that had subjected both the practice and ideology of social control to repeated attack. The "labeling" school sought to shatter the orthodox perspective on drug use and other detested forms of behavior (Becker 1963). Society created deviance out of difference (Kitsuse 1962). The process of labeling "deviant" behavior set in motion a series of events with dire consequences for people who were labeled as well as for society. Unlike the corrective posture of the "helping professions," the sociologists associated with the "labeling" school saw in behavioral diversity an intrinsic and vital aspect of social life (Matza 1969). To those drawn to the plight of psychiatric patients, the "antipsychiatrists" like Szasz and R.D. Laing suggested that medical dominance and control were every bit as repressive as the imposition of legal sanctions (Sedgwick 1972). Coercion by physicians buttressed the agencies of social control and imposed dreadful suffering on the patient.

Finally, for those concerned about the scope of the criminal law, the effort to restrict personal behaviors that posed no direct threat to others had created a "crisis of overcriminalization" (Kadish 1968). Gambling, prostitution, drug use, sexual behavior between consenting adults — the entire range of "victimless crimes" — had been mistakenly subject to the criminal law, with terrible consequences for the courts, the prisons, police departments, and the very status of the law. "The criminal law is an inefficient instrument for imposing the good life on others" (Morris and Hawkins 1970, 2).

The intellectual ferment of the 1960s and mid-1970s exhausted itself with little by way of demonstrable impact on the radical reform of drug abuse policy. The criminal law remained dominant, although the advocates of a therapeutic model had done much to reshape the social response to drug use. The most significant reflection of the effort to medicalize heroin addiction was in the methadone maintenance programs that had been provided with a niche in the clinical panoply. As the years passed, however, the initial therapeutic optimism that accompanied the rupture with the commitment to abstinence all but vanished. Methadone clinics were increasingly viewed with hostility, as community eyesores, where addicts met to engage in the commerce in drugs including methadone itself. Another change in outlook resulted when the fashion in drug use shifted from heroin to cocaine, rendering irrelevant many of the arguments for maintenance therapy rooted in the psychopharmacology of opiate use.

Finally, liberal intellectuals lost the capacity to inform the policy agenda across the full range of domestic problems as an aggressively conservative national administration came to Washington in 1980. When a renewed assault on drug use took shape—with its battle cry of "zero tolerance"—and a revitalized commitment to law enforcement took form, directed at both the international commerce in illicit psychotropic substances and at street-level trade, little by way of broad countervailing perspective was left to express the concerns that had animated the debate in earlier years.

The Revival of the Drug Policy Debate

Although David A.J. Richards, the legal philosopher, argued in 1981 that respect for human rights necessitated legalization of drugs, albeit under the supervision of physicians (1981), and William Buckley, the editor of the conservative *National Review*, announced his support for drug legalization in 1985 (Buckley 1985), they were the exceptions. Little sustained discussion took place until 1988, when suddenly a plethora of articles appeared calling for the decriminalization of drug use. At times these articles suggested that only outright legalization of all drugs would represent a coherent response to the crisis of drug use in America's cities. Thus Arnold Trebach of the Drug Policy Foundation, a center committed to fostering reformist thought, wrote in a special symposium issue of the *American Behavioral Scientist*:

> I am now convinced that our society would be safer and healthier if all of the illegal drugs were fully removed from the control of the criminal law tomorrow. . . . I would be very worried about the possibility of future harm if that radical change took place, but less worried than I am about the reality of the present harm being inflicted every day by our current laws and policies. (1989, 254)

Others supported legalization for some drugs, medical control for others. Pete Hamill, the popular columnist, thus declared:

> After watching the results of the plague since heroin first came to Brooklyn in the early fifties, after visiting the courtrooms and the

morgues, after wandering New York's neighborhoods . . . and after consuming much of the literature on drugs, I've reluctantly come to a terrible conclusion: The only solution is the complete legalization of these drugs. (1988, 26)

Cocaine, he asserted, should be sold through liquor stores, and heroin distributed through neighborhood health stations and drug stores to "registered addicts." Hamill would, however, retain the stiffest of criminal sanctions for those who "created new junkies" by selling narcotics to those not already addicted. Finally, in a strong attack on the social costs of prohibition that appeared in the *Atlantic Monthly*, Richard Dennis (1990) called for the legalization of cocaine but not of crack, the potent and smokable cocaine derivative that had so profoundly affected ghetto life in the late 1980s.

The Concept of Harm Reduction

Unlike the earlier appeals for the medical model of decriminalization that were predicated on a conception of narcotic addiction as a disease requiring the provision of maintenance doses as a form of treatment, support for medical intervention in the current period has assumed a different character. Borrowing from the experience and diction of Europe—but especially from Great Britain and Holland—reformers have embraced the concept of harm reduction (see the article by Oppenheimer in this issue). From this perspective the physician's role is not so much to treat—or normalize—the addict by providing drugs. Rather the task is to limit the potential injury associated with drug use. Thus, it became possible to consider the prescription of cocaine and other drugs in the hopes that the patient would be guided toward less self-destructive behavior. There is here no pretense of therapy, in the conventional sense.

From across the political spectrum the call for decriminalization has drawn support. U.S. District Court judge Robert Sweet (Kleiman and Saiger 1990) and Baltimore's black mayor, Kurt Schmoke (1989), have each denounced the prohibitionist strategy. Stephen J. Gould, writing in *Dissent* (1990), and Taylor Branch, in the *New Republic* (1988), have both issued attacks on the use of the criminal law. Most remarkable and in sharp contrast to the linkage between liberalism and drug reform in the 1950s, 1960s, and 1970s, noted conservatives in surprising numbers have been drawn to the reformist banner. The *National Review* has provided its pages to those who have claimed that decriminalization is a cause to which conservatives should give their support. Echoing the position first enunciated by Milton Friedman almost two decades earlier, D. Keith Mano wrote:

> Drug prohibition violates individual freedom . . . and the Jeffersonian pursuit principle. The *National Review* has done much to confer seriousness on the legalization debate and understandably, I think, it is a conservative issue at base. . . . Drug commerce between one consenting adult and another is nobody else's business. And a free market mechanism should obtain. Instead our welfare socialist approach has given monopoly privilege to organized crime by default. (1990,52)

Nothing more distressed the conservative proponents of decriminalization than the commitment of the Reagan and Bush administrations to the ever greater reliance on the instruments of legal repression in the "war on drugs," a strategy that could only result in the enhancement of state power and the withering of freedom. In an open letter to William Bennett, the nation's "drug czar," Milton Friedman sought to recall the common principles that united conservatives in their opposition to the statist programs of their liberal opponents:

> The path you propose of more police, more jails, use of the military in foreign countries, harsh penalties for drug users and a whole panoply of repressive measures can only make a bad situation worse. The drug war cannot be won by those tactics without undermining the human liberty and individual freedom that you and I cherish. (cited in Reinarman and Levine 1990)

To cultural conservatives who rejected the radical individualism so central to libertarians of whatever political stripe, and whose ideological roots could be traced to Burke rather than Mill, all such characterizations of the effort to repress drug use were profoundly mistaken, subverting the prospects of human virtue upon which the very existence of civic life in a democratic society was dependent (Kleiman and Saiger 1990). Thus was William Bennett archly critical of the intellectuals and fellow conservatives who would desert the struggle against drug use.

> Drug use—especially heavy drug use—destroys human character. It destroys dignity and autonomy, it burns away the sense of responsi-

bility, it makes a mockery of virtue. . . . Libertarians don't like to hear this. . . . Drugs are a threat to the life of the mind. . . . That's why I find the surrender to arguments for drug legalization so odd and so scandalous. (1990, 32).

Although their arguments are rooted in a very different political perspective on American social life, black leaders have been equally vehement in their reaction against the calls for decriminalization and especially toward the maximalist call for legalization. In part a reflection of the cultural conservatism of the black clergy, this response also reflects the despair of those who have seen their communities devastated by drug use and the drug wars and who fear that legalization would represent nothing more than the determination to write off an expendable population. Committed as they are to greater public expenditures for treatment, many leaders have denounced as genocidal the calls for legalization of drugs, and even for halfway measures motivated by the philosophy of harm reduction (Dalton 1989).

The Debate over Costs

Despite the expected ideological exchanges provoked by the call for fundamental drug policy reform, the crucial and most dramatic feature of the debate over decriminalization in the late 1980s has been the extent to which it has *not* been shaped by reference to issues of liberty and the role of the state as the guarantor of social cohesion. Rather a set of more prosaic concerns has dominated the debate: the social costs generated by the very effort to limit the social costs of drug use. Cost–benefit analysis has provided the yardstick of analysis (Warner 1991). It is the willingness to embrace that social accounting technique and to employ its apparently nonideological methods that has united the liberal and conservative critics of the status quo.

If the maximalist, radical option of legalization has drawn more support in the late 1980s than at any moment since the imposition of prohibition in the century's second decade, the structure of the argument made against the use of the criminal law has not changed much since the challenge to criminalization gained some currency in the post-World War II era. Indeed, if anything is striking about the contemporary debate, it is how reminiscent it is of earlier conflicts, despite its markedly more sophisticated character.

Although the upsurge of critical analysis had already begun, the appearance in the fall of 1989 of Ethan Nadelmann's "Drug Prohibition in the United States: Costs, Consequences and Alternatives" in *Science* marked an important juncture. Like those who preceded him, he painstakingly detailed the costs of drug prohibition. Vast expenditures—estimated at $10 billion in 1987—corruption, crime, violence, the spread of HIV infection, international misadventures could all be traced to the effort to suppress drug use and commerce. When balanced against the achievements, the price was for Nadelmann beyond all reason. But what of the potential costs that would follow upon legalization? Would drug use and, more important, the most disabling forms of drug use increase? These are questions that Nadelmann approaches with some caution. His conclusions, however, are unmistakable: the risks of pursuing such an agenda have been exaggerated, even grossly distorted; the costs of not advancing a reform agenda—of legalizing cocaine, heroin, and "other relatively dangerous drugs"—are too great. Legalization would not only produce enormous benefits for society in general, and America's ghettos in particular, but would enhance the health and quality of life of drug users who would be assured of access to drugs whose purity could be vouchsafed through government regulation.

Nothing more tellingly distinguishes the proponents of legalization and their antagonists than the very different estimations of the potential consequences that might attend an end to prohibition (Inciardi and McBride 1990). James Q. Wilson's "Against the Legalization of Drugs," which appeared in *Commentary* magazine, represents a forthright challenge to Nadelmann's optimistic characterization. Legalization, Wilson asserts, almost certainly would produce a vast increase in drug use with devastating impacts on the most vulnerable. There would be terrible implications for American social life. With a shallow bow to his critics, Wilson concludes:

> I may be wrong. If I am, then we will needlessly have incurred heavy costs in law enforcement and some forms of criminality. But if I am right and the legalizers prevail anyway, then we will have consigned millions of people, hundreds of thousands of infants, and hundreds of neighborhoods to a life of oblivion and disease. . . . Will we in the name of an abstract individualism and with the false comfort of suspect predictions decide to take the chance that somehow individual decency can survive amid a more general level of degradation? (1990, 28)

The current great debate over drug prohibition is being conducted in the face of an irreducible level of uncertainty about the potential consequences of legalization. Although the antagonists each acknowledge that there are many unknowns about the consequences of taking even modest steps toward legalization, they bring fundamentally, and in most instances, unbridgeable assumptions about how the risks and benefits of reform should be weighed.

Conclusion

Despite the fact that the range of advocates for decriminalization is broader now than at any point in more than a decade, and that the coalition favoring a maximalist strategy of legalization is more vital than it has ever been since prohibition was instituted in the early part of the century, there is little reason to believe that the demand for radical change will have an immediate impact on policy. In fact, the prospects for even minimalist steps toward decriminalization are far weaker than in the 1970s when, under the threat of returning heroin-addicted Vietnam soldiers, the U.S. government made a major commitment to the medical management of addiction, and when middle-class pressure moved the decriminalization of marijuana use and possession toward becoming a politically viable option in a number of states and local jurisdictions. Indeed, it is no small irony that the current move for decriminalization has arisen precisely at a moment when America may have entered a neoprohibitionist era, one in which the social tolerance for the use of intoxicants—both licit and illicit—may be declining.

What, then, is the significance of the debate over decriminalization? First, and perhaps most important, the sharp assault on the contours of American drug policy has exposed the profound imbalance between public expenditures for law enforcement designed to repress drug sales and use and the funds available for the treatment of individuals whose drug dependency has resulted in personal misery. Even some who reject the need for radical change now recognize that current efforts to support the treatment of drug users who express an interest in managing their addiction to opiates through methadone maintenance or in achieving abstinence from other drug use are grossly inadequate.

Second, the decriminalization debate has forced a consideration of the rationality of policies that currently prohibit the use of a wide range of drugs. By compelling a discussion of the extent to which our conventions have brought us to define some drugs as licit and others as illicit, causing us mistakenly to lump relatively less damaging drugs with more harmful substances, the proponents of decriminalization may foster a more reasoned discussion of public policy.

Finally, the advocates of decriminalization, no matter how limited or expansive their goals, have served to underscore the enormous economic and human costs of current prohibitionist policies. In so doing they have encouraged the search for alternatives to repression: the willingness of a number of state and local governments to tolerate or fund needle exchange programs in an effort to interdict the spread of HIV infection provides a striking example of such newly found openness.

In the end, the call for decriminalization — however broadly or narrowly defined — has revitalized the public debate over the fundamental structure of American drug policy. It has thus made possible a serious examination of the appropriate role of the state in regulating the behavior of competent adults, as well as its obligation to foster the conditions necessary for the existence of civic life and to provide care for the most vulnerable and even for the most socially despised. Perhaps more important, the decriminalization debate has shattered — if only for a moment — the dead weight of tradition that for more than a decade served to close off the possibility of critical inquiry. It is to the spirit of such inquiry that the two *Milbank Quarterly* issues on drug policy are devoted.

References

American Bar Association and American Medical Association. 1963. Drug Addiction: Crime or Disease? *Interim and Final Reports of the Joint Committee of the American Bar Association and the American Medical Association on Narcotic Drugs.* Bloomington: Indiana University Press.

Bayer, R. 1974. Repression, Reform and Drug Abuse: An Analysis of the Response to the Rockefeller Drug Law Proposals of 1973. *Journal of Psychedelic Drugs* 6:299–309.

————. 1975a. Liberal Opinion and the Problem of Heroin Addiction: An Examination of the Organs of Cultural Expression, 1960–1973. *Contemporary Drug Problems* 4:93–112.

————. 1975b. Drug Stores, Liquor Stores, and Heroin: An Analysis of the Libertarian Debate. *Contemporary Drug Problems* 4:459–82.

————. 1975c. Heroin Maintenance, the Vera Proposal and Narcotics

Reform: An Analysis of the Debate, 1971–1973. *Contemporary Drug Problems* 4:297–322.

———. 1976. Drug Addiction and Liberal Social Policy: The Limits of Reform. Ph.D. dissertation, University of Chicago. (Unpublished)

———. 1978a. Addiction, Criminal Culpability and the Penal Sanction: A Perspective on the Liberal Response to Repressive Social Policy. *Crime and Delinquency* (March):221–32.

———. 1978b. Heroin Decriminalization and the Ideology of Tolerance: A Critical View. *Law and Society Review* 12:301–18.

Bazilon, D.L. 1971. Drugs That Turn on the Law. *Journal of Social Issues* 27:47–52.

Becker, H. 1963. *The Outsiders*. New York: Free Press.

Bennett, W.J. 1990. Drug Wars: Drug Policy and the Intellectuals. *Police Chief* (May):30–6.

Berger, H. 1956. The Richmond County Medical Society's Plan for the Control of Narcotics Addiction. *New York State Journal of Medicine* 56:888–94.

Branch, T. 1988. Let Koop Do It. *New Republic* (October 24):22.

Buckley, W.F. 1985. Does Reagan Mean It? *National Review* 37:54.

Cloward, R.A., and K. Ohlen. 1960. *Delinquency and Opportunity: A Theory of Delinquent Gangs*. New York: Free Press.

Contemporary Drug Problems. 1973. Heroin Maintenance: A Panel Discussion. (Spring):165–200.

Dalton, H.D. 1989. AIDS in Blackface. *Daedalus* 118 (Summer):205–27.

Dennis, R.J. 1990. The Economics of Legalizing Drugs. *Atlantic Monthly* (November):126–32.

Dole, V.P. 1965. A Medical Treatment for Diacetyl-Morphine (Heroin) Addiction. *Journal of the American Medical Association* 193:646–50.

Drucker, P. 1972. How to Take the Profit Out of Hard Drugs. *Saturday Review of Literature* (May 13):26–7.

Epstein, E.J. 1974. Methadone: The Forlorn Hope. *Public Interest* (Summer):3–23.

Fort, J. 1962. Addiction: Fact or Fiction. *Saturday Review of Literature* (September 18):30–1.

Friedman, M., and R. Friedman. 1984. *The Tyranny of the Status Quo*. San Diego, Calif.: Harcourt, Brace, Jovanovich.

Georgetown Law Review. 1971. Emerging Recognition of Pharmacological Duress as a Defense to Possession of Narcotics: Watson v. United States. (February):761–76.

Goldstein, R.M. 1973. The Doctrine of Pharmacological Duress: Critical Analysis. *New York University Review of Law and Social Change* (Spring):141–58.

Gostin, L. 1991. Compulsory Treatment for Drug-dependent Persons: Justifications for a Public Health Approach to Drug Dependency. *Milbank Quarterly* 69(4):561–94

Gould, S.J. 1990. Taxonomy as Politics: The Harm of False Classification. *Dissent* (Winter):73–8.

Hamill, P. August 15, 1988. Facing Up to Drugs: Is Legalization the Solution? *New York* (August 15):21–7.

Inciardi, J.A., and D.C. McBride. 1989. Legalization: A High-Risk Alternative in the War on Drugs. *American Behavioral Scientist* 32:259–89.

Kadish, S. 1968. The Crisis of Over-Criminalization. *American Criminal Law Quarterly* 7:18–34.

King, R. 1953. The Narcotics Bureau and the Harrison Act: Jailing the Healers and the Sick. *Yale Law Journal* 69:736–49.

Kitsuse, J. 1962. Societal Reactions to Human Deviance. *Social Problems* 9:247–56.

Kleiman, M.A.R., and A.J. Saiger. 1990. Drug Legalization: The Importance of Asking the Right Question. *Hofstra Law Review* 18:527–65.

Lindesmith, A. 1947. *Opiate Addiction*. Bloomington, Ind.: Principia Press. (*Addiction and Opiates*, 2d ed., published in 1968. Chicago: Aldine.)

Lowenstein, R. 1967. Addiction, Insanity and Due Process of Law: An Examination of the Capacity Defense. *Harvard Civil Rights–Civil Liberties Law Review* (Fall):125–65.

Mano, D.K. 1990. Legalize Drugs. *National Review* (May 28):49–52.

Matza, D. 1969. *Becoming Deviant*. Englewood Cliffs, N.J.: Prentice-Hall.

Morris, N., and G. Hawkins. 1970. *The Honest Politician's Guide to Crime Control*. Chicago: University of Chicago Press.

Musto, D. 1973. *The American Disease: Origins of Narcotic Control*. New Haven, Conn.: Yale University Press.

Nadelmann, E.A. 1989. Drug Prohibition in the United States: Costs, Consequences, and Alternatives. *Science* 245:939–46.

Nation. 1970. The Menace and the Malady. (September 21): 228–9.

———. 1971. Opium: Sweeping the Sands. (November 1): 421.

———. 1972. Society Is Hooked. (January 24): 99–100.

New York Academy of Medicine, Committee on Public Health. 1955. Report on Drug Addiction I. *Bulletin of the New York Academy of Medicine* 31:592–607.

New York State Temporary Commission of Investigation. 1973. Interim Report Concerning the Operation of the Special Narcotics Parts of the Supreme Court, April 29. (Mimeo)

Packer, H.L. 1972. Decriminalizing Heroin. *New Republic* (June 3): 11–13.

Reinarman, C., and H.G. Levine. February 1990. A Peace Movement Has Emerged Against the War on Drugs. *Footnotes* 18(2).

Richards, D.A.J. 1981. Drug Use and the Rights of the Person: A Moral Argument for Decriminalization of Certain Forms of Drug Use. Symposium on Punishment: Critiques and Justifications. *Rutgers Law Review* 33:607–86.

Schmoke, K.L. 1989. First Word. *Omni* 11:8.

Sedgwick, P. 1972. R.C. Laing: Self, Symptom and Society. In *R.D. Laing and Anti-Psychiatry*, eds. R. Boyers and R. Orvill. New York: Harper & Row.

Szasz, T. 1972. The Ethics of Addiction. *Harper's Magazine* (April): 74–9.

———. 1974. *Ceremonial Chemistry: The Ritual Persecution of Drugs, Addicts, and Pushers.* New York: Anchor Books.

Stevens, A. 1952. Make Dope Legal. *Harper's Magazine* (November):40–7.

Trebach, A.S. 1989. Tough Choices: The Practical Politics of Drug Policy Reform. *American Behavioral Scientist* 32:249–58.

Warner, K.E. 1991. Legalizing Drugs: Lessons from (and about) Economics. *Milbank Quarterly* 69(4):641–62

Wilson, J.Q. February 1990. Against the Legalization of Drugs. *Commentary* (February):21–8.

The Social Demography of Drug Use

DENISE B. KANDEL

Columbia University; New York State Psychiatric Institute

E XCELLENT DATA BASES EXIST IN THE UNITED STATES to assess the extent of use of various drugs in the population and changes in patterns of use over time. Because of the striking increase in drug use during the 1970s, with its potential associated health hazards, particularly to young people, the federal government has played an important role in initiating and supporting systematic data-gathering efforts. However, most monitoring efforts have focused on the epidemiology of patterns of drug use rather than abuse and/or dependence and have examined drug use as a behavior rather than a clinical state.

In this review, I describe (1) overall current patterns of the use of mood-changing legal and illegal drugs; (2) the epidemiology of substance use disorders; (3) trends over time in patterns of use; and (4) variations in subgroups of the population—by sex, age, geographic location, socioeconomic status, and ethnicity.

The prevalence, patterns, and trends in nonmedical drug use can be assessed from two types of data: (1) data systems that compile statistics based on individuals whose drug use has brought them to the attention of official medical, treatment, or legal agencies; (2) surveys designed to determine the extent of various types of drug use in the noninstitutionalized population.

I will review the major sources of data briefly in order to highlight their strengths and limitations. Several data systems are ongoing and provide important information about trends in use over time. Major changes in these systems were implemented in 1991.

Data Sources

Institutional Data Systems

The two major institutional data systems ongoing at this time monitor medical and criminal drug-related cases.

The Drug Abuse Warning Network (DAWN), established in 1972, monitors the consequences of drug abuse using two indicators: drug-related hospital emergency room visits and drug-related deaths recorded in medical examiners' offices. Through 1990 information was obtained from 770 hospital emergency rooms, located primarily in 21 metropolitan areas, and from 87 medical examiners with offices in 37 metropolitan areas throughout the United States. (Over the last several years, the panel of hospitals was changed to a national representative sample of emergency rooms.) For several years, drug-related deaths occurring in New York City were not included in the data because of incomplete reporting by the medical examiner's office, which resumed reporting in 1988 (National Institute on Drug Abuse 1988b; 1990e; 1991d,e). Beginning in 1991, for the first time national estimates of drug-related admissions to emergency rooms were released by the National Institute on Drug Abuse (NIDA) for 1989, 1990, and 1991 (1991g; 1992).

The Drug Use Forecasting program (DUF), which was established in 1986 by the National Institute of Justice to measure the rates of drug use among persons arrested for serious crimes, included 22 participating cities in 1989. The DUF sample, however, is not at this time a national probability sample of arrestees. Drug use assessments are based on urinalysis for ten drugs, including cocaine, marijuana, phencyclidine (PCP), methamphetamine, heroin, and opium (National Institute of Justice 1990; 1991). The urine tests can detect most drugs used within the previous two or three days, and up to several weeks later for marijuana and PCP.

Periodic data on the scope and capabilities (e.g., services, slots) of drug and alcohol treatment and prevention programs in public and private agencies in the United States are currently provided by the National Drug and Alcohol Treatment Unit Survey (NDATUS), a point prevalence survey sponsored by NIDA and the National Institute on Alcohol Abuse and Alcoholism (NIAAA) and carried out intermittently since 1974. The two most recent surveys, conducted in 1987 and 1989, provide very limited information on the age, sex, and race/ethnicity of clients in the reporting units (National Institute on Drug Abuse 1989b; 1990e).

A continuing treatment-based monitoring system (the Client Data System) will be operative in 1992 and will provide regular and comprehensive data on clients in drug treatment programs (NIDA Notes 1991). Such data have not been systematically available since 1982, when the implementation of the block grant system eliminated federal mandatory requirements for reporting client admissions to the Client Oriented Data Acquisition Process (CODAP). Only a small number of selected states continued to submit data voluntarily to CODAP. As a result, comprehensive data on individuals currently in treatment are not available, and trend data are available only for a select subsample of states in a truncated period of time from 1979 to 1984.

These institutional data are based upon selected members of the drug-using population: those who are experiencing medical problems, are seeking treatment, have come to the attention of the criminal justice system, or have died from drug abuse. Institutional reporting can be spotty and uneven. Except for deaths, the data reflect counts of episodes or incidents and not individuals, which means that the extent of multiple admissions cannot be assessed in most cases. In addition, the population base from which the cases are drawn is not defined, making it impossible to ascertain what proportions of the general population and of various subgroups of users are represented by these data. Not only is the numerator ill defined in terms of independent individual units, but there is also no denominator.

Large-scale Surveys: The Epidemiology of Substance Use

Several large-scale population surveys of drug use, which include questions about the use of different classes of illicit drugs, were initiated in the early 1970s under the impetus of the National Commission on Marijuana and Drug Abuse. Most of our recent knowledge derives from two major continuing nationwide monitoring efforts sponsored by NIDA: the National Household Survey on Drug Abuse and Monitoring the Future. These two epidemiologic programs are evolving over time in order to provide data on groups that were previously either unrepresented or represented in numbers too small to provide stable estimates.

The National Household Survey on Drug Abuse is based on repeated cross-sectional household surveys of national multistage probability samples of household residents 12 years old and over, and has been carried out every two or three years up to 1988 and annually as of 1990 (National Institute on Drug Abuse 1991c). There have been eleven surveys since 1971. The drug questions are self-administered by respondents and the answers placed in a sealed envelope. To provide more precise estimates for certain subgroups in the population, in 1991 the sample was enlarged to over 32,000 respondents (National Institute on Drug Abuse 1991f). For the first time, six metropolitan areas were oversampled and persons living in college dormitories and homeless shelters, as well as civilians residing in military installations, were included in the sample. The last two surveys included an oversample of blacks and Hispanics to provide stable race-specific rates, which up to now have not been readily available. Larger sample sizes in these strata give rise to smaller standard errors and more precise parameter estimates.

Monitoring the Future uses a sophisticated cohort-sequential design, in which new cohorts of high school seniors are surveyed annually and a subsample of each cohort is followed over time. Initiated in 1975 by the Institute of Survey Research of the University of Michigan, the study involves successive annual surveys of over 16,000 high school seniors, drawn from 130 public and private schools throughout the United States, who answer structured, self-administered questionnaires in their classrooms; and biannual longitudinal mail follow-ups of 2,000 to 3,000 former students drawn from each senior cohort (Johnston, O'Malley, and Bachman 1991). There now have been 16 annual surveys. As of 1991, Monitoring the Future includes eighth and tenth graders, as well as twelfth graders.

These two studies are based on representative samples of the general population or well-defined population segments and have used the same methodology over time. Changes in reported rates of drug use can be attributed to changes in individuals' behaviors (or perhaps changes in the willingness to report drug use) rather than being confounded with changes in methods.

In addition to these regular monitoring activities, NIDA sponsors one-time data-collection efforts designed to assess drug use in special populations. These include the addition of questions on drug use in the 1988 National Maternal and Infant Health Survey and a National Pregnancy and Health Survey, designed to estimate the number of drug-exposed babies, which will be fielded in 1992. The Washington, DC,

Metropolitan Area Drug Study, initiated in 1990 as a series of 16 studies, aims to collect information on hidden and hard-to-reach populations, such as school dropouts, the homeless, and institutionalized populations. As of this writing, no data are available from any of these more specialized studies. Periodic national surveys also focus on a single legal drug, either smoking (e.g., National Center for Health Statistics 1989) or alcohol (Hilton 1988). Since 1980, the Department of Defense has sponsored four surveys of drug use among active military personnel worldwide (Bray et al. 1988). Because of the inclusion of a broad spectrum of substances and the repeated waves of data collection, I will discuss almost exclusively population-based data derived from the two NIDA-sponsored ongoing surveys.

In these surveys, respondents are typically asked whether they have ever used each class of drugs of interest and how frequently they have used each within specified periods of time. An individual is defined as a user if he or she reports having used the drug at least once. Rarely are questions included about problems related to drug use or any other information that could provide a basis for relating patterns of use to clinical syndromes. Limited questions regarding drug-related problems and dependence have been included in the household surveys beginning in 1985. However, these surveys provide excellent information about the prevalence of drug use in the general population, the distribution of users among different sociodemographic groups, and trends over time. Although these data provide information on the population at risk for problems of substance abuse, they offer little information about the extent of this risk.

The ECA Studies: Epidemiology of Substance Abuse Disorders

By contrast, in the early 1980s, the National Institute of Mental Health (NIMH) sponsored an epidemiologic program of research designed to measure the extent of psychiatric disorders in the American population, both household residents and persons in institutions or other group quarters, based on criteria specified by the American Psychiatric Association to define these disorders (American Psychiatric Association 1980; 1987). The criteria were incorporated in a structured interview administered by lay interviewers: the Diagnostic Interview Schedule (DIS). The Epidemiologic Catchment Area study (ECA) was implemented from

1980 to 1984 in five sites in the United States: New Haven, St. Louis, Baltimore, Durham, and Los Angeles (Robins and Regier 1991). A notable feature of the ECA is that the community sample was supplemented by a sample of individuals in institutions, drug and alcohol treatment centers, nursing homes, chronic hospitals, psychiatric hospitals, and prisons to provide more correct estimates of the prevalence of various disorders (Regier et al. 1990). Algorithms were developed to identify cases according to the nosologic rules presented in the third edition of the *Diagnostic and Statistical Manual of Mental Disorders* (DSM–III), using the version that was most current at the time the studies were conducted (American Psychiatric Association 1980; 1987). Because case identification in these community samples is not biased by factors leading individuals into treatment, the studies provide excellent information about the prevalence of various psychiatric disorders, including substance abuse disorders. However, because the ECA studies did not contain the usual measures of patterns of drug behavior included in the traditional epidemiologic drug surveys, the number of individuals who ever used specific classes of drugs and are therefore at risk for abuse of these drugs is mostly not available. In the ECA, the number of individuals who ever used *any* illicit drug was ascertained, but not those who ever used *each specific* class of illicit drugs.

Specific items were included in the interview schedule to measure the major groups of symptoms required for a diagnosis of substance use disorder, abuse and/or dependence, as specified in DSM–III. Substance use disorders subsume alcohol and other drug-related disorders. (In line with accepted terminology [e.g., Anthony and Helzer 1991], I use the term "drug abuse/dependence" to refer to disorders involving an illicit drug or the nonmedical use of substances that should only be used by medical prescription.) Substance abuse involves pathological use, impairment in social or psychological functioning resulting from substance use, and minimal duration of disturbance of at least one month. The more severe diagnosis of substance dependence requires tolerance or withdrawal for all substances, as well as pathological use or impairment in social or psychological functioning for alcohol dependence and cannabis dependence (slightly different criteria are specified for tobacco dependence) (American Psychiatric Association 1980; 163–4). In DSM–III, the diagnosis of abuse can be made for all classes of psychoactive drugs; the diagnosis of dependence can be made for all drugs, except cocaine, PCP, and hallucinogens. These diagnoses can be exclusive or concurrent. In DSM–IIIR,

by contrast, the same diagnostic rules apply to all classes of drugs, dependence requires the presence for one month of any three of nine
symptoms, and drug abuse becomes a residual category (American Psychiatric Association 1987; Kosten and Kosten 1990).

Preliminary results from the ECA were first published in 1984. More
detailed findings, especially for substance use disorders, were reported
only recently in *Psychiatric Disorders in America* (Robins and Regier
1991). I will draw heavily from one chapter in that volume, "Syndromes
of Drug Abuse and Dependence," by Anthony and Helzer.

Advantages and Limitations of the Epidemiologic Approach

These surveys, as well as others, are based on large, representative samples and, despite their limitations, have provided unique information
and new insights about the epidemiology of drug behavior.

By focusing on unselected samples rather than on the most extreme
and deviant groups included in treatment programs or clinical practices,
epidemiologic studies provide normative data from which new understanding of drug behavior can be gained. Especially when the studies are
based on large representative samples of the general population, epidemiologic data provide information on the distribution of the phenomenon in the population free from selection and referral bias into
treatment. Longitudinal studies, which follow individuals over time, enable researchers to assess the natural history of involvement across the life
span of individuals, to study changes in patterns of use over time and
among different groups, and to identify the risk factors and consequences of drug involvement. Epidemiologic data help refine nosologic
classifications and form a basis for assessment of the extent of comorbidity in the population, as well as the need for services.

It must be emphasized, however, that surveys based on household or
school samples generally exclude the individuals most likely to be involved in nonconforming activities, including drug use: those without
regular addresses, the homeless, the school absentees or dropouts, or
persons living in institutions (Ginsberg and Greenley 1978; Johnston,
O'Malley, and Eveland 1978; Johnston, O'Malley, and Bachman 1991;
Kandel 1975). Because these deviant individuals presumably constitute a

relatively small proportion of the general population, however, their exclusion does not significantly bias the overall epidemiologic estimates reported (see Clayton and Voss 1982; Kandel 1975), although the less frequently used drugs and the heaviest patterns of use may be underrepresented. The National Household Survey was expanded in 1991 in an effort to address this problem and to include certain of these hard-to-reach and/or institutionalized subgroups. Another limitation of the data is that self-reports of sensitive behaviors, such as drug use, may be subject to reporting bias, which is not randomly distributed throughout the population. In particular, blacks appear to be more likely than other ethnic groups to underreport their use of illicit drugs when it is infrequent (Mensch and Kandel 1988a).

The two types of measures—patterns of drug use and diagnostic assessments for drug use disorders—have not yet been included simultaneously in these national investigations. It is important, however, to assess the rates of drug use disorders among individuals who have ever used each class of drugs. The monitoring surveys, Monitoring the Future and the National Household Survey on Drug Abuse, provide very good information about the denominator, that is, the population of users who are at risk for abuse. The ECA provides very good data on the numerator: the population of abusers. Currently, it is very difficult to combine the two types of information and estimate the risk of dependence or abuse among those who ever experimented with specific drugs. Two newly initiated investigations promise to provide the necessary data: a study of the comorbidity of psychiatric disorders, directed by Ronald Kessler at the University of Michigan (Kessler 1990), and the National Longitudinal Alcohol Epidemiologic Survey, which was initiated in 1991 by the NIAAA and directed by Bridget Grant and Thomas Harford. This is a very ambitious three-wave longitudinal study of alcohol, substance use, and related disorders in a national panel of over 50,000 individuals.

Prevalence of Drug Use

Because patterns of use vary greatly over time, it is essential when examining the data to take account of the year of data collection. I will discuss only selected findings and trends in this chapter.

Overall Prevalence

The rates of self-reported experiences with various classes of drugs provide important information about the extent of the population at risk, not only for serious substance use disorders, but also for health and psychosocial consequences associated with patterns of use that do not necessarily meet criteria for abuse or dependence. Indeed, these consequences appear to increase linearly with degree of drug involvement (Kandel 1984). Traditionally, the illicit usage monitored in the drug surveys includes — in addition to alcohol, cigarettes, and illegal substances — the nonmedical use of psychoactive substances, such as minor tranquilizers or stimulants, which should only be used under medical prescription.

Illustrative data are presented in table 1 for the data most recently released from the 1991 surveys both for the high school seniors (University of Michigan 1992) and the population aged 12 and over (National Insti-

TABLE 1

Lifetime Prevalence Rates of the Use of Different Drugs in 1991 among High School Seniors and in the General U.S. Population Aged 12 and Over

Substance	Percentages ever using	
	Seniors[a]	General population[b]
Alcohol	88.0	84.7
Cigarettes	63.1	72.7
Marijuana	36.7	33.4
Stimulants	15.4	7.0
Inhalants	17.6	5.6
Cocaine	7.8	11.7
Crack	3.1	1.9
Hallucinogens	9.6	8.2
Analgesics	6.6	6.1
Tranquilizers	7.2	5.6
Sedatives	6.7	4.3
Heroin	0.9	1.4
Any illicit drug	44.1	37.1
Total (N)	(15,000)	(32,594)

[a] *Source:* University of Michigan 1992, table 1
[b] *Source:* National Institute on Drug Abuse 1991f

tute on Drug Abuse 1991f,g). As of this writing, only selected data were released from the two surveys. These will be cited as appropriate and will be supplemented by data from the earlier surveys (Johnston, O'Malley, and Bachman 1991; National Institute on Drug Abuse 1990a–c). By and large, the ranking of the various classes of drugs is identical in both samples, with the exception of cocaine. Differences in the age distribution of the two samples affect the overall prevalence levels reported in each study.

Prevalence of use differs markedly for various drugs: drugs that are legal for adults — alcohol and tobacco cigarettes — are used much more frequently than illegal substances. Overall, in 1991, 44.1 percent of the high school seniors have experimented with one illicit drug; in 1991, more than one-third (37.1 percent) of the American population aged 12 and over have done so. Marijuana is the most used illicit drug in both samples. Among adolescents, stimulants and inhalants (i.e., glue and gasoline) are next in prevalence and are twice as prevalent as cocaine. Among young adults, cocaine ranks next in prevalence after marijuana, and is twice as prevalent as stimulants (table 2). Thus, among adolescents aged 12 to 17, 2.4 percent have used cocaine compared with 3.0 percent for nonmedical use of stimulants; by contrast, among those 18 to 25 years old, 17.9 percent have used cocaine and 9.4 percent have used stimulants (National Institute on Drug Abuse 1991f). This age reversal in relative ranking is explained by the fact that the age-defined period of risk for initiation into cocaine lasts into the late twenties, a longer interval than exists for most other illicit drugs, which have usually been first tried in the late teens (Raveis and Kandel 1987).

In 1991, 40 percent of the cocaine users among the high school seniors (3.1 percent) had used crack. Crack appears to have spread rapidly across different communities in the last several years. Monitoring the Future identified crack use in half the sample schools in 1986, but recorded a rise to about 76 percent in 1988 (Johnston, O'Malley, and Bachman 1989, 63).

A substantial proportion of those who have used cocaine have smoked it, especially younger users. In the 1990 National Household Survey, among those who used cocaine in the last year, 31 percent of those aged 18 to 25 and 33 percent of those aged 26 to 34 reported having freebased it, compared with 57 percent of those aged 12 to 17 (National Institute on Drug Abuse 1991c, table 4.7). Thus, the majority of young people appear to have adopted a pattern of use that is particularly harmful to

TABLE 2

Lifetime Prevalence Rates of the Use of Different Drugs in 1991
in the General Population, by Age

Drug	Percentages ever using			
	Age 12-17	Age 18-25	Age 26-34	Age 35+
Alcohol	46.4	90.2	92.4	87.5
Cigarettes	37.9	71.2	76.4	78.0
Marijuana	13.0	50.5	59.5	23.9
Stimulants	3.0	9.4	12.2	5.4
Inhalants	7.0	10.9	9.2	2.7
Cocaine	2.4	17.9	25.8	7.0
Hallucinogens	3.4	13.2	15.6	5.4
Analgesics	4.4	10.2	9.8	4.1
Tranquilizers	2.1	7.5	10.1	4.2
Sedatives	2.4	4.3	7.5	3.5
Any illicit drug	20.1	54.7	61.8	27.5
Total (N)	(8,005)	(7,937)	(8,126)	(8,526)

Source: National Institute on Drug Abuse 1991f

their health. Data from clinical treatment centers indicate that individuals who freebase use much more cocaine than those who consume cocaine in other ways (Gawin and Kleber 1985). In the general population, those who freebase or smoke cocaine report experiencing more cocaine-related problems than other types of cocaine users (Adams, Rouse, and Gfroerer 1990).

Similar rankings among the various drugs obtain in the prevalence of annual or recent use (within the last 30 days) as lifetime, except for one reversal involving daily use of cigarettes.

Daily Drug Use. As noted above, with the exception of the ECA study, which I will discuss, epidemiologic studies do not include systematic criteria that would permit the identification of cases of drug abuse or dependence meeting diagnostic criteria. Daily use is taken as a measure of sustained and regular drug use. Data for daily use are reported mainly for high school seniors in Monitoring the Future. The National Household Survey on Drug Abuse reports mostly data on weekly use.

Daily use of most illicit drugs is rare in the noninstitutionalized population. Among high school seniors, almost no daily drug use is reported, with the exception of tobacco cigarettes, alcohol, and marijuana. In 1991, almost a fifth of seniors (18.5 percent) were smoking cigarettes daily (defined as use at least 20 times in the previous 30 days). Daily use of marijuana (2.0 percent) or alcohol (3.6 percent) was lower than that of cigarettes (University of Michigan 1992, table 4). In 1990, the same proportion (2 percent) of "daily" (i.e., used 20 days or more in the past month) marijuana users (the only drug for which such data are presented from the National Household Survey) was observed among young adults in the general population 18 to 25 years old as among high school seniors in 1990 or 1991; the proportion (1.6 percent) among those aged 26 to 34 was lower (National Institute on Drug Abuse 1991c, table 3.7). A much higher proportion of young people persist in their use of cigarettes than of any other class of drugs. In 1991, the proportions of current daily users represent 29.3 percent of high school seniors who ever smoked, but 5.4 percent of those who ever used marijuana and 4.1 percent of those who ever drank alcohol.

Daily marijuana users are much more likely than other users to be extensive users of other substances (Clayton and Ritter 1985; Johnston, Bachman, and O'Malley 1981; Kandel and Davies 1991c). Daily drug users are also much more likely than nonusers to experience drug-related problems, as illustrated by data from the ECA studies, which I will discuss in greater detail below. In the ECA, 24 percent of cocaine users who had ever used cocaine daily for at least two weeks reported that they felt dependent on the drug and 28 percent reported social problems with cocaine, compared with 2 percent and 4 percent, respectively, of cocaine users who had never used cocaine daily for at least two weeks (Anthony and Trinkoff 1989, table 1).

Symptoms of Dependence. The General Household Survey on Drug Abuse attempts to assess the extent of dependence experienced by users of selected drugs in terms of five components of use in the last year: attempts to cut down on use; use in larger amounts; daily use for two or more weeks; feelings of need for the drug and dependence on it; presence of withdrawal symptoms. A substantial proportion of all the past-year users 18 years old and over report having experienced at least one such symptom in the last year: 40 percent for marijuana, 38 percent for cocaine, 31 percent for alcohol, and 85 percent for cigarettes in 1990 (based on National Institute on Drug Abuse 1991a, tables 14, 19A, 20A, 21A; 1991c, tables 1.2, 9.3–9.6). However, the proportions reporting specific feelings of dependence are lower, especially for substances other than cigarettes: 9 percent reported such symptoms for marijuana, 6 percent each for cocaine and for alcohol, but 66 percent for cigarettes. From these data, I estimate that the proportions having experienced at least one symptom represent 4.1 percent of the general population 18 years old and over for marijuana, 1.2 percent for cocaine, 22.1 percent for alcohol, and 28.0 percent for cigarettes. As we will see shortly, except for marijuana, these rates differ somewhat from those observed on the basis of DSM–III diagnostic criteria observed among persons 18 and older sampled in from 1980 to 1984 by the ECA.

Age Patterns in Drug Use

To highlight the relative popularity of different classes of drugs, data from the General Household Survey have been presented for the U.S. population for all ages combined. However, striking differences in prevalence of use can be observed over the life cycle. Illicit drug use is a phenomenon of youth. The proportion in the general population having ever used any illicit drug is twice as high among those aged 18 to 34 as among those 35 and older (table 2).

In contrast to lifetime rates, annual age-specific rates are less likely to be confounded with historical factors and more closely reflect age-related maturational patterns. In order to place the age-related patterns in a broader behavioral context, data for drugs obtained legally (such as cigarettes or alcohol) or illegally (such as marijuana or cocaine) are compared with psychoactive drugs prescribed by a physician (such as minor tranquilizers) for narrowly defined age groups. The most current data on annual use of medically prescribed minor tranquilizers are available only for 1982, the most recent year in which data on prescribed psychotropic drugs were collected. The most recent, detailed age-specific data on the use of legal and illegal drugs in the general population are available from the 1991 survey (table 3).

The age-graded nature of the use of marijuana and other illicit drugs is highlighted when the use of these drugs is compared with the socially accepted substances such as alcohol or cigarettes, on the one hand, and the medically prescribed psychotropic drugs such as minor tranquilizers, on the other. The most striking age-related pattern of use is the peaking in the use of illicit drugs in the late teens and the twenties. The highest rates overall are observed in the age span 16 to 29 for marijuana and 18

TABLE 3

Annual Prevalence Rates of Selected Licit and Illicit Substances in 1991
and Medically Prescribed Psychotropic Drugs in 1982
in the General Population, by Age

| Age | 1991 | | | | 1982: any Rx psychoactive[b] (%) | Total (N) | |
	Cigarettes[a] (%)	Alcohol[a] (%)	Marijuana[a] (%)	Cocaine[a] (%)		1991	1982
12–13	10	18	2	.4	10	(2,632)	(515)
14–15	19	40	8	1	15	(2,659)	(511)
16–17	31	62	20	3	18	(2,714)	(555)
18–21	42	82	26	7	25	(4,060)	(546)
22–25	41	83	22	9	24	(3,877)	(737)
26–29	40	81	16	6	30	(3,554)	(693)
30–34	37	81	14	4	25	(4,572)	(878)
35–39	38	76	12	5		(1,862)	
40–44	38	76	5	1	{ 23[c]	(1,377)	{ (505)[c]
45–49	38	72	4	2		(1,026)	
50+	23	56	1	.6	27	(4,261)	(684)

[a] *Source:* 1991 National Household Survey on Drug Abuse (NIDA), unpublished data (Joseph Gfroerer: personal communication).
[b] *Source:* Miller et al. 1983, table 63. National Household Survey on Drug Abuse.
[c] Figures cited are for the age group 35–49.

to 34 for cocaine. The current use of illicit drugs declines sharply after age 39. (The same trends characterize the use of illicit drugs and the nonmedical use of psychoactive substances, such as the stimulants.) By contrast, following increases in adolescence, current use of cigarettes (or alcohol) and especially use of medically prescribed psychotropic drugs continue at approximately the same levels throughout adulthood, although the use of cigarettes declines gradually beginning in the late thirties and that of alcohol in the fifties.

Sex Differences

For most substances, a higher proportion of men than women are users. The sex differences increase with age and with increasing drug involvement. (In order to control for cohort differences, I present data for the prevalence rates of use in the last year. Similar results obtain for lifetime prevalence rates.) The sex differences in prevalence are small or even nonexistent in the teens (table 4). Overall, the proportion who has ever experimented with an illicit drug is 36 percent higher among men than among women.

The sex differences are accentuated with increasing degree of involvement. For instance, three times as many male as female high school seniors reported in 1990 that they were using marijuana or drinking alcohol on a daily basis (3.2 percent compared with 1 percent for marijuana; 5.2 percent compared with 1.9 percent for alcohol) (Johnston, O'Malley, and Bachman 1991, table 9). In the general population aged 12 and over in 1991, 3.6 percent of men but only 1.5 percent of women reported using marijuana at least once a week in the preceding year (National Institute on Drug Abuse 1991f, table 20A); 1 percent of men but .6 percent of women reported using it 12 or more times within the past year (based on data from the National Institute on Drug Abuse 1991f, table 21A). In 1991, more than twice as many men (2.6 percent) as women (1.2 percent) reported lifetime needle use of any illicit drug (National Institute on Drug Abuse 1991f, table 19).

These rates of drug use typically include anyone who reports having experimented with the drug, even if only once, and are obviously much higher than the proportions identified as cases. The only available epidemiologic data on cases of substance use disorders in the general population are available from the ECA program of research.

Prevalence of Substance Use Disorders

Overall Rates

The ECA data were gathered in the early 1980s, prior to the downturn in overall patterns of use in the general population and in drug-related medical cases, which I will discuss below. Were the study conducted now, the rates might well be lower, although, as we will see, there may be a lag of several years between starting to experiment with drugs and experiencing symptoms required for diagnosis as a case of drug abuse/dependence.

In the five sites aggregated and weighted to reflect rates in the United States as a whole, including the weighted representation of institutionalized persons, 6.2 percent of the population 18 and older receive a life-

TABLE 4

Annual Prevalence Rates of the Use of Selected Drugs in 1991 in the General Population, by Age and Sex

Percentages using in past year

Substance	Age 12–17		Age 18–25		Age 26–34		Age 35+		Total	
	M	F	M	F	M	F	M	F	M	F
Alcohol	43	38	86	80	85	77	71	60	73	64
Cigarettes	22	19	43	40	41	36	33	27	35	30
Marijuana	12	9	28	22	19	11	6	3	12	8
Cocaine	2	2	10	6	7	3	2	1	4	2
Stimulants	2	2	4	3	2	2	.7	.4	2	1
Tranquilizers	1	1	3	3	3	3	1	1	2	2
Any illicit drug	16	14	32	27	22	15	8	6	15	11
Total (N)	(3,995)	(4,010)	(3,470)	(4,467)	(3,416)	(4,710)	(3,541)	(4,985)	(14,422)	(18,172)

Source: National Institute on Drug Abuse 1991f

time diagnosis of drug abuse/dependence involving an illicit drug (Anthony and Helzer 1991) (see table 5). (The rate is almost identical, i.e., 5.9 percent, when the institutionalized cases are excluded [Regier et al. 1988].) The most frequent diagnosis is cannabis related. Only .2 percent of the total population receive a diagnosis of cocaine abuse (Anthony and Helzer 1991, table 6.4). (This low rate may be due to diagnostic criteria specified in DSM-III.) By contrast, one person in seven (13.8 percent) receives a lifetime diagnosis of alcohol abuse/dependence. Only one site (St. Louis) asked about cigarette smoking; more than a third of its respondents (36.0 percent) received a diagnosis of tobacco abuse/dependence. Substance abuse disorders involving an illicit drug are much less frequent than those involving a licit drug. For all diagnoses taken together, the lifetime rates of drug abuse/dependence are 60 percent higher among men than among women (7.7 percent compared with 4.8 percent). These rates are lower for cocaine and alcohol, but higher for tobacco, than those estimated for the 1990 general population regarding any of five dependence symptoms.

Of the cases with a drug abuse or dependence diagnosis, almost 40 percent among men and women involve abuse only, 25 percent involve dependence only, and about the same proportion involve both abuse

TABLE 5

Lifetime Prevalence Rates of DSM-III Drug Abuse/Dependence Disorders in the General Population, 1980-1984[a]

Lifetime disorder	Percentage
Any illicit drug	6.2
Cannabis	4.4
Stimulants	1.7
Sedatives	1.2
Opioids	.7
Hallucinogens[b]	.4
Cocaine[b]	.2
Alcohol[c]	13.8
Tobacco[d]	36.0

[a] *Source:* Anthony and Helzer 1991, ECA table 6.4. N = 19,417.
[b] Abuse only as per DSM-III.
[c] *Source:* Robins, Locke, and Regier 1991, table 13.7.
[d] Data for St. Louis site only: Robins et al. 1984, 952. N = 3,004.

and dependence. Thus, 59 percent of male and 55 percent of female drug abuse/dependence cases meet criteria for a drug dependence diagnosis (Anthony and Helzer 1991, table 6.8).

Rates presented for the total population are useful indicators of the relative prevalence of various disorders. However, substance use disorders, as is true of drug use more generally, are concentrated in the younger age groups in the population aged 18 to 29 (table 6). One in six males aged 18 to 29 meets criteria for a lifetime diagnosis of drug abuse/dependence. Among men and women, the prevalence is almost twice as high among those aged 18 to 29 as among those aged 30 to 44. There are almost no cases beyond the age of 44. The same age-related patterns appear among males and females. However, for each age group below age 45, the rates of diagnosed cases are about 50 percent higher among males than among females.

Rate of Drug Use Disorders among Users

From these data, we may begin to ascertain the rate of developing abuse or dependence, given that an individual has ever experimented with any illicit substance.

For the five sites together, this rate can only be ascertained for any il-

TABLE 6

Lifetime Prevalence Rates of DSM–III Drug Abuse/Dependence by Age in the Total Population and among Users of Any Illicit Drug from 1980 to 1984, by Sex[a]

	In population (%)			Among users of any illicit drug (%)		
Age	Total	Men	Women	Total	Men	Women
18–29	13.5	16.0	10.9	22.3	24.5	19.8
30–44	6.7	8.4	5.1	18.7	19.1	18.0
45–64	0.8	0.8	0.8	10.9	8.5	14.5[b]
65+	0.1	0.1	0.1	5.1	4.2	9.4[b]
Total	6.2	7.7	4.8	20.2	21.4	18.8

[a] *Source:* Anthony and Helzer 1991, ECA tables 6.6 and appendix table A–1a. Raw base frequencies not available.
[b] Rates reported in original table 6.6 were revised by the authors.

14 percent among those aged 65 and older (Anthony and Helzer 1991, table 6.27). The proportion is only half as large among young women aged 18 to 29 (14 percent), only a third as high among women aged 30 to 44 (9 percent), and a seventh as high among those aged 45 to 64 (3 percent). Only 1.5 percent of women aged 65 and over meet criteria for lifetime substance abuse/dependence disorders. This increasing sex differential in substance abuse disorders with increasing age reflects the growing prevalence of alcohol-related disorders among men compared with women.

Trends in Drug Use Prevalence Over Time

Patterns of Declining Use

General Population Samples.   The lifetime and period-specific prevalence rates observed in 1991 represent important downward trends in the usage of drugs, which began in 1980 for the use of most illicit drugs and in 1985 for cocaine. These peak periods in usage followed striking increases in the use of illicit drugs in the 1960s and 1970s.

The results of different studies, including studies carried out in Canada (Smart and Adlaf 1986), converge in documenting that throughout the 1980s there have been downward trends in the prevalence of licit and especially illicit drug use in all age groups in the population, although these appear to have slowed down over the last three years (1989–1991) compared with prior years. There have been downward trends in the proportions who ever experimented with illicit drugs, of those who used within the last year or within the last month. The trends seem to be stronger the more current the measure of use.

As a result, the proportion (44 percent) of high school seniors who report having ever used any illicit drug in 1991 represents a decline of 27 percent over the proportions recorded in the peak usage years of 1981 to 1982 and is lower than the proportion reported in 1975 (55 percent) (University of Michigan 1992, table 1). This trend characterizes also the prevalence of use of specific classes of illicit drugs, such as marijuana or cocaine. The lifetime prevalence of cocaine use in 1991 (7.8 percent) represents a 55 percent decline from the peak (17.3 percent) recorded in 1985. The trends are even stronger regarding current use compared with lifetime experience. More than half as many high school seniors report using any illicit drugs within the last month in 1991 as in 1975 (16.4

percent compared with 30.7 percent). The proportion of current (last 30 days) cocaine users is lower (1.4 percent) in 1991 than in 1975 (1.9 percent) (University of Michigan 1992, table 2). A third as many report using marijuana on a daily basis: 2.0 percent compared with 6.0 percent, and five times fewer than at the peak of 10.7 percent recorded in 1978 (University of Michigan 1992, table 4).

The very same trends appear in the general population. From 1985 to 1991, the proportion of those who had ever used any illicit drugs declined in all age groups, except those older than 35. Indeed, the latest data from 1991 indicate that the rates of illicit drug use are continuing to decline among adolescents 12 to 17 years, are leveling off among young adults 18 to 25, and are increasing slightly among those older than 35 (National Institute on Drug Abuse 1991f). By 1991, the proportions of lifetime marijuana users (13 percent) among adolescents aged 12 to 17 was similar to what it was in 1972 (14 percent). Because the lifetime rates in the older groups reflect the cumulative experiences of different birth cohorts who passed through the periods of risk for initiation into drugs at different historical periods, prevalence rates for more restricted and current periods of time, such as past year, more accurately reflect historical changes. In the six-year period from 1985 to 1991, the proportions of past-year users of any illicit drug declined by 32 percent, from 20 percent to 13 percent; the proportion of current (last month) users declined by 47 percent, from 12 percent to 6 percent (National Institute on Drug Abuse 1990a, tables 2.15 and 2.16; 1991a, table 2A; 1991f, table 2-A). The proportions who used cocaine at least once in the past month declined from 2.9 percent to .9 percent (National Institute on Drug Abuse 1988a, table 30; 1991f, table 4A). In 1991, among those 12 to 17 years old, the proportion of last month (current) marijuana users was actually lower (4 percent) than in 1972 (7 percent) (National Institute on Drug Abuse 1991c, table 2.10; 1991f, table 3A). In that same period, the decline in last-month marijuana use among those aged 18 to 25, the group with the highest rates of drug use of any age group, was even more striking: 13 percent versus 28 percent (National Institute on Drug Abuse 1991c, table 2.11; 1991f, table 3A). A smaller proportion of that same age group also reported using cocaine within the last month in 1991 than in 1974: 2 percent compared with 3 percent (National Institute on Drug Abuse 1991c, table 2.11; 1991f, table 4A). These changes, however, had all taken place by 1990. No further decline was observed between 1990 and 1991. Trend data for the annual use of various substances for three age groups in the general population from 1974 to 1991 are presented in table 7.

With the exception of cocaine, the downward trends are reflected not only in lifetime, annual, and current prevalences, but also in the proportions of individuals who are the most regular current users of those drugs. There has been a striking decline in daily use of marijuana, cigarette smoking, and alcohol drinking, both as a proportion of the total population and as proportions of the users (University of Michigan 1992, table 4). For example, among high school seniors from Monitoring the Future, daily marijuana users in 1991 represent 5 percent of those who ever experimented with marijuana, whereas they represented 18 percent in 1978.

The decline in daily use, however, does not appear to characterize cocaine users in the general population, undifferentiated as to age. On the contrary, heavy involvement in cocaine appears to have increased. Compared with 1985, in 1990 as in 1988, more than twice as many of those who used cocaine in the past year reported using it daily (4 percent in 1988, 5 percent in 1990 versus 2 percent in 1985). (Data on daily use for 1991 have not yet been released.) The proportions who used it at least once a week also continue to increase (11 percent in 1988 and 1990, 10.2 percent in 1991 versus 5 percent in 1985) (Adams et al. 1990, 8; National Institute on Drug Abuse 1990b; 1991a, table 20A). (Although data on daily use are not presented for specific age groups, there may be age-related differences in these patterns of change and possible similarity in the behavior over time of adolescents in the National Household Survey and of high school seniors in Monitoring the Future.) The proportions of last-year cocaine users in the general population reporting problems associated with the use of the drug, whether physiological, psychological, or family related, was almost double in 1990 and 1988 what it was among the users in 1985 (National Institute on Drug Abuse 1988a, table 72; 1990a, table 9.2; 1991c, table 9.2). These increases may have resulted from shifts in the manner of cocaine consumption, as reflected in the increases since 1985 in the proportions reporting that they freebased or smoked cocaine, especially in the group aged 18 to 25, which has the highest annual prevalence of self-reported cocaine use. In 1988 and 1990, 31 percent of those who used cocaine within the last year had freebased or smoked it, compared with 21 percent in 1985 (National Institute on Drug Abuse 1988a, table 34; 1991c, table 4.7; 1990a, table 4.7).

TABLE 7

Annual Prevalence of the Use of Selected Drugs in the Population from 1974 to 1991, by Age Group

Age group and drug class		1974 (%)	1976 (%)	1977 (%)	1979 (%)	1982 (%)	1985 (%)	1988 (%)	1990 (%)	1991 (%)
Youth (ages 12–17)	N =	(952)	(986)	(1,272)	(2,165)	(1,581)	(2,246)	(3,095)	(2,177)	(3,995)
Marijuana		18.5	18.4	22.3	24.1	20.6	19.7	12.6	11.3	10.1
Cocaine		2.7	2.3	2.6	4.2	4.1	4.0	2.9	2.2	1.5
Alcohol		51.0	49.3	47.5	53.6	52.4	51.7	44.6	41.0	40.3
Cigarettes[a]		–b	–b	–b	13.3	24.8	25.8	22.8	22.2	20.1
Any illicit use		–b	–b	–b	26.0	22.0	23.7	16.8	15.9	14.8
Young adults (ages 18–25)	N =	(849)	(882)	(1,500)	(2,044)	(1,283)	(1,813)	(1,505)	(2,052)	(3,470)
Marijuana		34.2	35.0	38.7	46.9	40.4	36.9	27.9	24.6	24.6
Cocaine		8.1	7.0	10.2	19.6	18.8	16.3	12.1	7.5	7.7
Alcohol		77.1	77.9	79.8	86.6	87.1	87.2	81.7	80.2	82.8
Cigarettes[a]		–b	–b	–b	46.7	47.2	44.3	44.7	39.7	41.2
Any illicit use		–b	–b	–b	49.4	43.4	42.6	32.0	28.7	29.2
Older adults (age 26+)	N =	(2,221)	(1,708)	(1,822)	(3,015)	(2,760)	(3,979)	(4,214)	(7,385)	(6,957)
Marijuana		3.8	5.4	6.4	9.0	10.6	9.5	6.9	7.3	6.8
Cocaine		–c	0.6	0.9	2.0	3.8	4.2	2.7	2.4	2.5
Alcohol		62.7	64.2	65.8	72.4	72.0	73.6	68.6	66.6	69.1
Cigarettes[a]		–b	–b	–b	39.7	38.2	36.0	33.7	31.9	32.0
Any illicit use		–b	–b	–b	10.0	11.8	13.3	10.2	10.0	9.6

Source: National Institute on Drug Abuse 1991c: National Household Surveys, tables 2.6, 2.7, and 2.8; National Institute on Drug Abuse 1991g. Annual prevalences not available for 1972 survey.
[a] Includes only persons who ever smoked at least five packs.
[b] Estimate not available.
[c] Low precision. No estimate reported.

Institutional Samples. The decline in the number of clinical cases related to illicit drug use began in 1989 or 1990, with a time lag of almost three years compared with school or community samples. The most recent data, however, suggest that a reversal in the downward trend may be followed by a new decline. The data from general population samples reflect, as I noted, a decline, starting in the mid-1980s in the proportion of individuals using cocaine, following stabilization from 1981 to 1985 and sharp increases in the late 1970s.

By contrast, the number of cocaine-related emergency-room admissions and cocaine-related deaths reported in medical examiners' offices and recorded in the DAWN system showed striking increases from 1980 to the first six months of 1989 and fluctuating trends since then. A substantial decline in 1990 has been followed by increases in the first three quarters of 1991 and new declines in the last quarter (National Institute on Drug Abuse 1992). The lowest number of admissions was recorded in the last quarter of 1990. The number of hospital emergency-room mentions of cocaine increased 300 percent, from 1981 to 1985, and almost doubled in the succeeding yearly interval. The number more than doubled again by 1988, when it reached 46,020 annual mentions (National Institute on Drug Abuse 1989a, C-84-04, 3; 1990c), continued to increase through the first two quarters of 1989, and peaked in the second quarter. Increases were also observed with respect to drug-related deaths recorded by medical examiners (National Institute on Drug Abuse 1989a, 3). Striking increases in cocaine admissions also appeared in a panel of 596 consistently reporting drug treatment programs in 15 states from 1979 to 1984, although not in the total number of admissions to these programs (National Institute on Drug Abuse 1988b). The number of clients admitted primarily for cocaine increased almost 400 percent. In great part, the increase in casualties may have been due to apparently sharper increases in the smoking of cocaine among clinical cases than among cocaine users in the general population (Schuster 1990a). Indeed, the percentages of cocaine-related emergency-room admissions of patients who reported smoking cocaine more than tripled from 1985 (11 percent) to 1989 (37 percent). In those same years, the percentages injecting cocaine decreased from 38 percent to 22 percent (Adams et al. 1990, 9).

A decline in drug-related emergency-room admissions began in the third quarter of 1989 and accelerated, especially for cocaine-related admissions, with the results that in 1990 the total number of drug-related mentions was 13 percent below the number for 1989 and the number of admissions specifically related to cocaine was 27 percent below 1989 (National Institute on Drug Abuse 1991d, table 4.03). However, the fourth quarter in 1990 marked the lowest point in admissions recorded since the peak in the second quarter of 1989. All drug-related admissions increased by 17 percent and admissions related specifically to cocaine increased 48 percent in the third quarter of 1991 compared with the number in the fourth quarter of 1990 (National Institute on Drug Abuse 1992). However, these admissions may not necessarily represent a systematic reversal of the downward trend because the number of all drug-related emergency-room admissions declined by 7.1 percent in the fourth quarter of 1991 compared with the third quarter, and the number of cocaine-related admissions declined by 4.1 percent. The rate of increase from 1988 to 1989 in drug-related deaths recorded in medical examiners' offices slowed down (Office of National Drug Control Policy 1990, 13); the number of these deaths recorded in 1990 was lower by 18.6 percent than the number recorded in 1989 (National Institute on Drug Abuse 1991e, table 4.03). The trends regarding arrestees are ambiguous; there appear to be declines in the rates of cocaine-positive urines among arrestees in selected cities (National Institute of Justice 1990). The rates of drug use in this group are extremely high compared with those observed in other institutionalized or clinical groups.

How Real and Widespread Is the Decline in Drug Use? The findings from population-based studies have been criticized and their validity questioned, with three particular criticisms emerging. One argument has been that the lower rates observed in surveys do not reflect a true decrease in drug use, but rather increasing social disapproval of drug use and respondents' reluctance to admit to their use in the face of this disapproval. A second argument has been that the decline characterizes middle-class conventional youths or adults who attend school and reside in stable households included in surveys, who may be for the most part casual users, but does not hold for other more disadvantaged and heavily using populations. In particular, Monitoring the Future omits data for about 35 percent of the age group: students absent from school on survey day and the dropouts. According to this argument, there are countervailing trends going on in the underclass and in the ghettos, with the rates there increasing rather than declining. The third objection has been based on the observation that, whereas the rates of use were declining in the population surveys, the morbidity and mortality indices based on

from first experiencing a problem to being currently diagnosed as a case of drug disorder (Anthony and Helzer 1991, 135). Data from selected treatment programs for the period 1979 to 1984 indicate that the average length of time between first use of cocaine and first admission ranged from 3.9 to 5 years (National Institute on Drug Abuse 1988b, 54). Because of changing methods of use and changing strength of cocaine, the time lag may be shorter in recent years than in the early 1980s. The recent increase in drug-related admissions to emergency rooms may reflect increasing medical complications among an aging cohort of drug users as well as changes in the purity of the drugs used, in route of administration, or in patterns of multiple use (National Institute on Drug Abuse 1991g).

Sociodemographic Distribution of Drug Use

The use of drugs varies across subgroups of the population. Age and sex differences were discussed earlier. Here, I focus in particular on ethnicity, as the epidemiologic data reveal an interesting paradox, reflected in the divergent ethnic distribution of drug users in general population and institutional samples. Data on marital status and income are not included in published reports for the National Household Survey on Drug Abuse.

Ecological Context

Prevalence varies according to areas of the country and population density (table 8). Lifetime experimentation with most drugs, in particular marijuana, and current cocaine use are most prevalent in the West; the other three geographic areas differ very little among themselves, although drug use is not as prevalent as in the West. Illicit drug use is less common in nonmetropolitan than in small or large metropolitan areas (National Institute on Drug Abuse 1991c).

Socioeconomic Status

Education. Lifetime prevalence reveals a curvilinear relationship of educational attainment with the use of illicit drugs and no relationship

TABLE 8
Lifetime Use, Last Month Use, and Persistence Ratios[a] of the Use of Marijuana, Cocaine, and Cigarettes in 1990 in the General Population, by Selected Demographic Characteristics

Demographic characteristic	Marijuana use (%)			Cocaine use (%)			Cigarette use (%)			(N)
	Ever	Last month	Ratio	Ever	Last month	Ratio	Ever	Last month	Ratio	
Region										
Northeast	29.9	5.5	.18	11.1	.9	.08	72.3	24.4	.34	(1,421)
North Central	35.4	5.7	.16	9.9	.7	.07	74.5	28.0	.38	(1,491)
South	29.0	4.0	.14	8.9	.7	.08	73.6	29.8	.40	(4,350)
West	40.2	5.7	.14	17.0	.9	.05	71.9	22.1	.31	(1,997)
Population density										
Large metropolitan	35.5	5.6	.16	13.2	1.0	.08	71.9	24.5	.34	(5,674)
Small metropolitan	33.1	5.1	.15	11.7	.6	.05	75.3	27.1	.36	(2,154)
Nonmetropolitan	28.4	4.0	.14	6.9	.6	.09	72.6	30.2	.42	(1,431)
Education										
Less than high school	23.8	5.2	.22	7.3	.8	.11	75.9	34.7	.46	(1,817)
High school graduate	36.0	5.1	.14	12.0	.9	.08	78.1	33.2	.43	(2,451)
Some college	43.3	6.6	.15	16.1	1.2	.07	80.1	37.2	.34	(1,482)
College graduate	38.7	3.2	.08	14.8	.4	.03	72.3	12.9	.18	(1,332)
Current employment										
Full time	45.5	5.7	.13	16.5	1.1	.07	81.7	32.3	.40	(3,969)
Part time	34.0	6.2	.18	11.3	—[b]	—	71.3	22.3	.31	(886)
Unemployed	44.0	12.3	.28	19.8	2.7	.14	78.4	43.2	.55	(454)

Source: National Institute on Drug Abuse 1991c: National Household Survey on Drug Abuse, tables 1.1, 3.1, 3.3, 4.1, 4.3, 8.1, 8.3.
[a] Persistence ratio = last month use divided by ever use.
[b] Low precision; no estimate reported.

53

with smoking. The lowest lifetime rates of illicit drugs are observed among those who have not completed high school; the highest rates occur among those with some college, but rates among college graduates are lower. However, for all substances, there is a substantial inverse relationship of education with current usage and with persistence of use among those who ever experimented with a particular substance. High school dropouts are much more likely and college graduates much less likely than any other group to be current users of the different classes of drugs. For instance, in 1991, 16.6 percent of those aged 20 to 34 years old who were school dropouts had used at least one illicit drug in the past month, compared with 9.9 percent of high school graduates (National Institute on Drug Abuse 1991f). Indeed, there is a positive relationship between education and cessation of drug use, once having experimented with a drug (table 8). The ratio of past month use to any lifetime use, which can be considered to constitute a measure of persistence of use, is much higher among those who failed to graduate from high school than among college graduates. In the ECA sample, drug abuse/dependence was highest among persons who had received no diploma, either from high school or from college (Anthony and Helzer 1991, table 6.15). Low educational attainment was a strong predictor of the onset of drug abuse/dependence over a one-year interval (Anthony 1990).

Employment. There is no consistent relationship between lifetime drug use patterns and current employment status. Unemployed persons, however, are much more likely to be current users and to persist in the use of drugs, following initiation, than those who are employed. For example, in 1990, among persons 26 to 34 years old, 6.8 percent of full-time workers reported using cocaine in the last year compared with 12.7 percent of unemployed persons (National Institute on Drug Abuse 1991c, table 4.2). However, in the ECA, an excess of diagnosed cases of drug dependence/abuse among the unemployed compared with the employed (10.4 percent versus 4.6 percent) was observed only among men aged 30 to 44 who had been currently using drugs within the last year. Among all other age and sex groups of active users or of individuals experiencing a drug-related problem within the last year, the proportions meeting criteria for a diagnosis were the same for both unemployed and employed (Anthony and Helzer 1991, table 6.17).

Income. Data on the relationship between income and patterns of drug use are rarely published. Selected data from the National Household Survey on Drug Abuse for employed men and women aged 18 to

40 in 1988 (described in an unpublished manuscript by Kopstein and Gfroerer, n.d.) were first published in 1990 for the entire population engaging in last-year use of marijuana and cocaine (National Institute on Drug Abuse 1991c, table 11.2). The data suggest a negative relationship between income and current (past month) use of any illicit drugs only among employed men and only for marijuana and not cocaine use (table 9). In the general population in 1990, there is a higher proportion reporting marijuana and cocaine use among those who earn less than $20,000 than among those earning more than $20,000 (National Institute on Drug Abuse 1991c, table 11.2). Similarly, in the ECA sample of persons in full-time employment, there is a strong inverse relationship of income with abuse/dependence among men, both lifetime and current: the rate among men earning less than $10,000 is four times higher than the rate among those earning $35,000 and over (Anthony and Helzer 1991, table 6.18). However, as Anthony and Helzer (1991, 143) point out, drug use and abuse/dependence are concentrated among younger workers who earn less than older ones. When the confound between age and income is controlled for, there are no consistent patterns of association between income and drug disorder diagnosis among employed males aged 18 to 29 (Anthony and Helzer 1991, table 6.18). By contrast, in a sample of junior and senior high school students from New York

TABLE 9

Prevalence Rates of the Use of Selected Drugs Among Full-time Employed Men and Women Aged 18–40 in the General Population in 1988, by Sex and Personal Income

	Past month use of any illicit		Past month use of marijuana		Past year use of cocaine	
Annual personal income	Male (%)	Female (%)	Male (%)	Female (%)	Male (%)	Female (%)
Less than $12,000	24.8	8.4	22.8	7.7	13.9	5.8
$12,000 to $19,999	19.6	9.3	18.9	7.4	10.0	7.3
$20,000 to $29,999	15.2	4.3	12.0	3.6	12.5	4.7
$30,000 or over	8.6	10.8	8.1	5.6	9.4	7.8

Sources: Kopstein and Gfroerer, n.d.; National Household Survey on Drug Abuse 1988, table 3. Base frequencies not available.

State schools, a positive relationship with family income was observed for measures of drug use similar to those reported for employed adult men in the National Household Survey (table 10).

In part, the inconsistencies between studies may stem from differences in samples, age, employment status, historical periods, and time frame used to define patterns of drug use. The cross-sectional nature of these data does not permit an assessment of the causal order between socioeconomic status and drug use. Longitudinal analyses from other studies suggest that drug use is a positive risk factor for dropping out of school in adolescence (Mensch and Kandel 1988b) as well as job instability in young adulthood (Kandel and Yamaguchi 1985). Correlatively, low job prestige, but not unemployment, was a risk for developing drug abuse/dependence in adulthood in the ECA sample (Anthony 1990).

Ethnicity

The relationships between ethnicity and drug behavior are complex, and appear to be changing rapidly. It should be noted that most published epidemiologic prevalence rates for different ethnic groups do not control for socioeconomic status.

Ethnic differences in patterns of use vary by age and recency of use, except for American Indians, who consistently report the highest rates of any group, and Asian Americans who report the lowest (e.g., Bachman et al. 1991; De La Rosa, Khalsa, and Rouse 1990; Gillmore et al. 1990; Harford 1986; Kandel, Davies, and Davis 1990; National Institute on

TABLE 10

Prevalence Rates of the Use of Selected Drugs by Household Income among Junior and Senior High School Students in New York State in 1988

Household income	Lifetime use of any illicit (%)	Past month use of any illicit (%)	Past month use of marijuana (%)	Past year use of cocaine (%)	Total (N)
Less than $20,000	26.2	10.5	8.0	3.2	(1,713)
$20–$49,999	33.0	14.0	12.1	4.0	(2,890)
$50,000 and over	35.3	16.7	14.1	5.1	(2,156)

Source: Kandel, Davies, and Davis 1990, tables 2.3, 2.4 and 2.5.

Drug Abuse 1991b; Oetting and Beauvais 1990). In adolescence and early adulthood, lower lifetime rates of reported drugs are observed among blacks than whites, with Hispanics in between these two groups, except in adolescence when Hispanics are the highest; at ages 35 and over, the lifetime rates are higher among blacks than whites. In the 1991 National Household Survey on Drug Abuse, 20 to 50 percent *fewer* blacks than whites report any *lifetime* experience with cocaine among persons younger than 35, whereas almost 50 percent *more* blacks than whites report such experience among individuals aged 35 and over (National Institute on Drug Abuse 1991f). Regarding use in the last year, higher rates for blacks than for whites appear among those aged 26 and older; the rates are still lower or the same at younger ages. Regarding use in the last month, rates are consistently higher among blacks than whites at all ages (table 11). These trends are displayed in graphic form for blacks and whites in figure 1. (In the national sample of high school seniors, the ethnic differences persisted with controls for sociodemographic characteristics, including parental education and urban–rural location (Bachman et al. 1991)).

The relative prevalence of the use of illicit drugs, especially cocaine, among blacks, compared with different ethnic groups in the general population, appears to be changing. Up to and including 1985, the higher rates of illicit drug use, especially cocaine use, among blacks, compared with whites and Hispanics, were observed only among those older than 35 for every prevalence rate, whether lifetime, last year, or last month. Consistently lower rates among blacks than whites were observed among individuals younger than 35. Over the last several years, however, the differential in favor of blacks, especially as compared with whites, appears to be gradually spreading into younger age groups and to be reflected first in the most current prevalence rates (table 12). Compared with whites, by 1988 higher annual and monthly rates were observed among blacks aged 26 to 34, and higher monthly rates were seen among those aged 18 to 25. By 1990, the higher annual rates were also observed among blacks 18 to 25 years old. A year later, by 1991, the trend had spread to the youngest age group. At least equal, or even slightly higher, annual and last month rates among blacks than whites were observed in the youngest age group, 12 to 17 years old. The relative position of Hispanics is less consistent over time.

Data in the National Household Survey are not available broken down simultaneously by sex, ethnicity, and age. In general, sharper eth-

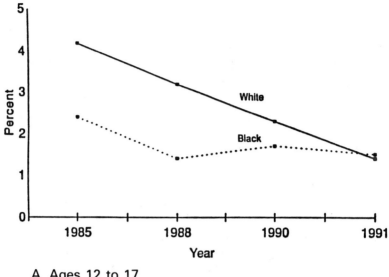

A. Ages 12 to 17

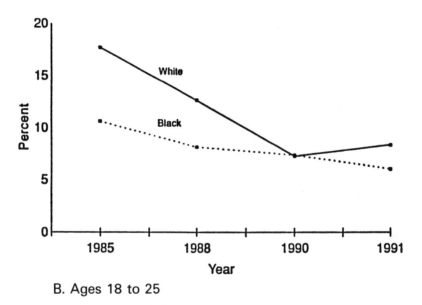

B. Ages 18 to 25

FIG. 1.   Trends in past year prevalence rates of cocaine use by race/ethnicity in the general population (1985, 1988, 1990, 1991).

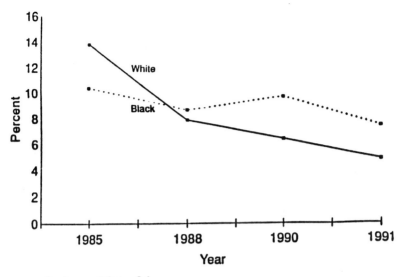

C. Ages 26 to 34

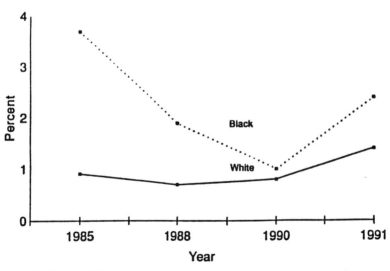

D. Ages 35+

FIG. 1. continued.

TABLE 11

Lifetime, Past Year, and Past Month Prevalence Rates of the Use of Cocaine in 1991 in the General Population, by Race/Ethnicity and Age Group

Age/ethnicity	Ever used (%)	Past year (%)	Past month (%)	Total (N)
Ages 12–17				
White	2.4	1.4	.3	(3,646)
Black	1.7	1.5	.5	(2,036)
Hispanic	3.7	3.0	1.3	(2,029)
Ages 18–26				
White	20.3	8.3	1.7	(3,689)
Black	10.1	6.0	3.1	(2,032)
Hispanic	15.0	7.1	2.7	(1,917)
Ages 26–34				
White	27.9	4.9	1.6	(4,001)
Black	22.2	7.5	2.7	(1,938)
Hispanic	18.6	4.5	2.0	(1,962)
Age 35+				
White	6.6	1.4	.2	(4,312)
Black	9.7	2.4	1.3	(2,044)
Hispanic	7.9	2.3	1.0	(2,008)
Total white	12.0	3.0	.7	(15,648)
Total black	11.3	3.9	1.8	(8,050)
Total Hispanic	11.2	3.8	1.6	(7,916)

Source: National Institute on Drug Abuse 1991f. National Household Survey on Drug Abuse, tables 1A,B; 4B–4C.

nic differences characterize patterns of cocaine use among women than men. Black women are especially likely to report lower lifetime experience with cocaine than other women. Black and Hispanic women also report lower rates of use of the legal drugs and of marijuana than whites. Among men, ethnic differences appear only with respect to illicit drugs other than marijuana.

Lower prevalence of reported use of a variety of drugs by blacks compared with whites has been reported by most other surveys that have examined ethnic patterns in drug use (Prendergast et al. 1989), whether the data are obtained by household interviews (Kandel and Davies 1991b) or in-school self-administered questionnaires (Bachman et al. 1991; Gillmore et al. 1990; Johnston, O'Malley, and Bachman 1991;

TABLE 12

Trends in Past Year Prevalence Rates of Cocaine Use in the General Population in 1985,[a] 1988,[b] 1990,[c] and 1991,[d] by Age Group and Race/Ethnicity

Race/ethnicity	Ages 12–17 (%)				Ages 18–25 (%)				Ages 26–34 (%)				Age ≥35 (%)			
	1985	1988	1990	1991	1985	1988	1990	1991	1985	1988	1990	1991	1985	1988	1990	1991
White	4.2	3.2	2.3	1.4	17.7	12.6	7.2	8.3	13.8	7.9	6.4	4.9	.9	.7	.8	1.4
(N)	(993)	(1,518)	(1,136)	(3,646)	(794)	(700)	(1,126)	(3,689)	(1,082)	(1,096)	(1,359)	(4,001)	(1,080)	(1,237)	(1,620)	(4,312)
Black	2.4	1.4	1.7	1.5	10.6	8.1	7.3	6.0	10.4	8.7	9.7	7.5	3.7	1.9	1.0	2.4
(N)	(590)	(747)	(448)	(2,036)	(461)	(320)	(414)	(2,032)	(499)	(366)	(460)	(1,938)	(395)	(455)	(520)	(2,044)
Hispanic	5.8	3.6	3.1	3.0	12.4	12.6	9.7	7.1	6.2	8.0	8.6	4.5	1.0	1.7	2.0	2.3
(N)	(627)	(763)	(526)	(2,029)	(528)	(454)	(448)	(1,917)	(534)	(475)	(462)	(1,962)	(307)	(501)	(479)	(2,008)

[a] *Source:* National Institute on Drug Abuse 1988a, table 29.
[b] *Source:* National Institute on Drug Abuse 1990a, tables 1.1, 4.2.
[c] *Source:* National Institute on Drug Abuse 1991a, tables 1B; 4B,C,D.
[d] *Source:* National Institute on Drug Abuse 1991f, tables 1B; 4B,C,D.

Kandel, Davies, and Davis 1990; Kandel, Single, and Kessler 1976; Maddahian, Newcomb, and Bentler 1986; Trimble, Padilla, and Bell 1987; Welte and Barnes 1987; Zabin et al. 1985). The household survey of a national sample of young men interviewed in 1974 by O'Donnell et al. (1976) is the only representative national study to report overall higher rates for blacks than for whites. As noted above, self-reported drug rates by blacks may be subject to greater underreporting than self-reports by other ethnic groups (Mensch and Kandel 1988a). Furthermore, representative national population samples are not the best source of data for comparing the ethnic distribution of treated cases, which tend to come disproportionately from large urban centers (Brunswick 1988). The only population surveys to report very high rates of illicit drug use for blacks are community surveys of urban low-income blacks (Brunswick, Merzel, and Messeri 1985). Such surveys, however, typically do not have matched comparison groups of poor urban whites. As the analysis of the data from successive general population surveys indicate, ethnic patterns of use seem to have evolved over time depending upon individuals' age and recency of use. Most studies do not have the data regarding trends, age, and pattern of use to reveal these complex patterns.

Ambiguous results regarding ethnic patterns in drug use disorders are provided by the ECA data. Slightly lower rates of cases of drug abuse/dependence meeting diagnostic criteria were observed among minorities in the general population from 1980 to 1984. The overall lifetime prevalence for drug use disorders was 6.4 among whites, 5.5 among blacks, and 4.4 among Hispanics; one-year prevalence was 2.7, 2.7, and 2.0, respectively (Anthony and Helzer 1991, table 6.6). The ethnic differences are more pronounced among women than among men (table 13). At ages 18 to 44, the years in the life span of highest rates for drug use disorders, whites have the highest rates of any group; Hispanics have the lowest rates of any group, although Hispanics generally report higher rates of drug use than blacks (Kandel, Davies, and Davis 1990; National Institute on Drug Abuse 1991a,c). There are no ethnic differences in the prevalence of currently (last month) active cases (Anthony and Helzer 1991, table 6.12). Furthermore, when restricted to those who had ever used one or more illicit drugs, the race differences are reduced and are small and nonsignificant (Anthony and Helzer 1991, table 6.6). In a prospective one-year follow-up of incidence of new cases, controlling for census tract location, race/ethnicity was not a risk factor for developing drug abuse/dependence in adulthood (Anthony 1990).

TABLE 13
Prevalence Rates of Lifetime Drug Abuse/Dependence Disorders,
from 1980 to 1984, by Sex, Age and Race/Ethnicity in ECA Sample

Age/ethnicity	Males (%)	Males (N)	Females (%)	Females (N)	Total (%)	Total (N)
Ages 18–29						
White	16.4	(1,363)	11.9	(1,387)	14.4	(2,750)
Black	12.7	(681)	8.5	(815)	10.5	(1,496)
Hispanic	10.7	(342)	3.9	(276)	7.4	(818)
Ages 30–44						
White	8.6	(1,335)	5.5	(1,488)	7.0	(2,823)
Black	7.6	(508)	3.6	(809)	5.4	(1,317)
Hispanic	5.0	(280)	2.9	(250)	3.9	(530)
All ages 18+						
White	—[a]		—[a]		6.4	(13,980)
Black	—[a]		—[a]		5.5	(4,962)
Hispanic	—[a]		—[a]		4.4	(1,620)

Source: Anthony and Helzer 1991, tables 6.6 and 6.12.
[a] Data not available.

Although there is ambiguity in the data, whether indexed by simple patterns of use or diagnostic criteria, at least as many, if not more, whites than blacks appear to be involved in using drugs, especially adolescents and young adults. The relative position of Hispanics is variable.

General Population versus Treated Cases: A Paradox. The juxtaposition of data on cocaine use from general population samples and data from cases that come to the attention of various treatment centers presents a paradox. As discussed above, a smaller or, at most, an equal proportion of blacks than whites among those younger than 35 report having ever experimented with illicit drugs, with the Hispanics generally in the highest position; at least as many whites as minorities meet criteria for drug disorders. Yet morbidity and mortality cases of illicit drug users, and especially of cocaine users who have come to the attention of various medical treatment or criminal institutions, such as drug-related emergency rooms, treatment programs, or medical examiners' offices, consistently show an overrepresentation of blacks compared with their distribution in the population (table 14).

For example, of cocaine-related emergency-room episodes recorded in

TABLE 14
Race/Ethnicity of All Drug Admissions, Cocaine Admissions, or Cocaine Users in Treated and General Population Samples, 1988–1990

Race/ethnicity	Drug abuse treatment programs[a] 1989 — All admissions (%)	Emergency room episodes[b] 1989 — All drug admissions (%)	Emergency room episodes[b] 1989 — Cocaine admissions (%)	Deaths in medical examiners[c] 1989 — All drug abuse deaths (%)	Deaths in medical examiners[c] 1989 — Cocaine deaths (%)	National household sample[d] 1990 — Cocaine users (%)	New York State high school survey[e] 1988 — Cocaine users (%)
White	49.0	42.4	25.2	51.2	36.1	81.1	72.4
Black	26.5	37.8	57.9	32.8	45.9	10.0	6.8
Hispanic	17.5	10.1	8.7	13.7	16.8	8.0	12.9
Other/unknown	7.0	9.8	8.2	3.0	1.2	10.9	7.9
Total (N)	(351,430)	(249,349)	(61,665)	(7,162)	(3,618)	(22,739)	(427)

[a] *Source:* National Institute on Drug Abuse 1990d, table 26.
[b] *Source:* National Institute on Drug Abuse 1990e, table 6.13.
[c] *Source:* Based on National Institute on Drug Abuse 1990e, tables 3.01, III–2.
[d] *Source:* National Institute on Drug Abuse 1991a, table 4A–D.
[e] *Source:* Based on Kandel, Davies, and Davis 1990, table 2.10a: 7th–12th graders.

1989, 25 percent involved whites and 58 percent blacks. In 1989, 49 percent of charts included in the NDATUS survey of drug treatment facilities covered white clients and 27 percent covered blacks. By contrast, in the 1991 household sample, 79 percent of the self-reported lifetime cocaine users were white and only 11 percent black (National Institute on Drug Abuse 1991f, tables 4A,B,D). The overrepresentation of blacks in clinical samples of drug users, compared with their representation in the population or their distribution among drug users in the community, seems to be increasing over time. The proportions of blacks in cocaine-related admissions in the DAWN system increased from 41 percent in 1984 to 54 percent in 1990; the proportions of whites and Hispanics declined from 36 percent to 30 percent and 14 percent to 8 percent, respectively (National Institute on Drug Abuse 1990c; 1991d). Similarly, the proportion of white admissions recorded in treatment programs by NDATUS declined from 58 percent in 1987 to 49 percent in 1989 (National Institute on Drug Abuse 1989b; 1990d).

One common explanation advanced to account for ethnic differences is that there is a bias involved in who appears for treatment, especially in public programs funded by states or the federal government. Whites may seek care from private physicians and may be underrepresented in government-financed programs.

I believe that another factor may also come into play. That is, although fewer blacks than whites experiment with various illicit drugs, a higher proportion of blacks than whites become heavily involved in using these drugs and develop problems with these drugs, although not necessarily to the extent of meeting criteria for drug abuse/dependence disorders.

Although fewer blacks than whites may initiate the use of cocaine, following initial experimentation blacks of all age groups are more likely than whites to persist in its use (table 15). Only 6 percent of whites who ever experimented with cocaine reported using the drug within the last 30 days preceding the 1991 household population survey, compared with 16 percent among blacks and 14 percent among Hispanics (based on National Institute on Drug Abuse 1991f, tables 4B,C,D). These ethnic differences in persistence of use have become accentuated over time. The proportions persisting were 1.3 times higher among blacks than whites in 1985, over 1.8 times higher in 1988, 3.4 times higher in 1990, and 2.7 times higher in 1991. In 1991, more blacks reported using crack than any other group. The proportions of lifetime users among those aged 26

TABLE 15

Persistence in the Use of Cocaine by Race/Ethnicity and Age
in the General Population in 1985,[a] 1988,[b] 1990,[c] and 1991[d]

Age/ethnicity	Persistence into[e] past year use				Persistence into[f] last month use			
	1985	1988	1990	1991	1985	1988	1990	1991
Total sample: 12+								
White	.52	.37	.24	.25	.24	.12	.05	.06
Black	.63	.47	.40	.34	.32	.22	.17	.16
Hispanic	.70	.52	.45	.34	.33	.24	.17	.14
Ages 18–25								
White	.63	.59	.34	.41	.29	.20	.09	.08
Black	.79	.78	.59	.59	.48	.41	.29	.31
Hispanic	.83	.67	.52	.47	.44	.36	.17	.18
Ages 26–34								
White	.51	.28	.23	.18	.25	.08	.05	.06
Black	.60	.44	.48	.34	.30	.15	.21	.12
Hispanic	.63	.37	.42	.24	.28	.18	.12	.11

[a] *Source:* National Institute on Drug Abuse 1988a, tables 28–30.
[b] *Source:* National Institute on Drug Abuse 1990a, tables 4.1,2,3.
[c] *Source:* National Institute on Drug Abuse 1991a, tables 4B,C,D.
[d] *Source:* National Institute on Drug Abuse 1991f, tables 4B,C,D.
[e] Ratio of last year over lifetime use.
[f] Ratio of last month over lifetime use.

to 34 were 9.2 percent, compared with 2.8 percent among whites and
3.7 percent among Hispanics (National Institute on Drug Abuse 1991f,
tables 5B,C,D).

Of those who ever used cocaine, blacks (and Hispanics) became more
heavily involved than whites. In the 1991 National Household Survey, .2
percent of whites, but 1.1 percent of blacks and .7 percent of Hispanics
had used cocaine at least once a week within the last year (National Institute on Drug Abuse 1991f, tables 21B,C,D), representing, respectively,
5.5 percent, 28.9 percent, and 18.8 percent of the last year 1991 users in
each ethnic group. Parallel differences were observed in a national sample of young men and women aged 19 to 27 surveyed in 1984 (Kandel
and Davies 1991b, table 8). The relatively greater involvement of black
cocaine users than whites increased in 1991 compared with 1990. In
1990, 8 percent of the past year cocaine users among whites and 17 per-

cent among blacks had reported being weekly users (National Institute on Drug Abuse 1991a, tables 20B,D), a doubling of the rate compared with a tripling in 1991.

Blacks are more likely than any other group to use drugs intravenously. In 1991, 2.4 percent of blacks, 2.2 percent of Hispanics, and 1.7 percent of whites reported having ever used cocaine, heroin, or amphetamines with a needle (National Institute on Drug Abuse 1991f, table 9). Furthermore, the blind seroprevalence surveys indicate much higher rates of HIV-positive childbearing women and HIV-positive newborns among blacks than any other group. In New York State, for the period from November 1987 to March 1990, the rate of HIV-positive newborns was 2.19 for blacks compared with .34 for whites and 1.43 for Hispanic babies (Novick et al. 1991). These results are free of any self-reported or sampling biases. Because of the known association between intravenous drug use and AIDS (DesJarlais et al. 1989), the seroprevalence results provide strong supporting evidence for ethnic differences in problematic drug use.

We would assume that persistence in use and degree of involvement would increase the risk of meeting criteria for drug abuse and/or dependence. The data from the ECA, however, are not consistent with this interpretation (Anthony and Helzer 1991). Although a higher proportion of drug users among blacks would be expected to meet these criteria, such does not appear to be the case (see table 14).

Discussion

Epidemiologic data about patterns of drug use in the population have important implications for our understanding of the nature of substance use and substance use disorders and for policy regarding drug abuse.

The downward trends observed over the last decade in the use of various illicit substances are as striking as the upward trends observed in the 1970s. The rates of decline appear to be slowing down, however, among the older age groups. Rates of drug-related medical morbidity, which increased again, following sharp declines over the previous two years, may be declining anew. The continuing decline among adolescents is encouraging because the adolescent years are those of highest risk for involvement in drugs. It is difficult to identify a single cause to account for the decline. The implementation of numerous school- and community-based drug-prevention programs, drug-treatment initiatives, extensive media interventions from the Partnership for a Drug Free America since 1987, the simple Just Say No campaign, the formation of parent groups against drinking and illicit drug use, the mobilization of communities against the use of drugs by young people, the AIDS epidemic, and associated national educational efforts linking it to drug use, a general emphasis in our society on health and diet, and the dynamic processes underlying the spread and constriction of epidemics all may play a role.

Whatever the causal factors, they probably have a major impact by changing social norms regarding the acceptability of using drugs and individuals' attitudes toward drugs and their willingness to use them. Several studies demonstrate convincingly that in the same period when the prevalence of drug use has declined, the perceived harmfulness and risks associated with using drugs have increased sharply. From 1986 to 1991, the proportions of high school seniors saying there is "great risk" to themselves of using cocaine occasionally increased from 54 percent to 76 percent (University of Michigan 1992). The proportions of seniors disapproving of people older than 18 trying cocaine increased from 80 percent to 94 percent (University of Michigan 1992, table 7). Among 12- to 17-year-olds in the population, the proportion who perceived "great risk" in smoking marijuana occasionally increased from 37 percent in 1985 to 52 percent in 1990 (Schuster 1990b; National Institute on Drug Abuse 1991c, table 11.1). There has also been increased perceived disapproval from peers and parents about using drugs (Johnston, O'Malley, and Bachman 1991, table 22 and figures 26–27.) Interestingly, the preliminary general population data for 1991 (National Institute on Drug Abuse 1991f) confirm the important linkage between drug behavior and attitudes. From 1990 to 1991, attitudes and perceptions have not changed or may even have become less negative at the same time that the downward trend in usage patterns is slowing.

Availability does not appear to be a strong facilitating factor for drug usage. In that same five-year period from 1985 to 1990 the perceived availability of illicit drugs actually improved slightly. For instance, among high school seniors, 51 percent said that it would be "fairly" or "very" easy for them to get cocaine (University of Michigan 1992). Attitudes appear to be the crucial proximal determinant of drug use.

The epidemiologic data further our understanding of the phenomenology of addictive states in the general population. Despite the limitations of DSM–III-based diagnoses, their implementation in the ECA community-based sample survey provides the most systematic information to date on substance abuse disorders in the population. Furthermore, data from three different data bases — the surveillance surveys of drug use patterns in the general population, the ECA program of research on the epidemiology of psychiatric disorders in the population, and drug-related emergency-room admissions — suggest that the mean length of time between first use of an illicit substance and the appearance of serious problems that form the basis of the diagnostic nosology seems to be around three to four years. A significant proportion of those who ever experiment with drugs progress to stages of abuse/dependence. The risk of abuse/dependence is not constant across all groups who experiment with a particular class of drugs, nor is it constant across the life span or across historical time. The overall risk of drug abuse/dependence decreases over the life cycle.

From a public health perspective, it must be emphasized that illicit drug use and substance abuse/dependence are a phenomenon of youth, adolescence, and young adulthood. Differences in usage patterns according to most socioeconomic characteristics are either small or inconsistent, although persistence of use appears to be inversely related to education. The contrast between the ethnic distribution of drug users in the community and in drug treatment, medical, or other institutional samples illustrates clearly that the treated and clinical population do not constitute a representative sample of users and abusers in the community. Indeed, the ECA study documents that only a fraction of drug abusers or drug-dependent individuals seek help for their drug-related problems. Only 30 percent of those with a lifetime or current diagnosis of drug abuse/dependence had mentioned their drug problem to a doctor or another professional (Anthony and Helzer 1991, table 6.25). Fifteen percent of cases active within the last year, who experienced a drug-specific problem in that period, received mental health services on an outpatient basis, 1 percent did so on an inpatient basis; 63 percent received medical care on an outpatient basis and 11 percent on an inpatient basis (Anthony and Helzer 1991, table 6.26). Consonant with the fact that women have more extensive contacts with health providers than men, the proportion of diagnosed individuals who told a doctor or other professional about their drug problems is one-third higher among females (37 percent) than among males (26 percent) (Anthony and Helzer 1991, table 6.25). Much remains to be understood about the pathways to treatment and care for drug abuse/dependence.

Planning for drug-related treatment facilities must take into account
that changes in the number of individuals using drugs over time and potentially in need of help will be a function not only of age-specific rates
of use, but also of the size of the groups at risk for abuse/dependence,
the age distribution of the U.S. population, and changes in that distribution over time. For example, although the rate of weekly use among
individuals who used cocaine within the last year did not change between 1988 and 1990 (10.5 percent and 10.6 percent), the estimated
number of these weekly users in the United States declined by 23 percent, from 862,000 to 662,000, because of declines in the absolute number of past year cocaine users (National Institute on Drug Abuse 1990b;
1991a). A certain ambiguity in the presentation and interpretation of
epidemiologic data occurs when a clear distinction between rates of use
within a particular age group and the absolute number of persons in that
age group is not made.

Epidemiologic studies, especially longitudinal studies, have clearly
demonstrated that drug initiation is influenced by contextual factors, especially peers (e.g., Elliott, Huizinga, and Ageton 1985; Kandel 1985).
The epidemiologic data reviewed in this chapter suggest that the behavior of users within a society is also determined by broader socio-cultural
factors, particularly the overall pervasiveness of the use of drugs in that
society. Concurrent with the decline in the overall rates of lifetime and
current experimentation with different drugs have been even more striking declines in the proportions of daily users, both of the total population and of lifetime users. For instance, from 1978 to 1991, lifetime rates
of marijuana use among all high school seniors declined by 38 percent
(from 59.2 percent to 36.7 percent), but rates of daily use declined by 81
percent (10.8 percent versus 2.0 percent) (University of Michigan 1992,
table 4). If dependence were solely under the control of physiological
factors, we could expect the number of daily users to constitute a constant fraction of the marijuana-using population—holding all other factors constant, including drug strength and purity. This does not appear
to be the case. In fact, as I noted several years ago on the basis of cross-
cultural studies, degree and persistence of drug involvement appear to
be directly related to the overall levels of use in a society (Kandel
1984b). There may be exceptions, however, particularly with respect to
cocaine. Generally, it appears that the higher the overall societal levels,
the greater the involvement in drugs on the part of the users, the more
persistent the use, the earlier the age of onset into the use of drugs, and

the greater the spread of the phenomenon throughout all groups in society, with an attenuation of intergroup differences in patterns of use (Kandel 1984b).

There may also be social–structural influences on drug behavior, which derive from demographic changes in the population. The downward trend in illicit drug use prevalence over the last decade since the peak in drug use prevalence observed in 1978–1980 has taken place in parallel with the aging of the population. The demographic shifts involve a decrease in the number of young people in the ages of greatest risk for initiation into drugs and an increase in the number of older age groups. From 1980 to 1990 the ratio of youths (aged 15 to 24) to the parental generation (aged 34 to 44) declined from 1.8 to 1.0 (based on data from U.S. Bureau of the Census 1988, 1989; 1990 data were projections). The upward trend in prevalence from 1960 to 1980 paralleled the upward trend in the ratio of youths to adults. Demographers have stressed that fewer members in the cohorts of young people and smaller relative cohort size will reduce opportunities for social interactions with peers (a most important factor in drug use initiation), and increase social control by the older generation (Easterlin 1987; Ryder 1965).

Structural factors may also partially explain rates of decline in drug use when changes in individual behaviors depend not only on opportunities for peer interactions, but also on group norms and drug users' characteristics. Perceived risks and disapproval associated with illicit drug use have increased. The rate of decline in drug use may follow a reverse diffusion process characteristic of epidemics in their expansion phase, and may accelerate as a function of the number of individuals initially exposed and at risk for initiation, especially if proscriptive norms also become more negative and individuals at risk for drug involvement are less deviant (Kandel and Davies 1991a). In periods with high prevalence of drug use, less deviant youths will be drawn into drug use, mainly through peer influence. These processes would be magnified with demographic changes. The rates of decline would accelerate when the pool of existing and potential users would include not only fewer individuals in the ages of greatest risk for initiation into drugs, but also fewer individuals committed to using drugs.

The mirrorlike trends characterizing the downward drug usage patterns and increasingly negative attitudes toward the use of drugs, despite the absence of changes in the perceived availability of drugs, provide strong support for the argument that changing the demand for drugs is

the key to controlling drug abuse. Changes at the individual level may
be amplified further by structural and demographic changes in society.

References

Adams, E.H., A.J. Blanken, L.D. Ferguson, and A. Kopstein. 1990.
    Overview of Selected Drug Trends. Rockville, Md.: National Insti-
    tute on Drug Abuse.
Adams, E.H., B. Rouse, and J. Gfroerer. 1990. Populations at Risk for
    Cocaine Use and Subsequent Consequences. In *Cocaine in the
    Brain*, eds. N. Volkow and A.C. Swann. New Brunswick, N.J.: Rut-
    gers University Press.
American Psychiatric Association. 1980. *Diagnostic and Statistical Man-
    ual of Mental Disorders*, 3d ed., Washington.
————. 1987. *Diagnostic and Statistical Manual of Mental Disorders*,
    3d ed., revised. Washington: American Psychiatric Association.
Anthony, J.C. 1990. The Epidemiologic Study of Drug Addiction and
    Related Syndromes. In *Handbook of Drug and Alcohol Addiction*,
    ed. N.S. Miller. New York: Marcel Dekker.
Anthony, J.C., and J.E. Helzer. 1991. Syndromes of Drug Abuse and
    Dependence. In *Psychiatric Disorders in America*, eds. L. Robins
    and D. Regier, 116–54. New York: Free Press.
Anthony, J.C., and A.M. Trinkoff. 1989. United States Epidemiologic
    Data on Drug Use and Abuse: How Are They Relevant to Testing
    Abuse Liability of Drugs? In *Testing for Abuse Liability of Drugs in
    Humans*, eds. M.W. Fischman and N.K. Mello, 241–66. NIDA re-
    search monograph 92. Rockville, Md.: National Institute on Drug
    Abuse.
Bachman, J.G., J.M. Wallace Jr., P.M. O'Malley, L.D. Johnston, C.L.
    Kurth, and H.W. Neighbors. 1991. Racial/Ethnic Differences in
    Smoking, Drinking, and Illicit Drug Use among American High
    School Seniors, 1976–89. *American Journal of Public Health*
    81:372–7.
Bray, R.M., M.E. Marsden, L.L. Guess, et al. 1988. *Substance Abuse
    and Health Behaviors Among Military Personnel*. Research Triangle
    Park, N.C.: Research Triangle Institute.
Brunswick, A.F. 1988. Black Males and Substance Use. In *Young, Black,
    and Male in America*, eds. J.T. Gibbs et al. Dover, Mass.: Auburn
    House.
Brunswick, A.F., C.R. Merzel, and P.A. Messeri. 1985. Drug Use Initia-
    tion among Urban Black Youth. *Youth & Society* 17:189–215.
Cacciola, J., and G. Woody. 1990. Cocaine Abuse vs. Dependence and

Levels of Severity: A Secondary Analysis for DSM–IV. Philadelphia: VA Medical Center. (Unpublished)

Clayton, R.R., and C. Ritter. 1985. The Epidemiology of Alcohol and Drug Abuse among Adolescents. *Advances in Alcohol and Substance Abuse* 4:69–97.

Clayton, R.R., and H.L. Voss. 1982. Technical Review on Drug Abuse and Dropouts. (Report) Bethesda, Md.: National Institute on Drug Abuse.

Coleman, J.S., and T. Hoffer. 1987. *Public and Private School: The Impact of Communities*. New York: Basic Books.

De La Rosa, M.R., J.H. Khalsa, and B.A. Rouse. 1990. Hispanics and Illicit Drug Use: A Review of Recent Findings. *International Journal of the Addictions* 25:665–91.

DesJarlais, D.C., S.R. Friedman, D.M. Novick, et al. 1989. HIV-1 Infection among Intravenous Drug Users in Manhattan. *Journal of the American Medical Association* 261:1008–12.

Easterlin, R.A. 1987. *Birth and Fortune: The Impact of Numbers on Personal Welfare*. Chicago: University of Chicago Press.

Elliott, D.S., D. Huizinga, and S.S. Ageton. 1985. *Explaining Delinquency and Drug Use*. Beverly Hills, Calif.: Sage.

Gawin, F.H., and H.D. Kleber. 1985. Cocaine Use in a Treatment Population: Patterns and Diagnostic Distinctions. In *Cocaine Use in America: Epidemiologic and Clinical Perspectives*, eds. N.J. Kozel and E.H. Adams, 182–92. NIDA research monograph 61. Rockville, Md.: National Institute on Drug Abuse.

Gillmore, M.R., R.F. Catalano, D.M. Morrison, E.A. Wells, B. Iritani, and J.D. Hawkins. 1990. Racial Differences in Acceptability and Availability of Drugs and Early Initiation of Substance Use. *American Journal of Drug and Alcohol Abuse* 16:185–206.

Ginsberg, I.J., and J.R. Greenley. 1978. Competing Theories of Marijuana Use: A Longitudinal Study. *Journal of Health and Social Behavior* 19:22–34.

Harford, T.C. 1986. Drinking Patterns among Black and Non-Black Adolescents: Results of a National Survey. *Annals of the New York Academy of Sciences* 472:130–41.

Hilton, M.S. 1988. Demographic Distribution of Drinking Patterns in 1984. *Drug and Alcohol Dependence* 22(1):37–47.

Johnston, L., J. Bachman, and P.M. O'Malley. 1981. *Highlights from Student Drug Use in America, 1975–1981*. Rockville, Md.: National Institute on Drug Abuse.

Johnston, L.D., P.M. O'Malley, and J.G. Bachman. 1989. *Drug Use, Drinking, and Smoking: National Survey Results from High School, College, and Young Adults Populations 1975–1988*. Rockville, Md.: National Institute on Drug Abuse.

————. 1991. *Drug Use among American High School Seniors, College Students and Young Adults, 1975–1990. Vol. 1: High School Seniors.* Rockville, Md.: National Institute on Drug Abuse.

Johnston, L., P. O'Malley, and L. Eveland. 1978. Drugs and Delinquency: A Search for Causal Connections. In *Longitudinal Research on Drug Use: Empirical Findings and Methodological Issues*, ed. D. Kandel, 132–56. Washington: Hemisphere–Wiley.

Kandel, D. 1975. Reaching the Hard-to-Reach: Illicit Drug Use among High School Absentees. *Addictive Diseases* 1:465–80.

————. 1984a. Marijuana Users in Young Adulthood. *Archives of General Psychiatry* 41:200–9.

————. 1984b. Substance Abuse by Adolescents in Israel and France: A Cross-Cultural Perspective. *Public Health Reports* 99:277–83.

————. 1985. On Processes of Peer Influences in Adolescent Drug Use: A Developmental Perspective. *Advances in Alcohol and Substance Abuse* 4:139–63.

Kandel, D.B., and M. Davies. 1991a. Decline in the Use of Illicit Drugs by High School Students in New York State: Comparison with National Data. *American Journal of Public Health* 81:1064–7.

————. 1991b. Cocaine Use in a National Sample of U.S. Youth (NLSY): Epidemiology, Predictors and Ethnic Patterns. In *The Epidemiology of Cocaine Use and Abuse*, eds. C. Schade and S. Schober, 151–88. NIDA research monograph 110. Rockville, Md.: National Institute on Drug Abuse.

————. 1991c. Progression to Regular Marijuana Involvement: Phenomenology and Risk Factors for Near-Daily Use. In *The Transition from Drug Use to Abuse/Dependence*, eds. M. Glantz and R. Pickens. Rockville, Md.: National Institute on Drug Abuse.

Kandel, Denise B., M. Davies, and M. Davis. 1990. New York State Youth Survey. Albany: New York State Office of Mental Health.

Kandel, D.B., E. Single, and R. Kessler. 1976. The Epidemiology of Drug Use among New York State High School Students: Distribution, Trends and Change in Rates of Use. *American Journal of Public Health* 66:43–53.

Kandel, D.B., and K. Yamaguchi. 1985. Job Mobility and Drug Use: An Event History Analysis. *American Journal of Sociology* 92:836–78.

Kessler, R. 1990. The National Comorbidity Study. *DIS Newsletter* 7(2):1.

Klerman, G.L., P.W. Lavori, J. Rice, et al. 1985. Birth-Cohort Trends in Rates of Major Depressive Disorder among Relatives of Patients with Affective Disorder. *Archives of General Psychiatry* 42:689–93.

Kopstein, A., and J. Gfroerer. n.d. Drug Use Patterns and Demographics of Employed Drug Users: Data from the 1988 National Household Survey on Drug Abuse. Rockville, Md.: National Institute on Drug Abuse. (unpublished)

Kosten, T.A., and T.R. Kosten. 1990. The Dependence Syndrome Concept as Applied to Alcohol and Other Substances of Abuse. In *Comprehensive Handbook of Drug and Alcohol Addiction*, ed. N.S. Miller. New York: Marcel Dekker.

Kosten, T.R., B.J. Rounsaville, T.F. Babor, et al. 1987. Substance-use Disorders in DSM-III-R: Evidence for the Dependence Syndrome across Different Psychoactive Substances. *British Journal of Psychiatry* 151:834–43.

Maddahian, E., M.D. Newcomb, and P.M. Bentler. 1986. Adolescents' Substance Use: Impact of Ethnicity, Income, and Availability. In *Alcohol and Substance Abuse in Women and Children*, eds E. Maddahian, M.D. Newcomb, and P.M. Bentler, 63–78. New York: Haworth Press.

Mensch, B.S., and D.B. Kandel. 1988a. Underreporting of Substance Use in a National Longitudinal Youth Cohort. *Public Opinion Quarterly* 52:100–24.

———. 1988b. Dropping out of High School and Drug Involvement. *Sociology of Education* 61:95–113.

Miller, J.D., I.H. Cisin, H. Gardner-Keaton, P.W. Wirtz, H.I. Abelson, and P.M. Fishburne. 1983. *National Survey on Drug Abuse: Main Findings 1982*. Rockville, Md.: National Institute on Drug Abuse.

National Center for Health Statistics. 1989. Smoking and Other Tobacco Use: United States, 1987. *Vital and Health Statistics*, series 10, no.169. Washington: Public Health Service, U.S. Department of Health and Human Services.

National Institute on Drug Abuse. 1988a. *National Household Survey on Drug Abuse: Main Findings 1985*. Rockville, Md.

———. 1988b. *Demographic Characteristics and Patterns of Drug Use of Clients Admitted to Drug Abuse Treatment Programs in Selected States: Trend Data 1979–1984*. Rockville, Md.

———. 1989a. Use and Consequences of Cocaine. Capsule C-84-04. Rockville, Md.: Press office. (Mimeo)

———. 1989b. *National Drug and Alcoholism Treatment Unit Survey (NDATUS) 1987: Final Report*. Rockville, Md.

———. 1990a. *National Household Survey on Drug Abuse: Main Findings 1988*. Rockville, Md.

———. 1990b. *National Household Survey on Drug Abuse: Population Estimates 1988*. Rockville, Md.

———. 1990c. *Semiannual Report*. Emergency Room Data: January 1987–December 1989; Medical Examiner Data, July 1986–June 1989. Statistical series G, no. 24. Rockville, Md.

————. 1990d. *National Drug and Alcoholism Treatment Unit Survey (NDATUS) 1989: Main Findings Report.* Rockville, Md.

————. 1990e. *Annual Data 1989. Data from the Drug Abuse Warning Network (DAWN).* Rockville, Md.

————. 1991a. *National Household Survey on Drug Abuse: Population Estimates 1990.* Rockville, Md.

————. 1991b. *National Household Survey on Drug Abuse: Highlights 1990.* Rockville, Md.

————. 1991c. *National Household Survey on Drug Abuse: Main Findings 1990.* Rockville, Md.

————. 1991d. *Annual Emergency Room Data 1990.* Rockville, Md.

————. 1991e. *Annual Medical Examiner Data 1990.* Rockville, Md.

————. 1991f. *National Household Survey on Drug Abuse: Population Estimates 1991.* Rockville, Md. (Revised tables: 2/92)

————. 1991g. Press Release: Assorted Statements and Statistical Documents, December 19. Rockville, Md.: Press Office.

————. 1992. Press Release. August 5. Rockville, Md.: Press Office.

National Institute of Justice. 1990. Arrestee Drug Use: January to March 1990. *Drug Use Forecasting* (October).

————. 1991. Drugs and Crime 1990: Annual Report. *Drug Use Forecasting* (August).

NIDA Notes. 1991. Vol. 5(5).

Novick, L.F., D.M. Glebatis, R.L. Stricof, P.A. MacCubbin, L. Lessner, and D.S. Berns. 1991. II. Newborn Seroprevalence Study: Methods and Results. *American Journal of Public Health* 81 (suppl.):15–21.

O'Donnell, J., H. Voss, R. Clayton, G. Slatin, and R. Room. 1976. *Young Men and Drugs—A Nationwide Survey.* Washington.

Oetting, E.R., and F. Beauvais. 1990. Adolescent Drug Use: Findings of National and Local Surveys. *Journal of Consulting and Clinical Psychology* 58:385–94.

Office of National Drug Control Policy. 1990. *Leading Drug Indicators* (White Paper). Washington: Executive Office of the President.

Prendergast, M.L., G.A. Austin, K.I. Maton, and R. Baker. 1989. *Substance Abuse among Black Youth.* Madison, Wis.: Wisconsin Clearinghouse, University of Wisconsin.

Raveis, V.H., and D.B. Kandel. 1987. Changes in Drug Behavior from the Middle to the Late Twenties: Initiation, Persistence, and Cessation of Use. *American Journal of Public Health* 77:607–11.

Regier, D.A., J.H. Boyd, J.D. Burke, et al. 1988. One-Month Prevalence of Mental Disorders in the United States. *Archives of General Psychiatry* 45:977–86.

Regier, D.A., M.E. Farmer, D.S. Rae, et al. 1990. Comorbidity of Mental Disorders with Alcohol and Other Drug Abuse. *Journal of the American Medical Association* 264:2511-18.

Robins, L.N., J.E. Helzer, M.M. Weissman, et al. 1984. Lifetime Prevalence of Specific Psychiatric Disorders in Three Sites. *Archives of General Psychiatry* 41:949-58.

Robins, L.N., B.Z. Locke, and D.A. Regier. 1991. An Overview of Psychiatric Disorders in America. In *Psychiatric Disorders in America*, eds. L. Robins and D. Regier, 328-66. New York: Free Press.

Robins, L.N., and D.A. Regier. Eds. 1991. *Psychiatric Disorders in America*. New York: Free Press.

Ryder, N.B. 1965. The Cohort as a Concept in the Study of Social Change. *American Sociological Review* 30:843-61.

Schuster, C.R. 1990a. Statement on the nature and extent of drug abuse in the United States. Presented to the Committee on the Judiciary, Subcommittee on Criminal Justice, U.S. House of Representatives, March 27. Washington.

Schuster, C.R. 1990b. Press Conference on the 1990 National Household Survey on Drug Abuse, December 19. Washington.

Smart, R.G., and E.M. Adlaf. 1986. Patterns of Drug Use among Adolescents: The Past Decade. *Social Science Medicine* 23:717-19.

Trimble, J.E., A.M. Padilla, and C.S. Bell. Eds. 1987. *Drug Abuse among Minorities*. DHHS pub. no. (ADM) 87-1474. Washington.

University of Michigan. 1991. Press release, January 23. Ann Arbor.

———. 1992. Most Forms of Drug Use Decline among American High School and College Students, U-M Survey Reports. Press release, January 27. Ann Arbor.

U.S. Bureau of the Census. 1988. Projection of the Population by Age, Sex and Race: 1988-2010. *Current Population Reports*, series P-25, no. 1017. Washington.

———. 1989. Population Profile of the U.S. *Current Population Reports*, series P-23, no. 159. Washington.

Welte, J.W., and G.M. Barnes 1987. Alcohol Use among Adolescent Minority Groups. *Journal of Studies on Alcohol* 48:329-36.

Zabin, L.S., J.B. Hardy, E.A. Smith, and M.B. Hirsch. 1985. Substance Use and Its Relation to Sexual Activity among Inner-City Adolescents. Presented at NIDA Technical Review on Drug Abuse and Adolescent Sexual Activity, Pregnancy and Parenthood, March. Bethesda, Md.

Acknowledgment: Work on this manuscript was partially supported by Research Scientist Award KO5 DA00081 from the National Institute on Drug Abuse.

Drug Policy:
Striking the Right Balance

AVRAM GOLDSTEIN and
HAROLD KALANT

Stanford University; University of Toronto

P SYCHOACTIVE DRUGS OBVIOUSLY PROVIDE PLEASURE
or relief to millions of users, but also can do enormous individual and social harm. The recurring debate about legalizing illicit
drugs arises from different perceptions of the degree of harm caused by
their prohibition, relative to the harm caused by the drugs themselves
(Nadelmann 1988, 1989a,b; Meisler 1989; Friedman 1989; Sweet 1989;
Schmoke 1989; Buckley 1989). At one extreme are libertarians who advocate removal of criminal sanctions from all drugs. At the other extreme are governments that apply the death penalty for even minor
levels of trafficking. The status quo in most of the world consists of different degrees of regulation for different psychoactive drugs, only caffeine being available without restriction. Accordingly, the debate is not
about the oversimplified dichotomy, legalization versus prohibition, but
rather about the specifics of regulatory policies for each drug.

An ideal policy for each drug would strike the best balance among all
the costs and benefits (Kalant and Kalant 1971). The right to enjoy the
pleasurable effects of drugs and freedom from state interference in citizens' private lives must be weighed against the benefits of governmental
measures to protect the well-being of drug users, people around them,
and society at large. The harm produced by excessive drug use must be
weighed against the costs, both monetary and social, of enforcing whatever degree of regulation is imposed. Every cost–benefit analysis carries
an implicit bias, which reflects the ethical, social, religious, and political

views of those doing the analysis. Our bias is toward a humane and democratic society that provides maximum individual freedom, but the exercise of such freedom must be consistent with the rights of others and the harmonious functioning of the community. All laws have potentially harmful effects, but policy recommendations based only on considering harm caused by the law would be just as unbalanced as those based only on considering harm caused by the drugs themselves.

All drugs can be dangerous; even when they are pure and are used on prescription to treat disease, they often have adverse effects. Most governments are required, by public consensus and demand, to protect citizens against numerous avoidable hazards and not merely to warn them of possible dangers. The U.S. Pure Food and Drug Laws, enacted in 1906, set up the technical machinery, the Food and Drug Administration (FDA), for assessing drug hazards, forbidding over-the-counter sale of the more dangerous drugs, requiring manufacturers to report on unanticipated adverse reactions, and exercising legal control over drug distribution. This legislation grew out of the recognition that innocent people, without the technical expertise needed to assess the risks, were being hurt by drugs with unacceptably high risk-to-benefit ratios.[1] ,

The use of drugs for nonmedical purposes carries risks not only for the user, but for society as well. A compassionate society ultimately pays the costs, not only of injury to nonusers, but even of self-inflicted injuries to users themselves. Society pays the costs of all acute and chronic toxicity through loss of productivity and by subsidizing medical care, providing welfare assistance to users' families, and dealing with the special educational needs of children whose brains were damaged in utero[2] (U.S. De-

---

[1] Examples of long-established legislation that protects as well as informs are laws requiring motorcycle helmets and automobile safety belts, pasteurization of milk, fluoridation of municipal drinking water supplies, and immunizations of school children. Temin (1980) recounts the history of drug regulation in the United States.

[2] Fetal damage associated with use of an illicit drug (Finnegan 1981; Hutchings, Brake, and Morgan 1989) is complicated by adulterants, malnutrition, and concurrent infections, making it difficult to implicate the drug itself with certainty. Even in the absence of these confounding factors, however, low birth weight and prematurity are associated with maternal smoking and alcohol use (Randall and Noble 1980). The fetal alcohol syndrome, characterized by abnormal facial features and mental retardation, is now recognized as a direct teratogenic effect of alcohol consumption during pregnancy (Clarren and Smith, 1978; Brown et al., 1979; Little and Streissguth 1981; Warren and Bast, 1988).

partment of Health and Human Services 1988). Thus, drug abuse is rarely a victimless crime. We think that society has a right to take the costs into account in formulating its drug policies.

We shall argue here the following points:

1. Psychoactive drugs are, to varying degrees, dangerous to users and to society.
2. Drug consumption is strongly influenced by availability.
3. Availability can be modified, not only by outright prohibition, but also in many ways that fall short of prohibition.
4. Although supply reduction is a desirable goal, demand reduction is the real key to lasting amelioration of the drug problem.
5. Rational drug policy ought to be tailored to the dangers presented by each psychoactive drug to users and to society.

Psychoactive Drugs Are Dangerous

Legalizing and regulating drugs that are now illicit would, through quality control measures, eliminate harmful effects due to unknown and variable potencies, adulterants (such as particulates responsible for embolism after intravenous injection), toxic byproducts of illicit manufacture, and bacterial or viral contamination. All other adverse effects, however, are due to intrinsic properties of each drug (table 1) and thus are independent of legal status. Harm to the user may occur immediately or only after chronic use and may be due to behavioral effects of the drug or to toxic actions on organ systems (Wallgren and Barry 1970; U.S. Department of Health Education and Welfare 1973; Institute of Medicine 1980; Lieber 1982; D.B. Goldstein 1983; Tarter and Van Thiel 1985; U.S. Department of Health and Human Services 1982, 1984a,b).[3,4]

An example of a significant threat to both the user and society is the paranoid psychosis, sometimes accompanied by violence, that can result

---

[3] (Gilman et al. 1985). Drug toxicity, in general, is dose related, and toxic dose thresholds vary widely among people. Only a small proportion of users will experience the most serious toxic effects listed in the table, but the larger the user pool, the greater the absolute number of people who are harmed. As with diets high in saturated fats, which lead to atherosclerosis in only a small percentage of consumers, the absolute numbers can be great enough to constitute a major medical problem with high health care costs.

from repeated use of amphetamines or cocaine (Connell 1958; Kalant, 1973; Arif, 1987). In classic experiments (e.g., Griffith et al. 1972) administration of amphetamine or cocaine to normal human volunteers on a regular dosage schedule produced paranoid psychotic behavior. Such studies showed that no previous psychopathology was required and that paranoid reactions to drugs of this class by addicts cannot be attributed to fear of law enforcement, but are the result of direct drug effects on the brain. Another example is the possibility of lasting brain damage from alcohol, volatile solvents, cocaine, phencyclidine (PCP), marijuana, and 3,4-methylenedioxy-methamphetamine (MDMA, which is also known as ecstasy) (Escalante and Ellinwood 1970; Peterson and Stillman 1978; Schmidt 1980; Heath et al. 1980; Popham, Schmidt, and Israelstam 1984; Olney, Labruyere, and Price 1989; McKenna and Peroutka 1990).

The addicting drugs have two special characteristics with policy implications. First, repeated long-term administration produces a state of physical dependence (D.B. Goldstein 1978; Sharp 1984; Jaffe 1985) so that neurochemical brain function is disturbed (withdrawal syndrome) if the drug is suddenly discontinued. This dependence occurs in animals as well as in humans. The pattern of dependence and the intensity of the withdrawal syndrome differ among drugs and among users. Dependence accounts, in part, for the compulsion to continue use of an addicting drug, and it complicates the treatment of addicts. However, there are effective medical procedures for ameliorating withdrawal distress during detoxification (Dupont, Goldstein, and O'Donnell 1979; Gold and Dackis 1984; Preston and Bigelow 1985).[3,5]

---

[4] A drug that delays reaction time or clouds judgment can endanger the lives of others if the user operates complex machinery or vehicles. A drug that causes violent paranoid behavior can endanger all who come in contact with the user. Behavioral effects, even at the moderate intensity sought by the average user, can present a major threat to society. For example, moderate doses of alcohol imbibed in ordinary social drinking are sufficient to cause a measurable decrement of performance in tests of reaction time, vigilance, or judgment, making for dangerous driving and hazardous operation of complex equipment (Moskowitz and Robinson 1988). Similar findings apply to marijuana (Yesavage et al. 1985). In general, any drug taken for the purpose of altering mood and behavior can, in some circumstances, endanger other people.

[5] Defense attorneys often claim that physical dependence exculpates crimes committed to obtain drugs. This argument is invalid if treatment is readily available as an alternative to criminal activity.

TABLE 1
Toxic Effects and Addiction Risk of the Major Psychoactive Drugs[a]

Drug category	Acute toxicity	Chronic toxicity	Relative risk of addiction
Alcohol and related drugs (benzodiazepines, barbiturates)	Psychomotor impairment, impaired thinking and judgment, reckless or violent behavior. Lowering of body temperature, respiratory depression.	Hypertension, stroke, hepatitis, cirrhosis, gastritis, pancreatitis.[b] Organic brain damage, cognitive deficits. Fetal alcohol syndrome.[b] Withdrawal effects: shakes, seizures, delirium tremens.	3
Cocaine, amphetamines	Sympathetic overactivity, hypertension, cardiac arrhythmias, hyperthermia. Acute toxic psychosis: delusions, hallucinations, paranoia, violence. Anorexia.	Paresthesias. Stereotypy. Seizures, withdrawal depression, chronic rhinitis, perforation of nasal septum.	1
Caffeine	Cardiac arrhythmias. Insomnia, restlessness, excitement. Muscle tension, jitteriness. Gastric discomfort.	Hypertension. Anxiety, depression, withdrawal headaches.	5
Cannabis (marijuana, hashish)	Psychomotor impairment. Synergism with alcohol and sedatives.	Apathy and mental slowing, impaired memory and learning (brain damage?). Impaired immune response.[c]	4

Nicotine	Nausea, tremor, tachycardia. High doses: hypertension, bradycardia, diarrhea, muscle twitching, respiratory paralysis.	Coronary, cerebral and peripheral vascular disease, gangrene. Gastric acidity, peptic ulcer. Withdrawal irritability, impaired attention and concentration. Retarded fetal growth, spontaneous abortion.[c]	2
Opiates	Sedation, analgesia, emotional blunting, dream state. Nausea, vomiting, spasm of ureter and bile duct. Respiratory depression, coma, synergism with alcohol and sedatives. Impaired thermoregulation. Suppression of sex hormones.	Disorders of hypothalamic and pituitary hormone secretion. Constipation. Withdrawal cramps, diarrhea, vomiting, gooseflesh, lacrimation, and rhinorrhea.	2
Hallucinogens (LSD, PCP)	Sympathetic overactivity. Visual and auditory illusions, hallucinations, depersonalization. PCP only: muscle rigidity, hyperpyrexia, ataxia, agitation, violence, stereotypy, convulsions.	Flashbacks. Depression, prolonged psychotic episodes.	5

83

[a] Listed here are effects due to the drugs themselves. The effects are dose related and subject to individual variation in sensitivity, so not all are expected to be seen in every user. Approximate rankings for relative risk of addiction are on a 5-point scale, where 1 is most severe.
[b] These effects result only from alcohol, not benzodiazepines or barbiturates.
[c] Bronchitis, emphysema, precancerous changes, lung cancer, pulmonary hypertension, and cardiovascular damage by carbon monoxide are consequences of smoking tobacco or marijuana, not due to the respective psychoactive drugs. Inhalation of smoke by nonsmokers is also a significant hazard (5). With equivalent smoking, these chronic toxic effects occur sooner with marijuana than with tobacco.

The second special characteristic, tolerance (D.B. Goldstein 1978; Sharp 1984; Jaffe 1985), which is typically associated with the development of physical dependence, is manifested by a tendency to escalate dosage because the same dose is no longer as effective as it was before. As with physical dependence, the degree of tolerance differs by drug and by user. An extreme form of dosage escalation is seen with heroin and cocaine under both experimental and real-life conditions (Meyer and Mirin, 1979; Fisher, Raskin, and Uhlenhuth 1987; Washton and Gold 1987). Dosage escalation complicates schemes for providing addicts with their favorite drugs free or at low prices; when British clinics tried this for heroin addicts, the addicts resorted to the black market for supplemental supplies when the dosage ceiling (high though it was) had been reached (Hartnoll et al. 1980).

Many people are able to use addictive drugs in moderation. There are coffee drinkers who take only a cup or two a day, occasional smokers who use only a few cigarettes a day, social drinkers who consume no more than a couple of drinks a day, and marijuana users who smoke a "joint" once in a while. Some people (at least for some period of time) can restrict their use of heroin to weekends, or of cocaine to an occasional party (Zinberg and Jacobson 1976; Kozel and Adams 1985). Others, in contrast, are vulnerable to escalation to compulsive heavy use, stopping only with great difficulty, if at all, and relapsing readily. There is no sharp separation between so-called social users and addicted users, but rather a continuum of increasing levels of use and risk (Smart and Whitehead 1972; Schmidt and Popham 1978; Makela 1978) (see table 1).

The compulsive quality of drug addiction presents a special danger because for most drugs there is no way to predict who is at greatest risk.[6] People who become addicted usually believe, at the outset, that they will be able to maintain control. After the compulsion takes control, addicts persist in using high doses, often by dangerous routes of administration. Because the heavy users constitute the heart of the drug problem, more research is urgently needed to explain why they doggedly

---

[6] We do not know to what extent predisposition is conditioned by experience, caused by endogenous depression or other psychiatric disorders, molded by drug-induced changes in brain chemistry, or genetically predetermined. We do not know whether, for a given person, the predisposition applies to all addicting drugs or is drug specific; in alcoholism, it seems to be drug specific. Researchers are attempting to identify genetic markers of predisposition to addiction (especially to alcohol) (Pickens and Svikis 1988; Martin 1989; Blum et al. 1990).

persist in a self-destructive activity despite full knowledge of its consequences.

Part of the explanation is in the pharmacology of the drugs themselves. Despite the acknowledged importance of peer group pressures, fads, personal and social stresses, price, and numerous other factors that affect drug use by humans, one cannot ignore the psychoactive drug actions, which are sought by the users. Experiments with rats, monkeys, and other species have shown that an animal fitted with an indwelling venous cannula, through which it can obtain an injection by pressing a lever, will establish a regular rhythm of lever pressing if (and only if) the injection contains one of the known addicting drugs.[7] One measure of the addictiveness of a drug is how hard the animal will work (that is, how many times it will press the lever) for each injection. Another measure is the extent to which the animal engages in drug self-administration to the exclusion of normal activities like eating, drinking, exploratory behavior, grooming, or sex. Yet another measure is the rapidity of relapse after a period of enforced abstinence. By these criteria cocaine is the most addictive drug known. Monkeys with unrestricted access in this laboratory procedure will actually kill themselves with cocaine by cardiovascular collapse, starvation, dehydration, or skin infections caused by self-mutilation (Aigner and Balster 1978; Fischman 1988).

Cognitive factors play a role in moderating the behavior of humans who try psychoactive drugs but do not become addicted. Nevertheless, the single-minded preoccupation of many cocaine, heroin, nicotine, and alcohol addicts with obtaining and using their respective drugs is disturbingly reminiscent of the animal experiments and reflects a major role of direct drug effects in driving addictive behavior. Research has begun to reveal where the addicting drugs act in the brain to produce the rewarding effects that give rise to self-administration behavior.[8] We are

---

[7] Animal experiments have the virtue that they permit direct study of the inherent reinforcing properties of the drugs themselves, uncomplicated by social factors (Schuster and Johanson 1974; Karoly et al. 1978; Brady and Lukas 1984; Clouet, Asghar, and Brown 1988).

[8] Microinjections directly into the brain have permitted the identification of a few specific sites and pathways that mediate the drug-induced positive reinforcement. One site is a cluster of dopaminergic neurons in the ventral tegmental area that project to the nucleus accumbens in the forebrain. Cocaine and amphetamines appear to stimulate this so-called reward pathway directly, whereas opiates evidently free the pathway from inhibitory controls (Koob and Bloom 1988; Kornetsky et al. 1988i; A. Goldstein 1989; Wise and Rompre 1989).

far from understanding fully how and where each psychoactive drug acts on these reward pathways, but the emerging picture suggests the following: Reward systems have developed over the course of evolution to reinforce useful behaviors and extinguish harmful ones and to maintain and adaptively regulate a fine-tuned set of drives related to pleasure and pain, emotional and sexual satisfaction, hunger, thirst, and satiety. Addicting drugs act on these same systems by substituting for the natural neurotransmitters that act at different points in the circuitry, thus producing an artificial state of reward (euphoria), a powerful compulsion to sustain that state, and possibly irreversible (or long persistent) dysfunctions of the reward mechanisms.

Availability Affects Consumption

As would be expected, the ease of obtaining a drug affects its consumption. Contrary to the prevalent view that prohibition failed, there is considerable evidence that it reduced alcohol consumption substantially, albeit at the price of bootlegging, gangsterism, violence, and disrespect for the law among some segments of society. De facto prohibition of alcohol was introduced in the United States around 1916 (Clark 1976)[9] and continued as a wartime restriction, at a time when the temperance movement (and then the war effort) enjoyed wide public support. A prompt fall occurred in the death rate from liver cirrhosis, which is a good index of the prevalence of alcoholism in the population and which correlates well with the mean per capita consumption of alcohol. The decrease in cirrhosis deaths from about 12 per 100,000 in 1916 to less than 7 in 1920 corresponds to a 50 percent fall in alcohol use (Klatskin 1961; Popham 1970; Schmidt 1977; Moore and Gerstein 1981).[10]

---

[9] Although the Eighteenth Amendment was not enacted until 1920, a variety of federal, state, and local measures were applied strongly and effectively, beginning in 1916. Measures included the strict regulation of interstate commerce in alcohol, prohibition of sale to persons under 21 years of age, local prohibition, and other restrictive measures. These measures constituted de facto prohibition, which was later formalized by the slower process of constitutional amendment (Clark, 1976).

[10] This decline also means that even alcoholics drank less when drinking became illegal, because the fall in cirrhosis death rate is due exclusively to the change in consumption by very heavy drinkers.

Conversely, lowering the legal drinking age in a number of states and provinces led to an immediate increase in alcohol-related driving accidents contributed by those under 21 (Whitehead et al. 1975; Whitehead 1977; Wagenaar 1983; Wechsler 1980). Thus, although drinking by persons under 21 had, no doubt, previously occurred, it increased sharply when the law permitted it. The potential effectiveness of legal restraints is also demonstrated by the ending of the Japanese methamphetamine epidemic through stringent police enforcement that was backed by an antidrug consensus among the general population (Brill and Hirose 1969).

An example of how availability affects drug use is provided by the experience of physicians, dentists, and nurses, who have easy (although illegal) personal access of psychoactive drugs that are forbidden to the general public. Despite the risk of heavy sanctions, such as loss of professional license and possible criminal prosecution, the per capita prevalence of addiction to opiates and other drugs was found to be much higher than in a matched control population (Vaillant, Brighton, and McArthur 1970; American Medical Association 1973; McAuliffe et al. 1986; Brewster 1986).[11]

Injudicious prescribing practices may allow diversion of a medically approved drug into the illicit market. In New York State, the simple step of imposing a triplicate prescription system for benzodiazepines, to permit accurate record keeping by the authorities, produced a dramatic drop in consumption (especially of Valium) and a steep increase in the street price of these widely abused drugs (New York State Department of Health 1989).

From the standpoint of the consumer, a rise in price is tantamount to decreased availability and vice versa. Thus, price affects drug use. The mean per capita consumption of alcohol in Ontario between 1928 and 1974 varied inversely with the unit price of alcohol in constant dollars, in

---

[11] A few other examples of availability affecting consumption are pub closing hours in Britain (Smart, 1974), cigarette vending machines in the United States (Altman et al. 1989), the change from clerk service to self-service in Ontario liquor stores (Smart 1974), and proximity to opium production areas in Laos (Westermeyer 1979). Court decisions holding establishments responsible, both in criminal and in civil law, for the consequences of serving liquor to someone already intoxicated (Insurance Law Reports 89-631, *O. Hague vs. Billings*, 27 April 1989, Supreme Court of Ontario, Grainger J.) exemplify yet another mechanism for reducing excessive consumption and ameliorating some adverse effects on society.

almost perfect mirror image fashion, and a similar relationship has been shown for several European countries. The cirrhosis death rate also varied inversely with price, indicating that alcoholics as well as social drinkers are affected by price changes. This price elasticity of alcohol use by alcoholics has even been demonstrated experimentally (Russell 1973; Popham, Schmidt, and deLint 1975; Babor et al. 1978; Davies 1983; Grossman 1989; Lewit 1989). Similarly, smoking has varied inversely with the level of taxation on cigarettes. The sudden large increase in the use of cocaine in North American cities following the introduction of crack, a crude form of cocaine free base, has been attributed to the lower price of crack than of cocaine salt preparations, as well as to the easier and more effective method of administration by smoking. These data suggest that anything that makes drugs less expensive, such as legal sale at lower prices, would result in substantial increases in use and in the harmful consequences of heavy use (Russell 1973; Popham, Schmidt, and de Lint 1975; Babor et al. 1978; Davies 1983; Grossman 1989; Lewit 1989).

Finally, education, fashion, and social consensus contribute to the shaping of public attitudes and practices with respect to drugs. Alcohol in Western societies, cannabis in the Moslem world, and hallucinogens in Native American religions illustrate how socially accepted psychoactive drugs are incorporated into the traditions, values, and practices of a society (Roueche 1960; La Barre 1975; Rubin 1975; Efron, Holmstedt, and Kline 1979). Social incorporation of a drug rests on a consensus regarding the circumstances, amounts, and patterns of use that are considered acceptable. There is therefore an important difference between behaviors with respect to a long-acculturated drug and a newly introduced one, especially in a society undergoing rapid change.[12] Illustrative are the current difficulties with cocaine in some American and Canadian cities in contrast to the stable or even declining use of longer established drugs in both countries (Abelson and Miller 1985; Crider 1985; Bachman et al. 1988; O'Malley, Bachman, and Johnston, 1988;

---

[12] Britain, in the eighteenth century, had successfully evolved a pattern of moderate use of ale, but suffered disaster with the introduction of gin at the time of the Industrial Revolution (Glatt 1958). Japan, which had long handled sake without major difficulties, experienced a serious epidemic of medical and social problems when huge military stocks of methamphetamine were dumped on the civilian market after World War II (Brill and Hirose 1969).

Adrian, Jull, and Williams 1989; Johnston, O'Malley, and Bachman 1989; Johnston 1990).[13]

Policy Options: The Polar Extremes

The pharmacologic, toxicologic, social, and historical factors noted above provide a basis for predicting the consequences of various options for reducing drug availability. One option would be an even more Draconian enforcement of current drug prohibition laws. However, greater expenditure on measures of the kind now being used seems unlikely; political difficulties would arise if funds were diverted massively from other high-priority programs. Consequently, a more militant antidrug policy might well take the form of new measures that do not cost more, but increase police powers by infringement of civil liberties, such as search without warrant, prolonged detention for interrogation without formal charges, or further dramatic increases in the severity of penalties.

Stern measures have, indeed, been credited with ending major drug problems. It is claimed that the serious opium problem in China was ended by stern measures, including the death penalty, after the Communists came to power (Yao 1958). The Japanese methamphetamine epidemic was stamped out by less brutal, but nonetheless forceful measures (Brill and Hirose 1969). However, the cost, if democratic governments were to adopt similar measures, would be a significant change in the character of the society. In addition, the explicit constitutional guarantees of the U.S. Bill of Rights and the Canadian Charter of Rights would pose formidable obstacles to such a drastic course.

The antithesis of this approach, the legalization of psychoactive drugs, has been proposed as a possible way to reduce the high costs of enforcing existing prohibitions. Not only would the police, courts, and prisons no longer have to deal with the huge load of drug cases that now burden them, but also the legal sale of drugs of known purity at moderate prices would, it is argued, drive illicit traffic out of existence. In ad-

---

[13] The rapid growth of cocaine use over the past decade has been attributed, at least in part, to the glamorization of cocaine in the mass media and its use by sports and entertainment celebrities (Crittenden and Ruby 1974).

dition, licit businesses and governments would allegedly earn huge revenues that now find their way into drug traffickers' bank accounts.[14]

On the cost side, however, would be the consequences of increased use and abuse of the drugs themselves. Even the proponents of legalization acknowledge some risk of increased drug use with its attendant problems, but they argue that the extent of such increase would be small. However, as an editorial in the *New York Times* remarked, "There is little evidence to support so stupendous a contradiction of common sense" (*New York Times* 1989); indeed, past experience suggests that the increase in use would be very large.

This common-sense expectation is generally confirmed by historical evidence. Alcohol and tobacco, which are now so freely available, are also the most widely abused drugs, but—as noted earlier—alcohol consumption was much lower when the drug was less readily available. Social custom made cigarettes effectively unavailable to women until after World War I; then consumption increased steadily as it became more acceptable for women to smoke, and the lung cancer rate for females eventually matched that for males. Opiates and cocaine were legal and freely available before passage of the Harrison Act in 1914 (Musto 1973). Despite the absence of sound nationwide surveys, there is evidence to suggest that this availability gave rise to widespread and serious misuse. According to an epidemiologic study conducted in 1913,[15] the percentage of adults addicted to these drugs appears not to have differed much from the percentage addicted to alcohol in present-day North America.

---

[14] Likely consequences of legalizing heroin in the United States were discussed by one of us over a decade ago during a previous war on drugs (A. Goldstein 1979).

[15] C.E. Terry, Health Officer for Jacksonville, Florida, persuaded the city council to set up a clinic at which known addicts could receive free prescriptions for the drugs they desired, in any amounts they wished (Terry and Pellens 1928). The prescriptions, duplicates of which were sent to Terry's office, bore the names and addresses of the recipients, enabling him to compile a detailed list of the individual users and the types and amounts of the drugs they habitually used. The results showed, remarkably, that almost 1 percent of the entire population of Jacksonville were habitual users. As Terry noted, this figure was a gross underestimate; at least half the population comprised children under the age of 15, who did not use drugs. Not included were over-the-counter purchases from pharmacists (still legal at that time) or direct provision of drugs to affluent patients by their own physicians (the clinic served primarily indigent or low-income users). Moreover, it was considered likely that the level of drug use in large urban centers was much higher than in Jacksonville (1913 population: 67,209).

The history of alcohol provides some basis for predicting what might be expected from the removal of all drug prohibitions.[16] The key question is whether legalization of opiates and cocaine would result in levels of addiction comparable to those seen currently among users of alcohol and tobacco. Opiates and cocaine are certainly not less addictive than alcohol or nicotine by any criterion. And although the intravenous route might never become widely popular, smoking (especially of crack) would be the route of choice for millions. There is no reason to doubt that the increased costs to society would rival those now attributable to alcohol. In that case the economic savings that might be achieved, even if it were possible to eliminate all the costs of drug law enforcement, might well be offset by the additional costs resulting from the consequences of increased drug use.

If the government were to attempt to prevent large increases in consumption by raising the prices for drugs sold through licit outlets, as suggested by some proponents of legalization, prices of illicit drugs could then be competitive, and drug traffickers could continue in business. Government would be in the unhappy position of having to choose between raising prices to discourage excessive use, thus allowing the illicit traffic to continue, and lowering prices enough to drive out the illicit trade, thus increasing consumption (Courtwright 1990).

It has been argued that legalizing and taxing drugs would provide financial resources for treatment of those who become addicted, but in Canada in 1984 the total social costs of alcohol were double the revenues generated from alcohol at all levels of government. In the United States in 1983, this ratio exceeded 10 to 1.[17]

A further inevitable consequence of legalization would be the impact

---

[16] The immediate post-Repeal increase in consumption in the United States was 43 percent, which led to a near doubling of the cirrhosis death rate. In addition, reflecting the inverse relation between real price and consumption, a 50 percent reduction in the price of alcohol in Ontario led to a 100 percent increase in consumption. Similarly, in California, a 50 percent increase in real income between 1953 and 1975 was associated with a 50 percent rise in per capita alcohol consumption (Bunce 1976). Thus, simultaneous removal of legal constraints on currently illicit drugs, and lowering of drug prices, would probably lead to at least a tripling of consumption, and this in turn would result in proportionately larger increases in all the health and social costs arising from heavy use.

[17] Canadian health care costs due to alcohol-related diseases were calculated at some $6.0 billion (Canadian), reduced labor productivity costs due to alcohol amounted to $2.5 billion, social welfare costs caused by alcohol totaled about

on public attitudes toward psychoactive drugs. The recent decline in drug use among high school students in the United States and Canada (Abelson and Miller 1985; Crider 1985; National Institute on Drug Abuse 1987; Bachman et al. 1988; O'Malley, Bachman, and Johnston 1988; Johnston 1989; Johnston, O'Malley, and Bachman 1989; Adrian, Jull, and Williams 1989) probably reflects a gradual acceptance of medical evidence that has been part of the justification for the continued illegal status of some drugs. Removal of the legal restrictions would risk conveying the message that drug use is not really as harmful as the students had come to believe and thus would weaken an important influence on consumption levels.

The right balance, we believe, lies somewhere between these policy extremes. The specific recommendations offered in the next section embody a variety of intermediate options based on two goals:

1. to reduce the recruitment of new addicts by making it more difficult and more expensive to obtain psychoactive drugs and by strengthening an antidrug consensus through education
2. to ameliorate the circumstances of those already addicted by regarding them as victims of a life-threatening disease (as indeed they are) requiring compassionate treatment

Current Extent of the Problem

The "War on Drugs" may be a useful metaphor, in the sense that war mobilizes social forces, sets priorities, marshals extraordinary resources,

---

$1.5 billion, and alcohol-related motor vehicle accidents were estimated to cost $0.3 billion. The total of these estimates comes to $10.3 billion. Revenue generated for all levels of government by the sale of alcohol in the same year was only $5.1 billion (Adrian, Jull, and Williams 1989, vol. 1, table 23). Comparable U.S. data for a population ten times greater showed about $117 billion in social and health costs, compared with an estimated alcohol revenue of $10.3 billion (Distilled Spirits Council of the United States 1984, table 42; U.S. Department of Health and Human Services 1987, table 13; Beer Institute 1987, tables 59, 60, 65). The Canadian estimates of alcohol-related revenue include not only excise taxes and duties and licensing fees, but also corporate income taxes and real estate taxes paid by the alcohol beverage industry, profits earned by the provincial government alcohol sales monopolies, and other indirect revenue. In contrast, the U.S. figures refer only to direct taxes on alcohol and therefore underestimate the total benefits to federal, state, and municipal governments.

and embodies shared societal goals. However, as with so many medical and social dysfunctions, total victory is an illusory goal. Psychoactive drugs have always been with us and probably always will be. The practical aim of drug policy should be to minimize the extent of use, and thus to minimize the harm. Because the best way to do this is often uncertain, budgets established in drug legislation should routinely mandate sufficient funds for evaluation. Inasmuch as behavior change comes slowly, it is also important, as the elements of an improved drug policy are put in place, to be patient and give them time to work; this may well prove the most difficult of our recommendations to carry out.

The first step toward a more rational and effective drug policy is for the media, the public, and governments to see the drug problem in correct perspective. The current degree of concern about illicit drug use, bordering on hysteria, is at variance with the actual data on the magnitude of the problem. As to how this distorted perception came about, one is reminded of Lincoln Steffens's description of how newspapers, in his day, created "crime waves" (Steffens 1931).

What is the magnitude of the problem? Regular sources of national U.S. data are the National Household Survey and the High School Seniors Survey (Abelson and Miller 1985; Crider 1985; National Institute on Drug Abuse 1987; Bachman, et al. 1988; O'Malley, Bachman, and Johnston 1988; Adrian, Jull, and Williams 1989; Johnston, O'Malley, and Bachman 1989; Johnston 1990), DAWN—the Drug Abuse Warning Network for emergency-room drug mentions (Swisher and Hu 1984), and surveys of military personnel (Burt 1981). These are supplemented by ad hoc (Leveson 1980) and local epidemiologic studies. In Ontario, surveys of students in grades 7 through 13 and of the adult general population have been carried out biennially since 1972.[17] The most recent estimates (table 2) (Gilbert 1984; National Institute on Drug Abuse 1989; U.S. Department of Health and Human Services 1989b)[18] show that our most serious problem drugs by far are alcohol

---

[18] Data from the National Institute on Drug Abuse (1989) and supplemental data quoted in *HHS News* (U.S. Department of Health and Human Services 1989b). For this population, daily users of heroin probably do not exceed a few hundred thousand, but heroin users are known to be underrepresented in the household population. Regular users of caffeine (as coffee, tea, chocolate, and soft drinks) are estimated conservatively at 90 percent of the population (Gilbert 1984).

TABLE 2
The Magnitude of the Drug Problem[a]

| | Frequency of drug use | |
Drug	Past month	Once or more weekly
Caffeine	178	178
Alcohol	106	47[e]
Tobacco		
Nicotine	57	57[d,e]
Smokeless	7.1	7.1
Marijuana	12	6.0
Nonmedical use of any psychotherapeutic drug	3.4	U[f]
Cocaine	2.9	0.9–2.2[g]
Crack[b]	0.5	0.3[h]
Inhalants	1.2	U
Hallucinogens	0.8	U
Heroin	1.9[c]	0.6[h]

Source: National Institute on Drug Abuse 1989.

[a] Data are numbers of users, in millions (18). The population base sampled for this survey consisted of 198 million people aged 12 and over, living in households. Tobacco use includes smokeless tobacco; cocaine use includes cocaine free base (crack).

[b] These values are included in the immediately preceding amounts.

[c] This estimate is for people who have ever used heroin, not just in the last month.

[d] These are our estimates, based on the fact that virtually all users of these two drugs, if they use monthly, also use at least weekly (and usually daily). See text for daily use of other drugs.

[e] Including 12 to 17 million functionally impaired alcoholics who use daily (the precise number depends on one's definition); virtually all tobacco users smoke or chew more than once daily.

[f] U, unknown.

[g] The lower number, from the 1988 Household Survey on Drug Abuse, is acknowledged to be an underestimate, as it excludes those living outside households. The higher number (50), could be an overestimate, biased by the fact that it is based on urine tests of arrestees (including those arrested for cocaine use), not on direct or indirect evidence of use once or more weekly.

[h] This estimate is for daily use.

and nicotine (tobacco), whether assessed by damage to users, harm to society, or numbers of addicts.[19]

The data in table 2,[18,19] which indicate use in the past month or week, obviously overestimate the size of the hard core of addicts who use

---

[19] Caffeine, the most widely used psychoactive drug, appears to be relatively benign, although not without dangers to users at high dosages (Curatolo and Robertson 1983); this refers to our table 1.

drugs several times daily (Kleiman 1990). On the other hand, all data sources tend to underestimate drug use in populations of low socioeconomic status (for example, homeless and transients). However, it is a fact (although not communicated by the media) that drug use, overall, has been declining—in all sections of the population, all parts of North America, and for all psychoactive drugs, whether licit or illicit (Abelson and Miller 1985; Crider 1985; National Institute on Drug Abuse 1987; Bachman et al. 1988; O'Malley, Bachman, and Johnston 1988; Adrian, Jull, and Williams 1989; Johnston, O'Malley, and Bachman 1989; Johnston 1990). The exception to this encouraging trend has been the recent increase in the number of people who use crack daily. This number is still relatively small, but it is of concern because of the peculiarly seductive quality of this form of cocaine[20] and because of the concentration of sales and associated violence in the inner cities.[21]

Recommendations

Supply Reduction and Appropriate Degrees of Regulation

Ideally, one would wish to match the degree of regulation and the effort expended in enforcement to the real dangers posed by each drug to the user and to society. This would respond effectively to the criticism that our present laws are hypocritical, in that dangerous, addicting drugs like alcohol and nicotine are freely available and even advertised, whereas marijuana, which is less dangerous than cocaine or heroin (but by no means harmless), is under stringent legal controls see.[22] (Peterson 1980; Fahr and Kalant 1983).

One way to use technical expertise instead of politics to formulate more rational policies would be to apply the model of the FDA, whose

---

[20] The smoking route delivers a drug to the blood flowing through the lungs. This blood, carrying a high concentration of cocaine, reaches the brain within a few seconds and without dilution. The chemical properties of crack (cocaine free base) suit it for efficient delivery by this convenient route. In this respect, crack is much like nicotine.

[21] However, the enormous sums of money being generated by the drug traffic imply that cocaine use (as distinct from trafficking) has a major middle- and upper-class component.

[22] A strictly rational approach is impractical because public acceptance and political feasibility of legislation depends not only on scientific evidence, but also

mission, with respect to therapeutic agents, is to match the degree of regulation to the actual danger each presents. Congress could delegate regulation of the nonmedical use of psychoactive drugs to the existing Alcohol, Drug Abuse, and Mental Health Administration (ADAMHA), with its three component institutes, the National Institute on Drug Abuse (NIDA), the National Institute on Alcohol Abuse and Alcoholism (NIAAA), and the National Institute on Mental Health (NIMH), much as it has delegated the regulation of therapeutic agents to the FDA. Under such a system, law enforcement responsibilities would remain with the Department of Justice. If removing the drug problem from politics is not yet feasible, the legislature should at least be guided, on a routine, ongoing basis, by the best factual information from nongovernmental experts on psychoactive, self-administered drugs, representing such fields as pharmacology, toxicology, medicine, psychology, psychiatry, criminology, law enforcement, and education.

Whatever degree of regulation is deemed, on balance, to be desirable for each drug, enforcement is essential for credibility and as a concrete expression of social disapproval. Enforcement has the desirable consequence of raising the black-market price of illicit drugs and making such drugs more difficult to obtain. The present situation, in which drug bazaars operate in full view of the police (Marriott 1989), seems intolerable in a society that claims to be ruled by law. It is unclear in such cases whether the police are corrupt or only demoralized, but it is noteworthy that corruption cuts through all strata of our governmental and private sectors, as numerous recent scandals have revealed. Thus, dealing effectively with the drug problem has broad implications for the rule of law in a democratic society.

Enforcement should be directed primarily at the higher levels of the distribution chain, but grandiose attempts to achieve a total interdiction of drug entry from abroad are a relatively poor investment. Advances in pharmaceutical chemistry are such that highly potent psychoactive drugs of every kind can be synthesized readily in clandestine laboratories, so

---

on long-established values and practices. It is extremely unlikely, for example, that present-day North American society would agree to put alcohol under stricter control than marijuana, even if currently available scientific evidence were to suggest that this is warranted. Polls show that the great majority, including those who were themselves users of marijuana, did not favor its legalization (Gallup Poll [Canada]: September 2, 1985); see also Peterson 1980, 54.

the illicit market would adjust quickly even to a complete sealing of our borders, were that possible. A modest level of highly visible interdiction activities should probably be continued, if only for their symbolic value. A massive shift of available funds is called for, however, from supply reduction to demand reduction (prevention education, treatment, and research). The federal drug war budget would be more cost effective if the presently proposed ratio of supply reduction to demand reduction—71 percent to 29 percent—were reversed.[23]

Enforcement will be most effective if coupled to community action, originating locally, but supported by adequate governmental funding and other forms of assistance. Especially in some inner-city, ethnic minority communities, enforcement is presently weakened by a widespread perception that the police apparatus behaves as a hostile, alien, and often racist force invading the community (Hamid 1990).

We advise retaining, for the present—and enforcing—the legal prohibitions on the importation, manufacture, distribution, and sale of opiates, amphetamines, cocaine, marijuana, and dangerous hallucinogens like PCP. At the same time, we suggest reducing the penalties for possession of small amounts of these drugs for personal use. Other differential enforcement options should be explored; without rewriting the laws, some laws could be enforced more strictly than others, according to the dangers of the particular drugs and the individual circumstances, as has been done for marijuana in some jurisdictions.[24] Unfortunately, recent U.S. legislation compels judges to inflict minimum five-year sentences

---

[23] In President Bush's fiscal 1991 budget request for the "National Drug Control Strategy," 29 percent was for interdiction and other offshore activities and 42 percent was for law enforcement: a total of 71 percent for supply reduction. Demand reduction totaled 29 percent. Data from Office of National Drug Control Policy.

[24] In Canada the legal status of cannabis has not been changed, but prosecutors do not oppose the use of discretionary powers by judges in sentencing, which permits them to grant absolute or conditional discharges, or to impose only a modest fine, in cases of possession of small amounts for personal use. As Single (1989) pointed out, decriminalization is not an appropriate term for the lessening of penalties for marijuana possession. Consequently, the fact that substantial increases in use did not occur in certain states does not indicate what would happen over a period of years if the possession and use of this drug were actually decriminalized. Very little solid data have yet been published in support of the frequent journalistic assertions that the relaxed Dutch policy has produced no increase in the use of cannabis or other psychoactive drugs (van de Wijngaart 1988; Engelsman 1989; Dorn 1989).

even for small-time users who sell or share small amounts of drugs (Taylor 1990).[25] We believe that criminalizing drug use per se is not productive, and we recommend that humane and constructive sentencing options be restored in drug cases.

It is sometimes argued that because marijuana seems to be the least harmful of the psychoactive drugs (excepting only caffeine), it could be legalized safely. However, the scientific evidence regarding the potential magnitude of long-term harm is still insufficient (Peterson 1980; Fahr and Kalant 1983), whereas the acute disturbance of psychomotor behavior is clearly dangerous under certain circumstances. It is not possible to predict with confidence the result of a vast expansion of the user pool, especially of heavy users. If prevention education achieves its goals, and public attitudes and other nonlegal controls over cannabis use become strong enough, it might eventually be possible to loosen the regulatory controls without risk of a major increase in use and the likely attendant problems. The experience of states like Oregon and Alaska, which have experimented with relaxing total prohibition, should be studied carefully with a view to understanding the effects on consumption. The much vaunted Dutch system deserves study; Holland did not institute sweeping drug legalization, however, but rather specifically reduced penalties for use of cannabis; at the same time, penalties on trafficking in other drugs were made more severe (Kleiman 1989).[24]

We advise increased taxation on tobacco and alcohol — as is already being done in some jurisdictions — inasmuch as this is known to be an effective means of discouraging consumption (Russell 1973; Popham, Schmidt, and deLint 1975; Babor et al. 1978; Davies 1983; Godfrey and Maynard 1989; Grossman 1989; Lewitt 1989). However, the resulting price increases must not be so great as to make an illicit market profitable. Uniformity of taxation across the country will be essential to avoid providing an incentive for interstate smuggling (Courtwright 1990). One problem is preventing tax revenues from becoming incentives for government agencies to promote increased consumption. In the government monopoly retail sales model (another means of discouraging consumption), sales revenues themselves have this potential. Therefore, tax revenues (or sales profits) should go only to drug-related research, education, and treatment, not into the general treasury.

---

[25] U.S. Code. As amended November 1, 1989. *U.S. Sentencing Commission Guidelines*, pursuant to ¶994(a) of Title 28.

The degree of regulation on tobacco should be increased. Social pressures are reducing consumption, especially in the adult, middle-class population, but sales to minors are still a problem. Federal and state laws abolishing cigarette vending machines would have a significant beneficial impact; with such machines accessible, laws forbidding sales to minors are completely ineffective, as shown in a recent study in the Washington, DC, metropolitan area.[26] Regulation on alcohol should also be increased. As with tobacco, there are many options short of total prohibition that would decrease consumption without stimulating a black market and associated criminal activities.[27]

In principle, routine or random drug testing is justifiable for people in sensitive jobs, whose use of psychoactive drugs (whether licit or illicit) could endanger public safety. Because the role of alcohol and other drugs in highway accidents is well documented, we believe that on-the-highway testing of drivers for alcohol on a nondiscriminatory basis at road blocks is justified as a protection for the innocent, and the U.S. Supreme Court has ruled that such tests are not unreasonable searches as specified in the U.S. Constitution (*New York Times* 1990). Moreover, lowering of the permissible legal limit (currently .10 percent in many jurisdiction) to .08 percent or .06 percent could have significant beneficial effects on highway safety (Kozlowski et al. 1989; Moskowitz 1989).[4] However, although urine testing for other drugs has improved greatly in accuracy (Foltz, Fentiman, and Foltz 1980; Hawks and Chia 1986), a significant problem in inferring psychomotor impairment from test results is that, whereas breath or blood tests give a real-time result, urine tests provide only a record of past use and therefore cannot determine whether a person is under the influence of a drug at the time the sample is obtained. Further research is needed for the development of noninvasive analytical methods for estimating concentrations of psychoactive drugs in blood.

---

[26] (Davis and Lyman 1989). A possibly useful step would be to restrict sale of tobacco to liquor stores, because they are accustomed to excluding minors as customers, and their compliance with proof-of-age requirements is monitored.

[27] Happy hours and other devices to promote increased consumption could be forbidden. A system like the British "pub closing hours" could be instituted. Tougher enforcement and tougher penalties on drunk driving (or, for that matter, driving in a condition impaired by any drug) could be implemented. Sale of distilled liquors, wine, and beer by the package could be restricted to licensed liquor stores or even to state-operated retail outlets, as it is in some states now and to a major extent in the Canadian provinces.

The North American demand for drugs is the driving force that creates major socioeconomic and political stress for the producer countries, especially in Latin America. The United States and Canada should assist these countries in reducing their economic dependence on drug exports. We should recognize and acknowledge that U.S. export of tobacco (especially to developing countries) undercuts any principled opposition to coca or opium export by other countries. A trade deficit does not justify our continuing in the role of major world supplier of a highly toxic and addictive substance.

Demand Reduction through Prevention Education, Treatment, and Research

All kinds of prevention efforts should be expanded as part of a broad strategy of demand reduction. Perhaps the most effective single factor in achieving this goal would be a social consensus on the appropriate circumstances and amounts of drug use. Changing attitudes, beliefs, and values at all levels of a society in order to achieve the desired consensus requires carefully planned, internally consistent, and sustained, long-term programs of education aimed at different ages, cultures, and socioeconomic groups.[28]

The time is long overdue to recognize officially, publicize, and incorporate into common speech and legislation the fact that tobacco (nicotine) and alcohol are potentially hazardous addicting drugs. We need to expunge from the language the phrases "alcohol and drugs" and "to-

---

[28] It is now recognized that neither mere drug information nor stern warnings about the dangers are effective. Recent programs, like that developed by National Institute on Alcohol Abuse and Alcoholism (U.S. Department of Health and Human Services 1989a) are aimed at the lower grades, which do not yet present drug abuse problems. They have tried to teach children to make value judgments on all matters (including but not limited to drug use), to have confidence in their own ability to do so, to resist peer pressure that goes against their own judgments, and to find alternative drug-free outlets for their drives and curiosity. Disappointingly, evaluation has not shown these elements to be effective in changing attitudes and behaviors; only an honest, calm, health-based message has proved to be effective (Moskowitz 1989; Kozlowski et al. 1989). Total expenditures on prevention education directed toward alcohol and other drugs by all federal and state departments and agencies in the United States in the current year is about $0.75 billion, 7.5 percent of the proposed budget for the War on Drugs. (Information supplied by the Office of the Director, National Institute on Alcohol Abuse and Alcoholism.)

bacco and drugs." This is not mere semantic nitpicking; language influences the way we think.

The ban on television advertising of cigarettes should be strengthened to prevent its circumvention by prominent, supposedly incidental, display of cigarette product names during television coverage of sports and other public events. Current U.S. and Canadian policies forbidding advertisements of distilled spirits on television acted as a useful first step, but there is not yet a well-founded policy on alcohol advertising in either country. A flood of beer advertisements has appeared, appealing primarily to youth, and linking beer to sports and sexual interests; international comparisons show that alcoholism can occur just as readily in predominantly beer- or wine-drinking as in spirit-drinking countries (Russell 1973; Popham, Schmidt, and deLint 1975; Babor et al. 1978; Davies 1983; Godfrey and Maynard 1989; Grossman 1989; Lewit 1989). To date, scientific studies have failed either to prove or exclude a short-term effect of alcohol advertising on consumption (Kozlowski et al. 1989; Moskowitz 1989). This is not surprising, given the ubiquity of drinking in films, television, and the print media, which probably have a greater impact on attitudes and behavioral norms than commercial advertising does. Nevertheless, we regard a progressive restriction of the right to advertise addictive drugs as an important and desirable first step in a long-term process of altering the present public perception of these substances as ordinary consumer products.

Ideally, classroom programs should not be drug specific, but should deal more broadly with the hazards of using psychoactive drugs. Integrated prevention efforts involving both the schools and the community are desirable. Finally, effective education is honest education; the educational message has to be the real dangers of each drug to the user and to society. It is useless merely to warn of the dangers of being caught, and health personnel (not law officers) should carry the drug message into the classrooms.

For specific populations with exceptionally severe drug problems, like American Indian communities or low-income African-American or Hispanic groups in major urban centers, effective prevention may be impossible without creating opportunities for economic advancement within a licit social framework and for enhanced self-respect through reinforcement of traditional social and cultural values.

Treatment should be available to all who desire it; long waiting lists are counterproductive. Having enough clinics to meet the demand will require large investments, but these could be cost effective in the long run. Adequate funding should be furnished for treatment research to test innovative therapeutic approaches, provided the research design will permit rigorous evaluation. Programs should be developed for making humane contact with addicts as a first step to treatment; needle exchanges may serve a useful purpose in this regard.[29]

We should consider developing and testing treatment programs that incorporate an initial phase in which the addict's drug of choice is made available. This approach might serve as a lure to bring some alienated users of heroin or cocaine into contact with health personnel, but it must be in the context of a genuine treatment and rehabilitation program. Many formidable practical difficulties would have to be overcome, not the least of which is to work out reliable methods of preventing the clinic itself from becoming a recruiting ground for new addicts.[30]

A different medical approach is illustrated by methadone maintenance, in which opiate addicts are stabilized on a long-lasting, orally

---

[29] As the addict group is now a major infectious focus of the acquired immunodeficiency syndrome (AIDS) epidemic in the United States, it is essential to educate them in how to stop the spread of AIDS. Means of education include informational programs about human immunodeficiency virus (HIV) transmission by blood and unsafe sexual practices, distribution of free condoms to men and women, free contraceptive advice and supplies for women, as well as access to sterilization and early abortion for HIV-positive women. Needle exchanges may be helpful primarily when used to bring intravenous drug users into a comprehensive treatment program (Hart et al. 1989). However, before the AIDS epidemic a British experiment that provided sterile equipment and pure heroin to registered addicts did not reduce the incidence of bloodborne infections; addicts shared their "sterile" equipment. Ironically, HIV is a fragile virus, easy to kill with brief heating or exposure to a disinfectant. Thus, simple means of sterilizing equipment are readily available to addicts, just as are condoms for preventing sexual transmission. But addicts do not necessarily govern their impulsive behavior according to rational guidelines, and persistent educational efforts are required (see Leukefeld, Battjes, and Amsel 1990).

[30] (A. Goldstein 1976; Trebach 1982). A similar medical model was tried in England for heroin addicts, but is now largely superseded by oral methadone maintenance. Heroin was not legalized; the drug remained illegal, but registered addicts were provided with it and with sterile syringes and needles (Judson 1974). The objective was to establish therapeutic contact and reduce the social harm caused by crimes that addicts committed in order to purchase drugs at high prices on the black market. Few of the expected favorable results were observed, however, probably because multiple intravenous injections of heroin every day represented a continuation rather than a change in addict lifestyle (Wiepert, d'Orban, and Bewley 1979; Kaplan 1983). No attempts have been made to apply this methodology to cocaine addicts.

administered opiate (Dole and Nyswander 1967; Dole 1988). Many methadone programs—provided they employ adequate dosages—have achieved the successful social rehabilitation of a considerable fraction of addicts (about one-half to two-thirds), some of whom continue to take methadone, whereas others eventually become opiate free. Reduction of street crime by addicts enrolled in methadone programs is well documented. Experts agree that methadone maintenance should not be the sole treatment for heroin addicts, but this treatment modality is well enough established to warrant expansion to meet the need (Wilmarth and Goldstein 1974; Sells 1974–76; Holmstrand, Abgaard, and Gunne 1978; Sells and Simpson 1980; Judson and Goldstein 1982a; Nurco et al. 1989).[31]

Some heroin addicts unquestionably benefit from drug-free residential environments (halfway houses). Extensive follow-up data show that some treatment is better than no treatment, but that a variety of therapeutic modalities is probably required to meet the needs of all heroin addict (Sells 1974–76; Sells and Simpson 1980). Although treatment programs of all types have achieved beneficial and humane results, there have also been practical difficulties, not the least of which is the relatively small proportion of addicts (especially to drugs other than opiates) who are treated during any given year (Hartnoll et al. 1985; Levin, Glasser, and Jaffee 1988). In addition, although some lessons can undoubtedly be learned from treatment experiences with heroin addicts, there is no agreement yet on appropriate treatment strategies for cocaine addicts.[32]

The funding should be increased for basic and applied research on all aspects of the drug problem. We predict that neurochemical and neurobiologic research will yield new understanding about the mechanisms of

---

[31] Methadone programs must be under the control of medical authorities to insure that adequate dosages are used; political and moralistic concerns have often interfered with treatment efficacy by mandating dosage ceilings that are too low and imposing too short a limit on the duration of treatment. An urgent need is to make widely available to physicians the long-acting methadone congener LAAM (levoalphaacetylmethadol), which is in several respects superior to methadone itself (Blaine and Renault 1976; Judson and Goldstein 1982b).

[32] The medical approach cannot be used in preventing recruitment of new addicts, except possibly to deglamorize addiction. Whenever a clinic offers psychoactive drugs as part of a treatment plan, it has to develop methods for excluding young experimenters who are not yet addicted, but who seek a convenient source of drugs.

the drug addictions. In the future, as in the past, such knowledge can be counted on to produce novel diagnostic, predictive, and therapeutic interventions. Specifically, learning more about the neurobiology and pharmacology of reward will lay a sounder basis for therapy. Testing for genetic vulnerability might permit better targeting of prevention efforts to those who are most vulnerable. Novel pharmacologic treatments that need to be developed include a long-acting agonist to supplant cocaine (analogous to methadone in opiate addiction), long-acting antagonists or immunization procedures, and drugs to facilitate detoxification and suppress craving. Finally, we need the patience to fund and carry out very long-term studies on the effectiveness of prevention education strategies; to do these studies well will be very expensive.[33]

Concluding Remarks

An atmosphere of desperation, which seems to prevail today in the War on Drugs, is not conducive to sound policy decisions or effective legislation. Until calm and reason can prevail, it may be better to do nothing than to act rashly, making matters worse. If we strike the right balance in drug policies, as we have suggested here, it should be possible to bring about a reduction in the demand for psychoactive drugs. A reduced demand for drugs offers the only real hope of eventually achieving, not a drug-free society, but one with substantially less drug abuse.

References

Abelson, H., and J. Miller. 1985. *A Decade of Trends in Cocaine Use in the Household Population*. NIDA research monograph 61:35–49. Rockville, Md.: U.S. Department of Health and Human Services.

Adrian, M., P. Jull, and R. Williams. 1989. *Statistics on Alcohol and Drug Use in Canada and Other Countries*. Vols. 1 and 2. *Statistics on Alcohol Use, Data Available by 1988*. Toronto: Addiction Research Foundation.

---

[33] (Bell and Battjes 1985; Pentz et al. 1989a,b). Educational efforts achieve their effects relatively slowly, compared with changes in the law or in the price of drugs, so it is essential to support education programs long enough to give them a chance to achieve whatever results they are capable of, and to permit scientific evaluation of their efficacy.

Aigner, T., and R. Balster. 1978. Choice Behavior in Rhesus Monkeys: Cocaine versus Food. *Science* 201:534-5.

Altman, D., V. Foster, L. Rasenick-Douss, and J. Tye. 1989. Reducing the Illegal Sale of Cigarettes to Minors. *Journal of the American Medical Association* 261:80-3.

American Medical Association, Council on Mental Health. 1973. The Sick Physician: Impairment by Psychiatric Disorders, Including Alcoholism and Drug Dependence. *Journal of the American Medical Association* 223:684-7.

Arif, A. Ed. 1987. *Adverse Health Consequences of Cocaine Abuse.* Geneva: World Health Organization.

Babor, T., J. Mendelson, I. Greenberg, and J. Kuehnle. 1978. Experimental Analysis of the "Happy Hour": Effects of Purchase Price on Alcohol Consumption. *Psychopharmacology* 58:35-41.

Bachman, J., L. Johnston, P. O'Malley, and R. Humphrey. 1988. Explaining the Recent Decline in Marijuana Use: Differentiating the Effects of Perceived Risks, Disapproval, and General Lifestyle Factors. *Journal of Health and Social Behavior* 29:92-112.

Beer Institute. 1987. *Brewers Almanac.* Washington.

Bell, C., and R. Battjes. Eds. 1985. *Prevention Research: Deterring Drug Abuse among Children and Adolescents.* NIDA research monograph 63. Rockville, Md.: U.S. Department of Health and Human Services.

Blaine, J., and P. Renault. Eds. 1976. *Rx: 3x/week LAAM Alternative to Methadone.* NIDA research monograph 8. Rockville, Md.: U.S. Department of Health and Human Services.

Blum, K., et al. 1990. Allelic Association of Human Dopamine D2 Receptor Gene in Alcoholism. *Journal of the American Medical Association* 263:2055-60.

Brady, J., and S. Lukas. Eds. 1984. *Testing Drugs for Physical Dependence Potential and Abuse Liability.* NIDA research monograph 52. Rockville, Md.: U.S. Department of Health and Human Services.

Brewster, J. 1986. Prevalence of Alcohol and Other Drug Problems Among Physicians. *Journal of the American Medical Association* 255:1913-20.

Brill, H., and T. Hirose. 1969. The Rise and Fall of a Methamphetamine Epidemic: Japan 1945-55. *Seminars in Psychiatry* 1:179-94.

Brown, N. et al. 1979. Ethanol Embryotoxicity: Direct Effects on Mammalian Embryos in Vitro. *Science* 206:573-5.

Buckley, W. 1989. The Panamanian Mess. *National Review* 41:70.

Bunce, R. 1976. *Alcoholic Beverage Consumption, Beverage Prices and Income in California 1952-1975.* Report no. 6. Sacramento, Calif.: State Office of Alcoholism.

Burt, M. 1981. Prevalence and Consequences of Drug Abuse among U.S. Military Personnel: 1980. *American Journal of Drug and Alcohol Abuse* 82:419–39.

Clark, N. 1976. *Deliver Us from Evil: An Interpretation of American Prohibition.* New York: Norton.

Clarren, S., and D. Smith. 1978. The Fetal Alcohol Syndrome. *New England Journal of Medicine* 298:1063–7.

Clouet, D., K. Asghar, and R. Brown. Eds. 1988. *Mechanisms of Cocaine Abuse and Toxicity.* NIDA research monograph 88. Rockville Md.: U.S. Department of Health and Human Services.

Connell, P. 1958. *Amphetamine Psychosis.* London: Chapman and Hall.

Courtwright, D. 1990. Drug Legalization and Drug Trafficking in Historical and Economic Perspective. Paper presented at Banbury Center Conference on Addictions, Banbury Center of the Cold Spring Harbor Laboratory, January 25–27. Cold Spring Harbor, New York.

Crider, R. 1985. *Heroin Incidence: A Trend Comparison between National Household Survey Data and Indicator Data.* NIDA research monograph 57:125–40. Rockville, Md.: U.S. Department of Health and Human Services.

Crittenden, A., and M. Ruby. 1974. Cocaine: The Champagne of Drugs. *Addictions* 21:62–74.

Curatolo, P., and D. Robertson. 1983. The Health Consequences of Caffeine. *Annals of Internal Medicine* 98:641–53.

Davies, P. 1983. In *Economics and Alcohol: Consumption and Controls,* eds. M. Grant, M. Plant, and A. Williams. New York: Gardner.

Davis, R., and A. Lyman. 1989. Hearings before the Subcommittee on Transportation and Hazardous Materials of the Committee on Energy and Commerce, House of Representatives (serial no. 101–85). Washington.

Distilled Spirits Council of the United States. 1984. *Annual Statistical Review 1983/84.* Washington.

Dole, V., and M. Nyswander. 1967. Heroin Addiction—A Metabolic Disease. *Archives of Internal Medicine* 120:19–24.

Dole, V. 1988. Implications of Methadone Maintenance for the Roles of Narcotic Addiction. *Journal of the American Medical Association* 260:3025–9.

Dorn, N. 1989. Sideshow: An Appreciation and Critique of Dutch Drug Policies. *British Journal of Addiction* 84:995–7.

Dupont, R., A. Goldstein, and J. O'Donnell. Eds. 1979. *Handbook on Drug Abuse.* Washington: National Institute on Drug Abuse.

Efron, D., B. Holmstedt, and N. Kline. 1979. *Ethnopharmacologic Search for Psychoactive Drugs.* New York: Raven Press.

Engelsman, E. 1989. Dutch Policy on the Management of Drug-related Problems. *British Journal of Addiction* 84:211–18.

Escalante, O., and E. Ellinwood, Jr. 1970. Central Nervous System Cytopathological Charges in Cats with Chronic Methedrine Intoxication. *Brain Research* 21:151–5.

Fahr, K., and H. Kalant. Eds. 1983. *Cannabis and Health Hazards: Proceedings of an ARF/WHO Scientific Meeting*. Toronto: Addiction Research Foundation.

Finnegan, L. 1981. The Effects of Narcotics and Alcohol on Pregnancy and the Newborn. *Annals of the New York Academy of Science* 362:136–57.

Fischman, M. 1988. Behavioral Pharmacology of Cocaine. *Journal of Clinical Psychiatry* 49(suppl.):7–10.

Fisher, S., A. Raskin, and E. Uhlenhuth. Eds. 1987. *Cocaine: Clinical and Biobehavioral Aspects*. New York: Oxford University Press.

Foltz, R.L., A. Fentiman, and R.G. Foltz. 1980. *GC/MS Assays for Abused Drugs in Body Fluids*. NIDA research monograph 32. Rockville, Md.: U.S. Department of Health and Human Services.

Friedman, M. 1989. An Open Letter to Bill Bennett. *Wall Street Journal*. September 7:A16.

Gilbert, R. 1984. Caffeine Consumption. *Progress in Clinical and Biological Research* 158:185–213.

Gilman, A., L. Goodman, T. Rall, and F. Murad. Eds. 1985. *Goodman and Gilman's The Pharmacological Basis of Therapeutics*, ed. 7. New York: Macmillan.

Glatt, M. 1958. The English Drink Problem: Its Rise and Decline through the Ages. *British Journal of Addiction* 55:51–67.

Godfrey, C., and A. Maynard. Eds. 1989. The Economics of Addiction. *British Journal of Addiction* 84 (special issue).

Gold, M., and C. Dackis. 1984. New Insights and Treatments: Opiate Withdrawal and Cocaine Addiction. *Clinical Therapeutics* 7:6–21.

Goldstein, A. 1976. Heroin Addiction. *Archives of General Psychiatry* 33:353–8.

———. 1979. Heroin Maintenance: A Medical View. *Journal of Drug Issues* (9):341–7.

———. Ed. 1989. *Molecular and Cellular Aspects of the Drug Addictions*. New York: Springer-Verlag.

Goldstein, D.B. 1978. Animal Studies of Alcohol Withdrawal Reactions. *Research Advances in Alcohol and Drug Problems* 4:77–109.

———. 1983. *Pharmacology of Alcohol*. New York: Oxford University Press.

Griffith, J., et al. 1972. Dextroamphetamine. *Archives of General Psychiatry* 26:97–100.

Grossman, M. 1989. Health Benefits of Increases in Alcohol and Cigarette Taxes. *British Journal of Addiction* 84:1193–1204.

Hamid, A. 1990. Paper presented at Banbury Center conference on addictions, Banbury Center of the Cold Spring Harbor Laboratory, January 25–27. Cold Spring Harbor, New York.

Hart, G., et al. 1989. Evaluation of Needle Exchange in Central London: Behaviour Change and Anti-HIV Status Over One Year. *AIDS* 3:261–5.

Hartnoll, R., et al. 1980. Evaluation of Heroin Maintenance in Controlled Trial. *Archives of General Psychiatry* 37:877–84.

Hartnoll, R., R. Lewis, M. Mitcheson, and S. Bryer. 1985. Estimating the Prevalence of Opioid Dependence. *Lancet* 1:203–5.

Hawks, R., and C. Chia. Eds. 1986. *Urine Testing for Drugs of Abuse.* NIDA research monograph 73. Rockville, Md.: U.S. Department of Health and Human Service.

Heath, R., A. Fitzjarrell, C. Fontana, and E. Garey. 1980. Cannabis Sativa: Effects on Brain Function and Ultrastructure in Rhesus Monkeys. *Biological Psychiatry* 15:657–90.

Holmstrand, J., E. Abgaard, and L. Gunne. 1978. Methadone Maintenance: Plasma Levels and Therapeutic Outcome. *Clinical Pharmacology and Therapeutics* 23:175–80.

Hutchings, D., S. Brake, and B. Morgan. 1989. Animal Studies of Prenatal Delta-9-tetrahydrocannabinol: Female Embryolethality and Effects on Somatic and Brain Growth. *Annals of the New York Academy of Science* 562:133–44.

Institute of Medicine. 1980. *Alcoholism, Alcohol Abuse, and Related Problems.* Washington: National Academy Press.

Jaffe, J.H. 1985. Drug Addiction and Drug Abuse. In *Goodman and Gilman's The Pharmacologic Basis of Therapeutics,* eds. A. Gilman, S. Goodman, T.W. Rall, and F. Murad. New York: Macmillan.

Johnston, L. 1990. Monitoring the Future: 1989 data, tables, and figures. Ann Arbor: University of Michigan. (Press release).

Johnston, L., P. O'Malley, and J. Bachman. 1989. *Drug Use, Drinking, and Smoking: National Survey Results from High School, College, and Young Adults Populations, 1975–1988.* DHHS pub. (ADM)89-1638. Rockville, Md.: U.S. Department of Health and Human Services.

Judson, B.A., and A. Goldstein. 1982a. Prediction of Long-term Outcome for Heroin Addicts Admitted to a Methadone Maintenance Program. *Drug and Alcohol Dependence* 10:383–91.

———. 1982b. Symptom Complaints of Patients Maintained on Methadone, LAAM (Methadyl Acetate), and Naltrexone at Different Times in Their Addiction Careers. *Drug and Alcohol Dependence* 10:269–82.

Judson, H.F. 1974. *Heroin Addiction in Britain: What Americans Can Learn from the English Experience.* New York: Harcourt Brace Jovanovich.

Kalant, H, and O. Kalant. 1971. *Drugs, Society and Personal Choice.* Toronto: Addiction Research Foundation.

Kalant, H., A.E. LeBlanc, and R.J. Gibbins. 1971. Tolerance to, and Dependence on, Some Non-opiate Psychotropic Drugs. *Pharmacology Review* 23:135–91.

Kalant, O. 1973. *The Amphetamines: Toxicity and Addiction*, ed. 2. Toronto: University of Toronto Press.

Kaplan, J. 1983. *The Hardest Drug: Heroin and Public Policy.* Chicago: University of Chicago Press.

Karoly, A., G. Winger, F. Ikomi, and J. Woods. 1978. The Reinforcing Property of Ethanol in the Rhesus Monkey. II. Some Variables Related to Maintenance of Intravenous Ethanol-reinforced Responding. *Psychopharmacology* 58:19–25.

Klatskin, G. 1961. Alcohol and Its Relation to Liver Damage. *Gastroenterology* 41:443–51.

Kleiman, M. 1989. *Marijuana: Costs of Abuse, Costs of Control.* New York: Greenwood.

———. 1990. Hard-core Cocaine Addicts. Measuring—and Fighting the Epidemic. Report prepared for Committee on the Judiciary, U.S. Senate. Washington.

Koob, G., and F. Bloom. 1988. Cellular and Molecular Mechanisms of Drug Dependence. *Science* 242:715–23.

Kornetsky, C., G. Bain, E. Unterwald, and M. Lewis. 1988. Brain Stimulation Reward: Effects of Ethanol. *Alcoholism* 12:609–16.

Kozel, N., and E. Adams. Eds. 1985. *Cocaine Use in America: Epidemiologic and Clinical Perspectives.* NIDA research monograph 61. Rockville, Md.: U.S. Department of Health and Human Services.

Kozlowski, L., R. Coambs, R. Ferrence, and E. Adlaf. 1989. Preventing Smoking and Other Drug Use: Let the Buyers Beware and the Interventions be Apt. *Canadian Journal of Public Health* 80:452–6.

La Barre, W. 1975. *The Peyote Cult*, ed. 4. Hamden, Conn.: Archon Books.

Leukefeld, C., R. Battjes, and Z. Amsel. Eds. 1990. *AIDS and Intravenous Drug Use: Future Directions for Community-based Prevention Research.* NIDA research monograph 93. Rockville, Md.: U.S. Department of Health and Human Services.

Leveson, I. Ed. 1980. *Quantitative Explorations in Drug Abuse Policy.* Jamaica, N.Y.: Spectrum.

Levin, B., J. Glasser, and C. Jaffee. 1988. National Trends in Coverage and Utilization of Mental Health, Alcohol, and Substance Abuse Services. *American Journal of Public Health* 78:1222–3.

Lewit, E.M. 1989. U.S. Tobacco Taxes: Behavioral Effects and Policy Implications. *British Journal of Addiction* 84:1217–34.

Lieber, C. 1982. *Medical Disorders of Alcoholism: Pathogenesis and Treatment*. Philadelphia: Saunders.

Little, R., and A. Streissguth. 1981. Effects of Alcohol on the Fetus: Impact and Prevention. *Canadian Medical Association Journal* 125:159–64.

Makela, K. 1978. Level of Consumption and Social Consequences of Drinking. *Research Advances in Alcohol and Drug Problems* 4:303–48.

Marriott, M. 1989. New York's Worst Drug Sites: Persistent Markets of Death. *New York Times*. June 1:1.

Martin, B. 1989. In *Molecular and Cellular Aspects of Drug Addiction*, ed. A. Goldstein. New York: Springer-Verlag.

McAuliffe, W., et al. 1986. Psychoactive Drug Use among Practicing Physicians and Medical Students. *New England Journal of Medicine* 315:805–10.

McKenna, D., and J. Peroutka. 1990. *Neurochemistry* 54:14–xx.

Meisler, S. 1989. Drug Legalization: Interest Rises in Prestigious Circles. *Los Angeles Times*. November 20:1.

Meyer, R., and S. Mirin. 1979. *The Heroin Stimulus: Implications for a Theory of Addiction*. New York: Plenum.

Moore, M., and D. Gerstein. Eds. 1981. *Alcohol and Public Policy: Beyond the Shadow of Prohibition*. Washington: National Academy Press.

Moskowitz, H., and C. Robinson. 1988. *Effects of Low Doses of Ethanol on Driving-related Skills: A Review of the Evidence*. Washington: Department of Commerce, National Technical Information Service.

Moskowitz, J. 1989. The Primary Prevention of Alcohol Problems: A Critical Review of Research Literature. *Journal of Studies on Alcohol* 50:54–88.

Musto, D. 1973. *The American Disease: Origins of Narcotic Control*. New Haven, Conn.: Yale University Press.

Nadelmann, E.A. 1988. U.S. Drug Policy: A Bad Export. *Foreign Policy* 70:83–108.

———. 1989a. *Science* 246:1104.

———. 1989b. Drug Prohibition in the United States: Costs, Consequences, and Alternatives. *Science* 245:939–47.

National Institute on Drug Abuse. 1987. *Drug Abuse and Drug Abuse Research, Second Triennial Report to Congress from the Secretary, Department of Health and Human Services*. Rockville, Md.

———. 1989. *National Household Survey on Drug Abuse: Population Estimates 1988*. Rockville, Md.

New York State Department of Health. 1989. Benzodiazepines: Prescribing Declines under Triplicate Program. *Epidemiology Notes* 4 (12).

New York Times. 1989. Why Rush to Surrender on Drugs. Editorial. December 14.

———. 1990. Court Approves Sobriety Checks Along the Road. June 15:1.

Nurco, D., T. Hanlon, T. Kinlock, and K. Duszynski. 1989. The Consistency of Types of Criminal Behavior over Preaddiction, Addiction, and Nonaddiction Status Periods. *Comprehensive Psychiatry* 30:391–402.

Olney, J., J. Labruyere, and M. Price. 1989. Pathological Changes Induced in Cerebrocortical Neurons by Phenecyclidine and Related Drugs. *Science* 244:1360–2.

O'Malley, P., J. Bachman, and L. Johnston. 1988. Period, Age, and Cohort Effects on Substance Use among Young Americans: A Decade of Change, 1976–1986. *American Journal of Public Health* 78:1315–21.

Pentz, M., et al. 1989a. A Multicommunity Trial for Primary Prevention of Adolescent Drug Abuse: Effects of Drug Use on Prevalence. *Journal of the American Medical Association* 261:3259–66.

Pentz, M., et al. 1989b. A Comprehensive Community Approach to Adolescent Drug Abuse Prevention: Effects on Cardiovascular Disease Risk Behaviors. *Annals of Medicine* 21:219–22.

Peterson, R. Ed. 1980. *Marijuana Research Findings: 1980.* NIDA research monograph 31. Rockville, Md.: U.S. Department of Health and Human Services.

Peterson, R., and R. Stillman. Eds. 1978. *Phencyclidine (PCP) Abuse: An Appraisal.* NIDA research monograph 21. Washington: U.S. Department of Health, Education and Welfare.

Pickens, R., and D. Svikis. Eds. 1988. *Genetic Vulnerability to Drug Abuse.* NIDA research monograph 89. Rockville, Md.: U.S. Department of Health and Human Services.

Popham, R. 1970. Indirect Methods for the Estimation of Alcohol Prevalence: A Review and Evaluation. In *Alcohol and Alcoholism*, ed. R.E. Popham. Toronto: University of Toronto Press.

Popham, R., W. Schmidt, and J. deLint. 1975. The Prevention of Alcoholism: Epidemiological Studies of the Effects of Government Control Measures. *British Journal of Addiction* 70:125–44.

Popham, R., W. Schmidt, and S. Israelstam. 1984. Heavy Alcohol Consumption and Physical Health Problems: A Review of the Epidemiologic Evidence. *Research Advances in Alcohol and Drug Problems* 8:149–82.

Preston, K., and G. Bigelow. 1985. Pharmacological Advances in Addiction Treatment. *International Journal of the Addictions* 20:845–67.

Randall C., and E. Noble. 1980. Alcohol Abuse and Fetal Growth and Development. *Advances in Substance Abuse: Behavioral and Biological Research* 1:327–67.

Roueche, B. 1960. *The Neutral Spirit: A Portrait of Alcohol.* Boston: Little Brown.

Rubin, V. Ed. 1975. *Cannabis and Culture.* The Hague: Mouton.

Russell, M. 1973. Changes in Cigarette Price and Consumption by Men in Britain, 1946–71: A Preliminary Analysis. *British Journal of Preventive and Social Medicine* 27:1–7.

Schmidt, W. 1977. In *Alcohol and the Liver*, eds. M.M. Fisher and J.G. Rankin. New York: Plenum.

———. 1980. Effects of Alcohol Consumption on Health. *Journal of Public Health Policy* 1:25–40.

Schmidt, W., and R. Popham. 1978. The Single Distribution Theory of Alcohol Consumption: A Rejoinder to the Critique of Parker and Harman. *Journal of Studies on Alcohol* 39:400–19.

Schmoke, K. 1989. Decriminalizing Drugs. *Omni* 11 (7):8–ll.

Schuster, C., and C.E. Johanson. 1974. The Use of Animal Models for the Study of Drug Abuse. *Research Advances in Alcohol and Drug Problems.* 1:1.

Sells, S. Ed. 1974–1976. *Studies of the Effectiveness of Treatments for Drug Abuse* (Vols. 1–5). Cambridge, Mass.: Ballinger.

Sells, S., and D. Simpson. 1980. The Case for Drug Abuse Treatment Effectiveness, Based on the DARP Research Program. *British Journal of Addiction* 75:117–31.

Sharp, C. Ed. 1984. *Mechanisms of Tolerance and Dependence.* NIDA research monograph 54. Rockville, Md.: U.S. Department of Health and Human Services.

Single, E.W. 1989. The Impact of Marijuana Decriminalization: An Update. *Journal of Public Health Policy* 10:456–66.

Smart, R. 1974. The Effect of Licensing Restrictions during 1914–1918 on Drunkenness and Liver Cirrhosis Deaths in Britain. *British Journal of Addiction* 69:109–21.

Smart, R., and P. Whitehead. 1972. The Consumption Patterns of Illicit Drugs and Their Implications for Prevention of Abuse. *Bulletin of Narcotics* 24:39–47.

Steffens, J. 1931. *The Autobiography of Lincoln Steffens.* New York: Harcourt Brace.

Sweet, R. 1989. Speech at Commonwealth Club, New York. Reported in the *New York Times* (December 13):1.

Swisher, J., and T. Hu. 1984. A Review of the Reliability and Validity of the Drug Abuse Warning Network. *International Journal of the Addictions* 19:57–77.

Tarter, R., and D. Van Thiel. Eds. 1985. *Alcohol and the Brain: Chronic Effects.* New York: Plenum.

Taylor, S., Jr. 1990. Ten Years for Two Ounces. *American Lawyer* 12:65–74.

Temin, P. 1980. *Taking Your Medicine.* Cambridge: Harvard University Press.

Terry, C., and M. Pellens. 1928. *The Opium Problem.* Reprinted 1970 with Foreword by J.C. Ball and Preface by C. Winick. (Montclair, N.J.: Patterson Smith.)

Trebach, A. 1982. *The Heroin Solution.* New Haven: Yale University Press.

U.S. Department of Health, Education, and Welfare. 1973. *The Health Consequences of Smoking: A Report of the Surgeon General.* DHEW pub. (HSM) 73-8704. Washington.

U.S. Department of Health and Human Services. 1982. *The Health Consequences of Smoking: Cancer: A Report of the Surgeon General.* DHHS pub. (PHS) 82-50179. Atlanta: Office of Smoking and Health.

———. 1984a. *The Health Consequences of Smoking: Chronic Obstructive Lung Disease: A Report of the Surgeon General.* DHHS pub. (PHS) 84-50205. Atlanta: Office of Smoking and Health.

———. 1984b. *The Health Consequences of Smoking: Cardiovascular Disease: A Report of the Surgeon General.* DHHS pub. (PHS) 84-50204. Atlanta: Office of Smoking and Health.

———. 1987. Alcohol and Health. Sixth Special Report to the U.S. Congress. Rockville, Md.: National Institute on Alcohol Abuse and Alcoholism.

———. 1988. *The Health Consequences of Smoking: Nicotine Addiction: A Report of the Surgeon General.* DHHS pub. (CDC) 88-8406. Atlanta: Office of Smoking and Health.

———. 1989a. *Helping Your Students Say No to Alcohol and Other Drugs.* Rockville, Md.: Alcohol, Drug Abuse, and Mental Health Administration.

———. 1989b. *HHS News* (July 31). Rockville, Md.

Vaillant, G., J. Brighton, and C. McArthur. 1970. Physicians' Use of Mood-Altering Drugs. *New England Journal of Medicine* 282:365–70.

van de Wijngaart, G.F. 1988. A Social History of Drug Use in the Netherlands: Policy Outcomes and Implications. *Journal of Drug Issues* 18:481–95.

Wagenaar, A. 1983. *Alcohol, Young Drivers, and Traffic Accidents: Effects of Minimum-Age Laws.* Lexington, Mass.: Lexington Books.

Wallgren, H., and H. Barry. 1970. *Actions of Alcohol* (Vols. 1 and 2). New York: Elsevier.

Warren, K., and R. Bast. 1988. Alcohol-related Birth Defects: An Update. *Public Health Reports* 103:638–42.

Washton, A., and M. Gold. Eds. 1987. *Cocaine: A Clinician's Handbook*. New York: Guilford.

Wechsler, H. Ed. 1980. *Minimum-Drinking-Age Laws: An Evaluation*. Lexington, Mass.: Lexington Books.

Westermeyer, J. 1979. Influence of Opium Availability on Addiction Rates in Laos. *American Journal of Epidemiology* 109:550–62.

Whitehead, P. 1977. *Alcohol and Young Drivers: Impact and Implications of Lowering the Drinking Age*. Ottawa: National Health and Welfare.

Whitehead, P. et al. 1975. Collision Behavior of Young Drivers: Impact of the Change in the Age of Majority. *Journal of Studies on Alcohol* 36:1208–23.

Wiepert, G., P. d'Orban, and T. Bewley. 1979. Delinquency by Opiate Addicts Treated at Two London Clinics. *British Journal of Psychiatry* 134:14–23.

Wilmarth, S., and A. Goldstein. 1974. *Therapeutic Effectiveness of Methadone Maintenance Programs in the Management of Drug Dependence of Morphine Type in the United States*. (Offset publication no. 3.) Geneva: World Health Organization.

Wise, R., and P. Rompre. 1989. Brain Dopamine and Reward. *Annual Review of Psychology* 49:191–225.

Yao, Y. 1958. The Single Convention on Narcotic Drugs and the Prevention of Drug Addiction. *Bulletin on Narcotics* 10 (1):1–8.

Yesavage, J., V. Leirer, M. Denari, and L. Hollister. 1985. Carry-Over Effects of Marijuana Intoxication on Aircraft Pilot Performance: A Preliminary Report. *American Journal of Psychiatry* 142:1325–9.

Zinberg, N., and R. Jacobson. 1976. The Natural History of "Chipping." *American Journal of Psychiatry* 133:37–40.

Drug Legalization and the Minority Poor

WILLIAM KORNBLUM

City University of New York

ONE OF THE EARLY AND BEST KNOWN STREET DRUG peddlers in Harlem was a failed jazz musician named Milton "Mezz" Mezzrow. A Chicagoan who had moved eastward with the jazz migration of the 1920s, Mezzrow in Harlem typified the street-wise rebel of the predepression years. Enamored of jazz and other African-American idioms, he believed the blues to be the embodiment of soul and the first original American form of self-expression. He took it for granted that marijuana was socially more desirable than alcohol, for it seemed to heighten the listener's appreciation of the new popular music. Mezzrow sold his product in the form of fat cigarettes soon called "mezeroles" by young Harlemites, many of them first-time buyers, who were black, Hispanic, Jewish, or Italian—representatives of the major population groups in the community at the time. Mezzrow himself was white and Jewish. His sources for the weed were Latinos (Mezzrow and Wolf 1946).

Although he was a relatively minor actor in what would soon become a larger public drama, Mezzrow's story is a timely reminder that illegal drugs are largely exogenous to African-American culture and its communities, certainly those of urban North America. Historically, new pleasurable commodities like marijuana, heroin, or cocaine were introduced by people who were not natives of the cities; among these were rural whites, West Indians, Italian Americans, Mexicans, Puerto Ricans, Africans, East Indians, Greeks, Colombian and others who migrated to cities from rural areas that grew these psychoactive products or from other urban centers (such as New Orleans) that had earlier developed markets for the drugs (Rubin 1975). Yet wholesale and retail markets for illegal drugs have tended to become especially well developed in minority ghettos, often, as in the case of heroin and now crack, with devastating effects. In large part this article is about the social forces that thrust illegal drugs so deeply into the fabric of minority communities.

Minority communities have been hardest hit by addictive drug epidemics over past decades and the sentiments of their representatives will of necessity carry great weight in legislative debates. The violence associated with the sale and use of drugs is found primarily in the minority communities of large and medium-sized cities. The majority of young males who have been killed in street violence over drug sales in the past three years are African Americans and Latinos. Overall, the homicide rate among black adolescent males is about six times higher than for whites (National Center for Health Statistics 1988). African-American, Latino, and white working-class males continue to be incarcerated for drug possession and sale at rates that severely tax the capacities of existing penal institutions. The majority of young women who become infected with the human immunodeficiency virus (HIV) are Latinas and African Americans, most of whom have histories of heroin addiction or of drug-related prostitution (Sterk 1989; Ayala 1991). Yet national statistics show that among the middle classes, where much of the demand for drugs originates, whites are significantly more likely than blacks to use illegal drugs and alcohol (Jaynes and Williams 1989; see also Kandel, this volume). This fact tends to refute suggestions that illegal drugs are a cultural trait of African-American or Latino communities. Yet the question remains as to why the ravages of addiction and the social problems associated with illegal drugs are so concentrated in lower-class minority ghettos.

Recent research demonstrates that the rate of sales and the incidence of addiction is higher in racially segregated ghettos than elsewhere (Williams 1989; Sullivan 1989). This is due in part to the large supply of illegal drugs available from ghetto-based merchants at far lower prices than buyers from the great middle-class, nonminority market are expected to pay. How this situation of economic specialization and ghetto drug supply came about and with what consequences for present generations of young people in the ghettos bears heavily on the issue of how to extricate the most pernicious drug markets from their niche in the nation's impoverished communities.

Theories of the ghetto underclass offer one set of explanations for the concentration of drug sales and addiction in impoverished minority communities. These theories trace the emergence of large proportions of people with "dysfunctional traits" (including criminal activities, drug use, and addiction) to large-scale, structural changes in the U.S. economy. Changes in the direction of a postindustrial service economy have deprived low-income minority individuals of better-paying, more secure industrial employment. Increasing numbers of the minority poor, some versions of the underclass theory argue, are left with few alternatives but to hang out, hustle, and seek welfare. Social scientists who developed the concept of the underclass have arrived at little consensus about its definition, its demographic size, or its specific consequences for criminality and drug abuse (Prosser 1991). Nonetheless, because the idea of the underclass has become such a dominant theme in policy discussions and in serious nonacademic thought about contemporary social problems, it requires attention in any treatment of drug use and the minority poor. In this article, I will develop the view that although deindustrialization and racial and class segregation clearly enhance the tendency for minority people to drift into selling and using drugs, the historical tendency for these markets to be localized in the ghettos in the first place is of primary significance.

In conclusion, I will argue for a community health perspective on drug control. This is a viewpoint that has growing numbers of supporters within minority communities and among critics of the failed prohibition strategies currently in practice. The plea often voiced by those most affected by drugs and drug-related violence is for strategies that do more than simply advocate drug decriminalization, while failing to address the consequences to their communities of generations of drug-use containment efforts and drug dealing. This view acknowledges, as Jerome Skolnick has concluded, "that there is no easy, or even difficult, solution to the American drug problem [but that there must be] a sharp reversal in our thinking regarding drugs, from a perspective centered on moral failure to a broader and more complex etiology highlighting public health and underlying social issues" (Skolnick 1992, p. 134).

Drug Market Segregation and Ghetto Segregation

Drug markets became hypertrophied in minority ghettos for a series of highly interrelated reasons, all having to do with race and class discrimi-

markets to areas of the cities seen as "off limits" for respectable classes. As Walter Reckless noted early in this century, this meant a proliferation of cabarets and bawdy houses for the Black Belt and the immigrant ghettos. As St. Claire Drake, Horace Cayton, E. Franklin Frazier, and other black social scientists saw quite clearly even before the postwar explosion of hard drug markets, it meant the creation of jobs for those who desperately needed them. During prohibition it meant that there would be a surge in the sale of bootleg alcohol and a concentration of speakeasies in the Harlems, Little Italys, and Poletowns of the cities. It also meant, however, that conflict within those communities would increase, as would violence, exploitation, and addiction.

In the case of alcohol prohibition, the passage of the Volsted Act in 1918 immediately shut down the cabarets of central-city entertainment districts. Almost overnight thousands of musicians, entertainers, and service workers of all kinds were forced out of work. Some found far less stable employment in the gangsters' speakeasies and roadhouses. The respectable classes discovered "slumming," and "darktown" came increasingly to be seen as the least threatening underworld, a part of the city where white people could briefly lose their inhibitions. Prohibitions have also created fleeting opportunities for business innovation in minority communities, as the case of marijuana illustrates extremely well.

Marijuana

During alcohol prohibition marijuana became a highly popular stimulant in many communities throughout the United States, especially in the ghettos. It was legal, relatively cheap, and pleasurable in social situations. It came to be associated with a bohemian lifestyle and a superficial form of class and racial integration. Its sale and distribution were not controlled by gangsters or large corporations and, unlike alcohol, it did not cause stupor, violence, or addiction. The mid-1920s, when a few hipsters like Mezzrow were selling marijuana in Harlem, to the late 1930s, when its sale was banned, marked a period of popular experimentation with the drug. Marijuana became integrated into the leisure life of communities like Harlem, which tolerated new ideas, racial mixing, and social experimentation. However, for reasons beyond the scope of this article, marijuana in the 1930s became the subject of a national fear campaign. Anti-marijuana legislation at the federal and state level became imminent when the now famous Laguardia Commission investigated its use and effects in New York from 1938 to 1941 (Solomon 1966).

The "sociological" component of the Laguardia Commission's report was actually conducted by undercover police officers. They noted that the drug was sold most commonly in the city in the form of "panatella" cigarettes, "occasionally referred to as 'meserole,'" the Harlem name for the fat joints Mezzrow had started selling years earlier. This description of the Harlem marijuana scene from the Laguardia Commission report is especially valuable for its discussion of the "tea pads."

> There are two channels for the distribution of marihuana cigarettes — the independent peddler and the "tea-pad." From general observations, conversations with "pad" owners, and discussions with peddlers, the investigators estimated that there were about 500 "tea pads" in Harlem and at least 500 peddlers. (quoted in Solomon 1966, 292)

The investigators defined a tea pad as a room or apartment where people gathered to smoke marijuana. The majority of such establishments were located in Harlem, where there was a distinct pattern of collusion between white landlords and the local authorities. Yet the vast majority of the tea houses did not sell alcohol or illegal drugs or allow prostitution, for there was ample legal money to be made in supplying the drug along with a venue for its consumption.

The Laguardia Commission's sociological study also noted that the atmosphere of the tea pads was congenial, "like that of a social club." Further, "a boisterous, rowdy atmosphere did not prevail and on the rare occasions when there appeared signs of a belligerent attitude on the part of a smoker, he was ejected or forced to become more tolerant and quiescent" (293). One of the most interesting setups of a tea pad, "which was clearly not along orthodox lines from the business point of view," was a series of pup tents arranged on a rooftop in Harlem. Those present, the undercover "sociologists" reported, "proceeded to smoke their cigarettes in the tents. When the desired effect of the drug had been obtained they all merged into the open and engaged in a discussion of their admiration of the stars and the beauties of nature" (293). One imagines them looking south over Central Park to the twinkling lights of midtown and the dreamy penthouses of the East Side, a smooth Duke Ellington tune on the breeze: elegant men and women, groups of friends, a hip and mixed crowd whose skin tones and backgrounds — African, West Indian, Spanish, Italian, Jewish, Asian American — are very New York. They are laughing and especially relaxed because for the briefest historical moment they are enjoying a substance whose use does not make them criminals.

Of course marijuana did become a controlled substance in the 1930s and its sale or use was made a criminal offense. The tea houses as economic institutions of interracial and ethnic sociability disappeared. The definition of marijuana as a dangerous drug, a precursor to the use of heroin and other narcotics, became official dogma and perhaps a self-fulfilling prophecy. Marijuana users became de jure deviants. Once the substance was banned, its users were forced to frequent the underworld drug markets where marijuana was merely one among a number of stimulants that might be offered. These markets continued to flourish in the ghettos and "less respectable" communities where the pattern of corruption and quasi-official containment policies followed practices established for other vices earlier in the century.

Heroin and Cocaine

Criminalization of marijuana and narcotics, as well as the interruption of the war, helped prepare the way for far more troublesome drug epidemics in minority communities like Harlem (see figure 1). As Kenneth Clark wrote in 1964, based on his research with the Harlem Youth Opportunities Unlimited Corporation (HARYOU), "Harlem is the home of many addicts; but as a main center for the distribution of heroin, it attracts many transients, who, when the panic is on, cannot buy drugs at home" (Clark 1965, 91). It became clear to Kenneth Clark, Cyril Tyson, Hylan Lewis, and all the HARYOU researchers that, following the time-honored practice of ghetto containment of deviance, the authorities were allowing illegal narcotics to be openly sold in the ghetto, behavior that was not tolerated in white communities. "It is known," Clark continued, "that when the panic is on in every other part of the city there are blocks in Harlem — 117th Street between Fifth and Lennox Avenues, for example, — where heroin can still be obtained" (1965, 104).

The disproportionate segregation of heroin markets in Harlem and other ghettos followed an historic pattern seen as well in earlier epochs in northern cities like New York and Chicago. Although never an avowed feature of public policy, the containment of market transactions

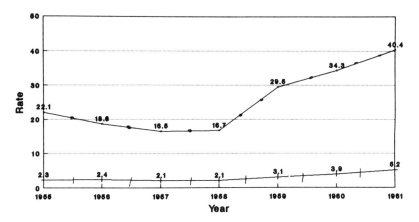

FIG. 1. Narcotics addiction rates (per 10,000) in Central Harlem and New York City from 1955 to 1961. (Adapted from HARYOU 1964.) Central Harlem, New York City.

for drugs and other deviant goods and services rested on a pattern of collusion between corrupt authorities and illegal merchants.

During the heroin epidemic, for example, East 116th Street in Harlem became an infamous open drug thoroughfare and marketplace, an identity that it retains to this day. Much of the heroin sold in retail quantities along this street came from the Pleasant Avenue neighborhood, at the East River border of the area, where Italian-American gangsters carried on a notorious wholesale drug trade. David Durk, one of the New York City police officers whose investigations of official corruption contributed to the success of the Knapp Commission Report on police corruption (1973), noted that during the heroin epidemic of the 1960s, "Pleasant Avenue was a street that never shut down. If you knew the right people you could go there and borrow fifty thousand in cash, or rent a submachine gun, or arrange to fix a judge, or pick up three kilos of heroin" (Durk 1976, 3).

In the 1970s African-American gangsters began to dominate wholesale and retail heroin markets as well as the growing retail market for powdered cocaine. Wherever possible they continued the pattern of collusion with corrupt officials. Harlem streets remained notorious for open-air drug transactions, a situation contributing to the public perception that retail drug markets in Harlem and other ghettos were impossible to control without curtailing importation of large quantities of drugs into the United States. This view of the situation gained new credibility during the crack epidemic of the 1980s and has been a justification for a "war on drugs," which tends to neglect the activities of retail markets in the ghettos in favor of efforts at large-scale interdiction. Government reports, such as that of the Knapp Commission, continually offered evidence of the greater tolerance for drug sales in ghettos than in middle-class, white communities. Rarely, however, was there any direct mention of the racism inherent in these disparities. The average citizen of the ghetto communities, on the other hand, often held extremely bitter views about drug use and sales in their communities, as evidenced in comments to Kenneth Clark and other HARYOU studies researchers by a 30-year-old Harlem male respondent:

> Most of us don't know anything about drugs or anything else, until we meet one of these types of people, and they introduce us to it — telling us about a way to make a dollar. That way we are deteriorating our race, by listening to them and by participating. But we don't have jobs, what can we do? We all need a dollar. We have to eat — we have to raise our families.
>   The MAN, he wants these things to exist in Harlem. Everything that exists in Harlem the government wants it to exist. If they didn't want it, they would stop it. (HARYOU 1964, 331)

A generation later, one hears even more of this sentiment expressed in Harlem and other black communities of urban America. The ghettos and immigrant neighborhoods of New York City, Los Angeles, Washington, D.C., and Miami are centers of the cocaine and crack trade, which has also made them centers of homicide and addiction. Cleveland, Chicago, St. Louis, Kansas City, Detroit, Milwaukee, San Francisco, and many other cities have drug problems as well, but they have not experienced the crack epidemic of the 1980s in equally murderous fashion. The reasons for this are instructive and help one understand the conspiratorial sentiments typically expressed by minority people in Harlem, East Capital Hill in Washington, D.C., and other hubs of the crack epidemic.

In those cities and their metropolitan regions there was (and to a decreasing extent still is) a large demand for cocaine in its powdered form. The drug became a recreational fad during much of the later 1970s and through the 1980s, especially among certain white, middle- and upper-class occupational groups (e.g., in politics, fashion, finance, and entertainment). Enormous cocaine supplies were built up and extensive networks of wholesale and retail suppliers developed, many of them from the minority groups, to meet the demand. Increasing numbers of dealers turned from trade in marijuana to the more easily transported and profitable cocaine; between 1983 and 1985, for example, the amount of marijuana seized by federal agents declined by about 30 percent, while Drug Enforcement Agency (DEA) seizures of cocaine increased by about 100 percent (National Center for Health Statistics 1988). In this period the street price for ordinary domestic marijuana almost doubled, while the price of cocaine fell. The smokable form of cocaine, known as "free base" or "crack," could only become widespread as the price for cocaine dropped and consumers could afford to burn the drug in higher volumes. As in the case of heroin, however, the addictive effects of the drug were felt most heavily in the places where the industry was based: in the ghettos and immigrant neighborhoods.

Research by Terry Williams and Edmundo Morales covers the history and ethnography of cocaine on the international and local New York levels in great depth. Their work forms one of the most comprehensive accounts now available of an illicit commodity, its institutions, and its culture (Williams 1978, 1989, 1992; Morales 1986, 1989). Both believe that alternative economic opportunities (e.g., crop substitution and job creation) are a vital aspect of drug control because of the way drug criminalization has so deeply imbedded production and distribution in the economies of low-income areas. (Neither, however, is sanguine about prospects for anything other than continuation of the failed policies of interdiction.) At the end of his *Cocaine Kids*, for example, Williams states: "The Cocaine Kids, and many of the kids coming behind them, are drawn to the underground economy because of the opportunities that exist there. The underground offers status and prestige—rewards they are unlikely to attain in the regular economy—and is the only real economy for many" (Williams 1989, 132). In his most recent work on the consumption side of the crack scene, Williams shows how personally debasing and self-destructive the crack milieu can become, and how deadly—due to high levels of violence and risk of infection by sexually transmitted diseases (STDs) (Williams 1992). In a fascinating parallel to the experience of the inner city, Morales' Peruvian research reveals that increasing numbers of the peasants who work in the cocaine laboratories and plantations are becoming addicted because of their prolonged contact with more powerful alkaloid doses than is to be found in the traditional form of coca leaf ingestion.

In summary, the disproportionate involvement of minority and recent immigrant groups in the illegal drug industry can be traced to historical patterns of vice market concentration in stigmatized, segregated communities. There is a rich but somewhat neglected literature on this subject, extending from the classic period of Chicago School social science to contemporary research from New York, Los Angeles, Detroit, New Orleans, and other major cities. Through this literature, one can trace the influence of alcohol and drug prohibitions and of vice "crackdowns" on the dispersal of deviant markets from urban central business districts to their subsequent concentration in the ghettos.

Contemporary research shows the continuing influence of this earlier "ecological niche" formation and of the connections between recent Hispanic immigration streams and opportunities for involvement in drug markets. Recent ethnographies of drug markets tend to stress the rational actions of successful retail level drug dealers, as opposed to the more commonly held notion that mere opportunity or attraction to the drugs explains involvement (Adler 1985; Williams and Kornblum 1985; Hagedorn 1988; Sullivan 1989; Williams 1989). Research on the changing course of the cocaine-crack epidemic, however, suggests that no matter how rational or successful groups of wholesale and retail dealers may be, the confluence of shrinking demand and persistent law-enforcement pressure results in increasing ghetto violence. Violence flares over turf defense as community protests and police actions push street-level dealers into the territories of other dealer groups. Underground markets are especially dangerous because those who operate in them do not have recourse to the normal institutions of social control and therefore must police themselves (Figueroa 1989). Guns are widely available in the United States. Because advantages may accrue to groups in the illegal markets with heavier firepower, there has been a grave escalation in weapons and a sensational increase in bystander deaths caused by automatic weapons.

As the consumption of cocaine diminishes in the nonminority, upper- and middle-class communities of metropolitan regions, and community mobilization against its use and sale increases in the same communities where its markets are concentrated, there are increasing reactions of defense, resistance, and violence among addicts and dealers. Similar patterns emerged with the heroin epidemic 30 years ago. The ill effects of a drug epidemic linger far longer in communities of the impoverished and stigmatized where addicts congregate from elsewhere and illegal markets are sustained, although at lower levels than during the epidemic.

Thus one sees that the history of illicit drugs in poor minority and immigrant communities has, among many other effects, helped to produce dependency and the increasing isolation of poor, minority people. This last trend immediately evokes images of the so-called urban underclass. It leads one to ask how drug markets are related to the existence of this supposed new class and what effects drug legalization might have on those whose life chances have been shaped by the drug epidemics.

Illicit Drugs and Theories of the Underclass

Perhaps the strongest legitimization for the theory that there is a new underclass emerging in U.S. central cities is represented by the publication in *Science* of a paper by economists Ronald Mincy, Isabel Sawhill, and Douglas Wolf (1990). The authors begin their analysis with a strict economic definition. They point out that if one counts in the underclass only those among the impoverished in America who have lived below the official poverty incomes for eight years or more, then about one fifth of the poor, or about six million people, could be considered members of the underclass. Tempering this view, if one considers as numbering among the underclass only those who have been impoverished over their entire lifetimes, the total would be perhaps no more than one or two million (admittedly an educated guess).

As important as these facts may be, they have little bearing on possible relationships between poor populations and the ghetto drug markets or addicts. The *Science* authors go further, however, and choose, as many who write on this subject do, to define the underclass in behavioral terms. This "behavioral underclass" could be measured, they assert, by simply counting "the number of people who engage in bad behavior or a set of bad behaviors." Crime (especially in the drug industry), failure to work when not physically or mentally handicapped, teenage pregnancy, dropping out of school, and long-term welfare recipiency are the bad behaviors they use, arguing that they characterize people who do not conform to the norms of work, family, and morality. Using a methodology developed by Erol Ricketts and Isabel Sawhill, which counts the population in neighborhoods predominantly composed of people with these bad behaviors, the authors come up with an estimate of a "behavioral underclass" of about 2.5 million people (based on the 1980 census) who live in 880 neighborhoods in American cities where there are high concentrations of other such ill-behaved people.

William Wilson and his coworkers in Chicago avoid labeling terms like "bad behaviors" and also seek to avoid having their research appear to blame the victims of poverty for evolving their own self-fulfilling "culture of poverty." On the contrary, for Loic Wacquant and Wilson (1989) the central issue is primarily social-structural. The ghetto is experiencing a "crisis," not because a "welfare ethos" has mysteriously taken over its residents, but because of joblessness and economic exclusion. These structural changes have reached dramatic proportions. They have triggered a process of "hyperghettoization" exemplified in the largely negative changes occurring in Chicago's Black Belt.

Wilson and his colleagues describe a racially segregated population on Chicago's South and West Sides where, between 1970 and 1980, the proportion of African Americans living in "extreme poverty areas" (neighborhoods where 40 percent or more live in "official poverty") increased from 24 percent to 47 percent, a number that only continued to rise during the 1980s. Over the same period in the ten largest cities in the United States the proportion of poor blacks living in such highly concentrated poor neighborhoods increased from 22 percent to 38 percent. Wilson could have extended this observation to scores of smaller cities like Newark, Gary, East St. Louis, Camden, and Bessemer, Alabama (once a thriving and largely black industrial satellite of Birmingham, now a dusty slum).

In Chicago, as in other large cities, the exodus of jobs and stable families with steady work has amounted to a form of social hemorrhage. Today's ghetto residents, Wacquant and Wilson argue, "face a closed opportunity structure." They are increasingly closed off from the opportunities afforded others in the society by the "rapid deterioration of housing, schools, businesses, recreational facilities, and other community organizations." A deterioration greatly aided, the authors continue, "by government policies of industrial and urban laissez-faire that have channeled a disproportionate share of federal, state, and municipal resources to the more affluent."

Jobs for people from Chicago's Black Metropolis were always more difficult to obtain then for others in the city, but Wilson and Wacquant show that deindustrialization of the city has hit ghetto residents particularly hard. From 1950 to 1980 the overall proportion of adults (including people over 65) of all races not employed in the city remained rather steady, around 43 percent. For ghetto blacks entering Chicago smokestack industries in the 1950s the proportions outside the labor force were only slightly higher than for the city overall. By 1970, however, rates of nonparticipation were 10 to 15 percentage points higher for ghetto residents, and by 1980 anywhere from two-thirds to three-fourths of ghetto adults were not in the (official, "above ground") labor force. As a further measure of how far the American Dream is slipping from the inner-city black poor, Wilson's research shows that in the extremely poor neighborhoods of Chicago's ghetto, over half (51 percent) of all residents live in households where the annual income is less than $7,500 (at the end of the 1980s). Three quarters have "none of six assets" (personal checking account, savings account, individual retirement account [IRA], pension plan, money in stocks or bonds, prepaid burial) and 97 percent owned no home, no business, no land.

These and other recent theories of the ghetto underclass are helpful in explaining the structural changes that have produced persistent minority poverty. One of their limitations is that they lump so many different populations that social scientists must use the concept with extreme care. Wilson himself now rejects the term "underclass" as too vague. Jencks (1990) argues that social scientists "should probably avoid the word altogether unless they are prepared to make clear which of its many meanings they have in mind." Still, he admits, the idea will continue to hold great appeal outside academic social science circles. "If the term underclass helps put the problems of America's have-nots back on the political agenda, it will have served an extraordinarily useful purpose" (Jencks 1990).

Much as one can agree with Jencks's last point, from the perspective of drug issues these theories of the underclass are of limited value in predicting or explaining the trends in ghetto drug markets noted here. These theories would suggest that the availability of large numbers of racially outcast, superfluous, undereducated teenagers and young adults provides a ready source of manpower for illegal industries in and outside the ghettos. In this sense, the underclass produces the people who too readily become enmeshed in the ghetto's drug institutions. Yet the drug ethnographies cited above show on balance that relatively few members of this population actually earn significant sums in the drug markets. More dabble in them and even more individuals get into trouble and circulate through the law-enforcement system by small-scale involvement in the drug trade or by becoming gravely addicted. Meanwhile the dominant illegal institutions of the wholesale drug industry continue to be located outside the ghetto. The ghettos typically become distribution centers of the more competitive and less profitable retail market. In industrial cities like Chicago, where the white middle class is not so accustomed to entering the ghetto to buy drugs, there is far less per-capita involvement in the drug industry than can be found in cities like Miami, New York, and Los Angeles.

Most current theories of the underclass fail adequately to consider the historical impact of vice market segregation in the minority ghettos. In consequence they generally fail to trace the influence of drug markets or to consider how the experience of young males in these markets may further stigmatize this population and further hinder its integration into the larger economy. In this sense it is the drug trade, with its experiences of addiction and the prison, that produces the most "strung-out," disabled members of the poverty population. This point was clear to the HARYOU researchers of the heroin period, but has figured less prominently in current, ahistorical discussions of the minority poor. Perhaps few of those who write structural analyses of the "underclass" have heard the modern version of the Harlem voices recorded by Kenneth Clark and his associates. For example, a 26-year-old addict told them:

> Work, work, some kind of work program set-up where a man can work and get ahead and support himself. Then he can go to some type of school at night, you know, to learn some type of trade, because in jail you can't learn a trade . . . you can't learn anything in jail, you know. All you can do there is learn to hate more. All you can learn there is how to stay out of the police's way as much as possible, even if it means ducking work. . . . I know that, because I started going to jail when I was a kid.
>
> I don't think I could be rehabilitated, you know, not now in this society. Maybe if I see something better offered. But I hope that in the future they offer kids, or my sister's kids, or someone's kids, a better opportunity than they offered me, because they didn't offer me anything. I either accepted a porter's job for the rest of my life regardless of how much education I had, or went to jail. In fact, I think jails were built for black men. You understand? If you look at the population up there, the black man is more popular in jail than the

white man. The black man makes parole less frequently than the white man, and the black man goes to the chair more often than the white man. Whitey gets all the breaks in this world. (HARYOU 1964, 330)

This century's history of ghetto containment of deviance — a specific feature of institutional racism — has compounded the extreme social and psychological difficulties of minority persons, especially the African-American male. It has stimulated the creation of thriving illicit markets and illegal economic institutions in the nation's racial ghettos and has gone far to produce a population debilitated by addictive drugs, alcohol, and fratricidal violence. It is not necessary to call upon a theory of the ghetto underclass to observe that there is a segment of highly alienated semicitizens in the heart of America's great cities. These are often the "survivors" among adults who come of age as poor adolescents in the ghettos. Each new drug fad is sustained by the cash from more affluent classes, but typically produces a tragic epidemic of drug addiction that is felt most bitterly in the ghettos and increases the number who are effectively lost from the institutions of the economy and the culture.

Given these historical truths it seems precipitous to declare that all the drugs, from the most addictive and potentially deadly to the rather benign, should become legal commodities. As James B. Jacobs has suggested, "Paralleling what occurred at the end of alcohol prohibition, some of the people who have gotten rich from illegal drugs would probably launder their images and play key roles in the now-legal distribution system" (1990, 29). Men like the addict quoted above would have to be content merely with further proof of the correctness of their sociological analysis of the society. Blanket legalization might prevent needless incarceration, but it offers no positive solutions to hyperghettoization and it would condone the escape to anodynes that helps make alcohol, legal and deadly, such a scourge of low-income communities. No nation in the world has legalized all mood- and mind-altering substances and it is extremely unlikely that the United States, a pioneer in failed prohibitions and symbolic crusades, will be the first to do so. The public at large has supported prohibitions it knows are not effective because, as Joseph Gusfield observes, to do so gives people assurance of a moral order, however symbolic. "It assures," according to Gusfield, "by demonstrating that there is authority and that it is on the side of the audience. It is a culture-creating and culture-validating mechanism" (1981, p. 183). Tragically, it has also been a mechanism that has contributed heavily to the stigma borne by racially distinct people in America for more than a century. By maintaining prohibitions on heavily addictive substances and experimenting with policies that legalize the less harmful ones, American political leaders have an opportunity to foster a moral order that is more than symbolic and is not applied selectively according to a person's income or skin color. But to garner any significant support in the communities themselves, decriminalization strategies will have to be part of broader policies that address a range of local problems, many of which can be understood in the framework of community health.

Community Health and Drug Policy

As the crack epidemic wanes somewhat in the United States, there remain active drug markets and relatively high rates of drug addiction in the nation's largest minority ghettos. Intertwined with addiction rates in a tangle of deadly causality are chronic unemployment, poverty, homicide, teen pregnancy, and high rates of AIDS, cirrhosis, and tuberculosis. Any discussion of the possibilities presented by drug legalization must also address these even deeper health and welfare problems in communities where drug use and sales have been so callously concentrated over the century.

This is not to deny the potential gains that would accrue to these same communities from drug decriminalization strategies. A shift in national policy to ease the more pernicious effects of the "War on Drugs" will result in lower rates of incarceration for drug-related charges. Municipalities would be able to spend more of their scarce resources on policing the violent crimes that contribute to local economic depression. Their burdens in dealing with youthful ex-offenders would be eased. Were we to legalize "but more tightly control marijuana than we do alcohol," Jerome Skolnick concludes, "we could end half or more of our current drug arrests without a significant impact on public health" (Skolnick 1992, 153).

Proposals to legalize cocaine or other more addictive drugs generate little support in the ghetto communities where their sale and use has had the most pernicious effects. Indeed, few proposals for dealing with the drug problems of minority communities will receive much support from those communities unless they are viewed as originating from the communities themselves. This is as true for AIDS and teen pregnancy as it is for drug use and sale. Despite all the media concern about the ravages of drugs and drug-related violence in the ghettos, most black community leaders and intellectuals do not trust white policy makers to understand their needs. Yale law professor Harlon Dalton, for example, asks of these policy makers, "Why do you offer addicts free needles but not free health care? Why do you show them how to clean their works but not how to clean up their lives?" He voices the concern of all black and minority community residents who wonder why policy experiments are so frequently tried out on them. "Instead of asking us to accept on faith that we won't be abandoned and possibly worse off once you move on to a new issue, why not demonstrate your commitment by empowering us to carry on the struggle whether you are there or not?" (Dalton 1989, 219).

In a recent survey of more than 800 residents of Harlem housing projects, Terry Williams and I found that adolescent pregnancy was the local problem that ranks highest among the concerns of adult respondents and teenagers. Crime and drugs are also high on their lists of concerns, of course. But the residents of Harlem's housing project buildings tend to perceive the depredations of criminals and drug dealers in the context of the health and development problems of their children and their neighbors. Policies like police sweeps to arrest small-scale dealers or drug legalization are not very popular. The community residents most often discuss drug issues as concerns that are less central than the health, education, and employment of their young people. They often speak of the need for accessible neighborhood health care facilities, preferably located in multipurpose community centers, that also provide opportunities for job-training and recreation programs developed by members of the local community. They often talk about massive arrests of local drug peddlers, most of whom are adolescents and young adults, as an irrational cycling of young men in and out of the criminal justice system. In our conversations with the residents of Harlem and other minority communities hit hardest by the consequences of drug markets and drug use, we do not find any great sympathy for drugs (with the possible exception of marijuana) or drug dealers. We do hear different expressions of the need to address local economic and health issues first or as part of any talk of drug wars. Indeed in many forms of expression the residents of the nation's urban ghettos seem to be agreeing with Baltimore's

Mayor Kurt Schmoke's plea, "If we're going to have a war against drugs, it shouldn't be headed by the attorney general; it should be headed by the surgeon general" (quoted in Nadelmann 1992).

References

Ayala, V. 1991. *Falling Through the Cracks: AIDS and the Minority Poor.* Unpublished Ph.D. dissertation, City University of New York Graduate School.

Clark, K.B. 1965. *Dark Ghetto: Dilemmas of Social Power.* New York: Harper and Row.

Dalton, H.L. 1989. AIDS in Blackface. *Daedalus* (Summer):165–204.

Drake, St.-C., and H. Cayton. 1946. *Black Metropolis: A Study of Negro Life in a Northern City.* New York: Harcourt, Brace and World.

Durk, D. 1976. *The Pleasant Avenue Connection.* Harper and Row.

Figueroa, J. 1989. *Survival on the Margin.* New York: Vantage Press.

Gusfield, J. 1981. *The Culture of Public Problems: Drinking–Driving and the Symbolic Order.* Chicago: University of Chicago Press.

HARYOU. 1964. *Youth in the Ghetto: A Study of the Consequences of Powerlessness and a Blueprint for Change.* New York: Harlem Youth Opportunities Unlimited.

Jaynes, G.D., and R.M. Williams Jr. Eds. 1989. *A Common Destiny: Blacks and American Society.* Washington: National Academy Press.

Jacobs, J.B. 1990. Imagining Drug Legalization. *Public Interest* 101 (fall):28–42.

Jencks, C. 1989. What Is the Underclass and Is It Growing? *Focus* 12 (1):14–26.

Knapp Commission. 1973. The Knapp Commission Report on Police Corruption. New York: Braziller.

Mezzrow, M., and B. Wolf. 1946. *Really the Blues.* New York: Random House.

Mincy, R., I. Sawhill, and D. Wolf. 1990. The Underclass. *Science* 252 (April 27):1–15.

Morales, E. 1986. Coca and Cocaine Economy and Social Change in the Andes of Peru. *Economic Development and Social Change* 35 (1):143–61.

———— 1989. *Cocaine: White Gold Rush in Peru.* Tucson: University of Arizona Press.

Nadelmann, E.A. 1992. America's Drug Problem. *Dissent* (Spring): 205–12.

National Center for Health Statistics. 1988. U.S. Statistical Abstract 1987, Table 298. *Vital Statistics Reports.* Washington: U.S. Department of Health and Human Services

Osofsky, G. 1963. *Harlem: The Making of a Ghetto.* New York: Harper and Row.

Ottley, R., and W.J. Weatherby. Eds. 1967. *The Negro in New York: An Informal Social History.* New York: Praeger.

Prosser, W.R. 1991. The Underclass: Assessing What We Have Learned. *Focus* 13 (2):1–18.

Reckless, W.C. 1933. *Vice In Chicago.* Chicago: University of Chicago Press.

Rubin, V. Ed. 1975. *Cannabis and Culture.* The Hague, Netherlands: Mouton.

Sifaneck, S., and W. Kornblum. 1990. Growing Up in Harlem Public Housing. In *The State of Black America.* New York: National Urban League.

Skolnick, J.H. 1992. Rethinking the Drug Problem. *Daedalus* (Summer): 133–60.

Solomon, D. 1966. *The Marihuana Papers.* New York: The New American Library.

Spear, A.H. 1967. *Black Chicago: The Making of a Negro Ghetto.* Chicago: University of Chicago Press.

Sterk, C. 1989. *Prostitutes and Their Health.* Doctoral dissertation, Erasmus University, Rotterdam.

Sullivan, M. 1989. *Getting Paid.* Ithaca, N.Y.: Cornell University Press.

Wacquant, L.J.D., and W.J. Wilson. 1989. The Cost of Racial and Class Exclusion in the Inner City. *Annals* (501):8–25.

Williams, T.M. 1978. *Cocaine in After Hours Clubs.* Unpublished Ph.D. dissertation, New York: City University of New York Graduate School.

———. 1989. *The Cocaine Kids.* Reading Mass.: Addison-Wesley.

———. 1992. *The Crack House.* Reading Mass.: Addison-Wesley.

Wilson, W.J. 1987. *The Truly Disadvantaged: The Inner City, the Underclass and Public Policy.* Chicago: University of Chicago Press.

Social Behavior, Public Policy, and Nonharmful Drug Use

CHARLES WINICK

City University of New York

A CENTRAL FEATURE OF AMERICAN DRUG POLICY has been the doctrine that the use of mood-modifying drugs like heroin, marijuana, and cocaine is hazardous, likely to lead to socially dysfunctional behavior, health problems, loss of control, and interference with work and other functioning.

The image of the out-of-control drug addict today contrasts with the situation in the early twentieth century, when drugs like opium, cocaine, cannabis, and chloral hydrate were freely available legally. One possible contributor to opium's becoming illegal in the United States was Samuel Gompers's claim that its use by Chinese immigrants increased their productivity so substantially that whites were at a disadvantage in the labor market (Michaels 1987).

How could opium be seen as encouraging productivity at one time and as destructive and antisocial at another? An answer to this question would involve study of the changing climate of opinion toward non-medical drug use since the closing of the opiate-dispensing clinics in the 1920s. American policy has grown consistently more opposed to non-medical drug use, decade by decade, culminating in the "zero tolerance" of the 1980s war on drugs, with its targeting of recreational users.

One recurring conclusion of the literature on mood-modifying drugs like heroin and cocaine is that their regular nonmedical use will almost inevitably lead to bleak personal and social outcomes. My article suggests that the conventional picture of uniformly negative consequences of regular drug use is not supported by the data. Because there are no studies attempting to test the hypothesis that Americans who illegally and regularly take psychoactive substances can do so without incurring significant losses in their lives, the relevant data derive from studies undertaken for other purposes.

A few studies involve persons in treatment interviewed about their former drug use; more of the data derive from investigations of users not in treatment. Although the studies vary in range and quality, they have appeared over a period of more than 60 years and have dealt with many different populations. A number of them were sponsored by government agencies.

Drug Use and the Ability to Work

The effects of regular drug use on work functioning are crucial because of the central role of work in defining social roles and the widespread belief that regular use of mood-modifying drugs is incompatible with the capacity to fulfill employment responsibilities. Two investigations of working addicts involve interviews with persons in treatment and others derive data from drug users in the community.

In one 1950s New York State investigation of 142 drug addicts in treatment, 71 percent were addicted to morphine and 19 percent to barbiturates (Morhous 1953). Physician (28 percent) and businessman (9 percent) were the most frequent occupations. The great majority of subjects worked steadily at their chosen careers and a number had exhibited upward mobility since the onset of addiction. Many entered treatment to reduce, but not to stop, their drug habit.

In a study of the work history of 555 former New York street heroin addicts in treatment, who held full-time jobs for at least three months while addicted, the typical respondent was a male aged 20 to 29; over half were black or Puerto Rican and actively involved in the drug subculture (Caplovitz 1976). Most subjects had held conventional jobs for more than two years and 70 percent held a full-time job for a year while addicted; 71 percent had used heroin while on the job. Most of the respondents felt that drug use made their jobs easier. Fifty-two percent of the respondents' fellow workers approved or tolerated the drug use and two-fifths of the subjects had bought or sold drugs on the job.

Perhaps the first systematic post-World War I study of the work effectiveness of opiate addicts was conducted by Kolb (1928), who found that three-fourths of the 119 addicts interviewed had good work records.

One 66-year-old woman, who had averaged 17 grains of morphine daily for 37 years, was typical; she had long successfully supported herself by working at a job that required substantial physical labor.

The first large-scale social science investigation of opiate addicts, who typically injected the drug and had been users for over five years, was conducted by Dai (1937) in Chicago. More than four-fifths of the 1,887 addicts he studied between 1929 and 1933 were functioning in conventional occupations.

Several decades later, in a statewide study (N = 266) of all the narcotic addicts who could be located in Kentucky, O'Donnell (1969, 132–3) noted that more than nine-tenths of the males receiving drugs legally were working effectively at established occupations. An improvement in work pattern typically followed an addict's securing a stable drug source, suggesting that this facilitated or caused the improved work situation.

In 1969, Arthur D. Little, Inc., was asked to conduct a thorough investigation of heroin addiction for a presidential commission and the National Institute of Mental Health (NIMH). On the basis of a three-year investigation of data from all available sources on the 120,000 addicts in the United States, the project director reported that approximately "30 percent of all the drug abusers actually are legitimate people, in the sense that they have a job which they keep. . . ." (Waldron 1969). These addicts included persons who worked at a wide range of jobs.

An investigation in New Orleans undertook to trace how older opiate addicts, over half of whom were steadily employed and who were not on methadone maintenance, were dealing with their addiction (Capel et al. 1972). The mean age of the men was 59. They adapted their drug use to changing circumstances. Where heroin had been preferred in the past, Dilaudid became popular because it was purer, easier to get, and could be taken orally. A number of addicts only stopped working when they became eligible for Social Security or pension income.

The war in Vietnam, in the 1970s, led to concern about how the widespread use of heroin was affecting the functioning of military personnel. Approximately 19 percent of the enlisted men were addicted to freely available and inexpensive heroin of 80 to 95 percent purity. By and large, there was no way to determine their addiction by work performance. Urine tests were introduced because the heroin use was otherwise not detectable. "A good many men were able to use narcotics heavily in Vietnam and still function acceptably" (Robins 1974). Undetected heavy users did not differ from occasional users in rates of either disciplinary action or promotions.

Zinberg (1984, 162) interviewed users of opiates and other drugs who took the substances on a controlled basis for an average of several years. Not only did they maintain conventional jobs in the community, but many also had a substantial commitment to work that went beyond earning a living. They valued the status gained from work: "I've done a lot of work in the union . . . I worked hard to get that . . . been with the union for about eight years . . . it doesn't counteract the good feeling that I get from the heroin."

During the period from 1959 to 1964, I led a panel study that investigated prevalence of drug use among functioning workers. When we originally recruited these illicit and regular opiate users from community sources, they were not known to authorities and had not been in treatment (Winick 1960, 1990, 1992). There were 43 physicians, 72 nurses, 94 jazz musicians, and 85 other people working in mass communications and distribution industries. The nurses were all female and the other subjects were all male. Of the 294 subjects, 9 percent were black, 4 percent were Hispanic, and 87 percent were white.

Follow-up interviews were conducted ten years after the first cycle of interviews. At that time, 37 percent of the physicians, 31 percent of the nurses, 35 percent of the musicians, and 27 percent of the other workers were still using opiates. The subjects generally reported that drug use hardly interfered with work functioning. Work dysfunction was mainly caused by an interruption in the availability of drugs. The work demanded the extremely arduous requirements of physicians and nurses, the need for the empathy and improvisational skills of the musicians, the urgent deadlines of mass communications specialists, and the repetitive tasks of warehouse workers.

Individuals in each of these occupational groups tended to use drugs for different but functionally facilitative purposes. One ophthalmic surgeon noted: "With Demerol, I can do three or four perfect operations a day. It builds up my resistance and makes it easier for me to concentrate when I am working double shifts and just couldn't keep up with it. The drugs help a lot." A trumpeter said: "With the heroin, I could feel and look cool and reach and hold the sound that I wanted." A warehouse worker stated: "It's a very slow and long day, taking plumbing parts out of bins. Without the drugs, I couldn't make it." A television cameraman observed: "I can't make a mistake on the job. I work a lot of overtime and the drugs make it easier for me to concentrate." No doubt other factors in the lives of these study subjects contributed to the relatively prosaic character of their drug habit and enhanced their ability to work: licit occupations, structured schedules, and participation in conventional family and community activities.

That some physicians are drug dependent has been especially troubling. However, in spite of the substantial consumer and professional concern about impaired physicians, there is evidence that some physicians function effectively while drug dependent. One noted case involved "Doctor X," who practiced medicine effectively and successfully for over 60 years (Cutting 1942). There appeared to be no significant professional or personal deficit as a result of his opiate addiction, which paralleled his entire career.

William S. Halsted, the father of modern surgery and a founder of Johns Hopkins Medical School, was cocaine dependent until the age of 34, when he turned to morphine, on which he probably remained continually dependent until his death at age 70. He was professionally active and medically creative during his whole life (Penfield 1969; Ingle 1971).

There are no reports demonstrating that addicted physicians are more likely to commit malpractice than others. Indeed, the country's largest program for addicted medical professionals reports that a physician's professional activities represent the last aspect of his or her life to be affected by drug dependence (Talbott and Wright 1987). Drug-using physicians typically have successful and active primary care practices (Winick 1990). As O'Donnell (1969, 227) noted in his report on addicts in Kentucky, some addicted physicians were described as "the best doctor in town."

A panel study of the natural history of male street addicts known to the authorities (N = 581) was conducted in California (Anglin et al. 1988). The men were interviewed during the period 1974–1975 and again 12 years later. Forty-nine percent were Hispanic, 40 percent Anglo, and 11 percent black. In the month preceding the final interview, 47 percent used marijuana or hashish, 44 percent took heroin, and 22 percent were cocaine users. Half were working full time at a legitimate occupation.

A multisite investigation of 124 urban male intravenous heroin users, not in treatment, found that about 30 percent were usually legitimately employed (Hanson et al. 1985). Their drug use provided stability, a sense of capability, increased drive, and feelings of control over their lives. The street addicts studied by Maddux and Desmond (1981) were employed an average of 62 percent of the time during their first decade of drug use.

If heroin use was the source of the greatest concern in the 1960s and 1970s, crack use seized center stage in the late 1980s. Although smoking crack is the most dependence-producing form of ingestion, it is not incompatible with regular work obligations. A 46-year-old practical nurse was observed driving his fairly new car to a Harlem crack house while parking his other car near his co-op apartment. He had been distilling and smoking cocaine for 22 years. "I smoke at least three times a week," he said. "But I don't chase it. It won't prevent me from going to work tomorrow night, from paying my bills. . . . Some people enjoy drinking wine. This is my enjoyment" (Treaster 1991). Among the other regular users at the crack house were social workers, a maintenance man, and other healthy-looking people with conventional jobs.

Finally, in view of concern over marijuana's links to an "amotivational syndrome," it is noteworthy that a psychoanalytic investigation of 150 heavy users of marijuana concluded that daily heavy marijuana use was compatible with significant career success (Hendin et al. 1987). Marijuana use was adaptive in occupations as demanding as corporation lawyer, executive, and theatrical director.

Users Who Are and Are Not in Treatment or Prison

Most studies of illegal drug use are based on retrospective interviews with former users in treatment programs. Users in prison represent another source of subjects. Such persons could be less competent and effective than the far larger number of unreported and unknown drug users. A user who is troubled and not doing well is more likely to seek help in treatment than someone who is healthy and functioning. Addicts usually enter treatment when their behavior has become dysfunctional (Ellis and Stephens 1976). A less alert user may be more prone to arrest than someone who is effective in "taking care of business."

Most drug-dependant persons never undergo treatment. The Institute of Medicine (1990) Committee for the Substance Abuse Coverage Study estimated that the point-in-time need for treatment on a typical day during 1987–1988 was approximately 5.5 million persons aged 12 or over. In 1989, the most recent year for which data are available, the United States had 433,647 slots for drug dependents, most of which were for drug-free outpatient counseling (National Institute on Drug Abuse 1990). There were 995,994 admissions to these 433,647 slots, so that each slot was used for approximately 2.3 admissions.

According to the Treatment Outcomes Prospective Study (TOPS), the most comprehensive study of the subject (Hubbard et al. 1989), representative clients will experience five different treatment episodes during the life cycle of their drug use. Multiple readmissions by such individuals account for the majority of total admissions.

The relatively small proportion of regular drug users undergoing treatment—one assessment reported that current programs treat fewer than a third of the nation's addicts (Treaster 1992)—reflects a lack both of available facilities and of interest on the part of many users. In one study, 70 percent of a sample of active New York City cocaine users, 40 percent of whom also regularly used heroine, had not been in, and had no intention of going into, treatment (Lipton 1992).

To clarify differences between drug dependents within and outside of institutional control, a number of comparisons of treated and untreated users of opiates and cocaine have been made. The largest national survey of young men in the high-risk age group reported that untreated heroin addicts were less likely than those in treatment to have impaired health or family situations (O'Donnell et al. 1976). Another study found that untreated addicts, compared with those in treatment, had more self-esteem, better family situations, and fewer legal problems (Graeven and Graeven 1983).

A New Haven investigation studied heroin addicts in and out of treatment who had drug habits that were comparable in duration, severity, and users' participation in illegal drug-procurement activities. The nontreatment group, however, functioned more effectively in a social context, had fewer legal problems, and was less likely to have dysphoric symptoms or a depressive disorder (Rounsaville and Kleber 1985).

Heavy cocaine users, not in treatment and living in communities participating in the NIMH Epidemiologic Catchment Area (ECA) study, were interviewed and their characteristics compared with those of similar cocaine users who were in treatment (Anthony et al. 1985). The ECA subjects had fewer health, social, psychological, or occupational problems. All relevant studies thus indicate that persons in treatment are less effective in dealing with their lives than street users not in treatment.

Upper-income Drug Users

Because they are not engaging in predatory criminal activity or using publicly supported treatment facilities, upper-income users are relatively invisible. Better information about these people could significantly alter our perception of the effects of drug use. Documentation of substantial drug use without noteworthy negative consequences, in this population, could enable us to make realistic assessments of the extent to which the destructive sequelae of drug use among inner-city residents are likely to reflect their position in the social system rather than the effects of drugs. In spite of widespread publicity given to the heroin and cocaine use of some children of the rich and famous, there are no large-scale studies of the subject. There is, however, at least one impressionistic report on "hidden" affluent young heroin users (Haden-Guest 1983).

Perhaps the only effort to determine the dimensions of drug use among a substantial sample of the upper classes was a statewide survey in New York (Frank et al. 1984). Families with an income of $50,000 per year or more reported more illicit drug use than any other income group. The upper-income group used cocaine at double the rate of the lower-income respondents, probably reflecting its relatively high price at the time. Combinations of substances were also used more heavily among the upper-income groups. Irrespective of measure, people with higher incomes had the most serious drug use, although there was no evidence of comparable levels of dysfunction.

Asked where they would go for help if they needed treatment, 72 percent responded that they would seek out a private professional and 26 percent preferred a self-help group. The larger the user's income, the greater the likelihood of the person going to a private professional. Thus, these upper-class users would not be in a hospital or publicly funded program that contributes to a national data collection system such as the Drug Abuse Research Program (DARP) or the Treatment Oriented Prospective Study (TOPS), the findings of which significantly influence policy decisions. Many non-upper-class working drug dependents serviced by employee assistance programs are also likely to go unreported, further contributing to an incomplete picture of the parameters of illegal drug use that underestimates upper-class and working users.

Upper-income users may find it easier to get drugs from physicians, and powerful people could have access that is not possible for others. Narcotics Commissioner Harry J. Anslinger, the leading foe of narcotics maintenance, secretly authorized the use of maintenance for specific persons on a number of occasions. Thus, in the 1950s he maintained influential United States Senator Joseph R. McCarthy, who was a political ally, on morphine for years (McWilliams 1986).

Field Studies of Street Addicts

A number of ethnographic and other field investigations of street addicts have looked at the career of the user and noted that it requires the kind of commitment that characterizes a demanding occupation, in which only some can succeed. Several reports described the street careers of the "cool cats," "stand-up cats," and "righteous dope fiends," for whom drug use provided vocational status and achievement (Finestone 1957; Sutter 1966; Feldman 1968; Huling 1985). Considering the dismal life choices confronting a youthful ghetto male, one research team noted, his most intelligent option might be to develop a drug career (Chein et al. 1964).

Several studies argue that, even though street addicts are not doing legitimate work, their activities can be assessed in terms of criteria of successful functioning. Anthropologist Edward Preble reported that young heroin addicts in New York City gangs worked very hard at "taking care of business," following a demanding daily routine seven days per week. They had to be energetic, flexible, resourceful, and alert achievers in order to carry out their exciting and challenging tasks (Preble and Casey 1969). Street addicts are often viewed by their peers as people with very demanding jobs who are models of vocational success (Hughes et al. 1971). Other reports have documented how the addict's hustling requires harder work than conventional jobs (Gould et al. 1974).

A large-scale natural history study of street addicts (N = 238) in Baltimore involved retrospective interviews about their first ten years of addiction (Nurco, Cisin, and Balter 1981 a, b, c). Thirty-one percent never had a nonaddiction period. Among black addicts, the most frequent pattern involved uninterrupted addiction and generalized social competence. These users tended to be in control of their destiny, to avoid jail, and to be able to manage their addiction. Blacks were apt to be more successful than whites in coping and achieving fulfillment of their goals.

Studies of Work and Drug Taking in Other Societies

Studies in different societies, both economically advanced and underdeveloped, and involving a range of substances, have documented the use of habituating drugs by persons who are effective workers. The four studies cited below are representative of a number of similar reports.

An investigation in Thailand found that some hill tribes reported that opium enabled them to function and it was not unusual to see a villager who had been addicted for 30 to 40 years and was still working actively (Suwanhala et al. 1978).

In Jamaica, where ganja plays a significant role in social and economic life, the drug often facilitates the accomplishment of work by individuals and groups. Dreher (1982) reported that its users generally feel that ganja enhances their ability to work by promoting strength and stamina. Supervisors agreed that the ganja helps workers in the arduous job of reaping sugar cane.

Dutch cocaine users not only used it while functioning effectively on the job, but typically worked while under the influence (Cohen 1989). American observers at national meetings of the Dutch "junky union" have been surprised at seeing members injecting heroin and then chairing the meetings with facility and skill.

A report by a British investigator concluded that a substantial proportion of the addicts receiving heroin at English clinics in the late 1960s could be characterized as stable, with high employment, legitimate income, and no hustling (Stimson 1973).

Federal Government's Opposition to Drugs for Addicts

What can account for the fact that a considerable body of research on the capacity of those who use drugs to work and fulfill their other social obligations has received so little attention in the shaping of public policy? What accounts for the hegemony of the perspective that only abstinence is compatible with normal functioning? Central to an understanding of this situation is the role of federal narcotics officials in shaping both public policy and the dominant social ideology.

Harry J. Anslinger, who directed the Bureau of Narcotics from 1930 to 1962, was the chief federal spokesman for the view that drug use inevitably produced dysfunction and pathology. Anslinger's strong views against drug maintenance were linked with his belief that addicts would typically come to the attention of the authorities in two years, so that there could be no "hidden" addicts. Federal authorities opposed efforts to provide drugs to users through the medical system and repressed information suggesting that medically maintained addicts could meet their social responsibilities.

Under Anslinger's guidance, the federal government systematically sought to distort the nature of heroin policy in England, especially through the 1960s when heroin was freely prescribed by physicians there. The British system had been described carefully in a number of publications, including a book by Schur (1962), an American sociologist. However, the Bureau of Narcotics consistently maintained that the system in England was equivalent to that in the United States. At the 1962 White House conference on addiction policy, a keynote speaker gave a lengthy speech on similarities of the British and American systems. Schur was given two minutes at the end of a session to present his contrary, and more accurate, perspective.

The FBN actively discredited scholars who expressed contrary views, such as sociologist Alfred R. Lindesmith, who taught at Indiana University and argued that drug maintenance was a possible option. When Lindesmith wrote the preface for the Indiana University Press publication of the American Bar Association–American Medical Association (1959) report suggesting some form of maintenance treatment for addicts, the bureau sent an agent to Bloomington to investigate the Press. Agents subsequently visited university officials to denounce Lindesmith (1965). On other occasions, federal agents placed him under extended surveillance and planted narcotics in his home.

The FBN published its own critique of the ABA–AMA report (Bureau of Narcotics 1959). The bureau's criticism has been described by one scholar as "the crudest publication yet produced by a government agency . . . [reflecting] the fury of the bureau's anti-intellectualism . . .

[and] propaganda that panders to provincial superstition of 'un-American' types" (DeMott 1962).

As part of the federal government's campaign to discredit programs of drug maintenance, considerable misinformation was disseminated about the 44 narcotic-dispensing clinics that were in existence between 1919 and 1923 (Bureau of Narcotics 1953).

When methadone maintenance emerged as a method for treating heroin addicts in the 1960s, it was actively opposed by the FBN. The bureau infiltrated clinics, stole records, spread false rumors, and encouraged attacks on the programs (Dole 1989). Marie Nyswander, who together with Vincent Dole pioneered the use of methadone maintenance, was under federal surveillance for years.

President Nixon, whose funding initiatives expanded methadone maintenance, never publicly identified himself with the modality and repeatedly rejected aides' insistence that he visit a methadone treatment program (Epstein 1977). Considering the climate of opinion, it is extraordinary that methadone became the dominant form of treatment for heroin addiction.

The Climate of Opinion

There was little interest in or support for heterodox views either of the relationship of drug dependence to social functioning or of drug policy until recently. The leading universities were not interested in drug dependence as a subject for teaching, research, or policy examination. There were no advocacy groups capable of challenging the orthodoxy and thereby serving as an alternative source of data for the media.

Before the National Institute on Drug Abuse was established in 1973, the NIMH provided policy guidance and leadership on matters of prevention of drug dependence and treatment of addicts. NIMH staff tended to express the traditional psychiatric view of drug users as deviants, for whom enforced abstention represented the primary treatment goal.

Contributing to the absence of discussion of alternative approaches to drug use was the dearth of prominent Americans who were willing to be identified as drug dependents. There was no lack of astronauts, generals, Nobel Prize winning writers, corporate executives, Academy Award winning actors, and other prominent Americans willing to be known as alcoholics, but entertainers and athletes are the only achievers who have borne witness to their drug use. Indeed, creation of the National Institute on Alcohol Abuse and Alcoholism in 1971 was in part the result of the efforts of two senators who publicly identified themselves as alcoholics. Very few national political leaders have been willing to become spokespersons for drug policy reform. President Carter was unable to get support for liberalizing marijuana laws and his drug policy adviser was forced to resign. The United States had no equivalent to writers like Graham Greene and Jean Cocteau, who ascribed their creativity, to some extent, to opium use.

Despite the heavy weight of both political and intellectual orthodoxy, there was a significant effort in the mid-1960s to reshape conceptualization of the drug problem. Propounded by a small group of sociologists, this dissenting perspective sought to present drug taking as a "victimless crime" (Schur 1965). Along with gambling, pornography, prostitution, homosexuality, and abortion, drug use was portrayed as an activity that should not be the subject of legal proscriptions because it involved willing associates. This challenge, which received support from a number of quarters, has had some impact on those committed to policy reform. Whatever decriminalization, however, either de facto or de jure, has occurred for some "victimless crimes" has not been extended to drug use.

Distinguished legal scholars and activists similarly had little impact on policy. Morris Ploscowe and Rufus King were nationally prominent attorneys who challenged America's approach to drugs. Ploscowe, a former New York City judge, was the staff director for the ABA–AMA report. King (1972), who chaired the ABA committee on narcotics, subtitled his book on America's drug problem "America's Fifty Year Folly."

In this climate of opinion, the recommendation by the conservative Commission on Marijuana and Drug Abuse (1973) that marijuana be decriminalized was completely rejected by Richard Nixon, although commission chairman, Raymond P. Schafer, was a close political ally of the president.

There were others who challenged prevailing views. Some were widely discussed, like Thomas Szasz (1979), the heterodox psychiatrist who portrayed drug users as victims of the mental health movement. Other writers included Andrew Weil (1972), who urged the recognition of a right to an altered state of consciousness, and several critics with a Marxist perspective (Yurick 1970; Karmen 1973; Helmer 1975). Dissenters also called for debureaucratizing treatment (Regush 1971), community control of drug prevention (Hartjen and Quinney 1970), and a critical examination of the official epidemiology on drug use (Epstein 1977).

However, these challenges had little impact on policy because of the political power of the prevailing ideology on "dope fiends" and the portrayal of drug use as a national threat requiring a "war on drugs" by President Nixon in 1971, President Ford in 1976, and President Reagan in 1982 and 1986. Given this climate of opinion, it is not surprising that scholars with heterodox hypotheses to examine could receive little support for their work from the preeminent source of research funds — the federal government.

Few established journals ran articles on drug dependence. A 1972 anthology that was representative of current thinking on drug use and social policy did not include even one contribution from a mainstream public health, medical, psychology, or sociology journal among its 42 articles (Susman 1972).

Until the advent of the recent reform movement, only one mainstream journal carried, in a 1957 issue, a varied and representative collection of views on American drug policy: *Law and Contemporary Problems*, the interdisciplinary quarterly published by the Duke University School of Law, each issue of which is devoted to a significant social problem (Shimm 1957). The nine contributors included key spokesmen for every significant approach to drug policy and the issue remains an important resource.

The first two American journals devoted to drug dependence were also, for some years, alone in being consistently open to a range of critical views: the *International Journal of the Addictions* (first published in 1965) and the *Journal of Drug Issues* (which began publication in 1970). Among the factors contributing to the journals' perspective has been the independence of each of its founding editors, an independence probably facilitated by the absence of institutional constraints.

Challenges to the prevailing ideology also came from the leading organization of persons interested in the drug problem, which was committed to open discussion of drug policies, the now defunct Student Association for the Study of Hallucinogens (STASH), in Beloit, Wisconsin. Controlled by students, STASH's program of publications, including books and the *Journal of Psychedelic Drugs* (now known as the *Journal of Psychoactive Drugs* and published in cooperation with the Haight-Ashbury Free Clinic), had considerable impact, especially on young people, in the late 1960s and 1970s.

The ferment of the 1960s, which brought into question the full range of American social institutions, provided a brief opening for fresh thinking about drug policy. The Ford Foundation, among other groups, underwrote the Drug Abuse Council (1972), which maintained a resource center, trained resident fellows, commented on policy, and funded papers and studies. After NIDA was established, the foundations felt that there was less need for the council and terminated their support.

AIDS and Functional Users

Any consideration of the functioning of drug users must address the realities of the AIDS epidemic. A substantial proportion of the drug injectors in parts of the United States will die from AIDS and many of their spouses or other sex partners will become infected.

In terms of our analysis, it would be necessary to examine the extent to which functional drug users adopt safer sex and injection practices, making them less likely to become infected. Such data are not yet available.

A variety of nongovernmental responses to AIDS could affect drug policies by identifying additional techniques for rendering the consequences of drug use less problematic. Such developments, including the spread of needle exchanges, the emergence of harm reduction as a viable goal, and vigorous community action may provide new perspectives on the characteristics of functional users.

Substance Abuse and the Functioning User

There is an analogy between the prevailing perspective on the use of heroin, cocaine, and other mood-modifying substances and the characterization of the course followed by heavy drinkers. In the case of the latter, it is typically assumed that a process of deterioration must occur (Jellinek 1952). However, deterioration is not inevitable. On the contrary, there is considerable evidence that heavy drinkers may function effectively, and that some addiction-level drinkers — a notable example being Winston Churchill — are leaders in culture, politics, and business. A number of American college graduates who averaged four drinks of whiskey, or six ounces daily, experienced no problems for a period of over 20 years (Vaillant 1983). In countries like France and Portugal, there is little relationship between heavy drinking and social distress.

Many of the daily users of alcohol and other drugs will "mature out" or otherwise stop using (Winick 1962; Maddux and Desmond 1980; Biernacki 1986; Edwards 1989). Public policy is predicated on assumptions that essentially ignore the large number of regular substance users who terminate drug use, just as it does not acknowledge the functioning user.

Findings from the study of heroin use by military personnel in Vietnam underscored the importance of the situational element in drug taking and the reversibility of addiction (Robins et al. 1980). A major follow-up study of Vietnam veterans, 10 to 15 years after discharge, concluded that the former heroin addicts were no more likely than other soldiers to be current drug users or otherwise to reflect enduring consequences of the experience (Roth 1986). The repeated drug use of the subjects studied by Zinberg (1984) typically did not involve escalation of dosage or the loss of conventional relationships with family and nonusers. Crucial to the pattern of controlled use was the adoption of rituals that defined the appropriate time and setting of use.

Even smoking crack can be normalized and routinized. A visitor to a Harlem crack house found that most of the smokers were in their thirties and forties and had been using crack for more than five years on a regular basis (Treaster 1991). Many clearly had the capacity to control use and had remained nonaddicted. An investigation of crack-using mothers has challenged some media stereotypes (Rosenbaum et al. 1990). The majority of the respondents reported that crack actually reduced their desire to have sex. The mothers shared basic American parenting values and expressed a great deal of concern for their children. Although tough, the mothers did not physically abuse their children. Crack did tend, however, to exacerbate already difficult socioeconomic living conditions. It was such underlying conditions, rather than crack use, that most effectively explained the extent to which such women departed from conventional norms of behavior.

In large measure, assumptions about the inevitability of the rapid onset of addiction with crack use is based on observations about the dominant mode of ingestion—smoking. There is some evidence, however, that when ingested differently, crack use may be less problematic. In one study by Siegel (1989, 308–11), over 200 California patients sniffed cocaine freebase ("Esterene"), or crack, under medical supervision, for the relief of arthritis, for more than two years without a single case of abuse. Some patients took 750 milligrams daily with no ill effects. Used intranasally, the crack was absorbed very slowly by the nostril's mucous membranes—the nose functioned like a time-release capsule. The program was halted by the state. However, 175 other persons in the Los Angeles area were found who were using intranasal cocaine freebase, outside of medical supervision. Few were experiencing problems, even with daily doses of 1000 milligrams. Their regular use without severe dysfunction suggested the possibility of safe use in nonmedical settings.

A largely middle-class population (N = 267) of heavy cocaine users was generally able to avoid experiencing major disruptions or significant distress in their lives (Waldorf, Reinarman, and Murphy 1991). Most who wanted to stop using were able to do so on their own and found that quitting was less difficult than had been expected. Cocaine use was neither immediately nor inevitably addictive, and controlled use was extremely common. Interaction with jobs, family, and friends helped to minimize problems. Many formerly heavy users were able to resume occasional use without relapse.

Conclusions

In any population of drug users, there will be some who can regulate their habit. Even the most intoxicating and addictive substances can be, and often are, used safely. Many of the negative consequences of drug taking may reasonably be attributed to preexisting problems of users or the interaction between their disadvantaged status and current policies regulating the price and availability of drugs.

Almost all the cocaine dealers described by Williams (1989) used cocaine, but most of the successful dealers did so in moderation whereas the least successful allowed themselves to become compulsive users. Reanalysis of the data from such studies could provide significant clues to the personal and social circumstances, factors, and variables that could explain the relative likelihood of either functional or dysfunctional consequences of psychoactive drug use.

However, with daily evidence of widespread negative consequences from addiction and nonmedical psychoactive drug use, it would be totally misleading to convey the impression that the use of psychoactive drugs holds no hazards. It is important, however, to note that the risks of taking such drugs are often overestimated because American society as a whole has rejected nonmedical drug use for almost a century.

A Calvinistic pharmacology prevails even in the medical use of drugs. A pattern of "opiophobia" (Morgan 1989) — manifested in the customary underprescription by clinicians of analgesics to postoperative patients — exists because of concerns about addiction. The Public Health Service is contemplating phasing out its program that permits a small number of patients (Hecht 1991) to smoke marijuana for relieving the nausea and vomiting that accompany some diseases and treatments, for reducing spasticity and pain in multiple sclerosis, and for easing intraocular pressure from glaucoma (Morgan and Zimmer 1991). Instead it proposes to substitute a synthetic form of marijuana containing a substance that prevents patients from getting high despite the belief by some that the substitute will be less effective (Siegel 1989, 312-13).

In this article I have provided evidence indicating that some people can regularly use drugs without harming themselves or inflicting losses on others. However, we do not currently know the probability of this outcome as opposed to more disastrous scenarios. We do not know how those whose lives have become profoundly disrupted by drug use differ from those for whom it poses no such difficulty. Most important, we do not know the relative impact of current prohibitionist policies on the patterns of dysfunctional drug use.

Other cultures provide clues that, without repressive laws, adult users may be able to regulate their own behavior and decide for themselves what constitutes appropriate use. The Dutch study of cocaine users, for example, demonstrated that a significant proportion of the sample experienced periods of increasing use (Cohen 1989). For others, cocaine use became so problematic that they abstained, either for long periods of time or entirely. So long as our government policy is based upon the assumption that nonmedical drug use is destructive, we cannot develop substantial knowledge of the factors that enhance such effective self-regulation of use.

In the case of alcohol and other drugs, former users help to define much of the discourse about drug policy. Like government officials, many feel a vested interest in extending their perception that psychoactive substance use is inherently dysfunctional. These expressions reinforce the dominant ideology, effectively ensuring little flexibility of outlook in American policy.

A more humane drug policy, grounded in a less distorted understanding of the existing patterns of drug use, would be more tolerant of benign drug use and would seek to prevent or control adverse consequences through appropriately fashioned public policy. The recent emergence of organizations committed to exploring policy alternatives, like the Drug Policy Foundation (founded in 1987), journals like the *International Journal for Drug Policy* (launched in 1989), and annual international meetings on the strategy of harm reduction (first held in 1990) suggest that the issue of nonharmful drug use could become more salient in the future. It is just possible that the prohibitionist ethos may loosen its hegemony, thus opening the way for the first time in almost a century for a fundamental rethinking of the issue of drug use.

References

American Bar Association and American Medical Association. 1959. *Drug Addiction: Crime or Disease?* Bloomington: Indiana University Press.

Anglin, M.D., Y. Hser, M. Booth, et al. 1988. *The Natural History of Narcotic Addiction.* Los Angeles: University of California.

Anthony, J.C., C.J. Ritter, M.R. Von Korff, et al. 1985. Descriptive Epidemiology of Adult Cocaine Use in Four U.S. Communities. In *Proceedings of the 47th Annual Scientific Meeting of the Committee on Problems of Drug Dependence,* ed. L.S. Harris, 283–9. Rockville, Md.: National Institute on Drug Abuse.

Biernacki, P. 1986. *Pathways from Heroin Addiction: Recovery without Treatment.* Philadelphia: Temple University Press.

Bureau of Narcotics, U.S. Treasury Department. 1953. *Narcotics Clinics in the United States.* Washington.

————1959. *Comments on Narcotics Drugs: Interim Report of the Joint Committee of the American Bar Association and the American Medical Association.* Washington.

Capel, W.C., B.M. Goldsmith, K.J. Waddell, et al. 1972. The Aging Narcotic Addict: An Increasing Problem for the Next Decades. *Journal of Gerontology* 27:102–6.

Caplovitz, D. 1976. *The Working Addict.* White Plains, N.Y.: Sharpe.

Chein, I., D.L. Gerard, R.S. Lee, and E. Rosenfeld. 1964. *The Road to H.* New York: Basic Books.

Cohen, P. 1989. *Cocaine Use in Amsterdam in Nondeviant Subcul-*

tures. Amsterdam: Institut voor Sociale Geografie, Universiteit van Amsterdam.

Commission on Marijuana and Drug Abuse. 1973. *Final Report.* Washington.

Cutting, W.C. 1942. Morphine Addiction for 62 Years. *Stanford Medical Bulletin* 1:39–41.

Dai, B. 1937. *Opium Addiction in Chicago.* Shanghai: Commercial Press. (Reprinted by Patterson Smith in 1970.)

DeMott, B. 1962. The Great Narcotics Muddle. *Harper's Magazine* 224:46–54.

Dole, V. 1989. Interview. In *Addicts Who Survived: An Oral History of Narcotics Use in America, 1923–1965*, ed. D. Courtwright, H. Joseph, and D. Des Jarlais, 331–43. Knoxville: University of Tennessee Press.

Dreher, M.C. 1982. *Working Men and Ganja: Marijuana Use in Rural Jamaica.* Philadelphia: Institute for the Study of Human Issues.

Drug Abuse Council. 1972. *Dealing With Drug Abuse: A Report to the Ford Foundation.* New York: Praeger.

Edwards, G. 1989. As the Years Go Rolling By: Drinking Problems in the Time Dimension. *British Journal of Psychiatry* 154:18–26.

Ellis, R., and R.C. Stephens. 1976. The Arrest History of Narcotic Addicts Prior to Admission: A Methodological Note. *Drug Forum* 5:211–24.

Epstein, E.J. 1977. *Agency of Fear.* New York: Putnam.

Feldman, H.W. 1968. Ideological Supports to Becoming and Remaining a Heroin Addict. *Journal of Health and Social Behavior* 9:131–9.

Finestone, H. 1937. Cats, Kicks and Color. *Social Problems* 5:3–13.

Frank, B., R. Marel, J. Schmeidler, et al. 1984. An Overview of Substance Use among New York State's Upper Income Householders. *Advances in Alcohol and Substance Abuse* 4:14–26.

Gould, L.C., A.C. Walker, L.E. Crane, and C.W. Lidz. 1974. *Connections: Notes from the Heroin World.* New Haven: Yale University Press.

Graeven, D.B., and K.A. Graeven. 1983. Treated and Untreated Addicts: Factors Associated with Participating in Treatment and Cessation of Heroin Use. *Journal of Drug Issues* 13:207–18.

Haden-Guest, A. 1983. Rich Kids on Smack: The Young, The Rich, and Heroin. *Rolling Stone* 399 (July 7):26–7.

Hanson, B., G. Beschner, J.M. Walters, and E. Bovelle. 1985. *Life with Heroin: Voices from the Inner City.* Lexington, Mass.: Lexington Books.

Hartjen, C.A., and R. Quinney. 1970. The Social Reality of the Drug

Problem: New York City's Lower East Side. *Human Organization* 30:381–91.

Hecht, B. 1991. Out of Joint: The Case for Medicinal Marijuana. *New Republic* (July 15):7–10.

Helmer, J. 1975. *Drugs and Minority Oppression*. New York: Seabury Press.

Hendin, H., A.P. Haas, P. Singer, M. Ellner, and R. Ulman. 1987. *Living High: Daily Marijuana Use among Adults*. New York: Human Sciences Press.

Hubbard, R.L., M.E. Marsden, J.V. Rachal, H.J. Harwood, E.R. Cavanaugh, and H.M. Guinzburg. 1989. *Drug Abuse Treatment: A National Study of Effectiveness*, 146–50. Chapel Hill: University of North Carolina Press.

Hughes, P., G.A. Crawford, N.W. Barker, S. Schuman, and J.H. Jaffe. 1971. The Social Structure of a Heroin Copping Community. *American Journal of Psychiatry* 1971, 128:551–8.

Huling, M. 1985. A Professional's View of Drug Abuse. In *Junkies and Straights: The Camarillo Experience*, ed. R.H. Coombs, 21–56. Lexington, Mass.: Lexington Books.

Ingle, J.I. 1971. William Halsted, Surgeon, Pioneer in Oral Nerve Block Injection and Victim of Drug Experimentation. *Journal of the American Dental Association* 82:46–7.

Institute of Medicine, 1990. *Treating Drug Problems*. Washington: National Academy Press.

Jellinek, E.M. 1952. Phases of Alcohol Addiction. *Quarterly Journal of Studies on Alcohol* 13:673–84.

Karmen, A. 1973. The Drug Abuse–Crime Syndrome: A Radical Critique. In *Sociological Aspects of Drug Dependence*, ed. C. Winick, 309–19. Cleveland: CRC Press.

King, R. 1972. *The Drug Hang-up: America's Fifty Year Folly*. New York: W.W. Norton.

Kolb, L. 1928. Drug Addiction—A Study of Some Medical Cases. *Archives of Neurology and Psychiatry* 20:171–83.

Lindesmith, A.R. 1965. *The Addict and the Law*, 243–68. Bloomington: Indiana University Press.

Lipton, D.S. 1992. Pathways Into Treatment: An Examination of the Entry Process. Paper presented to the Academy of Criminal Justice Sciences, March 30. Pittsburgh.

Maddux, J.F., and D.P. Desmond. 1980. New Light on the Maturing Out Hypothesis in Opioid Dependence. *Bulletin on Narcotics* 32:15–25.

———. 1981. *Careers of Opioid Users*. New York: Praeger.

McWilliams, J.C. 1986. *The Protectors: Harry J. Anslinger and the Federal Bureau of Narcotics 1930–1962*, 177–9. Ph.D. dissertation, Pennsylvania State University.

Michaels, R.J. 1987. The Market for Heroin Before and After Legalization. In *Dealing With Drugs: Consequences of Government Control*, ed. R. Hamowy, 327–52. Lexington, Mass.: D.C. Heath.

Morgan, J. 1989. American Opiophobia: Customary Underutilization of Opioid Analgesics. In *Advances in Pain Research and Therapy*, vol. 2, eds. C.S. Hill, Jr., and W.S. Fields, 163–73. New York: Raven Press.

Morgan, J., and L. Zimmer. 1991. U.S. Needs a Dose of Compassion. *New York Newsday* (August 28):91.

Morhous, E.J. 1953. Drug Addiction in Upper Economic Levels: A Study of 142 Cases. *West Virginia Medical Journal* 49:189–90.

National Institute on Drug Abuse 1991 *National Drug and Alcoholism Treatment Utilization Survey. Main Findings for Drug Abuse Treatment Units, 1989*. DHHS pub. no. 91-1729.

Nurco, D.N., I.H. Cisin, and M.B. Balter. 1981a. Addict Careers. I. A New Typology. *International Journal of the Addictions* 16:1305–25.

———. 1981b. Addict Careers. II. The First Ten Years. *International Journal of the Addictions* 16:1327–56.

———. 1981c. Addict Careers. III. Trends Across Time. *International Journal of the Addictions* 16:1357–72.

O'Donnell, J. 1969. *Narcotic Addicts in Kentucky*. Chevy Chase, Md.: National Institute of Mental Health.

O'Donnell, J.A., H.L. Voss, R.R. Clayton, et al. 1976. *Young Men and Drugs—A Nationwide Survey*. Washington: National Institute on Drug Abuse.

Penfield, W. 1969. Halsted of Johns Hopkins, the Man and His Problem as Described in the Secret Records of William Osler. *Journal of the American Medical Association* 210:2214–17.

Preble, E., and J.J. Casey. 1969. Taking Care of Business. *International Journal of the Addictions* 4:1–24.

Regush, N.M. 1971. *The Drug Addiction Business*. New York: Dial Press.

Robins, L.N. 1974. *The Vietnam Drug User Returns*. Special Action Office Monograph series A, no. 2. Washington.

Robins, L.N., J.E. Helzer, M. Hesselbrock, and E. Wish. 1980. Vietnam Veterans Three Years After Vietnam: How Our Study Changed Our View of Heroin. In *Yearbook of Substance Use and Abuse*, vol. 2, eds. L. Brill and C. Winick, 213–30. New York: Human Sciences Press.

Rosenbaum, M., S. Murphy, J. Irwin, and L. Watson. 1990. Women and Crack: What's the Real Story? *The Drug Policy Letter* 2:2–4.

Roth, L.M. 1986. Substance Use and Mental Health among Vietnam Veterans. In *The Vietnam Veteran Redefined: Fact and Fiction*, ed. G. Boulanger and C. Kadushin, 61–77. Hillsdale, N.J.: Lawrence Erlbaum.

Rounsaville, B.J., and H.D. Kleber. 1985. Untreated Opiate Adults: How Do They Differ from Those Seeking Treatment? *Archives of General Psychiatry* 42:1072–77.

Schur, E.M. 1962. *Narcotic Addiction in Britain and America: The Impact of Public Policy·* Bloomington: Indiana University Press.

———. 1965. *Crimes Without Victims.* Englewood Cliffs, N.J.: Prentice-Hall.

Shimm, M.G. Ed. 1957. Narcotics. *Law and Contemporary Problems* 22 (winter).

Siegel, R.K. 1989. *Intoxication: Life in Pursuit of Artificial Paradise.* New York: E.P. Dutton.

Stimson, G.V. 1973. *Heroin and Behavior.* New York: Wiley.

Susman, J. Ed. 1972. *Drug Use and Social Policy.* New York: AMS Press.

Sutter, A.G. 1966. The World of the Righteous Dope Fiend. *Issues in Criminology* 2:177–222.

Suwanhala, C., V. Poshyachinda, P. Tasanapradit, and A. Dharmkrong-at. 1978. The Hill Tribes of Thailand: Their Opium Use and Addiction. *Bulletin on Narcotics* 30:1–19.

Szasz, T. 1979. *Ceremonial Chemistry: The Ritual Persecution of Drug Addicts and Pushers.* London: Routledge and Kegan Paul.

Talbott, G.D., and C. Wright. 1987. Chemical Dependency in Health Care Professionals. *Occupational Medicine State of the Art Review* 2:581–91.

Treaster, J.B. 1991. In a Crack House: Dinner and Drugs on the Stove. *The New York Times* (April 6):24.

Treaster, J.B. 1992. Trying to Break Addictions, but in Less Time. *The New York Times* (June 20):1.

Vaillant, G.E. 1983. *Natural History of Alcoholism.* Cambridge, Mass.: Harvard University Press.

Waldorf, D., C. Reinarman, and S. Murphy. 1991. *Cocaine Changes: The Experience of Using and Quitting.* Philadelphia: Temple University Press.

Waldron, S. 1969. Statement to Select Committee on Crime, House of Representatives, 91st Congress, July 29.

Weil, A. 1972. *The Natural Mind.* Boston: Houghton Mifflin.

Williams, T. 1989. *The Cocaine Kids: The Inside Story of a Teenage Drug Ring*. Reading, Mass.: Addison-Wesley.

Winick, C. 1960. The Use of Drugs by Jazz Musicians. *Social Problems* 7:240–53.

———. 1962. Maturing Out of Narcotic Addiction. *Bulletin on Narcotics* 16:1–11.

———. 1990. Substance Dependence among Physicians and Nurses. In *The Sociocultural Matrix of Alcohol and Drug Use*, eds. B. Forster and J.C. Salloway, 342–66. Lewiston, Maine: Edwin Mellen Press.

———. 1992. A Ten Year Follow-Up of Working Opiate Users. *Journal of Addictive Diseases*. (Forthcoming.)

Yurick, S. 1970. The Political Economy of Junk. *Monthly Review* 22:22–35.

Zinberg, N.E. 1984. *Drug, Set and Setting*. New Haven: Yale University Press.

From Prohibition to Regulation:
Lessons from Alcohol Policy for Drug Policy

HARRY G. LEVINE and
CRAIG REINARMAN

Queens College, City University of New York;
University of California, Santa Cruz

M ORE THAN FIVE YEARS AFTER IT WAS LAUNCHED, America's latest war on drugs has given rise to a chorus of questions about its efficacy and its problematic side effects. Policy makers, journalists, and the general public have increasingly looked to alternatives to drug prohibition such as decriminalization and public health approaches. People have also been drawn to the history of America's experiences with alcohol prohibition and regulation.

In this article we review some major questions about the rise, fall, and effects of alcohol prohibition, and we examine the logic, rationale, and organization of alcohol regulation following its prohibition. We focus on lessons from alcohol prohibition that might be useful for understanding drug prohibition, and on various principles governing alcohol regulation that might apply to drug regulation. In the final section we try to assess the prospects for radical drug law reform by comparing current conditions with those prevailing at the time alcohol prohibition was repealed.

Historical analogies cannot, of course, provide simple and straightforward answers to the complex drug policy questions now confronting Americans. Closer attention to the story of alcohol prohibition and regulation, however, can help us to understand better the inherent problems and process of drug prohibition while illuminating a wider array of policy options. To set the stage, we begin with a brief overview of the

160

history of temperance, prohibition, repeal, and alcohol regulation in America.

Temperance, Prohibition, Alcohol Control

The antialcohol, or temperance, movement was created in the early nineteenth century by physicians, ministers, and large employers concerned about the drunkenness of workers and servants. By the mid-1830s temperance had become a mass movement of the middle class. Temperance was not, as is sometimes thought, the campaign of rural backwaters; rather, temperance was on the cutting edge of social reform and was closely allied with the antislavery and women's rights movements. Always very popular, temperance remained the largest enduring middle-class movement of the nineteenth century (Levine 1978, 1984; Tyrell 1979; Gusfield 1986; Rumbarger 1989; Blocker 1989).

The temperance campaign was devoted to convincing people that alcoholic drink in any form was evil, dangerous, and destructive. Throughout the nineteenth century, temperance supporters insisted that alcohol slowly but inevitably destroyed the moral character and the physical and mental health of all who drank it. Temperance supporters regarded alcohol the way people today view heroin: as an inherently addicting substance. Moderate consumption of alcohol, they maintained, naturally led to compulsive use — to addiction.

From the beginning, temperance ideology contained a powerful strand of fantasy. It held that alcohol was the major cause of nearly all social problems: unemployment, poverty, business failure, slums, insanity, crime, and violence (especially against women and children). For the very real social and economic problems of industrializing America, the temperance movement offered universal abstinence as the panacea.

From roughly the 1850s on, many temperance supporters endorsed the idea of prohibition. After the Civil War the Prohibition party, modeled on the Republican party, championed the cause. Nineteenth-century prohibitionists believed that only when sufficient numbers of party members held office would prohibition be practical because only then would it be fully enforced.

In the twentieth century a new prohibitionist organization — the Anti-Saloon League — came to dominate the movement (Odegard 1928; Timberlake 1963; Sinclair 1965; Gusfield 1968; Kerr 1985; Rumbarger

1989). The League patterned itself on the modern corporation, hiring lawyers to write model laws and organizers to raise funds and collect political debts. The League put its considerable resources behind candidates of any party who would vote as it directed on the single issue of liquor. By expanding the numbers of elected officials beholden to it, and by writing laws for those legislators to enact, the League pushed through many local prohibition laws and some state measures. In 1913 the League finally declared itself in favor of Constitutional prohibition. Increasing numbers of large corporations joined the many Protestant churches that had long supported the League. Then, during the patriotic fervor of World War I, prohibitionists mobilized the final support for a constitutional amendment. Among other arguments, prohibitionists claimed that in the United States the heavily German beer industry was sapping American will to fight.

By December 1917, both houses of Congress had voted the required two-thirds majority to send to the states for ratification a constitutional amendment prohibiting the manufacture, sale, transportation, import, or export of intoxicating liquor. In November 1918 Congress passed the War Prohibition Act, which banned the manufacture and sale of all beverages including beer and wine that contained more than 2.75 percent alcohol. On January 16th, 1919, Nebraska became the thirty-sixth state to ratify the Eighteenth Amendment, which was to go into effect in one year. In October 1919 Congress overrode President Wilson's veto to pass a strict enforcement act of prohibition known by the name of its sponsor, Andrew Volstead of Minnesota, chair of the House Judiciary Committee. The Volstead Act defined as "intoxicating liquor" any beverage containing more than 0.5 percent alcohol.

At midnight on January 16, 1920, the Eighteenth Amendment took effect. The famous minister Billy Sunday celebrated by preaching a sermon to 10,000 people in which he repeated the fantasy at the heart of the temperance and prohibition crusades:

> The reign of tears is over. The slums will soon be a memory. We will turn our prisons into factories and our jails into storehouses and corncribs. Men will walk upright now, women will smile, and the children will laugh. Hell will be forever for rent. (quoted in Kobler 1973, 12)

Prohibitionism was not, as is sometimes implied, a public health campaign to reduce mortality from cirrhosis of the liver or alcoholic admissions to state hospitals. As Joseph Gusfield (1968) has pointed out, prohibitionists were utopian moralists; they believed that eliminating the legal manufacture and sale of alcoholic drink would solve the major social and economic problems of American society.

The many literary, photographic, and cinematic images of the Prohibition era capture some of the essential features of the period. Prohibition was massively and openly violated, and alcohol was readily available in most of the United States. New institutions and cultural practices appeared: bootleggers and speakeasies, hip flasks and bathtub gin, rum runners smuggling in liquor, and prohibition agents like Elliott Ness smashing down doors. Adulterated and even poisonous alcohol was sold and many people were locked up for violating prohibition laws. (For rich descriptions of the prohibition era, see Allen 1931; Lyle 1960; Allsop 1961; Sinclair 1964; Mertz 1970; Kobler 1973; Everest 1978; and Cashman 1981. Burnham [1968] offers perhaps the only serious scholarly case for the success of prohibition. For the most recent evidence and discussions of its failures, see Miron and Zwiebel 1991; Morgan 1991; and Thornton 1991.)

Public opposition to prohibition began even before the Volstead Act passed, especially among labor unions, but organized opposition remained small and fragmented until 1926. Then one organization, the Association Against the Prohibition Amendment (AAPA), took over the campaign for repeal. Headed by Pierre DuPont and other powerful corporate leaders, the AAPA gathered increasing numbers of wealthy and prominent supporters, including many former prohibitionists. Although prohibition would have been repealed eventually, the AAPA unquestionably accelerated the process (Kyvig 1979; Levine 1985; Rumbarger 1989).

Just as World War I had provided the necessary context for rallying popular support to pass prohibition, the Great Depression provided the necessary context for repeal. Prohibition's supporters had long argued that it would ensure prosperity and increase law and order. In the late 1920s and early 1930s, prohibition's opponents made exactly the same argument. Repeal, they promised, would provide jobs, stimulate the economy, increase tax revenue, and reduce the "lawlessness" stimulated by and characteristic of the illegal liquor industry.

The Depression also played a crucial role in undermining elite support for prohibition. To some extent, alcohol prohibition had originally gained the support of large employers because they believed it would increase worker discipline and productivity and reduce other social problems. The mass violations of national prohibition in the 1920s, followed by the Depression of the 1930s, raised a new specter: prohibition, many came to believe, undermined respect for all law, including property law. This "lawlessness," as people then termed it, frightened many of the rich and powerful — like Pierre DuPont and John D. Rockefeller, Jr. — far more than problems with worker efficiency (Leuchtenburg 1958; Kyvig 1979; Levine 1985).

On top of "lawlessness," the threat of revolt and revolution was in the air in the early 1930s. There were food riots in many cities, unemployed people formed militant organizations, mobs stopped trains and took over warehouses of food. Socialists and communists held rallies of tens of thousands, angry armies of marchers camped in front of the White House, and some wealthy people had machine guns mounted on the roofs of their estates (Leuchtenburg 1958; Piven and Cloward 1971; 1977; Manchester, 1974).

Those with wealth and power increasingly supported repeal, in part because they felt the need to do something to raise public morale and show that the government was in some way responsive to popular pressure in a terrible depression. In 1931, Matthew Woll, vice-president of the American Federation of Labor and the sole labor member of the AAPA board, told President Hoover's National Commission on Law Observance and Enforcement (the Wickersham Commission) that workers were losing faith in the government's willingness to help them, and that prohibition was causing them further to distrust and resent government. By 1932 a number of influential leaders and commentators also had concluded that legalizing beer would make workers feel better about government and take their minds off their troubles. Senators were told, "Beer would have a decidedly soothing tendency on the present mental attitude of the working men. . . . It would do a great deal to change their mental attitude on economic conditions." Walter Lippman argued, "Beer would be a great help in fighting off the mental depression which afflicts great multitudes" (quotes from Gordon 1943, 104). The Wickersham Commission explicitly pointed to the class resentment and lawlessness engendered by prohibition in its report to Congress:

> Naturally . . . laboring men resent the insistence of employers who drink that their employees be kept from temptation. Thus the law may be made to appear aimed at and enforced against the insignifi-

cant while the wealthy enjoy immunity. This feeling is reinforced when it is seen that the wealthy are generally able to procure pure liquors, while those with less means may run the risk of poisoning. Moreover, searches of homes . . . have necessarily seemed to bear more upon people of moderate means than upon those of wealth or influence. (1931, 54-5)

On November 16, 1932, the Senate voted to submit the Twenty-first Amendment — repealing the Eighteenth Amendment and returning to the states the power to regulate alcohol — to state conventions for ratification. On March 13, 1933, a few days after he was sworn in as president, Franklin Roosevelt asked Congress to modify the Volstead Act to legalize 3.2 percent alcohol beer to provide needed tax revenue. By April 7, beer was legal in most of the country. On December 5, 1933, Utah became the thirty-sixth state to pass the Twenty-first Amendment. National alcohol prohibition was repealed, effective immediately.

In late 1933 and in 1934, bills creating state alcohol control agencies sped through state legislatures. The model for most of the legislation had been written by a group of policy-oriented researchers and attorneys associated with John D. Rockefeller, Jr., and with policy institutes he had created or financially supported (Levine 1985). Within two years of repeal nearly every state had an agency to supervise the sale and distribution of alcoholic beverages, and alcohol had ceased to be a controversial and politically charged issue. The production, sale, and distribution of alcoholic beverages today is still largely governed by the alcohol control structures designed and implemented at that time.

Effects of Prohibition on Consumption, Production, and Distribution

Consumption

It has frequently been observed that drug prohibition tends to drive out weaker and milder forms of drugs, and to increase the availability and use of stronger and more dangerous drugs (see, e.g., Brecher 1972). This has been so often reported that many analysts speak of it as an "iron law" of drug prohibition. This "law" holds because milder drugs are usually bulkier, harder to hide and smuggle, and less remunerative. People involved in the illicit drug business therefore frequently find it in their interest to do business in the more compact and potent sub-stances. For example, current interdiction efforts are most successful at capturing boats carrying many large bales of marijuana; therefore, many drug smugglers have turned to smuggling cocaine or heroin because it is easier and far more lucrative than smuggling marijuana (see Murphy, Waldorf, and Reinarman 1991).

This "law" of drug prohibition captures what happened during pro-hibition. The major effect of the Eighteenth Amendment and the Vol-stead Act on drinking was to dramatically reduce beer drinking (and therefore total alcohol consumption). At the same time, however, pro-hibition increased consumption of hard liquor (especially among the middle class). The fashionableness of the martini and other mixed drinks among the middle class is in part a historical legacy of prohibi-tion, when criminalization made hard liquor the most available form of beverage alcohol.

Table 1 is drawn primarily from data gathered by the Rutgers Univer-sity Center for Alcohol Studies and by historian William Rorabaugh (1979; see also Miron and Zwiebel 1991). We added estimates of beer and wine consumption for 1925 and 1930 based upon economist Clark Warburton's (1932) classic study and adjusted the total consumption figures accordingly. The table shows the per capita (15 years and older) consumption of absolute alcohol in spirits, wine, beer, and cider in America over nearly three centuries.

Two factors stand out in these figures. First, although total alcohol consumption declined after 1915, the sharpest drop occurred between 1830 and 1840, nearly a century before prohibition, when temperance first became a mass middle-class movement. Second, and more perti-nent here, prohibition led to a reduction in beer consumption, but an increase in consumption of wine and spirits. Warburton compared alco-hol consumption in the period of 1911 to 1914 with that during the prohibition years 1927–1930 and concluded that "the per capita con-sumption of beer has been reduced about 70 per cent, . . . the per cap-ita consumption of wine has increased about 65 per cent, . . . [and] the per capita consumption of spirits has increased about 10 per cent" (1932, 260).

From 1890 to 1915 beer accounted for more of the total alcohol con-sumed than did hard liquor. In 1915, for example, beer drinking ac-counted for nearly twice the total alcohol consumed as spirits did. This

TABLE 1
Alcoholic Beverage Consumption in the United States From 1710 to 1975[a]

Year	Spirits Bev.	Abs. alc.	Wine Bev.	Abs. alc.	Cider Bev.	Abs. alc.	Beer Bev.	Abs. alc.	Total Abs. alc.
1710	3.8	1.7	.2	<.05	34	3.4	–	–	5.1
1770	7.0	3.2	.2	<.05	34	3.4	–	–	6.6
1790	5.1	2.3	.6	.1	34	3.4	–	–	5.8
1800	7.2	3.3	.6	.1	32	3.2	–	–	6.6
1810	8.7	3.9	.4	.1	30	3.0	.3	.1	7.1
1820	8.7	3.9	.4	.1	28	2.8	–	–	6.8
1830	9.5	4.3	.5	.1	27	2.7	–	–	7.1
1840	5.5	2.5	.5	.1	4	.4	2.3	.1	3.1
1850	3.6	1.6	.3	.1	–	–	2.7	.1	1.8
1860	3.9	1.7	.5	.1	–	–	6.4	.3	2.1
1870	3.1	1.4	.5	.1	–	–	8.6	.4	1.9
1880	2.4	1.1	1.0	.2	–	–	11.1	.6	1.9
1890	2.2	1.0	.6	.1	–	–	20.6	1.0	2.1
1900	1.8	.8	.6	.1	–	–	23.6	1.2	2.1
1905	1.9	.9	.7	.1	–	–	25.9	1.3	2.3
1910	2.1	.9	.9	.2	–	–	29.2	1.5	2.6
1915	1.8	.8	.7	.1	–	–	29.7	1.5	2.4
1920	–[b]	–	–	–	–	–	–	–	–
1925	2.1	.9	1.0	.2	–	–	–	.3	1.4
1930	2.1	.9	1.0	.2	–	–	–	.4	1.5
1935	1.5	.7	.4	.1	–	–	15.0	.7	1.5
1940	1.3	.6	.9	.2	–	–	17.2	.8	1.6
1945	1.5	.7	1.1	.2	–	–	24.2	1.1	2.0
1950	1.5	.7	1.1	.2	–	–	24.1	1.1	2.0
1955	1.6	.7	1.3	.2	–	–	22.8	1.0	1.9
1960	1.9	.8	1.3	.2	–	–	22.1	1.0	2.0
1965	2.1	1.0	1.3	.2	–	–	22.8	1.0	2.2
1970	2.5	1.1	1.8	.3	–	–	25.7	1.2	2.5
1975	2.4	1.1	2.2	.3	–	–	28.8	1.3	2.7

Sources: Adapted from Rorabaugh (1979, 233) and Warburton (1932).
[a] Absolute alcohol for each beverage, per capita of drinking age (15+) population, in U.S. gallons.
[b] Estimates for 1920 vary considerably and have been omitted.

change was not permanent; spirits consumption fell after repeal while beer consumption rose. By 1935 the alcohol consumed from beer equaled that from spirits, and by 1945 Americans were getting 50 percent more of their total alcohol from beer than from hard liquor.

Consumption and Public Health
Under Prohibition

The new public debate about drug laws has increased interest in the effects of prohibition on public health, the economy, and social problems. These were very lively questions during the prohibition period but have been largely ignored since. However, in the last two decades alcohol researchers in a number of countries have investigated at length the relationship between total per capita alcohol consumption and specific illnesses, especially cirrhosis of the liver. The data available for the prohibition years in the United States will always be poor because it is impossible to get accurate consumption figures for an illegal substance. Nonetheless, changes in the last 50 years in many countries that have kept accurate consumption and health statistics do allow some inferences about the relationship between overall alcohol consumption and cirrhosis. Although not all liver cirrhosis is caused by heavy drinking, much is. Furthermore, cirrhosis rates generally follow overall per capita consumption rates. These effects are mediated by dietary patterns, by type of alcoholic beverages consumed, and by when they are consumed. The level of health care people receive also affects cirrhosis death rates. In general, however, the positive relationship between alcohol consumption and cirrhosis holds: when consumption increases, cirrhosis increases (Bruun et al. 1975; Mäkelaä et al. 1981; Moore and Gerstein 1981; Single et al. 1981).

One important way to evaluate the public health consequences of alcohol policies, then, is in terms of how they affect consumption. In 1932 Warburton pointed out that "except for the first three years, the per capita consumption of alcohol has been greater under prohibition than during the war period [1917–1919], with high taxation and restricted production and sale" (260). As table 1 suggests, both prohibition and postprohibition alcohol regulation kept overall consumption down compared with the decades prior to prohibition. Indeed, postprohibition regulatory policies kept alcohol use sufficiently low that it was not until the end of the 1960s, 35 years after repeal, that per capita alcohol consumption rose to the levels of 1915. Whatever public health benefits prohibition achieved in terms of reducing consumption, alcohol regulation in the 1930s and early 1940s accomplished them as well. Further, this occurred despite the fact that the postprohibition regulatory system had little or no public health focus, and despite the fact that the liquor industry (like most other U.S. industries) gained increasing influence over the agencies that were supposed to regulate it. Our point here is *not* that U.S. alcohol control is a model of effective public-health-oriented regulatory policy (it certainly is not). Rather, until at least 1960, alcohol control worked almost as well as prohibition in limiting alcohol consumption, and more effectively than preprohibition policies.

It is also important to note that other nations achieved even greater reductions in per capita consumption than the United States — without the negative consequences of prohibition. Robin Room (1988) has shown that in Australia a series of alcohol control measures instituted in the early twentieth century substantially reduced spirits consumption. More important, Australia's regulatory policies significantly reduced total alcohol consumption as well as the incidence of alcohol-related health problems, notably cirrhosis mortality. From a peak of 9.15 cirrhosis deaths per 100,000 in 1912, Australia's cirrhosis rate fell to 3.83 in 1933, and fluctuated between 3.15 and 5.12 for over 20 years. Room reports that mortality from alcoholic psychosis experienced a similar drop. All of this happened under regulated sale, not prohibition.

Great Britain's experience parallels that of Australia. England reduced overall consumption by instituting fairly stringent alcohol regulation at about the same time as the United States instituted prohibition. Moreover, as Nadelmann notes, it reduced "the negative consequences of alcohol consumption more effectively than did the United States, but it did so in a manner that raised substantial government revenues." By contrast, the U.S. government not only spent large sums attempting to enforce its prohibition laws, but was also unable to prevent the flow of money into criminal enterprises (1989b, 1102-3).

It is difficult to disagree with Nadelmann's conclusion that the "British experience [and, we would add, the Australian experience] strongly indicates that the national prohibition of alcohol in the United States was, on balance, not successful." Prohibition of course failed to fulfill the fantasies of prohibitionists about eliminating major social problems like poverty, unemployment, crime, and so on. Yet even in the less utopian terms of reducing total alcohol consumption, U.S. prohibition was no more effective than regulated sale in the 1930s and early 1940s. Prohibition, however, produced far more substantial negative side effects than did regulation.

Only a few other nations even tried prohibition laws, and only Finland instituted constitutional prohibition (repealing it before the United States and for many of the same reasons). Although there are today neotemperance movements in some Nordic and English-speaking (Great Britain, Canada, Australia, and New Zealand) countries, which focus on the public health dangers of alcohol, these are not prohibitionist groups. Contrary to the claims and worries of the U.S. alcohol industry, there are no neoprohibitionist movements and no serious discussion anywhere about returning to prohibition. In the United States even many local prohibition laws have been replaced by regulation of some kind. Over 50 years after repeal of the Eighteenth Amendment, the consensus remains that alcohol prohibition was not sound public policy.

Alcohol Production and Distribution During Prohibition

In the criminalized context of prohibition, alcohol consumption was influenced by the requirements of illicit production. It was much more profitable and cost effective to make and distribute distilled spirits (gin, vodka, whiskey, or rum) than beer. Beer is mostly water—only 3 to 6 percent alcohol. Production and storage of beer require enormous tanks, many barrels, and huge trucks and demand a substantial investment in equipment. Hard liquor is 40 to 50 percent alcohol; it contains up to 15 times more pure alcohol than beer. Because alcohol content was the main determinant of price, a gallon of spirits was much more valuable than a gallon of beer and also could be hidden and transported more easily. Furthermore, spirits could be preserved indefinitely, whereas beer spoiled very quickly. Large-scale beer bottling and refrigeration only developed in the 1930s, after repeal (Baron 1962; Kyvig 1979).

The rising supply of hard liquor came from many sources. Tens of thousands of people produced it in small, compact stills in sheds, basements, attics, and in the woods. It was also smuggled from Mexico, Europe, and Canada. Some of the largest names in distilling today entered the business or grew wealthy during the prohibition era—notably the Bronfmans of Canada, who own Seagram's. A considerable amount of alcohol was also diverted from purported industrial or medical uses.

Wine consumption also increased during prohibition, to about 65 percent more than the pre-World War I period, according to Warburton (1932). Standard table wine contains 10 to 14 percent alcohol. Much of the wine was made for personal consumption and as a profitable side business by immigrants from wine countries, especially Italy. After the first few years of prohibition, the California wine–grape industry experienced a boom and vineyard prices increased substantially. California grape growers planted hearty, thick-skinned grapes that could be shipped easily and used for small-scale and home wine making. Much of the California wine–grape crop was shipped to Chicago and New York in newly developed refrigerated boxcars. The grapes were bought right off the train by wholesalers, who resold them in immigrant neighborhoods. The home-made wine was then distributed to smaller cities and towns, where it was sometimes called "dago red" (Muscatine, Amerine, and Thompson 1984).

Although it is true that prohibition provided a major boost for organized crime, it is not true (although widely believed today) that gangsters and large criminal organizations supplied most prohibition-era alcohol. In Chicago and a few other large cities, large criminal gangs indeed dominated alcohol distribution, especially by the end of the 1920s. Most of the alcohol production and distribution, however, was on a smaller scale. In addition to home-made wines and family stills, people took station wagons and trucks to Canada and returned with a load of liquor. Lobster boats, other fishing boats, and pleasure boats did the same. Spirits and wine were also prescribed by physicians and available at pharmacies. Many people certified themselves as ministers and rabbis and distributed large quantities of "sacramental wine." Alcoholic beverages were made and sold to supplement other income during hard times. Prohibition thus shaped the structure of the alcohol industry in a distinctive way: it decentralized and democratized production and distribution (Lyle 1960; Allsop 1961; Sinclair 1965; Everest 1978; Cashman 1981).

Today as well, most people in the illicit drug business are small-scale entrepreneurs. Supporters of the drug war frequently suggest that elimination of the currently large-scale drug producers and distributors would have a lasting effect on drug production and distribution. There is no more evidence supporting this now than there was during alcohol prohibition. Much illicit drug production today is also decentralized and democratized. There is no criminal syndicate that, when eliminated, would stop the distribution of any currently illicit drug, or even reduce the supply for very long. Today some groups, families, and business organizations (like the so-called Medellin cocaine cartel) have grown very rich in the illicit drug business. However, just as Al Capone was quickly replaced, so have new producers taken the place of those cocaine "kingpins" who have been arrested. Indeed, after billions of dollars on interdiction have been spent by Customs, the Drug Enforcement Agency, and even the armed forces, there has been no lasting drop in the supply of cocaine. Even when interdiction does affect the supply of a criminalized substance, the effects are often ironic. The partial success of the Nixon administration's "Operation Intercept," for example, gave rise to what is now a huge domestic marijuana industry (Brecher 1972), which produces far more potent strains of marijuana and has become ever more decentralized and democratic as armed helicopter raids have increased.

In short, whereas prohibition regimes tend to be a boon to organized crime, they also increase the number and types of people involved in illicit production and distribution (Williams 1989; Murphy, Waldorf, and Reinarman 1991). Whether production occurs in a mob syndicate or a family marijuana patch, the result tends to be a shift toward production and sale of more concentrated forms of intoxicating substances. Recognition of such tendencies in the prohibition era accelerated the process of repeal and informed the search for alternative regulatory systems.

Establishing an Alcohol Control System

The Problem

In 1933, at the very end of the prohibition era, the difficulties of creating an alcohol control system seemed formidable. In the years before Constitutional prohibition in the United States, there had been little systematic control of the alcohol industry. The Eighteenth Amendment had not eliminated the business, but rather had profoundly altered its shape. Thus, in 1933 a sprawling illegal industry for producing and distributing alcoholic beverages was in place, composed of uncountable numbers of small independent distributors and producers, and some larger ones. For 14 years this industry had kept the United States well supplied with alcohol. The mass patronage of this illicit industry — and the political and economic implications of such a popular display of disrespect for law — was a major factor in convincing Rockefeller and other prominent supporters of prohibition to reverse field and press for repeal.

During prohibition the liquor business was wide open. In most cities and many towns, speakeasies closed when they wished or not at all; they sold whatever they wanted, to whomever they cared to, at whatever price they chose. They decorated as they wished and had a free hand in providing food and entertainment. Producers had complete control over the strength of their alcohol and the means of its manufacture, including the products that went into it. Neither producers nor distributors paid any taxes (except for payoffs to police and politicians) and they were not regulated by any government agency. During prohibition, the liquor industry was probably the freest large industry in America.

Alcohol control, on the other hand, was a highly coercive system. It was premised on government intervention into every aspect of the liquor business. Controversial issues such as whether food must be served, women admitted, music and games banned, bars and bar stools allowed, all had to be settled. The number, types, and locations of on- and off-premise outlets and their hours of sale had to be determined. Producers had to be regulated to ensure that products were safe and of a uniform alcohol content. In order to eliminate untrustworthy or disreputable persons, both producers and distributors had to be screened, licensed, and made to pay taxes. Legal drinking had to be socially organized in a way that would not be an affront to the abstaining half of the population. Conversely, the control system could not make regulation so tight, or taxes so high, that drinkers would prefer to patronize illicit bootleggers or speakeasies. Americans, after all, were by then quite used to disobeying liquor laws.

Prohibitionists had always argued that the liquor business was inherently unregulatable. The onus was now on reformers to show that this was not true, and that they could create structures to make the industry obey laws and yield taxes. The task, as expressed in the catchall title for alternatives to prohibition, was "liquor control" or "alcohol control" in the fullest sense of the term. In short, repeal posed an enormous problem of social engineering. Constructing alcohol control, in fact, involved problems of government regulation so large and complex as to make some of the classic Progressive-era reforms — regulating meat packing, for example — seem paltry in comparison. Except for national prohibition, postrepeal alcohol regulation is probably the most striking twentieth-century example of government power used directly to reshape both an entire industry and the way its products are consumed.

The Rockefeller Report

Prior to the passage of the Eighteenth Amendment, alcohol was regulated by cities, towns, and sometimes counties. State governments were rarely involved in regulating production or distribution. Prohibition then shifted control to the federal government. Postrepeal policy, however, made state governments chiefly responsible for devising and implementing a regulatory system. States could, and often did, then allow for considerable local option and variation.

By the end of the 1920s the Association Against the Prohibition Amendment had outlined some rough plans for alternatives to prohibition, but they had not been well worked out. The central principles of postprohibition alcohol control systems adopted by almost every state legislature were first fully laid out in a report sponsored by John D. Rockefeller, Jr. and issued in October 1933, shortly before repeal was ratified. Rockefeller's long-time adviser, Raymond Fosdick, was the senior author. Fosdick supervised the group of attorneys and policy analysts, most of whom worked with or for the Institute of Public Administration — a Progressive Era policy institute in New York that Rockefeller had funded for a number of years. The report was issued in press releases to newspapers and magazines over several weeks. Finally the Rockefeller Report (as it was called at the time) was released as a book, *Toward Liquor Control* by Raymond Fosdick and Albert Scott (1933).

Although few at the time recognized it, *Toward Liquor Control* had taken as its basic conclusions virtually all of the central recommendations made 30 years earlier by another elite-sponsored alcohol policy group called the Committee of Fifty. The Committee of Fifty, which was staunchly antiprohibitionist, had produced five books on various aspects of the "alcohol problem" around the turn of the century. Fosdick and the other study members had read the Committee of Fifty's reports and quoted them at length on the corruption and lawlessness resulting from earlier forms of local prohibition. The Rockefeller Report echoed the Committee of Fifty's conclusion that the legitimacy of the law must be of primary concern in liquor regulation. Both reports agreed that the specific content of the law mattered less than that the laws be obeyed.

Both reports argued that alcohol regulation required a flexible system that could be continually monitored and adjusted. Further, both reports advised that, if at all possible, government should take over the selling of alcoholic beverages (Billings 1905; Levine 1983; Rumbarger 1989).

The specific plan for alcohol control suggested by *Toward Liquor Control*, and the Rockefeller Report's most controversial proposal, was that each state take over as a public monopoly the retail sale for off-premises consumption of spirits, wine, and beer above 3.2 percent alcohol. As Fosdick and Scott explained: "The primary task of the [State Alcohol] Authority would be the establishment of a chain of its own retail stores for the sale of the heavier alcoholic beverages by package only." This is the source of the term "package stores" still used today for liquor outlets in many states. The state-run outlets of Canadian provinces, and of Sweden, Norway, and Finland, were cited as working examples of such a plan. This quickly became known as the "monopoly plan" and at the time was usually called "the Rockefeller plan."

For those states not willing to establish government liquor stores, Fosdick and Scott proposed an alternative system: "regulation by license." They cited England as the best example of a working license system. A single, nonpartisan board appointed by the governor would have statewide authority to issue liquor licenses and regulate the industry. "Tied houses" would not be permitted; no retail establishments could be owned directly by or under exclusive contract to a distiller or brewer.

Although it offered guidelines for a licensing system, *Toward Liquor Control* favored the monopoly plan. The possibility of increasing profits, they said, would encourage private businesses to sell more alcohol, to buy political influence and lax enforcement, and to violate laws. Rockefeller explained the chief advantage of government-owned liquor stores in his foreword to the book: "Only as the profit motive is eliminated is there any hope of controlling the liquor traffic in the interests of a decent society. To approach the problem from any other angle is only to tinker with it and to ensure failure." The irony of a Rockefeller warning about the dangers of the profit motive was not lost on observers in 1933. Rockefeller took such an anticapitalist position because, like others at the time, he had concluded, probably correctly, that government ownership brought greater powers to regulate and control behavior, and ensure obedience to the law.

For both plans, *Toward Liquor Control* outlined a detailed set of matters over which the state agency would have jurisdiction. These included the power to acquire real estate and other capital by purchase, lease, or condemnation; determine and change prices at will; establish a system of personal identification of purchasers; issue permits for and regulate the use of beer and wine for off-premises consumption and for on-premises consumption in hotels, restaurants, clubs, railway dining cars, and passenger boats; require alcohol manufacturers and importers to report on quantities produced and shipped; regulate or eliminate alcohol beverage advertising; determine the internal design, visibility from the street, hours and days of sale, number and locations of alcohol outlets.

In January 1934 a model law based on the guidelines of *Toward Liquor Control* and written by the staff of the Institute for Public Administration was published as a supplement to the *National Municipal Review*. The *Review* was the official journal of the National Municipal League, another Progressive Era policy organization supported by the Rockefellers. The model law and other supporting documents were widely circulated to legislators throughout the country in the months following repeal. State legislators, faced with difficult political choices, and with little personal expertise in the complexities of liquor regulation, turned to the authoritative and virtually unchallenged plans of the Rockefeller commission and the National Municipal League. In a letter in the Rockefeller Archives, one of the model law's authors estimated that the monopoly law was taken almost verbatim by 15 states, and the licensing law served as the text or draft for many more (Gulick 1977; Levine 1985).

Alcohol Control in Operation

Postrepeal regulation transformed the alcohol beverage industry. Finland, the only other nation to have experimented with constitutional prohibition, had nationalized production of spirits. However, such proposals were not seriously discussed in the United States. Instead, production took the form of an oligopoly of relatively few corporations. By the end of the 1930s, four or five years after repeal, roughly four-fifths of all distilled liquor made in the United States was manufactured by four corporations. The beer industry, although more diverse nationally because beer required quick and local distribution, was monopolized by region or area. Regulatory agencies preferred to deal with a few large corporations—they were easier to police and to make agreements with, and more likely to be concerned with keeping the image of the industry clean and respectable. This pattern of monopolization was not unique of course; most major American industries—steel, automobiles, soft drinks, chemicals, for example—were increasingly dominated by a few large corporations. (From at least the time of the National Recovery Act at the start of the New Deal, federal government policy often encouraged such concentration. The alcohol industry was exceptional only in how quickly many small producers were overtaken by a few dominant ones.)

Although production became oligopolistic, distribution was splintered and scattered. Perhaps the most important long-term innovation in postprohibition alcohol regulation was that it permitted the legal sale of alcohol at a wide variety of sites. Before prohibition, the saloon had been a single, all-purpose institution—there one drank beer, wine, or spirits, and there one purchased for off-premises consumption a bottle of spirits or a bucket of beer. After repeal, alcohol control created several different types of establishments to sell alcoholic beverages. In most states special stores were designated for selling distilled liquor and wine—often they could not sell any food at all, or even cigarettes. Beer, on the other hand, was made relatively widely available in bottles and cans—with grocery stores and small markets licensed to sell it. In other words, after prohibition, sale of bottled alcohol was increasingly separated from the public drinking place. This encouraged the privatization of drinking. Whether alone or with others, drinking became something more commonly done at home—where, it should be noted, drinking patterns were often moderated by family norms (see Zinberg 1984). By 1941, off-premises consumption accounted for the majority of alcohol sales (Harrison and Laine 1936; Kyvig 1979, 189).

The character of public drinking was significantly altered by these regulatory changes. A new class of licenses for on-premises consumption of beer only, or of beer and wine, was established and liberally issued to restaurants and cafeterias where eating moderated the character and effects of drinking. This separated the barroom selling distilled liquor and beer as a distinct institution. Many state alcohol control laws made provision for a local option whereby a county government could prohibit specific kinds of liquor selling within its borders. This option has been widely exercised. As late as 1973, of the 3,073 counties in the United

States, 672 prohibited sales of distilled liquor by the drink for on-premises consumption, and 545 totally prohibited sales of distilled spirits (Alcohol Beverage Control Administration 1973).

Under alcohol control, all establishments licensed for on-premises consumption of spirits were specifically restricted in ways that shaped the cultural practice of drinking. In some areas, control laws attempted to moderate the effects of drinking by encouraging food consumption (just as hosts of cocktail parties served hors d'oeuvres). For example, spirit sales often were limited to bona fide restaurants with laws specifying how many feet of kitchen space and how many food preparation workers there must be. Most states established restrictions on the number of entrances and their locations (back entrances are usually prohibited); the times of day and days of the week when sales may occur; permissible decorations; degree of visibility of the interior from the street; numbers and uses of other rooms; distance of the establishment from churches, schools, and other alcohol outlets; whether customers may sit at a long bar — a counter in close proximity to the source of alcohol — or whether they must sit at tables and order drinks as one orders food; and the ratio of chair seating to bar seating.

The public character of drinkers' comportment was also regulated. Many states, for example, prohibit dancing or live music except under special license. Most gambling or betting is prohibited, and other games are restricted as well. For many years, New York and other states did not allow barrooms to have pinball machines. Many states specifically ban the use of the word "saloon," others the use of the word "bar," and some forbid all words to indicate a drinking place. Until recently, most drinking establishments in California displayed only a name and a symbol: a tilted glass with a stirrer.

From a preprohibition or prohibition-era perspective, there are two surprising characteristics of postrepeal alcohol controls. First, most laws and regulations are *obeyed*. Almost all drinking places, for example, stop serving and collect glasses at the required hours; and they observe the regulations about tables, dancing, decorations, signs, entrances, and so on. By and large, this obedience has been relatively easily achieved through careful policing, coupled with the power to revoke or suspend licenses. Operating a liquor-selling business is usually quite profitable compared to other kinds of retail establishments, so owners tend to guard their licenses carefully. Minimum-age drinking laws constitute the one obvious exception to this regulatory success as well as being one of the few remaining forms of prohibition. Second, postrepeal alcohol regulation is usually *not* perceived as especially restrictive by customers. The many layers of laws and regulations are rarely noticed; most drinkers take them completely for granted.

A third, less surprising characteristic of postrepeal alcohol control is that policy has not been aimed specifically at maximizing what earlier reformers called "temperance"—meaning, above all, reducing habitual drunkenness or repeated heavy drinking. In his preface to *Toward Liquor Control*, Rockefeller maintained that such problems could not be effectively addressed by liquor regulation and that they would have to be taken up by other agencies as part of broader educational and health efforts. Since repeal, these tasks have been adopted by a number of independent and government groups, notably Alcoholics Anonymous and the National Council on Alcoholism, various state and local alcoholism agencies, and, since the early 1970s, the National Institute on Alcohol Abuse and Alcoholism. In recent years, some public health professionals have urged that the alcohol control system be used more self-consciously to reduce drinking and alcohol-related health problems. Such concerns have by and large been imposed on the system, however, and do not flow from its natural workings.

It is worth noting that whenever states propose adding public health concerns to the control system, the alcohol industry usually offers fierce opposition. This is why Rockefeller pushed to eliminate the profit motive from alcohol sales, even while advocating private production. This is also why Finland chose to organize both hard liquor production and sale as a state monopoly. As a result, the Finnish alcohol industry is relatively less powerful than the American industry, and the Finns have found it easier to make public health a part of their postrepeal control system.

On the other hand, despite all its flaws, postrepeal alcohol control did succeed in turning consumption away from hard liquor and back toward beer. Further, alcohol control (coupled with the Depression and World War II) did keep alcohol consumption below preprohibition levels. In fact, as noted earlier, it was not until 1970 that the total alcohol consumption level of the drinking-age population reached the levels of 1915.

In 1936 a second volume of the Rockefeller-sponsored Liquor Study Commission Report was issued. *After Repeal: A Study of Liquor Control Administration* (Harrison and Laine 1936) analyzed the results of liquor control after "a two-year trial," and described the most important changes and innovations in liquor administration instituted since repeal. The overall thrust of the report was that, with some understandable exceptions, alcohol control worked extremely well. Other observers at the time drew similar conclusions (Sheppard 1938; Shipman 1940). Legalizing alcohol and then regulating it had accomplished what most temperance and prohibition supporters claimed was impossible: alcohol moved from being a scandal, crisis, and constant front-page news story to something routine and manageable, a little-noticed thread in the fabric of American life. For over 50 years, alcohol control has quietly and effectively organized and managed the production, distribution, and sale of alcohol, as well as much of the social life associated with drinking.

The alcohol control system was and is coercive, although its coercion was not organized like that of prohibition. This coercion was designed with a certain pragmatic precision that continues to function effectively. Some prohibitionist critics observed at the time of repeal that this system was shaped around the preferences of drinkers and the alcohol industry (Garrison 1933). But as the Committee of Fifty had recommended at the turn of century, alcohol regulation was not designed to stop all drinking and eliminate the industry, but rather to promote "order, quiet and outward decency." This more modest goal has been largely achieved.

Despite frequent claims to the contrary, alcohol control has of course sought to legislate morality. It has not, however, sought to impose the morality of the nineteenth-century Victorian middle class, who took up the cudgel of temperance. Rather the alcohol control system legislates the more modern morality of the new business and professional middle class, of the corporate elite, and to some extent of the twentieth-century working class. Accordingly, unlike more stigmatized "vices" or "pleasures"—prostitution, gambling, and the use of marijuana, heroin, or cocaine—drinking has not been pushed by criminalization beyond the pale of normative and regulatory influence. Moreover, once it ceased to be outlawed, the alcohol industry was no longer dominated by unregulated, illicit entrepreneurs who shot at each other, developed organized crime syndicates, and paid off police and government officials. The leaders of the major alcohol industries are members of the economic establishment with an investment in maintaining order and obedience to law.

Now, over a half-century since prohibition, it is easy to forget that all this was the outcome of self-conscious public policy and not the "natural" result of market forces or national zeitgeist. The alcohol control system has worked sufficiently well that it usually goes unnoticed, even by students of prohibition or American history. For purposes of devising new drug policy options, however, it is important to remember that this particular system was the self-conscious creation of a political and economic elite with the power to institute what it regarded as good and necessary. The alcohol control system they devised is not especially democratic; it does not really address public health or social welfare concerns; it does not even attempt to address the range of alcohol-related health problems in our society; and it has produced enormous profits for a handful of large corporations that continue to fight public health measures. However, it has achieved what its designers sought to do: regulate and administer the orderly and lawful distribution of alcoholic beverages in a way that creates little controversy (Bruun et al. 1975; Beauchamp 1981; Levine 1984).

Lessons from the Regulatory Regime

There are many different (even contradictory) lessons that may be drawn from the story of alcohol control in the United States. Two seem particularly relevant for drug policy. First, although it may cut against the grain of our moral predispositions, drug control along the lines of alcohol control is a reasonable and practical policy option. Prohibitionists always claimed that alcohol was a special substance that could never be regulated and sold like other commodities because it was so addicting and dangerous. However, as the last 55 years of alcohol control and the experiences of many other societies have shown, the prohibitionists were wrong. The experiences of drug policy in other nations, and the experiences of U.S. pharmaceutical and drugstore regulation, suggest that most if not all psychoactive substances *could* be similarly regulated, sold, and used in a generally lawful and orderly fashion. It would mark a significant advance if the current U.S. debate on drug policy could be moved beyond the question of *whether* such a system of legalized drug control is possible; it is. Instead, we think debate should focus on whether a nonmoralistic assessment of the advantages and disadvantages of such a system make it desirable, and what different regulatory options might look like.

A workable system of drug control would have to be a flexible one, geared to local conditions, as Edward Brecher recommended 20 years ago in his landmark study *Licit and Illicit Drugs* (1972). The logic of such a flexible system was also outlined 90 years ago by the Committee of Fifty. As with alcohol control, drug control could be implemented so as to reduce substantially if not eliminate the illegal drug business and most of the crime, violence, and corruption it produces. Drug control with a public health orientation would also seek to encourage milder and weaker drugs and to make them available in safer forms accompanied by comprehensive education about risks, proper use, and less dangerous modes of ingestion. In other words, a public-health-oriented drug control regime would seek to reverse the tendencies that appear inherent under criminalization, where production, distribution, and consumption are pushed into deviant subcultures in which purity is not controlled, dosage is imprecise, and extreme modes of ingestion are the norm.

If a drug control system were designed according to rigorous public health criteria, then the experience of alcohol regulation suggests that, in the long run, drug problems would probably not rise significantly above the levels now present under drug prohibition, and overall consumption might not rise either (see also Nadelmann 1989a). Similarly, if such a public health model of drug control were coupled with increased social services and employment for impoverished inner-city populations, then the abuse of drugs like heroin and cocaine might well be expected to decrease (Brecher 1972; Jonas 1990).

Having said this, it is incumbent upon us to point to a second lesson that may be inferred from the history of alcohol control: it will be no simple matter to design such a drug control system. It took a full-time, multiyear effort for the researchers and planners at the Institute of Public Administration to come up with a workable beginning blueprint for postprohibition alcohol control. Furthermore, this system has been constantly adjusted ever since. A post-drug-prohibition control system will require even more study, research, and careful planning, which in turn will require a Rockefeller-like willingness to invest the necessary resources. Special commissions and policy study groups drawing on a wide range of expertise will be necessary, for it is unlikely that effective alternatives in drug policy can be designed by an individual scholar, however wise or visionary, in his or her spare time.

Useful lessons aside, all this begs a rather big question: does the political will exist even to study seriously alternatives to the drug policies that have dominated our thinking throughout the twentieth century?

That Was Then, This Is Now: The Political Context of Drug Reform

There are many differences between constitutional alcohol prohibition and drug prohibition that make drug law reform problematic. In the 1920s only one substance was at issue. Now there are several whole classes of them. Alcohol prohibition was repealed after only 13 years. But federal drug prohibition began over 75 years ago when opiates and cocaine were criminalized, and has been supplemented regularly ever since. Marijuana was criminalized over 50 years ago, lysergic acid diethylamide (LSD) 20 years ago, and MDMA (better known as "Ecstasy") in 1984 (Brecher 1972; Goode 1989).

Alcohol had been in popular recreational use for several millennia before prohibition. By the early 1930s half of the adults in the United States drank, and the vast majority of adults in most big cities wished to drink occasionally; they continued to do so during the prohibition era. Local police were rarely enthusiastic supporters of prohibition, and they themselves drank.

Today, however, despite widespread experimentation, even the most popular illicit drug, marijuana, was used by only about 20 percent of all adults in the last year. This is a sizable minority, but alcohol prohibition affected the majority. Further, unlike the 1930s, the prohibitionist ethos has attained legitimacy among nearly all police and politicians, most of whom believe that illicit drugs are extremely dangerous and that no one should use them. There are no longer any "wet" legislators to criticize prohibitionist policies and introduce alternatives, only "drys" debating other "drys." To imagine a political context comparable to that of repeal, we would have to assume that most police and at least half of the elected officials in the United States were moderate marijuana users, and that a sizable minority had used LSD and cocaine.

In the "Roaring Twenties" a new, urban middle-class generation came to maturity. They were the first post-Victorian generation and they tended to oppose what they saw as the repressive, puritanical restrictions of temperance. Further, by 1930 the political power of the

Anglo-American middle class had been diluted by a large number of immigrants from southern and eastern Europe, who brought with them cultural traditions that regarded drinking as a normal part of life. To them, alcohol prohibition seemed a bizarre custom imposed by moralistic fanatics. By the early 1930s, alcohol did not seem as threatening to as many as it once had. Antidrinking sentiment was weaker than it had been for 100 years, and it was becoming even weaker. Together with the widely perceived failures of prohibition, these demographic and cultural shifts helped render antialcohol ideology bankrupt.

There are today no comparable demographic or cultural changes. Most Americans are now as fearful of drugs as middle-class Americans were about alcohol at the start of the century. Current immigrants do not come from drug-using cultures. The baby-boomers who popularized the recreational use of marijuana and other drugs in the 1960s are in middle age. They are watching their health, restricting their consumption of illicit and licit drugs, and (like their own parents were) worrying about the drug use of their children.

Over and above natural citizen concern about very real drug problems, antidrug sentiment has been cultivated by politicians' drug war speeches, mass media scare stories, and multi-million-dollar advertising campaigns to a degree that turn-of-the-century temperance crusaders would envy (Reinarman and Levine 1989). Indeed, the use of drinking as a scapegoat explanation for social problems, which was so prominent in nineteenth- and early twentieth-century temperance and prohibitionist rhetoric, is reproduced today in antidrug campaigns. Long-standing problems like urban poverty, crime, and school failures are nowadays frequently blamed on drugs like crack and heroin. In another parallel with the nineteenth century, abstinence ("just say no") and the utopian wish for truly effective prohibition are held up as the solutions to urban problems. Billy Sunday's panacea, quoted earlier, of solving America's economic and social problems through alcohol prohibition remains alive in the dream that effective drug prohibition and a rigorous war on drugs can now solve the problems of America's poverty-stricken, urban neighborhoods. The result is that the political conditions for drug policy reform today are more like 1900 — when the prohibition movement was growing — than like 1933 when prohibition was repealed.

Another difference, as we discussed earlier, was the crucial role of the Great Depression in turning the political and economic elite against prohibition. With food riots and protest marches making headlines, popular discontent clearly helped shape the political context in which decisions about repeal and alcohol policy were debated. Despite all our contemporary crises, we are not yet facing the equivalent of the Great Depression. Even an economic catastrophe would not necessarily soften attitudes about drug prohibition as it did attitudes about alcohol prohibition. The ratio of drug users to drug prohibitors in the population today is too small to expect any such sharp shift in public opinion, even if the economy continues to deteriorate.

During the 1920s, and especially the early 1930s, repeal advocates argued that ending prohibition would result in a windfall of revenues from taxes on alcohol sales and from money saved on enforcement. This generally did not come to pass, for the economic needs of a growing government in a deep depression were so great that the new revenue was quickly expended. Thus it cannot be automatically assumed that if drug prohibition were lifted, excise taxes on legal drugs and reduced enforcement costs would provide a fiscal boon for governments. With worsening federal and state deficits, much of this money also would be absorbed. Given the shamefully inadequate level of support now provided for drug treatment, however, it is still conceivable that revenues from taxation and licensing could finance the expansion of treatment, counseling, and education that any sound drug control system would require (see Schmoke [1990] and *Hofstra Law Review* [1990] for detailed proposals). In terms of the politics of reform, however, it remains unlikely that the potential fiscal advantages of repeal will by themselves move us toward significant change in U.S. drug law.

The political and intellectual energy that fueled the repeal of alcohol prohibition came from outside the Democratic and Republican parties, and the situation is little different today. In 1928, Al Smith campaigned against prohibition, but the Democratic party provided no leadership, organizational skills, or intellectual support for repeal. A few current political leaders have criticized the ill effects of drug prohibition, but almost all elected officials of both parties have appealed to the electorate by trying to prove only that they are more committed drug warriors than their opponents. Some politicians may join in opposing the war on drugs and working for decriminalization, but it remains unlikely that many candidates for national office will soon take leadership roles in a campaign for drug law reform.

Conclusion

It is thus abundantly clear that the current context for repeal of drug prohibition does not compare favorably with the context in which alcohol prohibition was repealed. Historical, demographic, cultural, economic, and political conditions do not seem especially conducive for any radical change in U.S. drug policy at present.

We should note, however, that there are some signs of change. Many dissenting intellectuals have called attention to the immense costs, numerous casualties, and unintended consequences of extreme prohibitionist regimes like the current war on drugs (e.g., Nadelmann 1989a; Trebach and Zeese 1990; Goldstein et al. 1990; Jonas 1990). These include conservative publisher and writer William F. Buckley, Jr., Nobel Prize-winning economist Milton Friedman, former Reagan administration secretary of state George Shultz, federal judge Robert Sweet, and, at the other end of the ideological spectrum, Harvard science professor Stephen Jay Gould, Ira Glasser, head of the American Civil Liberties Union, and Mayor Kurt Schmoke of Baltimore, the first major political leader to proclaim publicly his support for decriminalization. In addition, a growing number of state legislators, federal judges, and even some police chiefs have openly criticized drug prohibition and urged consideration of repeal (e.g., Galiber 1990; Schuler and McBride 1990). The views of these prominent individuals have been echoed in periodicals such as the *Economist*, the *Nation*, *Harper's*, the *New Republic*, the *National Review*, and the *Wall Street Journal*.

Opposition voices have also taken institutional form. The Drug Policy Foundation in Washington, D.C., for example, has since 1987 published reformist newsletters and books, produced a regular television show on which experts debate alternative drug policies, and held a series of international drug policy reform conferences. There is as well the ongoing research on decriminalization and other alternative drug control regimes of the Princeton Working Group on the Future of Drug Policy, an interdisciplinary group of experts from across the United States, which convenes quarterly to develop long-range options for a postprohibition future. An international conference on drug legalization also was held last year at Stanford's Hoover Institution, one of a dozen such conferences on campuses across the nation in the last few years.

Although all this does not yet constitute a grass-roots movement for fundamental change in our drug laws, nevertheless the list of credi-

ble critics of drug prohibition who advocate some form of drug regulation regime has grown surprisingly long and their arguments have
gained a certain momentum. By showing the full social costs and questionable efficacy of unquestioning support for a regime of prohibition, and by exploring possible alternatives, the critics may help shift
the political climate within which drug policies are given shape and
force.

A consensus has emerged among dissenters and drug warriors alike on
at least one point: supply-reduction strategies like prohibition have inherent limits, so the future lies in *demand reduction*. Even Drug Enforcement Agency officials now admit that interdiction will never be
capable of halting the flow of currently illicit drugs. One need not be a
free market economist like Milton Friedman to understand that
criminalization is the sine qua non of black market profits, and that
these will continue to lure people into the illicit drug trade. Thus, a variety of unlikely bedfellows has concluded that any future success in
combating drug problems must center on reducing demand.

The use and abuse of drugs cuts across the social boundaries of class,
race, gender, and region. However, incidence and prevalence studies
have shown time and again that the most serious and sustained drug
problems are those found among the inner-city poor. According to surveys by the National Institute on Drug Abuse, almost all forms of illicit
drug use among the broad middle and working classes had been stable
or declining before the latest drug war was launched in the spring of
1986. The hard-drug problems that persist, and that animate both public concern and public policy, are those of the impoverished — precisely
those individuals who have neither a stake in conventional life to keep
them out of trouble with drugs nor the resources to obtain the treatment and social services they need to break away (Waldorf, Reinarman,
and Murphy 1991). In short, it is among the growing ranks of the impoverished that we find both the strongest demand for and the most serious problems with illicit drugs.

When it comes to the issue of *how* to reduce demand, there is little
consensus. Advocates of drug prohibition regimes often tacitly assume
that underlying economic and social problems have little to do with
drug problems; they tend to see strong drugs and weak individuals as
the cause. Public health professionals know that "environment" is just
as important as "agent" and "host" and have often supported alternative policies that speak to such underlying causal mechanisms. Other ad-

vocates of alternative control strategies assume that decriminalization coupled with expanded education and treatment will be enough. We are not so sure. The prohibitionist strategies, which have imprisoned hundreds of thousands of mostly young black males, only exacerbate the hardships faced by them, their families, and communities, thus helping to ensure continued or perhaps expanded demand. Decriminalization could help create the conditions for a radical reduction in the crime and violence of the illicit drug trade as well as for the development of more effective public health policies. By itself, however, decriminalization does not offer an adequate response to hard drug abuse among the urban poor.

In September 1988, at the height of U.S. efforts to persuade Latin American countries to reduce their production of cocaine, a Bolivian journalist wrote in the Sunday *New York Times* that interdiction to reduce supply as a means of reducing drug use can never succeed. He too suggested that the United States must work on reducing demand, and concluded by calling for "a Marshall Plan for cities" that would reduce the poverty and despair that are the source, if not the direct cause, of our worst drug problems.

The relatively low prevalence of drug problems in other industrialized democracies also suggests that such domestic reconstruction will be a necessary foundation for any effective drug control regime. Most Western European societies have lower levels of illicit drug use, abuse, and problems than the United States, largely because they have less inequality, poverty, and homelessness. E. L. Engelsmann (1990), head of Substance Abuse in the Ministry of Health of the Netherlands, recently made the same point at the Woodrow Wilson Center in Washington, D.C.: "The Dutch prefer a policy of social control, adaptation, and integration to a policy of social exclusion through criminalization. . . . Instead of a war on drugs, we prefer to wage a war against underdevelopment, deprivation, and [low] socioeconomic status" (also see Henk 1989).

Most Western European nations have been more successful than the United States in combating poverty with family allowances, full social and health services, and a welfare system that meets the basic needs of their citizens. There, as well as here, the heaviest abusers of hard drugs are still from the lowest strata in society. However, Germany, France, Belgium, The Netherlands, Switzerland, Denmark, Sweden, Austria,

Finland, and Norway all have a markedly smaller proportion of their citizenry living in poverty than does the United States, and markedly fewer drug problems.

Even if the context for drug policy reform were to shift and some form of a decriminalized drug control regime put in place, the underlying problems of the urban poor would remain. Without significantly improving schools and housing, eliminating homelessness, and providing universal medical care, well-paying jobs, and expanded delivery of other social services, our most serious drug problems will persist. The recent spread of both the sale and use of crack, for example, occurred despite an overall decline in all other forms of illicit drug use (Reinarman and Levine 1989). In part this is because the conservative social policies of the Reagan and Bush administrations have produced a sharp decline in the already tenuous quality of life of the poor. Instead of a Marshall Plan for the cities, the United States has been working under what might be called a Dresden plan—reduced social and health programs, urban blight, and bulging prisons.

Someday, Americans may, as Edward Brecher predicted, look back on drug prohibition as most people today look back on alcohol prohibition—as a mistake. In the twentieth century, a dozen major scientific commissions in Britain, Canada, and the United States have recommended alternatives to drug prohibition. The United States is the only nation where these recommendations have been so consistently ignored (Trebach 1989; Trebach and Zeese 1990). For starters, these recommendations should be more widely discussed and better understood in the United States. The experiences of other nations and cities—notably The Netherlands and Liverpool—also provide living examples of drug policies that are more humane and, because they are linked to better social policies, more *effective*. The full range of such alternatives to current drug policy should be studied and debated—from futuristic visions to pragmatic reforms that could be implemented immediately (Nadelmann 1989a; *Hofstra Law Review* 1990; Trebach and Zeese 1990).

We have shown that the United States is not yet in the position with regard to drugs that it was with alcohol in the 1920s and 1930s. We have also suggested, however, that there are a number of important lessons about future drug policy that may be learned from the postrepeal alcohol control system. We think the growing ranks of the peace movement against the War on Drugs and the broader public health community would do well to mine this policy vein for new approaches that blend some form of decriminalized drug control with expanded health and social services.

References

Alcohol Beverage Control Administration. 1973. *Licensing and Enforcement* (revised and updated by B.W. Corrado). Washington: Joint Committee of the States to Study Alcoholic Beverages Laws.

Allen, F.L. 1931. *Only Yesterday: An Informal History of the 1920s.* New York: Harper.

Allsop, K. 1961. *The Bootleggers and Their Era.* London: Hutchinson.

Baron, S. 1962. *Brewed in America: A History of Beer and Ale in the United States.* Boston: Little Brown.

Beauchamp, D. 1981. *Beyond Alcoholism: Alcohol and Public Health Policy.* Philadelphia: Temple University Press.

Billings, J.S. 1905. *The Liquor Problem: A Summary of Investigations Conducted by the Committee of Fifty and the Origins of Alcohol Control.* Boston: Houghton Mifflin.

Blocker, J. 1989. *American Temperance Movements: Cycles of Reform.* New York: Twane.

Brecher, E.M. 1972. *Licit and Illicit Drugs.* Boston: Little Brown.

Bruun, K., G. Edwards, M. Lumio, et al. 1975. *Alcohol Control in Public Health Perspective.* Helsinki: Finnish Foundation for Alcohol Studies.

Burnham, J.C. 1968. New Perspectives on the Prohibition "Experiment" of the 1920s. *Journal of Social History* 2:51–67.

Cashman, S.D. 1981. *Prohibition, the Lie of the Land.* New York: Free Press.

Englesmann, E. 1990. The Pragmatic Strategies of the Dutch "Drug Czar." In *Drug Prohibition and the Conscience of Nations*, eds. A.S. Trebach and K. Zeese, 49–55. Washington: Drug Policy Foundation.

Everest, A.S. 1978. *Rum Across the Border.* Syracuse, N.Y.: Syracuse University Press.

Fosdick, R.B., and A.L. Scott. 1933. *Toward Liquor Control.* New York: Harper.

Galiber, J.L. 1990. A Bill to Repeal Criminal Drug Laws: Replacing Prohibition with Regulation. *Hofstra Law Review* 18:831–80.

Garrison, W.E. 1933. Fitting the Law to the Lawless. *Christian Century* 50:1505–6.

Goldstein, P., H.H. Brownstein, P.J. Ryan, and P.A. Bellucci. 1990. Most Drug-Related Murders Result from Crack Sales, Not Use. *The Drug Policy Letter* (April). Washington: Drug Policy Foundation.

Goode, E. 1989. *Drugs in American Society.* New York: McGraw-Hill.

Gordon, E. 1943. *The Wrecking of the 18th Amendment.* Francestown, N.H.: Alcohol Information Press.

Gulick, L. 1977. Letter to Richard S. Childs, copy to Laurence S. Rockefeller, in Rockefeller Archives, May 2.

Gusfield, J.R. 1986. *Symbolic Crusade: Status Politics and the American Temperance Movement,* 2nd ed. Urbana: University of Illinois Press.

———. 1968. Prohibition: The Impact of Political Utopianism. *Change and Continuity in Twentieth Century America,* eds. J. Braeman et al. Columbus: Ohio State University Press.

Harrison, L.V., and E. Laine. 1936. *After Repeal: A Study of Liquor Control Administration.* New York: Harper.

Henk, J.V. 1989. The Uneasy Decriminalization: A Perspective on Dutch Drug Policy. *Hofstra Law Review* 18:717–50.

Hofstra Law Review. 1990. *A Symposium on Drug Decriminalization* 18(3).

Jonas, S. 1990. Solving the Drug Problem: A Public Health Approach to the Reduction of the Use and Abuse of both Legal and Illegal Recreational Drugs. *Hofstra Law Review.* 18:751–93.

Kerr, J.A. 1985. *Organized for Prohibition: A New History of the Anti-Saloon League.* New Haven, Conn.: Yale University Press.

Kobler, J. 1973. *Ardent Spirits: The Rise and Fall of Prohibition.* New York: G. P. Putnam.

Kyvig, D.E. 1979. *Repealing National Prohibition.* Chicago: University of Chicago Press.

Leuchtenburg, W.E. 1958. *The Perils of Prosperity: 1914–1932.* Chicago: University of Chicago Press.

Levine, H.G. 1978. The Discovery of Addiction: Changing Conceptions of Habitual Drunkenness in America. *Journal of Studies on Alcohol* 39:143–74.

———. 1983. The Committee of Fifty and the Origins of Alcohol Control. *Journal of Drug Issues* 13:95–116.

———. 1984. The Alcohol Problem in America: From Temperance to Prohibition. *British Journal of Addiction* 79:109–19.

———. 1985. The Birth of American Alcohol Control: Prohibition, the Power Elite, and the Problem of Lawlessness. *Contemporary Drug Problems* 12:63–115.

Lyle, J.H. 1960. *The Dry and Lawless Years.* Englewood Cliffs, N.J.: Prentice-Hall.

Mäkelaä, K., R. Room, E. Single, et al. 1981. *Alcohol, Society, and the State. 1: A Comparative Study of Alcohol Control.* Toronto: Addiction Research Foundation.

Manchester, W. 1974. *The Glory and the Dream: A Narrative History of America: 1932-1972.* Boston: Little, Brown.

Mertz, C. 1970. *The Dry Decade.* Seattle: University of Washington Press.

Miron, J.A., and J. Zweibel. 1991. Alcohol Consumption During Prohibition. *American Economic Association Papers and Proceedings* 81:242-7.

Moore, M., and D.R. Gerstein. Eds. 1981. *Alcohol and Public Policy: Beyond the Shadow of Prohibition.* Washington: National Academy Press.

Morgan, J. 1991. Was Alcohol Prohibition Good for the Nation's Health? Working paper. School of Medicine, City University of New York.

Murphy, S., D. Waldorf, and C. Reinarman. 1991. Drifting into Dealing: Becoming a Cocaine Seller. *Qualitative Sociology* 13(4):321-43.

Muscatine, D., M. Amerine, and B. Thompson. 1984. *The University of California Book of California Wine.* Berkeley: University of California Press.

Nadelmann, E. 1989a. Drug Prohibition in the U.S.: Costs, Consequences, and Alternatives. *Science* 245:939-47.

———. 1989b. Response to Letters. *Science* 246:1102-3.

Odegard, P. 1928. *Pressure Politics: The Story of the Anti-Saloon League.* New York: Columbia University Press.

Piven, F.F., and R. Cloward. 1971. *Regulating the Poor: The Functions of Public Welfare.* New York: Pantheon.

———. 1977. *Poor People's Movements.* New York: Pantheon.

Reinarman, C., and H.G. Levine. 1989. Crack in Context: Politics and Media in the Making of a Drug Scare. *Contemporary Drug Problems* 16:535-77.

Room, R.G.W. 1988. The Dialectic of Drinking in Australian Life: From the Rum Corps to the Wine Column. *Australian Drug and Alcohol Review* 7:413-37.

Rorabaugh, W.J. 1979. *The Alcoholic Republic: An American Tradition.* New York: Oxford University Press.

Rumbarger, J.J. 1989. *Profits, Power, and Prohibition: Alcohol Reform and the Industrializing of America, 1800-1930.* Albany: State University of New York Press.

Schmoke, K.L. 1990. An Argument in Favor of Decriminalization. *Hofstra Law Review* 18:501-25.

Schuler, J.T., and A. McBride. 1990. Notes From the Front: A Dissident Law-Enforcement Perspective on Drug Prohibition. *Hofstra Law Review* 18(3):893–942.

Sheppard, Mrs. J.S. 1938. After Five Years, What Has Repeal Achieved? *New York Times Magazine* (December 4).

Shipman, G. 1940. State Administrative Machinery for Liquor Control. *Law and Contemporary Problems* 7:600–20.

Sinclair, A. 1964. *Era of Excess: A Social History of the Prohibition Movement.* New York: Harper.

Single, E., P. Morgan, and J. Delint. Eds. 1981. *Alcohol, Society, and the State. 2: The Social History of Control Policy in Seven Countries.* Toronto: Addiction Research Foundation.

Timberlake, J.H. 1963. *Prohibition and the Progressive Movement, 1900–1920.* Cambridge, Mass.: Harvard University Press.

Thornton, M. 1991. Alcohol Prohibition Was a Failure. Policy analysis report no. 157. Washington: Cato Institute.

Trebach, A.S. 1989. Ignoring the Great Commission Reports. *The Drug Policy Letter* (Sept.–Oct.):5.

Trebach, A.S., and K.B. Zeese. Eds. 1990. *Drug Prohibition and the Conscience of Nations.* Washington: Drug Policy Foundation.

Tyrell, I. 1979. *Sobering Up: From Temperance to Prohibition in Antebellum America, 1800–1860.* Westport, Conn.: Greenwood Press.

Waldorf, D., C. Reinarman, and S. Murphy. 1991. *Cocaine Changes: The Experience of Using and Quitting.* Philadelphia, Pa.: Temple University Press.

Warburton, C. 1932. *The Economic Results of Prohibition.* New York: Columbia University Press.

Wickersham Commission [National Commission on Law Observance and Enforcement]. 1931. *Report on Enforcement of the Prohibition Laws of the United States.* H.R. 722, 71st Congress, 1st Session. Washington.

Williams, T. 1989. *Cocaine Kids: The Inside Story of a Teenage Drug Ring.* Reading, Mass.: Addison-Wesley.

Zinberg, N.E. 1984. *Drug, Set, and Setting: The Basis for Controlled Intoxicant Use.* New Haven, Conn.: Yale University Press.

Acknowledgments: The authors would like to recognize the many helpful comments made on earlier drafts by Lynn Zimmer, John Morgan, Robin Room, and Ethan Nadelmann. Work on this paper was supported, in part, by grants from PSC-CUNY Faculty Research Program. The material on alcohol control draws upon Levine (1985).

To Build a Bridge:
The Use of Foreign Models by
Domestic Critics of U.S. Drug Policy

GERALD M. OPPENHEIMER

Brooklyn College, City University of New York

FROM THE BEGINNING OF THE U.S. POLICY DEBATE over narcotics control, drug use has been perceived as a significant domestic problem linked inextricably to international commerce. To gain influence over that traffic, the United States initiated the Shanghai Commission of 1909, the first multinational conference on the opium trade. Three years later, the U.S.-inspired Hague Opium Conference met to reconsider the possibility of controlling international commerce in drugs (Musto 1987). The conference, in its final convention, proposed that each signatory agree to strong domestic controls over the production and use of narcotics and cocaine (Musto 1987). Since those meetings, the United States has often used international conferences and agencies to attempt to police cross-national drug traffic, an important adjunct to its internal policy of narcotics prohibition and enforced drug abstinence.

Despite its involvement in international conferences and its recognition of the cross-national existence of drugs, drug traffic, and addiction, the U.S. government has shown almost no interest in how other countries treat their domestic drug problems. This is all the more remarkable when one considers that the United States has failed repeatedly to achieve the stated aims of its internal narcotics policy. Instead, it has been domestic critics of American policy who have historically looked to other nations for answers to the U.S. drug problem. Why have they done so?

For domestic critics of U.S. narcotics policy, foreign models have served three related purposes. First, critics searching for alternatives to current policy have rarely been able to find them within the United States. Because the federal government has played such a dominant role in crafting drug policy and because it has supported a powerful, often intolerant, prohibitionist ideology, there have been few relevant social experiments, even at the state or local level. (By contrast, a problem like health care financing has generated a plethora of private and public initiatives.) Although critics could perhaps extract some few examples from the American past, the narcotics clinics of 1919–1923 specifically, foreign models proved richer in detail and experience.

Secondly, by introducing foreign models into political discourse on drug policy, domestic critics forced comparisons. Americans tended to see U.S. narcotics policy as standard, if not universal. Placing that policy into an international context, critics insisted on its "relativity" and on the empirical need to weigh the efficacy and efficiency of the American system against that of other nations. When critics found that foreign models performed better on selected measures, these data were used to support arguments for changes in U.S. policy. In sum, American critics used comparative studies to weaken U.S. ethnocentrism and to open the policy process to alternative approaches.

Finally, foreign models served as vehicles for the expression of political, moral, or ideological positions. The analysis of and elaboration upon foreign systems provided a social text from which arguments against the U.S. system or for reform could be mustered. Foreign models were appropriated as field experiments that validated one's particular stance in American policy debates (Klein 1991). Those who used foreign experience in this manner were often guilty of "selective perception" (Klein 1991, 4), focusing on those dimensions of a multidimensional policy that best suited their needs.

In this essay, I will examine two periods in which American critics successfully introduced discussion of foreign models into the domestic discourse over drug policy. In the process, the foreign models came to represent important alternatives to contemporary U.S. approaches to drugs, narcotics in particular. During the first period, the post-World War II era, from the late 1940s to the early 1970s, critics suggested the possibility of adopting a British-style solution to the U.S. drug crisis. During the second period, beginning in the mid-1980s, domestic policy critics found in Holland a response appropriate to drug use during the human immunodeficiency virus (HIV) pandemic.

Background: U.S. Narcotics Policy

In the postwar period, American critics attracted to British policy governing addiction wrote against a background of profound pessimism about the U.S. approach, seeing in the former a striking success, in contrast to domestic failure. As Edwin Schur, a sociologist who would emerge as a forceful proponent of the British system observed:

> American efforts at controlling traffic in illicit drugs, as well as the various attempts to treat the addict, have not produced the desired results. Many large drug importers continue to evade enforcement officials; the number of addicts in this country is alarmingly high, and seems by many estimates to be increasing. . . . These discouraging facts might lead us to accept addiction as a permanent feature of our society. Yet another Western Country — Great Britain — reports a very small number of addicts and almost no market in illegal drugs. Why does this difference exist? (Schur 1962, 66)

The U.S. narcotics policy, the baleful effects of which Edwin Schur described, was quite different from that of Britain. Central to the American policy is the 1914 Harrison Act, passed in part to comply with U.S. obligations under the Hague Opium Convention. The act required that physicians, dentists, pharmacists, and other "legitimate" drug handlers register with the Treasury Department, pay an annual tax, and maintain appropriate records. The implicit aims of the Harrison Act were disputed at the time of its enactment, and the dispute has continued (Musto 1987; Trebach 1982). Ultimately, the most important arbiter of the law's meaning was the Treasury Department's Bureau of Internal Revenue, administrator of the act, which held that, under the new legislation, the federal government could restrict physicians and pharmacists from dispensing narcotics for other than, in the words of the law, "legitimate medical purposes" (Terry and Pellens 1974, 984).

What that phrase denoted led to further disputes. Some, including physicians, believed that addiction was a disease and that drug maintenance therapy to prevent withdrawal symptoms constituted appropriate treatment (Musto 1987). For a brief moment, between 1919 and 1920, the Treasury Department, fearing that addicts deprived of narcotics could threaten the public order, joined with maintenance forces to support public clinics where poor addicts might be prescribed narcotics (Lindesmith 1965; Musto 1987). Otherwise, the department supported

elite medical, legal, and social groups opposed to therapeutic maintenance, arguing that it fed the vice of degenerate individuals while enriching dishonest doctors (Bayer 1976; Musto 1987). These groups held
that appropriate medical therapy consisted of drug detoxification within
an institutional setting where an addict could be treated for withdrawal,
isolated from narcotics, and assisted in remaining abstinent.

Unfortunately, the cure of addiction remained elusive, and relapse
rates were high (Musto 1987). Belief in cure for addicted persons began
to diminish by 1920 and disappeared almost entirely by 1930 (Musto
1987). Presciently, the Public Health Service concluded in 1918 that all
approaches that weaned addicts away from drugs were equally good; the
answer to narcotics abstinence lay less in medicine, which could do very
little, than in law enforcement (Musto 1987). Soon after the passage of
the Harrison Act, therefore, "narcotic users were treated almost exclusively as criminals. . . . If the addict was to change, such change was to
occur from behind prison bars, the principal agency of rehabilitation being punishment" (Bayer 1976, 76).

Consequently, the number of narcotics-associated prosecutions rose
during the 1920s. The point prevalence of narcotic law violators in three
federal penitentiaries on April 1, 1928, was approximately 30 percent
(Musto 1987). The proportion in state and local prisons was also high,
particularly with adoption by the states of the Uniform Narcotics Law in
1932, after which state laws tended to be patterned on, and to follow
the trends in, federal narcotics legislation (King 1972).

This early trend toward a uniformly restrictive and punitive national
narcotics policy was accelerated after World War II. An upsurge in heroin use spurred the passage of new, draconian federal laws—the Boggs
Act of 1951 and the Narcotics Control Act of 1956—followed by similarly harsh state legislation. These laws significantly hiked minimum
sentences and almost completely eliminated parole for those found
guilty of selling or possessing narcotics (King 1972). In many states the
status of addiction became unlawful (Lindesmith 1965). Yet such coercive measures in support of a prohibitionist narcotics policy failed, as
had earlier legislation with the same aims (Bayer 1976). They neither
stemmed the rise in heroin use nor checked public fears, which at times
during the 1960s approached panic levels.

Compounding the inefficacy of draconian legislation was the burden
it placed on the criminal justice system, threatening to overwhelm
courts and prisons (Bayer 1976). When, subsequently, a movement

emerged in the 1950s against the failed policy of rigid, punitive law enforcement, it had two critical components: the medicalization of addiction and the creation of alternative mechanisms to free overburdened agencies of law enforcement (Bayer 1976).

Any reform had to face multiple barriers, not least an ideology that tended to be as rigid and inclusive as the policy itself. That ideology, which treated the addict as an insidious "other," had powerful racist and xenophobic roots, and contained a strong prohibitionism, which held that drugs led to immorality and, in the worst instances, to insanity (Musto 1987; Trebach 1982). Such elements — immorality, the dangerous outsider — came together in the association between addiction and crime. By the 1920s it was dogma, supported by federal authority, that addicts were thieves and thugs who took drugs (Anslinger and Tompkins 1953). During the 1950s and 1960s most urban crime was falsely attributed to addicts (Bayer 1976).

In brief, from 1914 through the early 1960s, narcotics, heroin in particular, were demonized, and drug users were caricatured to the point of dehumanization. Because their depredations were perceived as willful, however, addicts bore moral and legal responsibility for their acts. As a consequence, society was within its rights to prosecute addicts forcefully until they chose to give up addiction and drugs (a source of moral disorder and pathology). Legal repression was required to save "civilized society" (Bayer 1976, 3).

Nevertheless, during the 1960s, American policy broadened to include a therapeutic response to addiction. Supporters of that response were medical professionals, jurists, and politicians who believed a purely punitive approach had failed (or was undermining the judicial system), and urban residents who feared the spread of heroin into the middle class. Although many supporters of a therapeutic response continued to caricature addicts as dangerous deviants and heroin as a "demon's brew," they also argued that heroin addicts suffered from a chronic disease that was largely the outgrowth of psychosocial stressors beyond their conscious control (Bayer 1976). Most addicts, therefore, were not responsible for their condition, and consequently should not be subject to legal sanctions.

Yet many who supported a therapeutic response still held to a policy of abstinence, believing that, for the good of addicts and the social order, drug users required incarceration, albeit under medical auspices. Some public figures called for "maximum security hospitals," others for indefinite quarantine of chronic narcotics users (Bayer 1976; Gostin 1991). During the 1960s, state and national governments passed into law policies of civil commitment to, and compulsory treatment of addicts in, hospitals (Bayer 1976). When, in that decade, alternatives to prolonged hospitalization appeared—therapeutic communities and methadone maintenance clinics specifically—addicts were often "benevolently forced" into treatment by the diversion programs of the criminal justice system or by the threatened denial of public welfare payments (Bayer 1976). The existence of such compulsory, closed ward, or even outpatient care serves to underscore the continuation of a morally coercive policy in the United States—of penal incarceration by other means for many addicts. In the words of Alfred Lindesmith, the leading critic of U.S. drug policy, these programs of control offered liberals "a gesture toward a new and more humanitarian approach and a new vocabulary for old practices" (Lindesmith 1965).

Lindesmith was an important spokesperson for those who held the most appropriate therapeutic response to addiction was not mandatory abstinence, but rather narcotics maintenance. In his writings he reconstructed the history of the U.S. narcotics clinics of the 1920s, positing that they demonstrated the viability of maintenance therapy (Lindesmith 1965). His main arguments, however, rested upon his reading of the British experience; his ideal was to adopt a policy comparable to one Britain had evolved.

The British Approach

Prior to 1920, narcotics were freely available without prescription in Britain (Schur 1962). Parliament that year passed the Dangerous Drugs Act, which, like the Harrison Act, was in partial fulfillment of the Hague Convention of 1912. The act stringently restricted Britain's international commerce in narcotics and regulated their manufacture. Further, it limited to physicians the right to dispense narcotics, specifying, much like the Harrison Act, that a doctor could do so "only as necessary for the practice of his profession" (Judson 1975). To clarify the meaning of that phrase, the Home Office, administrator of the new law, asked the Ministry of Health for an expert opinion of what constituted appropriate medical practice in this area. In response, the ministry convened a special investigatory committee of physicians under Sir Humphrey Rolleston, president of the Royal College of Physicians.

The Rolleston Committee, in its final report of 1926, developed a number of definitions and observations that deeply influenced British narcotics policy and radically distinguished it from U.S. policy. The committee concluded that narcotics addiction was not a vice but a disease, one in which drugs "relieve a morbid and overpowering craving" (Trebach 1982, 93). Unfortunately, the committee found that medical practice infrequently produced permanent cures. Therefore, while urging physicians to treat their patients strenuously in order to free them of addiction, the committee recognized also that some patients required indefinite maintenance on narcotics: "those in whom a complete withdrawal of morphine or heroin produces serious symptoms which cannot be treated satisfactorily under the ordinary conditions of private practice [and] those who are capable of leading a fairly normal and useful life so long as they take a certain quantity, usually small, of their drug of addiction, but not otherwise" (Trebach 1982, 94). The precise clinical needs of each addict should, however, be determined only by his or her physician, possibly in consultation with a specialist.

The Rolleston Committee did not so much create a new system to treat narcotics addiction as "simply codify the best of the common law of medical practice" (Trebach 1982, 90). A conservative body, the committee maintained what it felt was realistic therapy for drug-addicted patients. Yet the committee could afford to act compassionately because the problem of narcotics addiction was rare in Great Britain (Judson 1975). When the first government figures were compiled in 1936, they showed 616 known addicts, a number that declined thereafter, reaching 290 in 1953 (Spear 1969); in the United States, when the Harrison Act was passed and interpreted, estimates of the number of addicts ranged from a million to 110,000 (Musto 1987).

In 1958, after the number of addicts began to rise in Britain, the government empanelled a new medical commission headed by Sir Russell Brain. The Brain Commission, in its second report, issued in 1965, noted a relatively sharp rise in narcotics use associated with a new type of addict. Whereas in the past addicts had largely been medical professionals or persons addicted in the course of medical treatment, there was now a growing number of younger, urban, "deviant" addicts who came to drugs through a black market. Because that market was supposedly linked to irresponsible prescribing practices of some private physicians, the committee recommended that only specialists working in drug-dependence clinics dispense heroin to treat addicts, recommendations that were instituted in 1968.

Gradually, these clinics implemented significant modifications in therapy—changes, however, that were controlled by the practitioners heading those clinics and varying by locality. In the early 1970s, for example, physicians decreasingly prescribed injectable narcotics and, in time, increasingly relied upon oral methadone. Nevertheless, during this period, as before, addicts were treated in Britain as sick people with access to narcotics maintenance.

In contrast to the United States, therefore, the British, from the Rolleston to the Brain Committees, neither demonized narcotics nor dehumanized the addict. Heroin and morphine remained therapeutic agents with powerful addictive properties, not sources of social and personal disorder. Regardless of how they came to be addicted, addicts were persons with a chronic disease who required medical care. Their responsibilities lay in seeking medical help and in attempting cure, that is, abstinence from drugs. Where that was impossible, they were expected to live as productively as possible, given their deficit.

Narcotics Maintenance Reform and the British Model

U.S. reformers in the 1950s and early 1960s who supported the British narcotics maintenance model might have found historical precedent in this country, particularly in the narcotics clinics of the early 1920s. Such clinics were of little practical interest to them, however; no contemporary country used a clinic system to treat its addicts (Lindesmith 1965). Instead, to define policy alternatives, the reformers looked abroad, using a comparative approach. Edwin Schur, for example, in the preface to *Narcotic Addiction in Britain and America*, wrote: "My purpose in this book is to indicate, more fully than has been done elsewhere, what the British approach to addiction is, how it works in practice, and whether it might be applicable to the drug problem in America" (Schur 1962).

A major reason U.S. domestic critics undertook comparative studies was to bolster their position at home. In studying policy in Britain and other countries, Lindesmith, Schur, Rufus King, and other reformers hoped to disabuse Americans of their ethnocentric assumptions about the possibility of narcotic maintenance, arguing that the contrary was true: narcotics maintenance therapy was normative in many Western nations—and it led, cost effectively, to policy success.

Because they produced the most articulate and comprehensive arguments for the maintenance approach, the work of Alfred Lindesmith and Edwin Schur will be the central focus of this discussion. In addition, I will examine perhaps the most important instance of an effort to give institutional life to the maintenance position, the Vera Institute's proposal for a narcotics maintenance clinic in New York City.

In his books, *Opiate Addiction* (1947) and *The Addict and the Law* (1965), as well as numerous articles in journals of political opinion, Alfred Lindesmith trenchantly analyzed what he saw as shortfalls in American addiction policy. He sought alternative ways of framing the addiction problem and its solution. Like Schur and other supporters of narcotics maintenance, he was attracted to Britain's medical approach to addiction.

Lindesmith argued that addiction was essentially a physiological and cognitive process over which the individual had no willful control. Regardless of the original reason for coming to narcotics, the moment of "conversion" was universal: once a person recognized that his or her withdrawal symptoms were due to the absence of drugs, that person was "hooked," with little chance for permanent cure.

For Lindesmith, U.S. policy following the Harrison Act had failed in its objectives because it contradicted the physiological fact of addiction. Instead, that policy had produced undesirable, even dangerous, outcomes. These included a primitive, inhumane treatment of addicts, the development of an addict subculture that reenforced addictive behavior, an illicit traffic in needlessly expensive drugs, and a subsequent surge in urban crime. From these followed an escalation in the size of police agencies, police corruption, and the erosion of civil liberties in the service of drug eradication. Ultimately, American policy produced chaos: having criminalized a disease and driven the diseased underground, the United States had lost the capacity to control either narcotics or the addict.

Instead of perpetuating this ruinous policy, Americans, Lindesmith argued, should craft an alternative approach that conformed to the physiological requirements of addicts. The United States could find that alternative in Europe, where virtually all countries treated addicts as patients under the care of physicians (Lindesmith 1947). Instead of cruelly caricaturing addicts as moral monsters or social deviants, these nations defined them as patients with a debilitating disease. The exemplar of this approach was Britain, the model for most other countries (Lindesmith 1965).

The British program, Lindesmith held, had multiple advantages over the American model. The drug-dependent individual, under the treatment of a private physician, was free of the need to commit crime and the personal disgrace associated with criminality. He or she was exploited neither by the pusher nor the police, and in fact could lead a decent private and public life. The distribution of narcotics through medical professionals controlled the amount of drugs used by addicts under treatment. It also reduced the need for an illicit traffic in narcotics; consequently, drugs were rarely available to unaddicted susceptibles in the population (Lindesmith 1965). This accounted for the low rate of addiction in Britain and other nations with comparable narcotics policies. Finally, the private nature of the patient–doctor relationship, by isolating the addict, did not foster the emergence of an addict subculture, which might draw both "susceptibles" and illicit drugs.

Lindesmith bolstered his position in favor of a British-style system through a series of cross-national comparisons. Using United Nations documents, for example, he showed that, in each of 13 Western countries that permitted narcotic maintenance, the estimated number of addicts was exceedingly low. More interesting, perhaps, was his use of a "migratory study," the experiences of 50 expatriated Canadian addicts in London. In Canada, whose narcotics policies were comparable to those of the United States, 80 percent of that group fit the description of criminal addicts: "Few of these patients had ever worked steadily, all had been dependent on an illicit supply of drugs and none had been normal, gainfully employed members of society" (Lindesmith 1965, 185). Once cared for by the British system, a majority of the 50 was rehabilitated. Nineteen, maintained on heroin, held regular employment, while 18 were reportedly drug free (a proportion left unexplained by Lindesmith, for whom permanent cure of addiction was rare).

Finally, Lindesmith relied on comparative analysis to argue that U.S. drug policy consistently produced destructive effects. The United States, according to Lindesmith, with hegemony over its allies during World War II and over Japan thereafter, insisted on exporting its antimaintenance policy into Asia. What followed with monotonous regularity was the transformation in each country of a limited opium-smoking problem within the Chinese community into a broad-based narcotics problem involving heroin, morphine, and other manufactured opiates. Along with these drugs, new practices appeared in Hong Kong, Formosa, Thailand, Indonesia, and Japan: the increased use of hypodermic needles, the growth of drug traffic and organized crime, and the spread of addiction to young, impoverished urban males who acquired narcotics through underworld contacts (Lindesmith 1965). Having introduced the American punitive-prohibition system of narcotics control, the Far East suffered an Americanized drug problem. The countries that followed the British example experienced significantly different results from countries that chose the U.S. policy. Thus Lindesmith could write: "There is a close relationship between the type of [narcotics] control program used and the characteristics and origins of the addicted population" (Lindesmith 1965, 188).

Edwin Schur, like Alfred Lindesmith, had little patience with causal theories of addiction (explanations based on psychodynamic or deviance theories), arguing that no definitive, unbiased research existed to support them. Like Lindesmith, he stressed the central role of addiction policy, portraying it as the crucial intervening variable between the raw physical fact of addiction and the characteristics or behavior of a country's addicts. Through its social policy, each nation crafted its addict population; to change the latter, one had to transform the former. A comparative study of two countries—the United States and Great Britain, similar in so many ways—supported the crucial role of addiction policy.

"The content of behavior," wrote Schur, "is very largely determined by social definitions" (Schur 1962, 207). The United States had labeled addiction a crime and prohibited the use of drugs. Britain, following a nonpunitive course, had medicalized the problem. As a consequence, British addicts behaved differently from their American counterparts. In Britain, no strong correlation existed between addiction and criminal acts. With access to relatively inexpensive drugs, addicted individuals need not rob, burgle, or push narcotics, nor construct a protective subculture, to survive. Britain might well have had many individuals predisposed to addiction. However, because drugs were freely available, resulting in a dearth of illicit substances and the absence of an addict subculture, those susceptibles were precluded from readily obtaining drugs and, perhaps more important, from the opportunity of learning how to use them. Certainly the effects of British policy served to contradict the American belief that narcotics maintenance could not curb addicts' criminality because addicts were never satisfied with a limited, legal dose.

British experience also contradicted American assumptions about who became an addict. In Britain, a large proportion of addicts were from the middle and upper classes, at least half were female, and most tended to be older rather than younger. In brief, British addicts were not from marginal or despised social groups or from the "dangerous classes." British policy, unlike American, did not produce addicts who were a threat to the social order. On a theoretical note, the cross-cultural differences between addicts undercut, according to Schur, much "scientific" discussion about universal psychological, or behavioral effects of opiates (Schur 1982, 115).

British policy worked; the U.S. policy did not and could not. Whenever a policy seeks to curtail the satisfaction of a strong demand, it encourages the development of a profit-oriented illicit market whose size and wealth creates a vested interest on the part of many for its survival. Alcohol and abortion prohibition were further examples of the failure of morally repressive laws. In Britain, where in contrast to its narcotics policy there were inadequate opportunities for legal abortions, illicit facilities existed that were similar to those in the United States. For Schur, policy was destiny.

Neither Schur nor Lindesmith expected the United States to adopt the British system in its entirety. According to Lindesmith:

> What is suggested is that successful foreign programs, including the British, should be intensively studied and intelligently adapted to American needs and to the special conditions existing in this country. (Lindesmith 1965, 271)

Nonetheless, in broad outline, the proposals recommended were strikingly similar to the British approach. First, their programs would be under strict medical control. Addicts should, if possible, be treated by private physicians (not clinics, which would encourage the congregation of drug users and the social reinforcement of the drug subculture). Physicians should be able to tailor dosage to the needs of the patient and be permitted to maintain them on narcotics. Relatively few would be cured of drug addiction. Despite this therapeutic pessimism, however, the proposed program would not rule out the possibility of abstinence.

Lindesmith wrote that doctors should act as if maintenance therapy were a temporary expedient, keeping dosages as low as possible, while attempting to persuade their patients to undergo hospital-based detoxification (Lindesmith 1965).

Nevertheless, addicts should enter such programs voluntarily. Neither Lindesmith nor Schur held that most addicts should be coerced into treatment. On the one hand, mandatory therapy did not work. On the other, both reformers fervently believed that most addicts would use treatment if available:

> Despite assertions to the contrary, there are very few addicts who do not desire to be freed of their habits. This is true also in countries where addiction is not a criminal matter. (Lindesmith 1965, 272)

Both reformers were interested in developing "humane and workable policies" (Schur 1962, 211). Humane policies and programs would make coercion and moral manipulation of most addicts superfluous. Their belief that coercion of addicts was generally unnecessary profoundly separated the reformers from most of their American contemporaries.

Lindesmith and Schur's advocacy of a narcotic maintenance approach based on the British example forced supporters of American prohibitionist policies to look abroad (or at least pretend to do so) in order to respond. Essentially four lines of argument were levied against the reformers. The first, used by the Federal Bureau of Narcotics (FBN) and its allies to discredit their opponents, was that the differences between the British and American systems were in fact spurious. The two systems were actually fairly similar — as they would be, given that both subscribed to the same international agreements (Harney 1960; Larimore and Brill 1960; Lindesmith 1965). The second rebutting argument was that the British system, far from being an efficacious alternative, had significant drug problems of its own. For example, Harry Anslinger, the U.S. Commissioner of Narcotics, wrote:

> In England, the British government reports annually only 350 addicts known to authorities. . . . England during the past year has had a surge of hashish addiction among young people. A year ago they were looking at the United States with an "it can't happen here" attitude. (Anslinger and Tompkins 1953, 279)

His successor, Harry Giordano, made similar claims a decade later, as did others in the FBN (Harney 1960; Lindesmith 1965). The reformers, for their part, flatly rejected both arguments (Lindesmith 1965; Schur 1962).

In the remaining, more sophisticated rebuttals, the critics asserted that reformers had improperly reversed the causal associations between public policy and addiction rate and between addiction and crime. Opponents of narcotics maintenance argued that because Britain had always had a small number of drug abusers, it could support a maintenance approach, not the other way around. Larimore and Brill, for example, in a report to the governor of New York State, claimed that Britain, with a deep cultural abhorrence of narcotics, had few individuals in its population susceptible to narcotics addiction (Larimore and Brill 1960). Others attributed the relatively low rate of addiction less to susceptibility than to a far more efficient police and judicial system (Harney 1960).

Finally, those who criticized the reformers held that criminals became addicts, not the reverse. According to Harry Anslinger, in the United States, "the person is generally a criminal or on the road to criminality before he becomes addicted" (Anslinger and Tompkins 1953, 170). The absence of an addict-criminal "class" in Britain was a peculiarity of that country's culture and irrelevant to American policy.

To the extent that the British approach was a historical product of unique cultural and social conditions, how could it be transplanted successfully to another nation with a different set of historical experiences? The issue of "portability," raised by opponents of narcotic maintenance, was significant — and difficult to answer (Schur 1960, 1962). Lindesmith responded by denying the singularity of the British approach, claiming that other Western nations — the Netherlands and Argentina, for example — also had British-style systems (Lindesmith 1965). Schur, more tentative, asserted that the cultural relativists had produced no real arguments to support their claims (Schur 1962). For both sides, the issue, while powerful, remained academic, as it could not be solved empirically (except later, by analogy, using the methadone maintenance clinic experience).

In addition to these four arguments, opponents of the reformers, the federal authorities in particular, were not above shrill personal attacks on their critics. Commissioner Anslinger, when describing Alfred Lindesmith and others in a letter to the *Journal of the American Medical Association*, wrote:

Several years ago a professor of sociology at an American university who is a self-appointed expert on drug addiction, after interviewing a

few drug addicts wrote an article in which he advocated that the
United States adopt the British system of handling drug addicts. The
professor followed the method used by dictators to "make it simple,
say it often"; true or false the public will believe it. "Adopt the British system" is now urged by all self-appointed narcotics experts who
conceal their ignorance of the problem by ostentation of seeming wisdom. (Anslinger 1954, 787)

Between the reformers like Lindesmith and Schur and their opponents, little substantive dialogue was possible. Each side represented alternative paradigms, with significantly different definitions of the
addict, the roots of addiction, and the role of moral and legal coercion
in rehabilitation. In appealing to foreign experience each side appropriated what it needed to support its claims, although the reformers appear
to have done so with considerably more commitment to veracity and
good faith.

In addition to individual reformers, prominent institutions also supported narcotics maintenance. During the early 1950s, both the Medical
Society of Richmond County, in New York City, and the New York
Academy of Medicine did so. More significantly, the Joint Committee
on Narcotic Study of the American Medical Association and the American Bar Association, two organizations that had previously supported
the prohibitionist policy, issued a report in 1959 recommending the creation of an experimental clinic to evaluate treatment protocols for narcotic addiction, drug maintenance among them. The report contained
an appendix written by Rufus King, which praised narcotics maintenance policies in several European countries. Perhaps the most dramatic
proposal, in that it came close to putting a limited heroin maintenance
program into effect in the early 1970s, was that of the Vera Institute of
Justice in New York City.

Up to that time, proposals for heroin maintenance had had little effect on policy. In fact, during the late 1960s, their thunder had been almost completely stolen by the successful proliferation of methadone
clinics. Methadone, a synthetic narcotic, had been intensively studied
between 1964 and 1966 by Vincent Dole and Marie Nyswander at Rockefeller University in New York. They found that patients, once "stabilized" on a sufficiently high dose of oral methadone, ceased to crave
heroin and substantially attenuated their criminal behavior (Epstein
1974). Methadone maintenance was soon supported by municipal and
state governments and, most crucially, by the federal authorities in

Washington. It was, in fact, in the context of methadone maintenance that the Vera Institute proposed a new role for heroin maintenance.

A private foundation formed in 1961, the Vera Institute had created a number of innovative programs designed to reduce pressures on the criminal justice system (Bayer 1976; Robinson 1978). When, in the late 1960s and early 1970s, New York City committed itself to a large-scale program of methadone maintenance, it asked the Vera Institute to tailor a version for Bedford-Stuyvesant, a ghetto neighborhood with a high rate of addiction and associated crime (Robinson 1978). In 1971, even before the city's methadone program had expanded to the point of treatment on demand, the Vera Institute, with municipal support, embarked on a more radical venture: heroin maintenance to "lure" into treatment those hard-core addicts who had failed to stay in the program ("program failures") or who had rejected treatment in any form (Bayer 1976; Robinson 1978). In planning, the Vera Institute was influenced by the British approach to addiction, particularly the post-Brain Commission "clinic system," which the Institute "credit[ed] . . . with stabilizing the number of addicts at a level below that of 1968" (Judson 1975).

The final treatment model, as it emerged in a cautious proposal in May 1972, called for a research project consisting of 130 male methadone-maintenance "treatment failures"; they were to be maintained on heroin, dispensed intravenously in the clinic, for up to one year (the "lure period"). Over that time, bolstered by a range of rehabilitative services, addicts would establish a strong therapeutic bond with the clinic staff that would empower them to transfer from heroin maintenance to more orthodox forms of addiction treatment. Outcomes in addicts maintained on heroin would be compared with those of a control group composed of similar patients maintained from the beginning on oral methadone.

The Vera Institute's proposal found support among some high-ranking law enforcement officials in New York and many jurists, most of whom were concerned with lowering crime rates and reducing pressures on the overburdened criminal justice system (Bayer 1976). Among treatment professionals, the Vera proposal generated considerable debate; most professionals associated with therapeutic communities and the leadership of the methadone maintenance programs strongly opposed the heroin maintenance experiment (Bayer 1976). The black community, with some exceptions, was hostile to the project, leveling charges against its proponents that ranged from genocide against, to indifference toward, black people. An example of the latter was the testimony of Harlem congressman Charles Rangel:

> Heroin maintenance is the cry of some Americans who would like to sweep the addict under the rug. It is the call of those who are afraid to deal with the causes of addiction . . . that lead young men and women to narcotics. It is the instant solution of those who think that with free heroin will come — as if from heaven — an end to crime and violence. (Bayer 1976, 262)

Most damaging to the project was federal opposition that included an ad hoc Congressional alliance of conservative white and liberal black representatives from New York State, the director of the Bureau of Narcotics and Dangerous Drugs, and, ultimately, President Nixon, who attacked heroin maintenance in no uncertain terms (Bayer 1976).

The defeat of the Vera Institute's proposal raised a number of issues. First, despite the precedent of narcotic (methadone) maintenance in the United States — a new modality supported by the Nixon administration and by many members of the black community — heroin maintenance could not be freed from its earlier demonization, a striking example of the institutional and ideological rigidities of U.S. narcotics policy. In fact, methadone maintenance had been marketed less as an exception to America's prohibition policy than, paradoxically, as an "antinarcotic agent," which could effectively "eliminate heroin addiction and criminal behavior" (Epstein 1974, 6). Through this linguistic legerdemain, methadone maintenance prudishly retained the old taboos, thereby failing to extend the parameters of legitimacy sufficiently to allow for more radical policy changes.

Secondly, the rejection of heroin maintenance, even as a treatment lure, marked the end of therapeutic liberalism in the United States. By 1973, the number of treatment slots in most major U.S. cities exceeded demand; yet less than half the addicts in those cities had entered drug programs. (The estimated proportion ranged from 45 percent in New York City to 7 percent in Los Angeles [Bayer 1976].) The assumption of liberal reformers like Lindesmith that most addicts would voluntarily opt for treatment, if offered, proved incorrect (Lindesmith 1965). As a consequence, many who initially supported methadone maintenance and other modalities as a means of "capturing" addicts, and thereby reducing crime, shifted back to more coercive enforcement, by calling again for compulsory quarantine and treatment of *all* addicts, or by supporting some form of old-fashioned "get tough" incarceration, stripped of any pretense to treatment (Bayer 1976).

On the federal level, support for demand reduction, that is, treatment and primary prevention, relative to law enforcement, as measured in share of total drug budget, declined after the mid-1970s (Falco 1989). Whereas under the Nixon administration, up to two thirds of the drug budget had gone to demand reduction, that proportion dropped to 43 percent under Jimmy Carter (Falco 1989; Trebach 1982). The Reagan administration initiated the most radical shift, allocating approximately 20 percent to prevention and treatment and 80 percent to law enforcement between 1982 and 1988 (Falco 1989; Moore 1991). Under President Reagan, drug policy was defined almost entirely as a law enforcement problem, much as it had been prior to the early 1960s (Falco 1989).

Drug Policy during the HIV Epidemic

The HIV epidemic produced a notable change in the debate over narcotics policy. In the past, one could dispute the extent to which drug addiction was a disease or simply a willful criminal act. Now the use of drugs, when taken intravenously, was clearly associated with a fatal infectious disorder, a "real" disease, one that threatened to spread into the "general" or respectable population.

In the early 1960s, the fear that heroin might further expand into the middle class mobilized the population and politicians to support a radical therapeutic response, methadone maintenance (Bayer 1976). Ten years later, the failure of narcotics maintenance to attract most of the urban addict population served to undercut the support of a public interested in a mechanism to "capture" and neutralize these antisocial "others." With punitive legislation or treatment unsuccessful in absorbing the second largest risk group for AIDS, what alternatives were possible? How could one reach a group that remained, as Lindesmith had described it 20 years earlier, forced to live underground and beyond the control of medical or police authorities?

As before, policy alternatives were a function of one's conception of the drug user (and, by extension, of addiction and narcotics). One of the early reports on the epidemic, published under the auspices of the Institute of Medicine and the National Academy of Sciences, cited the many public health officials who believed that intravenous drug users were impervious to public health interventions because "the target population simply will not listen" (Institute of Medicine 1986a, 94). Addicts, by implication, were ignorant, hedonistic, and heedless of consequences, a view still expressed by Mirko Grmek, historian of the acquired immune deficiency syndrome (AIDS) epidemic, in 1990:

> In contrast to homosexuals, who carefully heeded new data, the addicts were refractory to educational campaigns. . . . Too often the act of taking drugs is no more than acting out their desire to destroy themselves. . . . The uncaring victim becomes a peddler of death. (Grmek 1990, 168)

Researchers in the early 1980s demonstrated more positive possibilities. They found that by 1984 most addicts in New York City had heard of AIDS and its transmission through needle sharing; over half had changed their high-risk behaviors (Des Jarlais, Friedman, and Stoneburner 1988). The researchers therefore suggested that drug users might be open to public health interventions. The question remained, Which interventions were appropriate?

Because of the pandemic nature of AIDS, many U.S. public health and policy researchers, providers, and ethnographers engaged in working with intravenous drug users (IVDUs) began to exchange information with their European colleagues at meetings like the annual AIDS conferences and the 1985 International Conference on AIDS and Drug Injectors in Newark, New Jersey (S.R. Friedman of Narcotic and Drug Research, Inc., 1991, personal communication on July 15). Specifically, these workers began to learn of Holland's innovative programs for IVDUs. As a consequence, American researchers and policy analysts began to visit the Netherlands with the hope of finding appropriate strategies that might be applied to the United States.

Little of the Netherlands' narcotics policy originated with the HIV epidemic, but preceded it by a number of years. That policy developed slowly over the decade following the first significant rise in heroin addiction in the country in 1972 (van de Wijngaart 1988). The Dutch have adopted what they call a pragmatic and tolerant approach to drug addiction (Engelsman 1989). Their aim is to reintegrate the stigmatized addict into Dutch society by "normalizing" the addict and his or her problems, primarily by using a public health model that provides treat-

ment for addiction, while also offering services to attenuate the consequences of continued drug use.

In a public health model, legal rules play a diminished role. Prosecution of drug users is decidedly less stringent and more pragmatic in Holland than in most Western countries. Since 1976, the Dutch have
distinguished between "drugs presenting unacceptable risks" (van de
Wijngaart 1990, 668) like heroin and cocaine, and hashish or marijuana
(which have been decriminalized de facto). Although users of the
harder drugs may be prosecuted, the public prosecutor has considerable
license in implementing the law. According to a statement by the
Dutch Ministry of Welfare:

> One of the basic premises of Dutch Criminal procedure is the expedi-
> ency principle laid down in the Code of Criminal Procedure, whereby
> the Public Prosecutions department is empowered to refrain from
> bringing criminal procedures if there are weighty public interests to
> be considered. . . . The law thus steps aside, as it were, in cases
> where prosecution would have no beneficial effect in reducing the
> risks involved. (van de Wijngaart 1990, 668)

Central to the Dutch strategy is the concept of "harm reduction." For
the individual addict who cannot or will not give up the addict lifestyle,
harm reduction means learning to take responsibility for one's behavior;
for society, the concept denotes providing assistance in various forms to
improve the addicts' physical and social welfare (Buning 1986; Engelsman 1989; van de Wijngaart 1990). That assistance should encompass a
spectrum of easily accessible and "user friendly" services.

Dutch harm reduction policy includes outreach work in streets and
hospitals, medical assistance to addicts in jails, and low-threshold facilities that dispense methadone and health care while keeping "hassles" to
a minimum (e.g., no mandatory urine checks) (Buning et al. 1986;
Buning, van Brussel, and van Santen 1988). Perhaps the best known of
the low-threshold projects are the methadone buses initiated by the
Amsterdam Municipal Health Service in 1979. These mobile clinics, following a prescribed route, provide a daily dose of methadone to a client
pool of narcotic addicts. (These clients have already undergone medical
and social evaluation and agree to be listed in a central registry and to
visit a physician quarterly.)

In 1981, the Municipal Health Service organized higher-threshold
methadone clinics for addicts willing to end their use of illegal drugs,

submit to urine checks, and work with counselors (Buning, van Brussel, and van Santen 1988). For those committed to chemical abstinence, drug-free programs were also available. In the various programs, participants receive medical attention and a range of rehabilitative and social services intended to integrate addicts into society. By 1987, an estimated 70 percent of Amsterdam's 7,000 addicts had some contact with those programs (Buning, van Brussel, and van Santen 1988).

One of the most recent additions to Amsterdam's drug policy was the needle and syringe exchange program. Intrinsic to its development were the *Junkiebonden* (junky unions), which exist in Amsterdam, Rotterdam, and other major cities (Friedman, de Jong, and Des Jarlais 1990). Addicts created these unions in the early 1980s to promote their interests, including more services from the government and from health facilities (Friedman and Casriel 1988). The *Junkiebonden* demanded needle exchanges because they feared for addicts' health.

When an inner-city pharmacist refused to sell injection equipment in 1984, the Amsterdam junky union convinced a reluctant Municipal Health Service to underwrite a needle exchange to forestall a possible hepatitis B outbreak (Buning, van Brussel, and van Santen 1988). The next year, as public officials became alarmed over AIDS, Amsterdam expanded the exchange to enable a program that had traded 25,000 needles and syringes during the last half of 1984 to exchange approximately 820,000 in 1989 (Buning 1990; Buning, van Brussel, and van Santen 1988). By 1990, needle exchanges existed in 40 Dutch municipalities (Buning 1990).

A preliminary study of the Amsterdam needle exchange found that participants reported a lower rate of high-risk activities, like needle sharing or drug use, than nonparticipants (Buning, van Brussel, and van Santen 1988). Another investigation, which prospectively followed a group of exchange users for more than two years, observed a decline in needle sharing over that period (van den Hoek, van Haastrecht, and Coutinho 1989). During the years of the needle exchange, the number of narcotic addicts and of drug injectors has stabilized in Amsterdam, suggesting that the exchange has not been associated with an increase in the number of IVDUs in that city (Buning et al. 1986; Buning, van Brussel, and van Santen 1988).

By 1985, when the HIV epidemic became of major concern to Dutch authorities, they had in place a network of services to offer addicts and a philosophy that emphasized accessibility. Although new policies had to be added, condom distribution for example, the Dutch, unlike other governments, did not suddenly have "to build bridges to addicts" (Engelsman 1989, 11). Having defined addiction as a public health problem, the Netherlands easily incorporated their drug policy into the larger public health effort against HIV infection.

Dutch narcotics policy was a powerful lesson to American workers interested in reaching as many addicts as possible with HIV-related interventions, particularly the majority of IVDUs with no interest in drug treatment programs. Following harm reduction principles, these workers moved to introduce various preventive measures designed to reduce the probability of HIV transmission through shared, contaminated needles and syringes and through high-risk sex. Influenced by the Dutch example, they attempted, in particular, to introduce the concept of needle exchange into the United States.

Signaling that policy was a new report under the auspices of the Institute of Medicine and the National Academy of Science, written by the Committee on a National Strategy for AIDS (Institute of Medicine 1986b). The committee, while recommending expansion of the current methadone and drug-free treatment programs, added:

> Clearly it will not be possible to persuade all IV drug users to abandon drugs or to switch to safer, noninjectable drugs. Many may wish to reduce their chances of exposure to HIV but will neither enter treatment nor refrain from all drug injection. (Institute of Medicine 1986b, 109–10)

Although the committee recognized that increasing access to licit sterile needles would be controversial, it pointed out that Amsterdam had already begun to distribute sterile injection equipment, and it called for similar policy experiments in the United States.

In New Jersey, at approximately the same time, the deputy commissioner of health, influenced by Dutch policy, proposed an experimental needle exchange program (Bayer 1989; Sullivan 1986). The governor blocked the experiment, despite his state's status as the first in which over half of AIDS cases were IVDUs. Elsewhere in the nation, elected officials, as well as the National Institute on Drug Abuse, rejected needle exchange as a threat to drug control programs (Bayer 1989).

In the absence of a public initiative, local activists began to press for needle exchange. In some instances, this meant ignoring the law. Eleven states (New York, California, New Jersey, Connecticut, Pennsylvania,

Delaware, Rhode Island, Massachusetts, New Hampshire, Maine, and Illinois) forbid the sale of needles and syringes without prescription. In the remaining 39, possession of needles is illegal when found with illicit drugs (Lambert 1991). Despite these restrictions, almost all U.S. needle exchanges were started or catalyzed by local activists who secured governmental approval at some point before or after initiating the exchange, or who continue to operate illegally (Joseph and Des Jarlais 1989).

As early as 1985, AIDS researchers who had studied IVDUs locally and visited the Netherlands asked the health commissioner of New York City to develop a needle exchange in that municipality. (New York, the epicenter of the HIV epidemic in the United States, has approximately 200,000 IVDUs, over half of whom are reportedly seropositive.) A small experimental program started only in November 1988, after protracted negotiations between the city and state departments of health, negotiations that were catalyzed earlier that year by threats from a private group, ADAPT (Association for Drug Abuse Prevention and Treatment), to distribute needles as an act of civil disobedience (Gillman 1989). In 1987, Outside In, a private organization offering medical services to street kids in Portland, Oregon, began organizing a needle exchange, influenced by discussions with Dutch officials and by American researchers who had visited Holland (S.R. Friedman 1991, personal communication; Oliver 1990). Because of difficulty obtaining insurance, the Outside In program began only in November 1989, with the state health department providing consultation.

The first functioning needle exchange program in the United States opened in August 1988 in Tacoma, Washington. (By that date, such programs existed not only in Holland, but also in other countries, including Britain, Australia, and Sweden.) Dave Purchase, an experienced drug counselor who had read of the Dutch experience, began the exchange without government approval, using private funds. By January 1989, however, the Tacoma–Pierce County Board of Health adopted the program and began supporting it (Davidson 1990).

Other legal needle exchange programs in the United States exist in a number of cities, among them Seattle, Washington; Boulder, Colorado; New Haven, Connecticut; and the state of Hawaii. Exchanges operate illicitly in a number of places, including San Francisco and Boston; in New York City, the exchanges were illicit from February 1990, when a new mayor canceled the legal pilot program, until mid-1992, when he accepted a new needle exchange plan, but one that did not rely upon municipal funds. Activists operating those programs have been arrested, but charges against defendants in those cases have been dropped or they have been acquitted by the courts (Health/PAC 1990).

Although each of these programs, developed under local initiative, have unique features, all share two basic purposes. The first is to exchange new, sterile hypodermic syringes for used injection equipment, almost invariably on a one-for-one basis. Secondly, the exchange functions as a "bridge" between street addicts and health workers, allowing the latter to offer risk reduction counseling, services like condom distribution, and referrals to other facilities, like drug treatment programs (Joseph and Des Jarlais 1989). Workers claim to build that bridge to IVDUs through frequent encounters, the sharing of a common language, and the slow establishment of mutual trust (Health/PAC 1990).

This low-threshold approach has been attacked severely as condoning drug use, or worse, leading to an increase in IVDUs (Davidson 1990; Lambert 1988). Critics question the scientific validity of studies in the United States and abroad that provide justification for the exchanges (Joseph and Des Jarlais 1989; Marriott 1988). Many African-American and Latino leaders in New York City have accused the authorities of cynically distributing needles to addicts who would prefer treatment if that option existed (Lambert 1988). In language reminiscent of the debate over heroin maintenance in 1972, some African-American officials have called the exchanges "genocidal" or a symbol of white indifference to minority lives (Lambert 1988); implicit in those charges is black distrust of public health "experiments," particularly since the 1972 revelations concerning the infamous Tuskegee syphilis study (Thomas and Quinn 1991).

However, supporters of needle exchange argue that the programs should not be used as substitutes for treatment but, as in Europe, a link to addicts who, rejecting treatment, remain isolated and underground. Moreover, the needle exchanges are not genocidal, but rather designed to reduce mortality in all affected populations through the use of harm reduction measures. Finally, although ethical and practical limitations prevent definitive evaluation of the syringe exchange programs, the results to date across many study sites prove remarkably consistent. No data presently available demonstrate that exchanges are associated with increased drug injection; instead, investigations have shown either no change or lower rates of injection over the study period (Joseph and

Des Jarlais 1989). In addition, preliminary data from Tacoma, New Haven, San Francisco, and other North American cities appear to show that participants, like those studied in Europe and Australia, have reduced AIDS risk behavior, with a concomitant decline in HIV infection (Altman 1989; Navarro 1991a; Watters, Cheng, and Prevention Point Research Group 1991; Hagan et al. 1991). Naturally, evaluators must continue monitoring all needle exchange programs before definitive conclusions can be drawn.

Although opposition led to temporary termination of the needle exchange in New York City, other programs continued, uncompromised by New York's decision. Contrary to the experience of the last half-century, localities are able to initiate and, to a degree, control drug policy options. In fact, for the first time since the narcotic maintenance clinics of the 1920s, states have become social laboratories in the area of drug policy. They will be able to accumulate a body of epidemiological data that can be used to test American experience against that of Europe, Canada, and Australia. What is perhaps more important is that localities and states will be able to use these specifically American data and experiences to learn from each other, and to influence the further development of U.S. drug policies and programs. In fact, such a learning process has already begun; deeply influenced by the success of the needle exchange in New Haven, the same New York City mayor who terminated the small pilot program in 1990 recommended in November 1991 that the city assist community groups to design and run needle exchanges (Navarro 1991b).

States and localities have introduced other initiatives that, based on the public health/harm reduction models, are designed to reduce HIV transmission. For example, because needle sharing remains fairly common among addicts, most of whom cannot afford a supply of sterile "works," and needle exchanges are rather rare, a number of outreach programs have taught addicts to disinfect their injecting equipment with household bleach before use. One of the earliest of these outreach programs was ADAPT, formed in 1985 in New York City by ex-users and health professionals. ADAPT negotiates with shooting-gallery owners to make bleach and sterile needles available and conducts AIDS-prevention education among drug users in the streets and among ex-addicts in treatment programs (Friedman, de Jong, and Des Jarlais 1990). In San Francisco, beginning in the mid-1980s, a five-agency consortium trained community health outreach workers to teach addicts to clean their hypodermics with household bleach (Newmeyer et al. 1989). In Chicago, a program recruits drug users to teach harm reduction (bleach and condoms) to their peers (Friedman, Des Jarlais, and Goldsmith 1989). Similar "bleach and teach" programs exist in other municipalities.

An interesting and remarkable aspect of many of these programs is that they have appropriated the drug subculture — abhorred by an earlier generation of reformers — to reach out to and locate the target populations. To what extent will such appropriations — incorporation of the shooting gallery, the hypodermic, and the addict into the public health model — eventually lead to social tolerance, if not acceptance, of them as unavoidable social phenomena?

A more immediate question is the extent to which the HIV epidemic can galvanize addicts to organize. Some involved in the public health/harm reduction effort have been inspired by the examples of the *Junkiebonden* and the U.S. gay community to promote drug users' organizations (Friedman and Casriel 1988). With the probability of collective self-organization among current users rather low, these reformers have suggested that sympathetic outsiders work to empower addicts, helping them develop an internal leadership and a set of goals (Friedman and Casriel 1988). Consequently, sympathetic ex- or nonaddicts have used needle exchanges and other interventions to promote individual and group empowerment among IVDUs and their families (Friedman et al. 1991; Health/PAC 1990). Unfortunately, despite the HIV crisis and several attempts by outsiders to organize IVDUs, the early results were at best equivocal (Friedman et al. 1991). More recent experiences in Baltimore, St. Paul, and New York City, however, appear to promise greater success (S.R. Friedman 1991, personal communication). Given the multiple barriers addicts must contend with — illegal status, the need to support their habits, illnesses, and poverty — it still remains to be seen whether American addicts can develop a movement, even during a pandemic.

Over the last five years, those who advocate the public health model have appropriately focused almost entirely on the vehicles (needles and syringes) and behaviors that are implicated in transmission of HIV. These interventions have successfully reached street addicts outside the prison and drug-treatment systems. Interestingly, preliminary results from Hawaii, Tacoma, New Haven, and elsewhere have found that once needle exchanges are instituted, drug treatment referrals begin to rise, sometimes significantly (Davidson 1990; Lichty 1990; Navarro 1991a).

Unfortunately, treatment programs are often too full to accommodate new patients, particularly in larger municipalities (Navarro 1991a). In New York City, according to city and state sources, "there has been no expansion of drug treatment facilities . . . within the past 10 years, and slight expansion of treatment slots in light of the crisis" (Joseph and Des Jarlais 1989, 5). Yet current programs in the city accommodate 38,000 patients, approximately half the number who would enter treatment if it were available (Joseph and Des Jarlais 1989). The next addition to the public health model should therefore be increased availability of drug treatment facilities. Ideally, this would mean not only more treatment slots, but also low threshold programs that would attract a larger proportion of street addicts, and experimental ventures that could reach out to subgroups like addicted women and to persons on crack.

Conclusion

For at least half a century, critics of American drug policy have had occasion to turn to foreign models for answers to the questions they have raised. Three of their major purposes for looking abroad were adumbrated earlier: (1) to discover alternatives to current programs in the United States; (2) to undertake comparative, empirical studies that might weaken American ethnocentrism and open the policy process to alternative approaches; or (3) to appropriate foreign experience in order to bolster political or ideological positions at home.

To explain the attraction of foreign models to the postwar critics of U.S. policy, the first two reasons are probably the least important. The United States had had its own experience of maintenance, including narcotic clinics; the search for new approaches was not a prime motivation for looking abroad. A stronger reason to do so was an attempt to make empirical, cross-national comparisons (for example, of the number of addicts) and to undercut ethnocentric assumptions about addict behavior or characteristics; but these comparative studies were often subordinate to, or part of, political and moral arguments. Despite attempts at scholarly research and careful documentation, promaintenance reformers, engaged in a struggle with an ascendant adversary with radically different beliefs, tended to use the British model to validate their posture, which was that change as they defined it was both possible and preferable.

Conversely, faced with a pandemic that is transmitted, in part, by intravenous drug use, contemporary critics are most strongly attracted to foreign experience for the first two reasons. Their aim is to build bridges to street addicts in order to encourage behavioral change, the only means available to stanch the spread of HIV. Knowing from past experience that neither punitive enforcement nor treatment facilities will reach more than a minority of users, they learned of and adopted alternative approaches already in place in the Netherlands.

Significantly, these alternative approaches have as their dependent variable, not drug use, now understood as a vital independent variable, but the rate of HIV, which theoretically affects the entire population. This change in variables ironically allows the critics to press for dramatic changes in drug policy (using techniques of civil disobedience where necessary), which the authorities accept or connive with for the sake of the public's health.

In the near future, critics and others may look abroad for a second reason. As part of the public health campaign against HIV, epidemiology has played a crucial role in measuring and evaluating AIDS-related phenomena, including intervention programs in the United States and elsewhere (Oppenheimer 1988). For example, relatively objective data from abroad have proved useful to advocates of needle exchange at home. The U.S. experience, currently being measured, will be part of the international pool of data. Soon, perhaps for the first time in the history of U.S. drug policy, objective cross-national empirical comparisons of specific drug-related programs will prove possible. As a consequence, we may discern to what degree the U.S. drug problem requires unique policy responses, and under what circumstances selected programs, like needle exchange, can be transferred from other countries and cultures.

Can the consensus for change in U.S. drug policy, where it exists, expand beyond the parameters fixed by the current public health emergency? It is possible that local initiatives, once institutionalized, could develop a logic and constituency of their own. (It is also conceivable that such a constituency might include active drug users.) Moreover, should needle exchanges prove successful in this country, they could generate interest in other drug-related interventions developed elsewhere. AIDS has created a formal system of information exchange among nations—

the International Working Group on Drug Users and AIDS, for example—which could provide communities in this country with relevant intelligence and expertise. However, the current consensus for change, supported by local officials and health workers (with the federal government maintaining an ominous silence), is fragile. Should attempts be made to push beyond the perceived needs of the epidemic, the result may be divisive moral and ideological debates, similar to the heroin maintenance experience of the postwar years. Predictably, both sides would turn to the accumulated pool of international data; they would do so, however, selectively, to validate and to bolster their particular political texts.

References

Altman, L.K. 1989. Needle Exchange Programs Hint a Cut in AIDS Virus Transmission. *New York Times* (June 7): B5.

Anslinger, H.J. 1954. Letter. *Journal of the American Medical Association* 156(8):787–8.

Anslinger, H.J., and W.F. Tompkins. 1953. *The Traffic in Narcotics.* New York: Funk and Wagnalls.

Bayer, R. 1976. Drug Addiction and Liberal Social Policy: The Limits of Reform. Ph.D. dissertation, University of Chicago. (Unpublished)

———. 1989. *Private Acts, Social Consequences: AIDS and the Politics of Public Health.* New York: Free Press.

Buning, E.C. 1990. AIDS-Related Interventions among Drug Users in the Netherlands. *International Journal on Drug Policy* 1(5): 10–13.

Buning, E.C., R.A. Coutinho, G.H.A. van Brussel et al. 1986. Preventing AIDS in Drug Addicts in Amsterdam [Letter]. *Lancet* 1(8494): 1435.

Buning, E.C., G.H.A. van Brussel, and G. van Santen. 1988. Amsterdam's Drug Policy and its Implications for Controlling Needle Sharing. In *Needle Sharing Among Intravenous Drug Abusers: National and International Perspectives*, eds. R.J. Battjes and R.W. Pickens, NIDA research monograph 80. Washington.

Davidson, D.C. 1990. Tacoma's Point Defiance. *Health PAC/Bulletin* 20(3):16–17.

Des Jarlais, D.C., S.R. Friedman, and R.L. Stoneburner. 1988. HIV Infection and Intravenous Drug Use: Critical Issues in Transmission Dynamics, Infection Outcomes, and Prevention. *Reviews of Infectious Diseases* 10(1):151–8.

Engelsman, E.L. 1989. The Netherlands' Policy on AIDS and Drug Abuse. Testimony before the U.S. House of Representatives Subcommittee on Health and the Environment for Hearings on AIDS and the Intravenous Use of Drugs. (Mimeo).

Epstein, E.J. 1974. Methadone: The Forlorn Hope. *Public Interest* (summer):3–24.

Falco, M. 1989. *Winning the Drug War: A National Strategy.* New York: Priority Press.

Friedman, S.R., W.M. de Jong, D.C. Des Jarlais et al. 1987. Drug Users' Organizations and AIDS Prevention: Differences in Structure and Strategy. Poster presented at the Third International AIDS Conference, Washington.

Friedman, S.R., and C. Casriel. 1988. Drug Users' Organizations and AIDS Policy. *AIDS and Public Policy Journal* 3(2):30–6.

Friedman, S.R., D.C. Des Jarlais, and D.S. Goldsmith. 1989. An Overview of AIDS Prevention Efforts Aimed at Intravenous Drug Users Circa 1987. *Journal of Drug Issues* 19(1):93–112.

Friedman, S.R., W.M. de Jong, and D.C. Des Jarlais. 1990. Organizing Intravenous Drug Users for AIDS Prevention. In *The Effectiveness of Drug Abuse Treatment: Dutch and American Perspectives*, eds. J.J. Platt, C.D. Kaplan, and P.J. McKim. Malabar, Fla. Dreiger.

Friedman, S.R., M. Sufian, R. Curtis et al. 1991. AIDS-Related Organizing of Intravenous Drug Users from the Outside. In *Culture and Social Relations in the AIDS Crisis*, eds. E. Schneider and J. Huber. Newbury Park, Calif.: Sage.

Gillman, C. 1989. Genesis of New York City's Experimental Needle Exchange Program. *International Journal on Drug Policy* 1(2):28–32.

Gostin, L. 1991. Compulsory Treatment for Drug-dependent Persons: Justifications for a Public Health Approach to Drug Dependence. *Milbank Quarterly* 69(4):561–94.

Grmek, M.D. 1990. *History of AIDS: Emergence and Origin of a Modern Epidemic.* Princeton: Princeton University Press.

Hagan, H., D.C. Des Jarlais, D. Purchase et al. 1991. Lower HIV Seroprevalence, Declining HBV Incidence and Safer Injection in Relation to the Tacoma Syringe Exchange. Presentation at the Seventh International Conference on AIDS, Florence, June 19th. (Abstract #WC3291)

Harney, M.L. 1960. Drug Addiction. *Commentary* 30(6):531–2.

Health/PAC. 1990. Drug Use and AIDS in New York City, Health Policy for the '90's. *Health/PAC Bulletin* 20(3):23–31.

Institute of Medicine. 1986a. *Mobilizing against AIDS, the Unfinished Story of a Virus.* Cambridge, Mass.: Harvard University Press.

———. 1986b. *Confronting AIDS, Directions for Public Health, Health Care, and Research.* Washington: National Academy Press.

Joseph, S.C., and D.C. Des Jarlais. 1989. Needle and Syringe Exchange as a Method of AIDS Epidemic Control. *AIDS Updates* 2(5):1–8.

Judson, H.F. 1975. *Heroin Addiction: What Americans Can Learn From the English Experience.* New York: Vintage.

King, R. 1972. *The Drug Hang-Up, America's Fifty-Year Folly.* New York: W.W. Norton.

Klein, R. 1991. Risks and Benefits of Comparative Studies: Notes from Another Shore. *Milbank Quarterly* 69(2):275.

Lambert, B. 1988. The Free-Needle Program is under Way and under Fire. *New York Times* (November 13):E6.

———. 1991. AIDS Protesters Test State Needle Laws. *New York Times* (April 14):E6.

Larimore, G.W., and H. Brill. 1960. The British Narcotic System, Report of a Study. *New York State Journal of Medicine* 60(1):107–15.

Lichty, P. 1990. "The Point is to Save Lives": Needle Exchange in Hawaii. *Health/PAC Bulletin* 20(3):11–15.

Lindesmith, A.R. 1947. *Opiate Addiction.* Bloomington, Ind.: Principia Press.

———. 1965. *The Addict and the Law.* Bloomington: Indiana University Press.

Marriott, M. 1988. Needle Exchange Angers Many Minorities. *New York Times* (November 7):B1,8.

Moore, M.H. 1991. Drugs, the Criminal Law, and the Administration of Justice. *Milbank Quarterly* 69(4):529–60.

Musto, D.F. 1987. *The American Disease: Origins of Narcotic Control.* Expanded edition. New York: Oxford University Press.

Navarro, M. 1991a. Yale Reports Clean Needle Project Reduces AIDS Cases. *New York Times* (August 1):A1.

———. 1991b. Dinkins Endorses Privately Financed Needle Swap Plan. *New York Times* (November 5):B3.

Newmeyer, J.A., H.W. Feldman, P. Biernacki, and J.K. Watters. 1989. Preventing AIDS Contagion among Intravenous Drug Users. *Medical Anthropology* 10(2–3):167–75.

Oliver, K. 1990. Outside In: Portland's Syringe Exchange. *Health/PAC Bulletin* 20(3):17–18.

Oppenheimer, G. 1988. In the Eye of the Storm: The Epidemiological Construction of AIDS. In *AIDS, the Burdens of History*, eds. E. Fee and D.M. Fox. Berkeley: University of California Press.

Robinson, C.D. 1978. The Politics of a Heroin Maintenance Proposal in New York City. In *Drugs, Crime and Politics*, ed. A. Trebach. New York: Praeger.

Schur, E.M. 1960. Drug Addiction. *Commentary* 30(6):534–5.

————. 1962. *Narcotic Addiction in Britain and America: The Impact of Public Policy*. Bloomington: Indiana University Press.

Spear, H.B. 1969. The Growth of Heroin Addiction in the United Kingdom. *British Journal of Addiction* 64(2):245–55.

Sullivan, J.F. 1986. Jersey "Willing" to Give Addicts Clean Needles. *New York Times* (July 24):A12.

Terry, C.E., and M. Pellens. 1974. *The Opium Problem*, 2d ed. Montclair, N.J.: Paterson Smith.

Thomas, S.B., and S.C. Quinn. 1991. The Tuskegee Syphilis Study, 1932 to 1972: Implications for HIV Education and AIDS Risk Education Programs in the Black Community. *American Journal of Public Health* 81(11):1498–1504.

Trebach, A.S. 1982. *The Heroin Solution*. New Haven: Yale University Press.

van den Hoek, J.A.R., H.J.A. van Haastrecht, and R.A. Coutinho. 1989. Risk Reduction among Intravenous Drug Users in Amsterdam under the Influence of AIDS. *American Journal of Public Health* 79(10):1355–7.

van de Wijngaart, G.F. 1988. Methadone in the Netherlands: An Evaluation. *The International Journal of the Addictions* 23(9):913–25.

————. 1990. The Dutch Approach: Normalization of Drug Problems. *Journal of Drug Issues* 20(4):667–8.

Acknowledgments: This paper depended upon conversations with and the generous support of the following individuals, most of whom also served as patient and helpful readers of earlier drafts of the manuscript: Charles Eaton, Christine Epifania, Samuel Friedman, Robert Padgug, Bernard Pollack, Edith Springer, and Anne Stone.

Drugs, the Criminal Law, and the Administration of Justice

MARK H. MOORE

Harvard University

A COMMONLY HELD, BASIC TENET OF LIBERAL jurisprudence is that, in a free society, the criminal law should be used sparingly (Feinberg 1984; Packer 1968). Its use should be limited to controlling actions that harm others (Feinberg 1984, 10–16). It should not be casually available to those who wish to impose their particular views of virtuous conduct on others.

The most famous (and in many ways, most extreme) statement of this position was made by John Stuart Mill in *On Liberty*, originally published in 1859 (revised edition, 1956).

> The only purpose for which power can be rightfully exercised over any member of a civilized community, against his will, is to prevent harm to others. His own good, either physical or moral, is not a sufficient warrant. (1859 [1956, 13])

Relying on this principle, Mill found it necessary to oppose laws prohibiting the sale of alcohol.

Other classical philosophers have held less extreme positions about the proper use of the criminal law. Burke (1790 [revised edition, 1955]), for example, might well have been suspicious of Mill's principle and the particular application to laws prohibiting alcohol. He states:

> Government is a contrivance of human wisdom to provide for human *wants*. Men have a right that these wants should be provided for by this wisdom. Among these wants is to be reckoned the want, out of civil society, of a sufficient restraint on their passions. Society requires

not only that the passions of individuals should be subjected, but that even in the mass and body, as well as in the individuals, the inclinations of men should frequently be thwarted, their will controlled, and their passions brought into subjection. (1790 [1955,68])

Burke would have been particularly suspicious of developing a position on the desirability of a particular law based only on an abstract principle:

But as the liberties and restrictions vary with times and circumstances and admit to infinite modifications, they cannot be settled upon any abstract rule; and nothing is so foolish as to discuss them upon that principle. (1790 [1955,69])

Instead, he would have looked for guidance to the "practice of their ancestors, the fundamental laws of their country," or the "convention" that informs those fundamental laws.

From these observations, one cannot easily predict what position Burke would have taken with respect to the prohibition of alcohol. To the extent that he viewed drinking as a vice that undermined the requirements of civil society, Burke might well have supported prohibition. On the other hand, to the extent that drinking seemed to be a well-settled custom of the free men of England, and to be reasonably well regulated by convention, Burke, like Mill, might have objected to efforts to restrict liberty and ignore established conventions.

Recently, contemporary philosophers have followed Burke in questioning the primacy that Mill would give to the protection of individual liberty in the construction of social institutions. (I am following Amy Gutmann's interpretation of such contemporary philosophers as Alasdair MacIntyre, Charles Taylor, Roberto Unger, and Michael Sandel [Gutmann 1985, 308].) Indeed, the "communitarian critics" of liberalism have argued that justice does not reside in institutions that protect individualism at all costs, but rather in "a community whose primary bond is a shared understanding both of the good for man and the good of that community" (MacIntyre 1981, 232-3). Because a common history plays an important role in developing these crucial shared understandings, traditions have an important position in these modern theories as well as in Burke's.

Yet the contemporary theorists want to go beyond Burke's commitment to tradition and found the justice of their "shared understandings" in practical reason as well as in tradition. (This much has reason gained in stature as a guide to individual and social virtue since Burke's time!) Thus, for example, Alasdair MacIntyre observes that "when a tradition is in good order it is always partially constituted by an argument about goods the pursuit of which gives to that tradition its particular point and purpose" (MacIntyre 1981, 42). Closer to the subject at hand, John Kaplan recommends abandoning Mill's principle as a guide to formulating heroin policy, attempting instead a serious effort to estimate the good and bad consequences of relaxing current restrictions on its availability (Kaplan 1983, 109–10).

The point is that while the liberal philosophical tradition makes a virtue of economizing on the use of the law to protect individual liberty, the law may also be seen within that tradition as an important instrument in *establishing* a liberal community.

The question to be addressed in this article is whether criminal laws directed at the sale and use of drugs like heroin and cocaine are helpful in establishing a liberal community. It is an important question.

United States law enforcement agencies now arrest more than 1,300,000 citizens each year for the possession, distribution, and sale of prohibited drugs (Bureau of Justice Statistics 1990, 418). More than 250,000 citizens, many of them minorities, are now in jails or prisons for drug offenses.

If the laws that put so many nonconformist citizens in "a terror of apprehension, rendering [their] privacy precarious, and [their] prospects in life uncertain" (Feinberg 1984, 4) cannot be justified as contributing to the maintenance of a liberal community, they should be abandoned. To explore this question, I begin by looking for philosophical guidance from Mill, Burke, and the contemporary theorists. In particular, I start with Mill's principle to explore the possibility of justifying laws against drug use even within its strict purview. This analysis exposes the various ways in which drug use does result in harms to others, and therefore properly makes drug use a concern of others. It also reveals some of the ways in which a liberal community can make moral claims on what might be seen as the purely private conduct of individuals, thereby giving scope for intrusive uses of the law in regulating individual conduct.

Then, because I am also impressed by Burke's advice that laws to curb passions might be necessary to civil society, and that, in any case, it is desirable to understand how the law is functioning in the "particular contrivances" that men have made to deal with the problem of drug abuse, I turn to a brief historical exploration of the role that drug laws have played in contemporary drug policy.

Finally, because I am also influenced by John Kaplan, I turn to the question of whether the laws have any important practical benefits, and whether they can be enforced fairly without doing too much damage to the institutions of the criminal justice system.

The Philosophical Question

In seeking a philosophical justification for applying criminal law to the control of drug use, there are two reasons why it is helpful to start with Mill's classic statement about the proper role of the criminal law in a liberal society.

First, many agree with Mill's principle. Indeed, his ringing celebration of individual liberty has been echoed by scores of liberal political philosophers (see, for example, Rawls 1971). In somewhat less extreme forms, it has also formed the core of much liberal jurisprudence (Feinberg 1984; Packer 1968). Furthermore, it has found wide, durable appeal in the American political culture, which remains deeply suspicious of governmental interference—particularly when cloaked in claims of beneficence.

Second, on its face, Mill's strict principle seems to be the strongest indictment against using the criminal law to control drug use. Consequently, if an argument can be made for the propriety of regulating drug use even under Mill's extreme principle, it seems far more likely that one could justify its use under the different (and probably more favorable) principles associated with Burke and contemporary communitarian philosophers.

Mill's Position on Alcohol Prohibition

To begin the analysis of Mill's position, one must first understand his position on efforts to prohibit the commercial distribution of alcohol in England. Not surprisingly, he was opposed to such laws. More surprising are his reasons. Two seem key.

First, although the defenders of such laws (including an organization called simply the "Alliance") had sought to insulate themselves from the criticism that they attacked private liberty by focusing control efforts

on the commercial distribution of alcohol, Mill understood their ultimate purpose to be to discourage the private consumption of alcohol
(Feinberg 1984; Packer 1968). Because Mill believed that the act of
drinking belonged clearly in the private domain, and did not inevitably
impose substantial and unavoidable harms on others, it was wrong for
the state to discourage such conduct. In short, the Alliance, and particularly their secretary, who was the principal spokesperson, was wrong on
the merits of the case.

However, Mill also objected to what he took to be the disingenuousness of the legislative proposals, "since the State might just as well forbid [the consumer] to drink wine as purposely make it impossible for
him to obtain it" (Mill 1859 [1956, 90]). The disingenuousness was ob-
jectionable because the implicit deception made it difficult to have the
kind of rational discourse that Mill thought was necessary to the proper
formulation of public policy.

Second, and far more important, Mill objected to the philosophical
basis for the prohibitionists' argument. He quotes the philosophical position of the secretary of the Alliance at some length to reveal the error
of their position:

> The Secretary . . . says, "I claim, as a citizen, a right to legislate
> whenever my social rights are invaded by the social act of an-
> other. . . . If anything invades my social rights, certainly the traffic
> in strong drink does. It destroys my primary right of security, by con-
> stantly creating and stimulating social disorder. It invades my right of
> equality, by deriving a profit from the creation of a misery I am taxed
> to support. It impedes my right to free moral and intellectual devel-
> opment, by surrounding my path with dangers, and by weakening
> and demoralizing society, from which I have a right to claim mutual
> aid and intercourse." (Mill 1859 [1956, 90])

With the target clearly outlined, he delivers his objection:

> A theory of social right, the like of which probably never before
> found its way into distinct language: being nothing short of this —
> that it is the absolute social right of every individual, that every other
> individual shall act in every respect exactly as he ought; that whoso-
> ever fails thereof in the smallest particular, violates my social right,
> and entitles me to demand from the legislature the removal of the
> grievance. So monstrous a principle is far more dangerous than any
> single interference with liberty; there is no violation of liberty which

it would not justify. . . . . The doctrine ascribes to all mankind a vested interest in each other's moral, intellectual, and even physical protection, to be defined by each claimant according to his own standard. (Mill 1859 [1956, 90-1])

Thus, Mill is attacking the broad philosophical position taken by the leaders of the Alliance as well as their particular proposed policy.

Whether Mill would have been as opposed to the prohibition of alcohol if the leaders of the Alliance had been less disingenuous or extreme in their positions remains unclear. What is clear is that Mill was *not* opposed to some forms of alcohol regulation. He was willing, for example, to allow the continued taxation of alcohol on the grounds that something needed to be taxed, and it might as well be something that people could do without. What was wrong was to tax alcohol with the intent of discouraging consumption (Mill 1859 [1956, 102]).

He was also willing to allow some restrictions on who could sell alcohol. As he explained:

All places of public resort require the restraint of a police, and places of this kind peculiarly, because offenses against society are especially apt to originate there. It is, therefore, fit to confine the power of selling these commodities (at least for consumption on the spot) to persons of known or vouched for respectability of conduct; to make such regulations respecting hours of opening and closing as may be requisite for public surveillance, and to withdraw the license if breaches of the peace repeatedly take place through the connivance or incapacity of the keeper of the house, or if it becomes a rendezvous for concocting and preparing offenses against the law. (Mill 1859 [1956, 103])

What was wrong, again, was to limit licenses "for the express purpose of rendering them more difficult of access, and diminishing the occasions of temptation." Such actions were suitable only for the government of children, not free persons.

He was even willing to punish those individuals who had shown their inability to control their drinking by committing crimes while intoxicated.

Drunkenness, for example, in ordinary cases, is not a fit subject for legislative interference; but I should deem it perfectly legitimate that a person, who had once been convicted of any act of violence to others under the influence of drink, should be placed under a special legal restriction, personal to himself; that if he were afterwards found drunk, he should be liable to a penalty, and that if when in that state he committed another offense, the punishment to which he would be liable for that other offense should be increased in severity. (Mill 1859 [1956, 99])

Thus, even Mill was open to some discussion and debate about harms to others that could be caused by purveying or using psychoactive substances, and to search for some devices for controlling those harms. To the extent that drug use harmed others, a justification for legislative control could be established even under Mill's strict principle.

The Link Between Drug Use and Crime

Perhaps the most obvious harm caused by drug use is crime. Indeed, many who support criminal laws against drug use do so precisely because they believe that drug use prompts otherwise law-abiding citizens to commit crimes. As evidence, they point to the fact that many of those arrested for murder, robbery, and burglary use drugs, and that criminal offenders who use drugs are among the most active and dangerous criminal offenders (Chaiken and Chaiken 1982; Chaiken and Johnson 1988; National Institute of Justice 1990).

The problem with this argument is that these facts do not prove that drugs cause crime (Chaiken and Chaiken 1990, 203–39). Perhaps those who are most prone to commit crimes also like to use illegal drugs. Perhaps the reason that drug users commit crimes is that crime is the only way they can earn enough money to pay for the drugs whose cost has been increased by making their sale illegal. Indeed, these alternative explanations gain increased credibility from experiments indicating that the direct pharmacological effects of many illicit drugs (including heroin and marijuana) is to make users pacific rather than aggressive—at least while they are under the influence of the drug (Miczek et al. 1990).

On the other hand, there is also physiological evidence indicating that some drugs do encourage aggression in humans and animals, and some crimes do seem to have been committed under the influence of drug-induced changes in perception or other physiological states (Miczek et al. 1990, 23). In addition, some drugs that make users pacific at one stage of metabolism, change their character at a later stage. As alcohol is metabolized, for example, it eventually releases compounds that tend to make people irritable and angry; when drug-dependent opiate users are deprived of opiates they too become irritable (Fagan 1990, 251; Miczek et al. 1990, 7). Finally, there is the worrisome fact that the drug most consistently linked to violence in the home and assaults among strangers in public locations is alcohol—a drug that is freely available (Miczek et al. 1990, 8).

Consequently, although the current observed correlation between drug use and crime cannot prove that drugs cause crime, it cannot be assumed that all of the observed relationship is accounted for solely by the personality of the users or the perverse effects of making drugs illegal. To be sure, if all drugs were made as freely available as alcohol, the observed relationship between drug use and crime might well change. Perhaps a smaller proportion of those using drugs would commit crimes, and more of the drug-related crimes would be associated with periods of intoxication and temporary irritability than with sustained economic need. The point is, however, that the relationship between drugs and crime would not disappear. Indeed, if the overall level of drug use increased as a result of the more ready availability and diminished moral stigma associated with use, the net effect of drug legalization on crime could be to *increase* the absolute level of drug-related violence. This could be true even as the *proportion* of drug users involved in crime diminished.

Drug Use and Other Harms

Even if drug use does not cause crime, it may result in different kinds of harms to others. Some of these effects are tangible and directly attributable to drug use independent of the unintended side effects of current policies. Others are less tangible, or less immediately attributable to drug use in itself.

Physiological Effects on Infants. With one important exception, drug use (unlike smoking) does not usually affect the health of others with whom one is in contact. When a pregnant woman uses drugs, it produces an adverse effect on the fetus she nurtures (Besharov 1989, 6–11, 42; Ryan, Ehrlich, and Finnegan 1987, 295–9; Zuckerman 1989, 762–8). This has led some legislators to propose criminalizing such conduct, and a few prosecutors to prosecute pregnant women who use drugs under statutes designed to control other offenses (e.g., drug dealing, or child abuse and neglect [Gomez-Ibanez 1990; *New York Times* 1989; Patner 1989]).

Accidents Affecting Others. Drug use also intoxicates people. When intoxicated people drive cars, or work with moving equipment, or direct aircraft landings, they pose immediate hazards, and sometimes inflict real harms on others (Kolata 1990; National Committee for Injury Prevention and Control 1989, 6146; *New York Times* 1987; *Washington Post* 1989). Indeed, researchers in New York and Philadelphia have discovered that when traffic fatalities are tested for cocaine as well as alcohol use, cocaine shows up in a large and disproportionate number of cases (National Committee for Injury Prevention and Control 1989, 119,123).

Intoxicated Attacks on Others. Being intoxicated makes people careless and negligent as well as clumsy. In such a state, ordinarily compelling internal inhibitions and external rules can be undermined. As our experience with alcohol teaches us, an assault against a spouse, a friend, or a child is far more likely when one is drunk than when one is sober (Room and Collins 1983). The same could turn out to be true for psychoactive drugs if they were even more commonly used than they are now.

Dependence-induced Neglect of Others. Some drugs also produce dependence; they motivate use long beyond prudential limits of finances and reasonable pyschological commitment. Often, the dependence interferes with the ability of the drug user to discharge his responsibilities to employers, spouses, or children. As a consequence, these individuals are injured: the employer loses money, the spouse becomes impoverished and dispirited, the children lose the guidance and assistance they need to develop into responsible and resourceful citizens (Johnson et al. 1990, 44–55; National Commission on Marijuana and Drug Abuse 1973, 113–99).

The Drain on Public Resources. Finally, because we are all now connected to one another through systems of private and public insurance (to say nothing of the obligation of charity), when a drug user injures himself, or leaves his dependents in an impoverished state, he affects the material well-being of those who will be asked to share the burden of caring for him and his dependents. This, too, is a harm that drug users do to others (Bartels 1973, 460–1).

These are all tangible, direct, important ways in which drug use can affect the well-being of others in the society. Insofar as these are accepted as important harms to others that can be linked directly to drug use (rather than to the policies now regulating drug use, or to the characteristics of the people who tend to use drugs), they establish part of the justification for criminalizing drug use—even under Mill's strict principle.

Drug Use and Paternalism

Mill offered an exception to his general principle that criminal laws should be used only to reduce harms done to others for those whose judgment about their own best interests was unreliable. The obvious example was children. As Mill put it:

> It is, perhaps, hardly necessary to say that this doctrine is meant to apply only to human beings in the maturity of their faculties. We are not speaking of children. . . . Those who are still in a state to require being taken care of by others must be protected against their own actions as well as against external injury. (Mill 1859 [1956, 125])

On these grounds, Mill, and presumably we, would have had no objection to prohibiting drug use among children.

However, this exception may apply to more than just children. In Mill's formulation, children are used as an example of a broader class of people who are "still in a state to require being taken care of by others." That definition could conceivably cover those who are mentally ill. Another possibility is that it could cover those who had specifically shown themselves to be unable to use drugs in ways that did not interfere with their responsibilities to the rest of the society; for example, those who were referred to drug treatment programs because their drug use was implicated in criminal offending, or neglect of their children, or failures in school.

John Kaplan (1983) also raises the question of whether Mill would have "countenanced" broader laws to achieve the practical goal of protecting children (and others) from drugs, and offers the following points:

> There is no doubt that, in a society such as ours, making heroin freely available to adults would render completely unenforceable any effort to prevent the young from having access to the drugs. . . . In all probability, Mill would have regarded this kind of reasoning (that such laws were necessary) as allowing the tail to wag the dog. . . .

At the very least, Mill would require that the benefits of protecting youth by prohibiting all access to heroin be balanced against the interference this would cause to the legitimate freedom of adults. . . . In reaching such a balance, we would have . . . to decide difficult empirical questions. . . . This kind of inquiry . . . seems to remove the issue from the realm of principle and place it in that of practicality. (1983, 104)

Thus, the broad exception for "paternalism" given by Mill offers substantial room for justifying the use of state authority to regulate drug use. Regulation may be appropriate for all who cannot be trusted to judge their own interests, or use them wisely. Furthermore, depending on empirical judgments, the controls may have to be wider to protect those who need to be protected. Mill, no doubt, would have resisted many of these extensions, but political philosophers who have a less atomistic vision of society, and a weaker commitment to the protection of liberty, might find room for these extensions.

Drugs, Slavery, and Responsibility

Mill offered a second exception to his principle as an explanation of why a liberal state might reserve the right to prohibit individuals from selling themselves into slavery.

The reason for not interfering unless for the sake of others, with a person's voluntary acts, is consideration for his liberty. But by selling himself for a slave, he abdicates his liberty; he foregoes any future use of it beyond that single act. He therefore defeats, in his own case, the very purpose which is the justification of allowing him to dispose of himself. . . . The principle of freedom cannot require that he should be free not to be free. It is not freedom to be allowed to alienate his freedom. These reasons, the force of which is so conspicuous in this peculiar case, are evidently of far wider application. (Mill 1859 [1956, 125])

Whether drug use fits into this exception is unclear. It depends on whether we understand freedom in a liberal society as a right, or as a responsibility; and how we regard such psychological states as "intoxication" and "dependence."

Most liberal political theory sees liberty as a right, and assumes that it is desired. One could equally well argue, however, that liberty, in the form of being accountable for oneself, is also a *responsibility* in liberal societies. It is inalienable not only because it is desired by individuals, but also because society expects and requires people to keep themselves free so that whatever happens to individuals can be justly attributed to them.

Viewed from this perspective, a liberal society could reasonably consider it not only morally unattractive, but also an offense for someone knowingly and intentionally to place himself in a position of irresponsibility. Slavery is the most extreme example. One might, however, view making oneself dependent on drugs, or becoming intoxicated as similar problems of a lesser degree.

Community Standards and the Limits of Principle

Thus, as John Kaplan argued almost a decade ago, Mill's principles are not a bar to the state regulation of drugs like heroin and cocaine (Kaplan 1983, 109–10). There are substantial harms to others that can be more or less directly attributed to the use of these drugs. There are members of society whose judgment about their own interests in drug use cannot be relied upon. Use of some kinds of drugs may arguably put citizens in a dependent, irresponsible state that is inconsistent with the rights and responsibilities of citizens in a liberal society.

Of course, none of these points implies that drug use, possession, or sale should necessarily be the object of a criminal prohibition. Other lesser forms of state regulation may be more appropriate.

Moreover, it is by no means clear that these arguments apply with equal force to all currently illicit drugs. It seems clear, for example, that among the currently illegal drugs the arguments for state control apply far more convincingly to cocaine and heroin than to marijuana or the hallucinogens.

Indeed, going through this analysis, one begins to sense the limitations of arguing the issue of drug regulation solely on the basis of abstract principles without reference to particular drugs, and specific policies. It is simply too hard to make the principles do the work of dictating a differentiated, detailed policy. The principles are too loose, and their application depends on too many uncertain empirical judgments.

Further, the principles seem to require a kind of consistency that, in the real world, is impossible to achieve. The current drug laws are writ-

ten so that if a psychoactive drug has some abuse potential and no legitimate medical use, it must be placed in a category that prohibits all but
research uses of the drug regardless of the magnitude of its abuse potential. In effect, the law blots out the differences in these drugs on the
grounds that they all represent some abuse potential and have no important medical application.

The strongest reasons that can be mustered for regulating heroin and
cocaine provide equally strong justifications for regulating alcohol and
tobacco, which are currently beyond the scope of the legislation that
regulates the availability of psychoactive and dependence-producing
substances.

Many of the extensions of Mill's principle that could be used to justify state regulation of drugs could be applied to gambling, borrowing
money, and having children, as well as to the use of psychoactive substances. Yet it is inconceivable that these activities would be regulated
in the same way that we regulate drugs.

These problems, of course, could be taken as evidence of the failure
of our drug laws to meet the requirements of principle and consistency,
and therefore of their immorality. That, in turn, can be seen as an important reason for changing them.

A different way of looking at the inconsistencies, however, is to see
them as reflections of a historical process that properly makes claims on
drug policy (Sandel 1982). In this conception, the reason we treat tobacco and alcohol differently from heroin and cocaine is not only that
their pharmacological impact is different, but also because society en-
countered them in various ways and learned about them at a slower
pace. To contemporary citizens, these drugs carry various meanings with
their own philosophical weight and significance.

Indeed, it may be that our experience with alcohol constitutes one of
the strongest reasons *not* to legalize drugs such as heroin and cocaine:
We already have one huge drug problem. Why add another simply to
be consistent? It may also be that we are sociologically better prepared
to deal with the threat that alcohol represents than we are to deal with
heroin and cocaine because we have accumulated a great deal of experience with this drug. That fact may also be relevant in deciding what our
policy should be.

The point is simply that it is not only impractical, but also philosoph-
ically wrong to address the issue of drug policy solely from the vantage
point of abstract principle (Sandel 1982). The principled arguments; the
tests of the logic that connects principles to specific judgments about

drug policies; the search for inconsistencies in our handling of different drug problems; and the concern that the principles we use to justify (or rationalize) drug policy are far too broad because they would also justify actions that are clearly inappropriate are all helpful devices for criticizing and adapting our current drug policies. These devices push in a direction that is almost certainly right: toward a more precise and refined policy that narrows the scope of drug regulation and makes less glaring the observable inconsistencies in the regulatory treatment of varied psychoactive substances.

Nonetheless, in reaching a philosophical conclusion about a proper drug policy, some respect must be given to current community understandings of what these drugs are, and how they might properly be regulated, as well as to abstract principle. We cannot stand entirely outside our history or current politics in reaching a principled conclusion about drug policy without risking significant philosophical and practical errors. For that reason, as part of our philosophical investigation, it is important to understand how society and its policy makers seem to have understood the role of drug laws in the recent past.

Drug Laws and Drug Policy: A Brief History of Thought

The Law Enforcement Era

From about 1930 to 1960, one could say that law enforcement constituted the entirety of the nation's drug policy (Musto 1987, 210–29; Schur 1962, 191–8). The use of drugs was seen almost entirely as a moral question, with the proper state response being to establish and enforce a criminal prohibition against sale and use. If such use continued, it was not a sign that the laws were wrong or ineffective, only that more people needed to be educated about the moral hazards of drug use, and that more or tougher enforcement was needed to exorcise the evil of drug use from society. It was a time when society was most comfortable with the broad extensions of the Mill harm principle outlined above. Drug use did look like something that produced only harm, irresponsibility, and slavery.

The Emergence of Drug Treatment

Starting in 1960, a new theme emerged in drug policy: the theme that drug users might be viewed as ill people who needed treatment rather than immoral people who deserved punishment (Musto 1987, 239). This view was championed by psychiatrists and physicians, who believed that they had something important to contribute to the solution of what was then only a small national problem.

In response, special treatment facilities for helping drug users recover were funded at both national and state levels (Musto 1987, 239). Equally important, authority was granted to divert drug users who had committed crimes to compulsory treatment programs, and also to compel drug users who had not been convicted of crimes to undergo treatment under civil commitment laws (Musto 1987, 239). The hope was that voluntary and compulsory drug treatment could achieve what the moral injunctions, threats, and purchasing inconveniences associated with laws criminalizing drug use alone could not: reduction of drug use among those who were simply not deterred by the laws.

Supply Reduction and Demand Reduction Strategies

The late 1960s brought substantial increases in illicit drug use. The geological force in this epidemic was the growing, widespread use of marijuana. However, the wave of illicit drug use was capped by a virulent epidemic of intravenous heroin use in the nation's cities, and the widely celebrated use of psychedelics among some of the nation's cultural elites. In devising a response, the nation struggled between a "law enforcement" approach and a "medical" approach—between trusting in "cops" or trusting in "docs."

The ultimate response was a new formulation of the choices in drug policy. Instead of viewing the choices as between law enforcement and medical approaches, policy makers began discussing the issue in terms of "supply reduction" versus "demand reduction" approaches (Domestic Council Drug Abuse Task Force 1975, 1). To some degree, these terms continued to reflect the basic ideological and bureaucratic forces that had previously given us the choice between the law enforcement and medical approaches. Supply reduction efforts seemed to rely principally on enforcement activities, thereby capturing the attention of previous supporters of the enforcement approach. For their part, demand reduction efforts seemed to rely mainly on drug treatment, thereby gaining the support of earlier champions of the medical approach.

Despite the close parallels in these conceptual schemes, the concepts of supply and demand reduction brought some important new developments to drug policy. For one thing, the shift from the medical approach to demand reduction created more conceptual room for the development of drug abuse *prevention* programs—including, in particular, the growth of drug education and mass media advertising about the hazards of drug use.

More significantly, however, the shift from law enforcement to supply reduction substantially narrowed the scope of law enforcement. In the era from 1930 to 1960, enforcement had been seen as a strategy that reduced *demand* as well as *supply*. Through the law's moral injunctions and threats, users were being targeted along with traffickers and pushers. In the era from 1970 to 1980, law enforcement was more narrowly targeted on drug dealers.

In this later era, the principal justification for investing in law enforcement efforts was the belief that laws and enforcement efforts directed against manufacturers, importers, and distributors would decrease the volume of drugs available at any given price, and would increase the average effective price of drugs. That, in turn, could be expected to reduce overall drug consumption—particularly among those who were not yet fully committed to drug use, but also among the committed by motivating them to seek treatment (Domestic Council Drug Abuse Task Force 1975, 2–4). Indeed, in theory, these measures would work to reduce overall levels of consumption even if the underlying factors influencing demand did not change.

There is some evidence to indicate that this approach worked to halt the most urgent part of the drug problem of the late 1960s and early 1970s, namely, the threatened growth of intravenous heroin use (Bartels and DuPont 1975). It did not, however, roll back heroin use substantially except through the process of attrition of current users. Some of the continuing problems of heroin use were mitigated by the development of publicly supported treatment programs specifically for heroin users (e.g., methadone maintenance clinics, and therapeutic communities) (Anglin and Hser 1990, 417–24).

The Cocaine Epidemic and the Limits of Federal Supply Reduction

In the mid to late 1970s, an epidemic of cocaine use began in the United States. It started in the professional classes, where the adverse consequences of cocaine use were at first shielded from public view. The wealth and social position of the early cocaine users could, for a while, absorb the bad effects that cocaine was having on them. Thus, for a while, the epidemiological data made cocaine look more like marijuana use than heroin: lots of use, but few adverse consequences (Moore 1990a, 11).

By the early to mid 1980s, however, the disastrous consequences of cocaine use began to appear. The number of cocaine users showing up in the nation's emergency rooms and jails began to increase dramatically (Moore 1990a, 12). This was partly the result of the fact that the demands of frequent cocaine use had finally exhausted the resources of the relatively well-off people who were the leading edge of the epidemic. It was also the result, however, of the fact that cocaine use had migrated downward in the socioeconomic scale and was affecting people whose troubles showed up more rapidly in public facilities and registers. Another factor was the appearance of "crack" — a form of cocaine that proved particularly quick and powerful in inducing dependence, and was especially attractive to those with less money to spend on drugs (Moore 1990a, 12).

Federal drug policy was slow to respond to the particular threat represented by cocaine because it tended to see cocaine use against the backdrop of a much larger, more chronic drug problem. Nonetheless, when it responded, it tended to emphasize federal supply reduction efforts over all other approaches (Falco 1989, 25–8). The Department of State increased aid to foreign source countries, and pressured them to increase their drug control efforts. The Department of Defense was mobilized to assist the United States Customs Service, the Immigration and Naturalization Service (INS), and the Coast Guard in dramatically increased efforts to interdict drugs crossing the border by air, land, and sea (*National Journal* 1986, 2106–9; Simon 1990; U.S. Congress 1987). The Federal Bureau of Investigation (FBI) was at long last coaxed into joining the Drug Enforcement Administration (DEA) in investigating cases focused on high-level drug traffickers here and abroad.

The Reagan "Demand Reduction" Strategy

The increased expenditures on supply reduction efforts, coupled with limited spending for drug prevention and treatment programs, "unbalanced" federal drug policy. It led many to claim that the Reagan administration neglected the demand reduction approaches that were a necessary complement of the supply reduction efforts.

In fact, one could argue that there *was* a Reagan demand reduction strategy; it was just one that was based on instruments other than drug treatment. The "Just Say No" campaign launched by Nancy Reagan had a remarkable resonance in the country. Many previously quiescent parents were mobilized to establish local community standards about drug use, and to advocate for more restrictive drug policies. These efforts came a little before an observed change in the attitudes of high school seniors toward drugs, and may partially account for that change (Black 1988).

Potentially as important was the huge effort made to encourage corporate America to crack down on drug use in their workforce, and to rely more on drug testing (Tysse and Dodge 1989). These were unconventional demand side instruments, and both their propriety and efficacy may be doubted. In describing trends in drug control policy, however, it would be wrong to ignore them.

Drug Laws as Demand Reduction

Indeed, from the perspective of this article, there are two important features of the Reagan demand-side strategy. First, it emphasized the mobilization of private community groups, such as parents or employers, to control drug use rather than public agencies, such as schools or public health hospitals. Second, in seeking to discourage drug use, it took for granted the idea that drug use was wrong and dangerous, and sought to discourage it by establishing new standards of conduct and holding people accountable for misconduct rather than by trying to educate or make it easier for people to stop their drug use.

These characteristics of the Reagan demand-side strategy created a context in which law enforcement could once again be seen as a demand-side, as well as a supply-side, strategy. The imagined mechanisms by which criminal laws directed at drug use could practically reduce drug use are essentially three.

First, the promulgation and enforcement of the laws can be seen as serving the same function as public education. The law is seen as a collective understanding about the dangers of drug use, and the establishment of an individual responsibility to avoid drug use. Its promulgation seeks to remind individuals about the reasons for the law, and to increase the law's moral force and legitimacy. It produces its practical results by promoting voluntary compliance among those who are persuaded, and by authorizing others in the community to comment informally on behavior that lies well outside the law. In effect, the law and its promulgation are seen as a way of establishing, or sustaining, or giving force to a community norm.

A second is that where education and moral exhortation fail, deterrence through the threat of penalties for misconduct might still succeed. To hold users accountable for their actions, however, required the development of credible sanctions. Thus, for serious offenses, many states passed minimum mandatory sentences for drug laws; for lesser offenses, many states experimented with the use of novel forms of punishment such as "boot camps"; and for relatively minor offenses, states experimented with the confiscation of drivers' licenses (Task Force on Drugs and the Courts 1991, 5).

If deterrence fails, a third mechanism can be brought into play, namely, the use of continuing state control over individuals convicted of drug offenses to provide them with the motivation and assistance to abandon their drug use. In the case of ordinary crimes, this mechanism is called "rehabilitation," and is widely (but perhaps erroneously) discredited (DiIulio 1991, 104–13; Sechrest et al. 1979, 279). In the case of drug offenses, or of drug users convicted of nondrug offenses, rehabilitation takes the form of compulsory urinalysis programs imposed as a condition of probation or parole, compulsory drug treatment programs, or drug treatment programs inside prisons (Anglin and Hser 1990, 424–8, 437–9; M. R. Chaiken 1989; Wish, Toborg, and Bellassai 1988). The literature on these sorts of programs indicates that they are successful in suppressing drug use and criminal conduct among their participants (Anglin and Hser 1990, 425–6, 429, 438–9).

The Effectiveness of Drug Laws

Thus, the current conception of the role of laws and law enforcement in drug policy encompasses the idea that these mechanisms can be effective in reducing the supply of drugs (and through that mechanism, reduce overall consumption) and that they can directly affect the demand for drugs (through the mechanisms of moral exhortation, deterrence, and rehabilitation). An important question is whether there is any empirical evidence to support these views.

Supply Reduction Effectiveness

The view that the drug laws can reduce the overall supply of drugs and thereby reduce consumption below what it would have been if the drug laws were not affecting the supply must overcome skepticism about the efficacy of enforcement efforts to reduce the supply, increase the price, and limit the availability of drugs. It must also overcome the belief that the demand for drugs is constant or "perfectly inelastic" so that the same quantity is consumed no matter what the price.

In considering the question of whether drug laws can reduce supply, it is important to keep in mind what is being claimed. It is not being claimed that the drug laws will eliminate all drugs being supplied to illicit markets in the United States, nor is it being claimed that the efforts will price the drug out of the reach of all consumers nor that all drug dealers will be arrested and prosecuted. The only claim is that the quantity of drugs supplied to illicit markets at any given price will be less than would be true in a world in which the drugs were legal, and that this will, given a constant demand for drugs, tend to increase the price and reduce the quantity of drugs actually consumed. Thus, evidence that drugs continue to come into illicit markets, or that some users still purchase the drugs, or that many dealers are still active is not necessarily evidence of a "failure" of supply reduction efforts. The crucial question is whether the quantity of drugs supplied at any given price has gone down, and by an amount sufficient to discourage a meaningful amount of drug use that would otherwise occur.

Note also that laws prohibiting the manufacture and sale of drugs produce their effects on the supply of drugs through two quite different mechanisms. The obvious one is that the laws expose drug dealers to arrest and prosecution by law enforcement agents. That risk must be taken into account by dealers, forcing them to engage in expensive activities to minimize the risk, and to demand a higher price from consumers as compensation for the risks they run (Moore 1977). That is what reduces the supply and increases the price of illicit drugs.

The less obvious mechanism is that the drug laws deny drug dealers the ordinary protections they would have as legitimate businessmen. They cannot rely on the law to enforce contracts, nor to protect them from extortion or theft. In short, they are exposed to thieves as well as law enforcement agencies. That, too, increases their risk and forces them to invest in expensive security efforts, and to demand additional compensation for their danger.

The net effect of these mechanisms is to increase the price of illicit drugs substantially beyond the price that would be charged in a legal market for these drugs. Heroin is 60 times more expensive than legal morphine; illegal cocaine is 15 times the legal price (Moore 1990b). Illegality probably accounts for most, if not all, of these price differentials.

It is also true that there have been periods in our recent history when supply reduction efforts have clearly succeeded in limiting the supply of drugs. These are periods in which the measured price of drugs in illicit markets has increased even as the measured quantity of drugs consumed has fallen (Boyum 1989). There were supply reduction successes in dealing with heroin from Turkey in the early 1970s, and from Mexico in the late 1970s (Moore 1990b). There may also be a supply reduction success in dealing with marijuana over the last eight years (Moore 1990b). However, there has also been a supply reduction failure: the supply of cocaine seems, until very recently, to have increased despite enormous efforts to reduce it (Moore 1990b).

Supply reduction successes are not particularly valuable if they do not result in reduced consumption. Indeed, if the only consequences of law enforcement pressure are that the prices increase, with higher revenues to dealers, while quantity consumed remains constant, one might conclude that supply reduction efforts made the problem worse by enriching (at least in financial terms) the drug dealers who were part of the problem. To be valuable to drug policy, supply reduction efforts must succeed in reducing drug consumption. That claim runs up against the common view that, because many drug users are addicted, or because the underlying causes of drug use remain unaffected, supply reduction efforts will not succeed in reducing consumption.

In assessing these arguments, however, it is important, once again, to keep in mind what is being claimed. Some confuse the reasonable view that drug use is "inelastic" (i.e., *relatively* unresponsive to changes in price and availability) with the claim that drug use is "perfectly inelastic" (i.e., *entirely* unresponsive to changes in price and availability). Furthermore, they base their claims on the addictive quality of drugs.

Yet, they ignore the fact that there are many new users whose desire for drugs might be less than absolute. They also ignore the fact that many users "mature out" of drug use voluntarily, and that the availability of drug treatment programs might provide a path out of drug use. The presence of new users, maturing-out users, and treated users in the overall population of drug users would make the aggregate demand for drugs far more elastic than one might at first assume (Moore 1977). In fact, the best estimates of the price elasticity of demand for drugs like heroin center around 0.2, which means that a doubling in the price of drugs would result in a 20 percent decrease in the level of use (for estimates of elasticity of demand for drugs other than heroin, see Moore 1990). This may not seem particularly significant until one remembers that the drug laws increase the price of drugs by much more than 100 percent.

Thus, there are some analytic and empirical reasons to believe that drug laws, operating on the supply of drugs, can reduce drug consumption even if the demand for drugs remains constant.

Demand Reduction Effectiveness

The claim that drug laws can effectively reduce demand through moral injunction, deterrence, and rehabilitation is far more difficult to evaluate because it is a relatively new claim.

The first part of that argument (that moral injunction can succeed in reducing drug use) must overcome skepticism, based on beliefs about the assumed inelasticity of demand and the idea that "forbidden fruits" are more attractive than those that are legal and normal (Nadelmann 1988, 28–9). Empirical evidence here is harder to come by. It may well be that some whose inclinations are already antisocial and risk favoring may be additionally attracted to drug use by the fact that its use is officially discouraged. There may be others, however, for whom the official disapprobation works to reduce their inclinations to experiment — either directly by persuading them that drug use is a bad idea, or indirectly by the effect of the laws in mobilizing a more determined, sustained opposition to drug use by parents and others in the community. The net effect will depend on the initial distribution of individual orientations throughout the society, the credibility of the messages, and the reasonableness with which the obligations are enforced.

What seems more solid, however, is that both urinalysis and treatment under court order as an alternative to jail is successful in suppressing crime and encouraging employment, improved parenting, and so on.

There is some evidence to indicate that a program of continued urinalysis can motivate drug users to reduce their drug use, and presumably, improve their social functioning. There is also evidence to indicate that compulsory treatment programs as an alternative to jails and prisons can reduce drug use and criminal misconduct, and enhance employment (Anglin and Hser 1990). This part, at least, of the demand-side strategy seems to work.

It is thus by no means obvious that these laws are without practical effect in shaping the character of the drug problem the nation faces. They may prevent some drug use that would otherwise occur and help to encourage current drug users to abandon the habit.

Indeed, it is heartening that the laws finally seem to be taking effect even with respect to cocaine use (Black 1988; Office of National Drug Control Policy 1991, 4). Of course, one could claim that the changing attitudes and reduced cocaine use are really the result of hard-earned, concrete experience with the drug and the social learning that accompanies that experience, rather than the effect of laws. In this view, the laws simply float on top of social attitudes and neither influence nor are affected by them.

One could also say that when the community learns about something (for example, that cocaine use is dangerous for people), it wants to encode that learning in laws so that it can remember. Perhaps laws emphasize what has been learned, and extend that learning not only across individuals in the society without first-hand experience, but also into the future to try to warn future generations of the problem. In short, the laws may help to strengthen informal community norms, and to allow the passage of information from one generation to the next (Parachini 1986).

The Fairness of the Laws

Over the long run, the effectiveness of the drug laws in mobilizing communities to resist drug use depends not only on the sense that they are, in fact, focused on a serious problem, and that they are effective in dealing with it, but also on whether they are perceived to fall fairly on the general population, and deliver their benefits somewhat equally. There is a worry here, for the drug laws may be applied differently and produce different effects in well-organized communities on the one hand, and in less well-organized communities on the other. The concern is less about the fairness of the arrests than about the overall effects of drug enforcement.

Begin with the assumption that the illicit drug trade is far more likely to find a foothold in disorganized, poor communities than in better-organized wealthy communities. This will be true to some extent because the ties that bind the less well-organized communities to the norms of the broader society are weaker, in part because individuals in the communities might be more easily tempted by the economic opportunities associated with selling and the pleasures of drug use, and to a certain degree because police services are less adequate and more easily corruptible.

The effect of these forces is to create a world in which the poor community's commitment to controlling drug use will be weaker than that of other communities. Their loyalties will be divided. Most will want to resist drug use and drug dealing, but there will be others who wish to continue. Dealers, users, and relatives of both have an interest in maintaining the trade. Indeed, these incentives may become particularly strong if the local drug markets are supported by buyers from outside the community. These revenues will make local drug dealers even more economically powerful.

The net result is to create communities in which a great deal of drug enforcement will occur, but with little positive impact on the local communities. The arrests will not necessarily trigger any other response in the community because there are few other resources to be used in combatting the local problem, and many who are implicated in the trade. Lack of resources will prevent those arrested from defending themselves against the charges and shaping the disposition to their interests. In these communities, then, drug law enforcement may seem to be a vicious and cynical effort.

In contrast, in a better-organized, wealthier community with more economic opportunities, drug using and dealing will be attractive to a far smaller fraction of the population. Instead of building local markets that would be vigorously resisted, the users will go outside the community, usually to the poorer, less well-organized communities. The local dealers who operate will remain small scale. Law enforcement, which enjoys the support of the local community, will be able to keep the problems small and localized. Indeed, any arrests that occur are likely to galvanize the community into more effective action across a wider front.

Moreover, the parents and friends of the person arrested are likely to be able to defend the arrested person effectively, and to shape the dispositions in useful directions.

The net result of these dynamics, of course, is that the disorganized communities end up paying much of the price associated with having and enforcing laws against drugs while receiving few of the benefits. The better-organized communities pay less of the price, and obtain far more of the benefits. This observation has two crucial implications for the administration of the drug laws.

First, enforcement efforts must be supplemented with treatment and prevention efforts, not only generally, but particularly in communities that are disorganized and besieged by drug problems. This is important, not only to be effective, but also to be just and fair. Anything less than that leaves the entire system vulnerable to a charge of neglect and discrimination that must ultimately undermine the effectiveness of the laws.

Second, the drug laws must be enforced so as not only to respond to the interests and concerns of the local communities, but also to help build the community's own efforts to control the problem. Both the overall operations and the handling of individual cases should be influenced by the community's ideas about what is in their best interest in controlling the drug problem. This is no easy task — particularly in a world where the criminal justice system is already under pressure and overused.

Effects on the Criminal Justice System

In reckoning the effects of using the criminal law to deal with drugs, one must also keep track of the impact of these laws on the institutions of the criminal justice system, and their ability to live up to their fundamental values and principles. One's first impression is that the heavy involvement of the criminal justice system in dealing with drug use cannot help but corrupt and demoralize the system.

One important consequence of using the criminal law to combat the drug problem is that the criminal justice institutions will be enlarged relative to other social institutions. Spending on police, courts, and prisons is growing faster than spending on welfare and education (Strasser 1989, 36–41). That may be an important effect in its own right.

In addition, the sheer volume of drug cases may be weakening the state's capacity to dispense justice in other areas. Corrections expenditures as a proportion of state-level general expenditures have risen from 1.6 percent in 1979 to 2.4 percent in 1989 (Herman B. Leonard, personal communication, 1991). The response to cases of rape, robbery, and burglary may now be degraded, to say nothing of our ability to deliver any kind of civil justice (Task Force on Drugs and the Courts 1991, 7–9). That too may be a distorting corruption of the system.

The biggest concern is that the increased scale of drug arrests will end up corrupting the institutions of the criminal justice system because drug cases are intrinsically corrupting. To make drug arrests, police agencies must rely on some of their most intrusive investigative methods, including informants, undercover operations, and wiretaps (Manning 1980). In conducting such operations, police may be tempted by bribes, misled by informants, or spurred on to inappropriately aggressive investigations.

To handle the press of cases the police generate, the courts transform their process of adjudication into an administrative process in which procedural steps are eliminated and deals are made (Task Force on Drugs and the Courts 1991, 26–35). In this transformation, both the rights of defendants and the interests of the broader community may be sacrificed. Even in the best of circumstances, judges facing drug-involved defendants are motivated to consider offender characteristics as well as the seriousness of offenses in making their disposition, with significant implications for the apparent justice of the sentences meted out and the training that is demanded of court personnel.

In short, the institutions of the criminal justice system may be dramatically transformed by the difficulties of dealing with such a large quantity of drug cases. These effects may last long after the current drug crisis has abated.

There is some good news here. The pressure of dealing with the drug cases has occasioned important improvements in the orientations and performance of the criminal justice system. Among police agencies, many police executives have rediscovered their fundamental dependence on local communities to help them achieve their objective, and they have begun experimenting with new ways of policing cities that are designed to build working partnerships to deal effectively with local neighborhood problems (Sparrow, Moore, and Kennedy 1990). These fledgling efforts promise to change the face of policing in the future, and to make the police less aloof and more helpful in restoring civility to urban streets. In the courts, some long overdue management reforms have been implemented that will not only reduce the costs of court processing, but also increase consistency and enhance accountability (Task Force on Drugs and the Courts 1991, 11–13, 19–35). Probation and corrections departments are undertaking a great many innovations and experiments with alternatives to incarceration (DiIulio 1991, 60–102). These are all innovations, partly occasioned by the drug crisis, that will improve the performance of the system in the future.

Conclusion

The nation is paying a heavy price for confronting its drug problem, specifically the current epidemic of cocaine use, with the criminal justice system. By rolling out the criminal law, and the institutions of the criminal justice system, we are committing some of our most powerful (and precious) weapons to the fight. In judging whether this is wise, it is proper to be keenly aware of the potentially corrupting effect of this effort on the principles that properly guide a liberal state, and on the institutions of the criminal justice system. It is also proper to be skeptical of their effectiveness. Viewed from this vantage point, it seems clear that we are probably at (if not beyond) the limit of these systems to be used justly and well in dealing with drug use. Over the next few years, we should work hard to reduce our reliance on them and to build up our treatment and prevention systems.

At the same time, one should not let our concerns about these effects distract our attention from the consequences of failing to deal effectively with drug use in general, and the cocaine epidemic more particularly. True, there may have been natural limits to the cocaine epidemic that we are now living through. Left to expand according to its own rules, however, a cocaine epidemic will inflict a great deal of damage on the society. And not all of the adverse consequences of cocaine are caused by its illicitness.

Moreover, dealing with the cocaine epidemic through other institutions such as schools, public health system, and so on, would have created enormous consequences for those systems, which are already straining under other demands. Indeed, it is hard to imagine a world in which school systems had to confront drug use without the assistance of criminal agencies, and in which the country's health system had to cope suddenly with more casualties of drug use.

Laws against drugs and the criminal justice system both have an important role to play in helping the nation deal with its drug problem. The challenge is to use these instruments skillfully, and with attention to the potential damage that using them can have for the society at large and for the instruments themselves. Indeed, as noted above, the challenge to criminal justice institutions might even be used to strengthen rather than weaken them. As the police reach out for more effective partnerships with communities, particularly poor, minority communities; as the courts reach for more varied dispositions and a principled basis for making them; and as the probation and corrections departments invent new forms of punishment alternatives to incarceration, we may come to see the criminal justice system as it ought to be seen: not as a device for exacting vengeance or for banishing individuals from the society in the vain hope that they will not return, but instead as a device for imposing collectively agreed-upon obligations on one another, and for ordering relations in a civil society.

The institutions of the criminal justice system are hardly society's favorites. Yet when they are used skillfully and well and justly to remind us of our duties to one another, they become an important part of what limits drug use in the society, and makes a liberal society possible.

References

Anglin, M.D., and Y.-I. Hser. 1990. Treatment of Drug Abuse. In *Drugs and Crime*, eds. M. Tonry and J.Q. Wilson, 393–460, vol. 13 of *Crime and Justice: A Review of Research*, eds. M. Tonry and N. Morris. Chicago: University of Chicago Press.

Bartels, J.R., and R.L. DuPont. 1975. Testimony before the Subcommittee on Future Foreign Policy Research and Development, House Committee on Foreign Affairs, April 23. Washington.

Bartels, R. 1973. Better Living Through Legislation: The Control of Mind Altering Drugs. *Kansas Law Review* 21:439–92.

Besharov, D.J. 1989. The Children of Crack: Will We Protect Them? *Public Welfare* (Fall):6–12.

Black, G.S. 1988. Changing Attitudes Toward Drug Use: 1988 Report. The First Year Effort of the Media-Advertising Partnership for a

Drug-Free America, Inc. Rochester, N.Y.: Gordon S. Black Corporation.

Boyum, D. 1989. *A Second Look at Drug Supply Reduction Effectiveness: New Methods and Applications.* Working paper no. 89-01-17, prepared for the Program in Criminal Justice Policy and Management, John F. Kennedy School of Government, Harvard University, Cambridge, Mass.

Bureau of Justice Statistics. 1990. *Sourcebook of Criminal Justice Statistics — 1989,* eds. T.J. Flanagan and K. Maguire, table 4.1, 418. Washington.

Burke, E. 1790. *Reflections on the Revolution in France.* (Revised ed. 1955, ed. H.D. Mahoney. New York: Macmillan.)

Chaiken, J.M., and M.R. Chaiken. 1982. *Varieties of Criminal Behavior.* Santa Monica, Calif.: RAND.

———. 1990. Drugs and Predatory Crime. *Drugs and Crime,* eds. M. Tonry and J.Q. Wilson, vol. 13 of *Crime and Justice: A Review of Research,* eds. M. Tonry and N. Morris. Chicago: University of Chicago Press.

Chaiken, M.R. 1989. *In-Prison Programs for Drug-Involved Offenders. Issues and Practices in Criminal Justice.* Washington: National Institute of Justice.

Chaiken, M.R., and B.D. Johnson. 1988. *Characteristics of Different Types of Drug-Involved Offenders.* Washington: National Institute of Justice.

DiIulio, J.J., Jr. 1991. *No Escape: The Future of American Corrections.* New York: Basic Books.

Domestic Council Drug Abuse Task Force. 1975. *White Paper on Drug Abuse.* A Report to the President. Washington.

Fagan, J. 1990. Intoxication and Aggression. In *Drugs and Crime,* eds. M. Tonry and J.Q. Wilson, vol. 13 of *Crime and Justice: A Review of Research,* eds. M. Tonry and N. Morris. Chicago: University of Chicago Press.

Falco, M. 1989. *Winning the Drug War: A National Strategy.* New York: Priority Press.

Feinberg, J. 1984. *Harm To Others,* vol. 1 of *The Moral Limits of Criminal Law.* New York: Oxford University Press.

Gutmann, A. 1985. Communitarian Critics of Liberalism. *Philosophy and Public Affairs* 14(3):308–22.

Gomez-Ibanez, J.A. 1990. *Cocaine Mothers.* Case no. C16-90-944.0, John F. Kennedy School of Government Case Program. Cambridge, Mass.: Harvard University.

Johnson, B.D., T. Williams, K.A. Dei, and H. Sanasbria. 1990. Drug

Abuse in the Inner City: Impact on Hard-Drug Users and the Community. In *Drugs and Crime*, eds. M. Tonry and J.Q. Wilson, vol. 13 of *Crime and Justice: A Review of Research*, eds. M. Tonry and N. Morris. Chicago: University of Chicago Press.

Kaplan, J. 1983. *The Hardest Drug: Heroin and Public Policy* Chicago: University of Chicago Press.

Kolata, G. 1990. Study Finds Cocaine in Many Motorists Killed in New York. *New York Times* (Jan. 12):A1.

MacIntyre, A. 1981. *After Virtue*. Notre Dame, Ind.: Notre Dame University Press.

Manning, P.K. 1980. *The Narc's Game*. Cambridge, Mass.: MIT Press.

Miczek, K.A., J.F. DeBold, M. Haney, J. Tidey, J. Vivian, and E.M. Weerts. 1990. Alcohol, Drugs of Abuse and Violence. Paper prepared for National Academy of Sciences Panel on the Causes and Control of Violence, March. Washington.

Mill, J.S. 1859. *On Liberty*. (Revised ed. 1956, ed. C.V. Shields. Indianapolis: Bobbs-Merrill.)

Moore, M.H. 1977. *Buy and Bust: The Effective Regulation of an Illicit Market in Heroin*. Lexington, Mass.: Lexington Books.

———. 1990a. Drugs: Getting a Fix on the Problem and the Solution. *Yale Law & Policy Review* 8:8–35.

———. 1990b. Supply Reduction and Drug Law Enforcement. In *Drugs and Crime*, eds. M. Tonry and J.Q. Wilson, vol. 13 of *Crime and Justice: A Review of Research*, eds. M. Tonry and N. Morris. Chicago: University of Chicago Press.

Musto, D.F. 1987. *The American Disease: Origins of Narcotic Control*, expanded edition. New York: Oxford University Press.

Nadelmann, E.A. 1988. The Case for Legalization. *Public Interest* 92 (summer): 3–31.

National Commission on Marijuana and Drug Abuse. 1973. *Drug Use in America: Problem in Perspective*, second report. Washington.

National Committee for Injury Prevention and Control. 1989. *Injury Prevention: Meeting the Challenge*. New York: Oxford University Press.

National Institute of Justice. 1990. Arrestee Drug Use. *Drug Use Forecasting: January to March 1990*. Washington.

National Journal. 1986. Saddling Up for the War on Drugs. (September 6):2106–9.

New York Times. 1987. Drug Traces Found in Two Conrail Workers After Fatal Crash. (January 15):A1.

———. 1989. Mother Charged in Baby's Death from Cocaine; Illinois Prosecutor Cites Rise in Similar Cases. (May 10): A10.

Office of National Drug Control Policy. 1991. *National Drug Control Strategy*. Washington: Executive Office of the President.

Packer, H.J. 1968. *The Limits of the Criminal Sanction*. Palo Alto, Calif.: Stanford University Press.

Parachini, A. 1986. Drug Abuse Afflicts U.S. in Cycles; Inevitable Lure. *Los Angeles Times* (July 31):I-1.

Patner, A. 1989. Handful of Prosecutors Start Treating Pregnant Drug Users as Child Abusers. *Wall Street Journal* (May 12): A3C.

Rawls, J. 1971. *A Theory of Justice*. Cambridge, Mass.: Harvard University Press.

Room, R., and G. Collins. Eds. 1983. *Alcohol and Disinhibition: Nature and Meaning of the Link*. Proceedings of a Conference, February 11–13, 1981, Berkeley/Oakland, California. Research monograph no. 12. Rockville, Md.: National Institute on Alcohol Abuse and Alcoholism.

Ryan, L., S. Ehrlich, and L. Finnegan. 1987. Cocaine Abuse in Pregnancy: Effects on the Fetus and Newborn. *Neurotoxicology and Teratology* 9:295–9.

Sandel, M. 1982. *Liberalism and the Limits of Justice*. Cambridge: Cambridge University Press.

Schur, E.M. 1962. *Narcotic Addiction in Britain and America: The Impact of Public Policy*. Bloomington: Indiana University Press.

Sechrest, L., et al. Eds. 1979. *Rehabilitation of Criminal Offenders: Problems and Prospects*. Washington: National Academy of Sciences.

Simon, H. 1990. The Pentagon and the War on Drugs. Case no. C16-90-934.0, John F. Kennedy School of Government Case Program. Cambridge, Mass.: Harvard University.

Sparrow, M.K., M.H. Moore, and D.M. Kennedy. 1990. *Beyond 911: A New Era for Policing*. New York: Basic.

Strasser, F. 1989. Making the Punishment Fit the Crime . . . And the Prison Budget. *Governing* (January):36–41.

Task Force on Drugs and the Courts, New Jersey. 1991. *Supreme Court Task Force on Drugs and the Courts. Draft Final Report*, February 28. (Unpublished.)

Tysse, G.J., and G.E. Dodge. 1989. *Winning the War on Drugs: The Role of Workplace Testing*. Washington: National Foundation for the Study of Employment Policy.

U.S. Congress. 1986. *Anti Drug Abuse Act of 1986*, 99th Congress, 2nd session. *United States Code Congressional and Administrative News*. St. Paul, Minn.: West Publishing Company.

Wish, E.D., M.A. Toborg, and J.P. Bellassai. 1988. *Identifying Drug*

Users and Monitoring Them During Conditional Release. Issues and Practices in Criminal Justice. Washington: National Institute of Justice.

Zuckerman, B., D.A. Frank, R. Hingson et al. 1989. Effects of Maternal Marijuana and Cocaine Use on Fetal Growth. *New England Journal of Medicine* 320(12):762–8.

Compulsory Treatment for Drug-dependent Persons: Justifications for a Public Health Approach to Drug Dependency

LAWRENCE O. GOSTIN

American Society of Law and Medicine

MY GOAL IS TO PROPOSE A PROGRAM FOR compulsory treatment for persons who are dependent on illicit drugs and who can benefit from services. Compulsory treatment involves a serious diminution in autonomy and liberty. Thus, a heavy burden rests on proponents to justify compulsory treatment by careful reasoning and specific evidence (Aronowitz 1967). I will seek to accomplish this by demonstrating benefits both to the individual and to society, and by showing the efficacy of compulsory treatment. I will then propose a specific program for effecting the policy of compulsory treatment.

In making these proposals, I am acutely sensitive to the historic failures of compulsory treatment,[1] and to the current beliefs of many, perhaps most, drug-treatment specialists that compulsory treatment makes little sense in a political environment where even those who want treatment cannot receive it (National Institute on Drug Abuse 1987). The need for, and the right to, drug treatment services therefore must be integrally connected to any mandatory program.

I will describe and analyze two different forms of mandatory treatment: civil commitment and diversion from the criminal justice system. A clear theoretical distinction exists between these two forms of mandatory treatment, although in practice they overlap and the terms are of-

---

[1] Despite the creation of civil commitment statutes throughout the United States in the 1960s, no state is currently committing significant numbers of persons for drug treatment.

ten used interchangeably. Civil commitment authorizes the state to confine a person for treatment with due process, but without bringing a criminal charge. Diversion from the criminal justice system involves diverting a person already charged with, or convicted of, an offense from indictment, trial, or sentencing.

I am often encouraged by my colleagues to address the question of legalization in *any* article I write on the drug epidemic (Gostin 1991a,b). Civil libertarians, in particular, argue that the issue of mandatory treatment cannot arise unless what Joel Feinberg has termed the "clutchability" of the state to assert control over the drug user has first been determined (Feinberg 1970). Put another way, if the state does not have the constitutional authority to prohibit and criminalize the use or sale of drugs, then surely it has no authority to restrict the person's liberty for the purposes of mandatory treatment.

I am both a pragmatist and a realist. My convictions are as follows:

1. The academic debate on legalization of drugs, while conceptually useful, has so dominated discourse that it has actually impeded creative ideas for a public health approach within the extant legal system.
2. The critical data needed to come to a conclusion on legalization are unavailable and perhaps unknowable (e.g., whether drug use, morbidity, mortality, and criminality would increase, or decrease, and by how much).
3. In any event, the current academic discourse on legalization will not lead to decriminalization of drugs in the foreseeable future.

The constitutionality of imposing criminal sanctions against persons who use or sell drugs is so well established that successive Supreme Courts have dismissed constitutional challenges without argument and with a single phrase.[2] The Court's implicit reasoning is that drug use

---

[2] See, e.g., *Whipple v. Martinson*, 256 U.S. 41, 45 (1921). ("There can be no question of the authority of the state to regulate the . . . use of dangerous habit forming drugs. This power is so manifest in the interest of public health and welfare, that it is unnecessary to enter a discussion of it."); *Robinson v. California*, 370 U.S. 660 (1962) (quoting *Whipple* with approval); *Powell v. Texas*, 392 U.S. 514 (1968) (upholding constitutionality of criminalizing public drunkenness); *Harmelin v. Michigan*, 1991 LEXIS 3816 (June 27, 1991), Kennedy J. concurring. (Harmelin's suggestion that simple possession of cocaine was nonviolent and victimless is "false to the point of absurdity.")

manifestly contributes to morbidity, mortality, and associated criminal behavior, rendering the state's power to control beyond question.[3]

Two separate, but important, questions are worthy of study. First, do the barely spoken assumptions of the Supreme Court about the constitutionality of criminal sanctions against drug use withstand jurisprudential analysis? Second, even if the state has the constitutional authority to criminalize drug use or sale, should the state exercise its criminal jurisdiction? This requires further policy assessment that carefully balances the health benefits of prohibition, with its economic and social costs, and the human rights burdens. Addressing either of these two important issues in this article would be distracting to the arguments on mandatory treatment in lieu of criminal punishment, and the allotted space would permit only superficial treatment of the weighty social problems raised by legalization.

The Advent and Demise of "Civil" Commitment

The Supreme Court in *Robinson v. California* held that a state statute making it an imprisonable offense to "be addicted to the use of narcotics" inflicts a cruel and unusual punishment in violation of the Eighth and Fourteenth Amendments.[4] The Court would not allow criminal punishment for the "status" or "chronic condition" of being a narcotics addict; a status offense would render an addict subject to prosecution "at any time before he reforms."[5] Any law that made it a criminal offense to have a disease such as a drug dependency, mental illness, or leprosy "would doubtless be uniformly thought to be [unconstitutional]." This strong statement, however, did not prevent the Court from ruling only six years later that it was constitutional for a state to convict an alcoholic for public drunkenness.[6] Although the Court argued that the person was convicted because of his *behavior* of appearing

---

[3] Harmelin, op. cit. ("Studies demonstrate the grave threat that illegal drugs, particularly cocaine, pose to society in terms of violence, crime, and social displacement.")

[4] *Robinson v. California*, 370 U.S. 660 (1962).

[5] *Robinson v. California*, 370 U.S. at 666.

[6] *Powell v. Texas*, 392 U.S. 514 (1968).

in public, not his *status* of alcoholism, this comes perilously close to punishing a person because of his physical dependence.

Oddly, the Supreme Court's rejection of punishment for addicts in *Robinson* paved the way for federal and state statutes designed to involuntarily confine drug-dependent persons. The purpose of this confinement was expressed as "therapeutic" and not "punitive." More than 40 years before *Robinson*, the Supreme Court ruled that "there can be no question of the authority of the state in the exercise of its police power to regulate the . . . use of dangerous habit forming drugs. . . . The right to exercise this power is so manifest in the interest of public health and welfare, that it is unnecessary to enter a discussion of it."[7] The Supreme Court in *Robinson* said that states could constitutionally establish "a program of compulsory treatment for those addicted to narcotics," including "periods of involuntary confinement" enforced through penal sanctions.[8]

Although the California commitment statute had already been adopted in 1961, the dicta in *Robinson* provided the impetus for the enactment of federal and state programs of mandatory treatment (Aronowitz 1967). Governor Nelson Rockefeller specifically referred to the *Robinson* decision in urging the adoption of New York's civil commitment statute (Rockefeller 1966). By the mid-1960s, the federal government,[9] California,[10] Massachusetts,[11] and New York[12] each had enacted major civil commitment statutes for "narcotics addicts."[13]

The statutes enacted in these four major jurisdictions were broadly similar in approach, but differed in their specific application. All the statutes used the term "civil commitment" (Abromovsky and McCarthy 1977; Aronowitz 1967). The courts held that confinement had "none of

---

[7] *Whipple v. Martinson*, 256 U.S. 41, 45 (1921).

[8] *Robinson v. California*, 370 U.S. at 665.

[9] *Narcotic Addict Rehabilitation Act of 1966*, P. L. 89-793 (Nov. 8, 1966).

[10] Cal. Welfare and Institutions Code, paras. 3000–3005 (West 1966).

[11] Mass. Ann. Laws, ch. 111A, paras. 1–10 (Supp. 1965).

[12] N.Y. Mental Hygiene Law, paras, 200–17 (McKinney Supp. 1966).

[13] Earlier civil commitment statutes had been enacted in the 1950s in such states as Alabama, Arkansas, Delaware, Georgia, and Maryland. These statutes, however, were used very little, apparently because relatives refused to initiate commitment, and few specialized treatment facilities were established. At that time much of the "treatment" for drug dependency took place in the mental health system (Aronowitz 1967).

the attributes of a criminal or penal sanction,"[14] and was "not to be considered as a punishment for a crime" (Ginnow 1974).[15] Yet these "civil commitment" statutes actually encompassed at least three distinct forms of mandatory treatment, some of which were closely connected to the criminal process[16]:

1. *pure civil commitment,* where the person was detained for mandatory treatment not connected with any current arrest or charge for a criminal offense
2. *civil commitment in lieu of a criminal trial,* where eligible persons were detained for mandatory treatment after being arrested and charged with a criminal offense, and the treatment took place in lieu of continued prosecution of the offense, that is, mandatory treatment while a criminal charge was held in abeyance
3. *civil commitment following a criminal conviction,* where the person convicted received mandatory treatment in lieu of a prison sentence or other criminal disposition

True civil commitment, as used in the mental health context, would be confinement without any connection to an arrest, charge, or conviction for a criminal offense.

These mandatory treatment statutes applied to persons who, by reason of repeated use of illicit drugs, were addicted or in "imminent danger of becoming addicted." The statutes appeared, even then, to limit confinement to persons who were not merely casual users, but who were emotionally or physically dependent on drugs (Gulick and Kimbrough 1990).[17]

In order for a drug-dependent person to be eligible for mandatory treatment in lieu of a trial or sentencing, he or she had to come within the specifications of the statute. Typically, persons charged or convicted

---

[14] *Showers v. Lloyd,* 296 F. Supp. 441 (D.C. Cal. 1969); *ex parte De La O,* 28 Cal. Rptr. 489, 378 P.2d 793 (1963); *in re Whisaker,* 134 F. Supp. 864 (D.C. 1955).
[15] *People v. Reynoso,* 50 Cal. Rptr. 468, 412 P. 2d 812 (1966).
[16] All the statutes, except Massachusetts, also permitted addicts to be committed on their own petition.
[17] *People v. Victor,* 42 Cal. Rptr. 199, 398 P. 2d 391 (1965).

of violent offenses, or who had a record of such offenses, were ineligible for mandatory treatment.[18]

Eligibility for mandatory treatment for persons charged or convicted of an offense was determined in the criminal proceeding.[19] However, prior to mandatory treatment, the person had a right to a *civil* hearing when the sole issue was his dependency on drugs. The civil proceedings, however, had such an immediate effect upon his personal liberty that the person was entitled to a full due process hearing, including the right to counsel, notice, and the right to compel and question witnesses.[20]

Mandatory treatment meant that persons were confined in specialized drug-treatment facilities with the goal of attaining total abstinence from drugs. If a drug-dependent person was deemed ready for the next phase of treatment, he or she would be released from the facility as an outpatient. Once released, the person was subject to intensive supervision similar to that required of a person on parole. This might involve specified living arrangements such as a group home, periodic visits from supervisors, and drug testing. Breach of any condition would require the person to be readmitted to an inpatient facility.[21]

Persons were committed for mandatory treatment for indefinite periods of time, subject to a statutory maximum. The prescribed maximum periods depended upon whether the person was charged or convicted of an offense, and differed under each statute. Maximum detention for those charged with or convicted of an offense ranged from three to ten years (Myers 1974). The duration of detention, within the statutory minimums or maximums, was a medical rather than a judicial decision.[22]

---

[18] *U.S. v. Taylor*, 689 F.2d 1107 (D.C. Cir. 1982); *Macias v. U.S.*, 484 F.2d 1292 (5th Cir. 1972); *Neria v. U.S.*, 493 F.2d 913 (5th Cir. 1974); *People v. Navarro*, 102 Cal. Rptr. 137, 497 P.2d 481 (1972); *U.S. v. Krehbiel*, 493 F.2d 497 (9th Cir. 1974).

[19] *People v. Strickland*, 52 Cal. Rptr. 215 (1966).

[20] *People v. Moore*, 76 Cal. Rptr. 150 (1969); *People v. Malins*, 101 Cal. Rptr. 270 (1972); *People ex rel. McNeill v. Morrow*, 302 N.Y.S. 2d 933 (1969); *People v. Fuller*, 300 N.Y.S. 2d 102, 248 N.E. 2d 17 (1969); *Pannell v. Jones*, 368 N.Y.S. 2d 467, 329 N.E. 2d 159 (1975).

[21] The person still had civil rights, however, and had *some* due process protections before he was compelled to be reinstitutionalized. *Re Bye*, 115 Cal. Rptr. 382, 524 P.2d 854, cert. denied, 420 U.S. 996 (1975). *Re Murillo*, 110 Cal. Rptr. 494, superseded 115 Cal. Rptr. 393, 524 P.2d 865 (1974).

[22] *Baughman v. U.S.*, 450 F.2d 1217 (8th Cir. 1971).

Successful termination of mandatory treatment meant a great deal to persons because it affected their liberty and determined whether any pending criminal charges would be dismissed. Persons were therefore entitled to a periodic hearing on termination, but it often involved a pro forma review of affidavits or depositions.[23]

Mandatory treatment statutes were widely upheld as constitutional whether[24] or not[25] the person had been charged with, or convicted of, a crime (Schopler et al. 1964). The courts upheld these statutes as a valid exercise of the police power because they were reasonably necessary to protect the public health and welfare.[26]

Encouraged by the courts' approval of existing laws, numerous states enacted mandatory treatment statutes in the years to follow (i.e., from the mid-1960s through the 1970s). Although a few states repealed their statutes,[27] today some 18 states and the federal government have mandatory drug-treatment laws.[28] However, the enthusiasm for mandatory treatment rapidly waned throughout the 1980s until now, where it is, for all intents and purposes, a relic of the past, never utilized. The National Conference of Commissioners on Uniform State Law (NCCUSL) published a lengthy model treatment statute in 1973.[29] The Uniform Act was coolly received by the states, and not one has adopted it in whole or in part (*American Jurisprudence 2d* 1990).

Remarkably little has been written about the reasons mandatory treatment was devised with such promise, used in such earnest, and then quietly allowed to wither—all in the space of a couple of decades. Were a post mortem to be written, undoubtedly it would mention several factors responsible for the demise of mandatory treatment. Certainly, the advent of methadone maintenance enabled treatment to take place on a voluntary basis in the community, as opposed to compulsory admission to an institution. Many heroin addicts simply did not need to

---

[23] *U.S. v. Thornton*, 344 F.Supp. 249 (D.C. Del. 1972).

[24] *In re Trummer*, 36 Cal. Rptr. 281, 388 P.2d 177 (1964); *Narcotic Addiction Control Commission v. James*, 285 N.Y.S. 2d 793, 29 A.D. 2d 72 (1967).

[25] *Ex parte Raner*, 30 Cal. Rptr. 814, 381 P.2d 638 (1963).

[26] *Blinder v. State Department of Justice*, 101 Cal. Rptr. 635 (1972).

[27] For example, Connecticut in 1990.

[28] AK, CA, GA, HI, IN, MA, MI, ND, NV, NY, RI, SC, SD, WV, WI (NJ, NM, and TX are for juveniles only). See also Anderson and Keilitz (1991).

[29] Uniform Drug Dependence Treatment and Rehabilitation Act, published by NCCUSL in 1973. See 25 Am. Jur. 2d. Supp. para 75 (April 1990).

be forced to take methadone. Apart from methadone, adequate treatment facilities were never established. Authorities simply stopped using mandatory treatment because specialized treatment facilities were not available. Today, the U.S. Public Health Service has virtually abandoned any attempt to provide treatment as a diversion from the criminal justice system.

Connected to this reason was the growing belief in the 1970s that "treatment does not work." Well-publicized analyses of treatment outcomes declared that treatment was valueless both in stopping or even impeding drug use, and in stemming associated crime (Martinson 1974).

The hope of effective treatment began to turn sour, and drug dependence began to be viewed as a hopeless, chronically relapsing condition without any effective intervention. In addition, there was the pronounced shift in ideology from the 1960s through the 1980s. The ideology of social welfarism that emerged in the 1960s rested on the central belief that drug dependence was a disease amenable to public health interventions. David Musto (1989) characterized the period as follows: "Reform-minded lawyers, academics, and physicians found the harsh penalties toward addicts to be inhumane. Rather than depriving addicts of heroin, heroin should be provided them. Rather than jailing addicts, they should be hospitalized. . . ."

By the 1980s, drug users were beginning to be perceived as more bad than ill, and law enforcement and criminal punishment began to emerge as the predominant public strategy (U.S. Office of National Drug Policy 1990a). By the end of the 1980s, the policies then in vogue of user accountability and zero tolerance made it acceptable to direct the state's formidable powers toward drug-dependent persons themselves (Gostin 1991a). Indeed, this shift in political ideology can be traced in the expenditure of the federal budget devoted to treatment and prevention compared with law enforcement, interdiction, and eradication. Two decades ago, more than 50 percent of the total drug-abuse budget went to treatment and prevention; it was reduced to between 18 and 27 percent during the Reagan years in the 1980s, and is approximately 29 percent for Fiscal Year 1991 (Brecher 1989; Shenon 1990; U.S. Office of National Drug Policies 1990b). Some policy makers today are calling for at least half of the drug budget to be spent on treatment and prevention (Majority Staffs of the Senate Judiciary Committee 1990; Pear 1990).

A final reason for the disuse of mandatory treatment probably rested with the fact that the laws themselves were out of touch with contemporary thinking about the legitimacy of the state's power to confine, which reflected the influence of the civil libertarian challenge to the agencies of social control. The premise of these laws was that it was acceptable to label mandatory treatment as "civil" and shelter the entire process from a hard-headed review of the philosophical purposes, public health efficacy, and human rights aspects of the confinement[30] (Abromovsky and McCarthy 1977).

Throughout the 1970s, the federal courts were making revolutionary changes in the analogous concept of civil commitment of the mentally ill (Brakel, Parry, and Weiner 1985; Perlin 1989; Note 1975). Courts required rigorous procedural due process prior to civil commitment of persons with mental illness or mental retardation;[31] extended the right to due process to adolescents voluntarily committed to institutions;[32] required recent dangerous overt behavior as a basis for commitment;[33] refused to allow purely custodial confinement in the absence of treatment for nondangerous persons;[34] and provided a limited right to refuse treatment for institutionalized persons.[35] Drug-dependency statutes were clearly deficient in the rights afforded to individuals when measured against the mental health decisions of the federal courts.

Whatever the real reasons for the demise of mandatory treatment, it is certain that many drug-dependent people charged or convicted of offenses preferred treatment to criminal punishment. (Some offenders charged with minor offenses, of course, preferred a noncustodial sentence or a short term of imprisonment to indeterminant periods of treatment.) Much of the litigation of the time was targeted at federal or state authorities who refused to divert them to treatment[36] or simply argued

---

[30] Uniform Drug Dependence Treatment and Rehabilitation Act. 1973. Prefatory Note.
[31] *Lessard v. Schmidt*, 349 F.Supp. 1078 (E.D. Wisc. 1972).
[32] *Parham, Commissioner, Department of Human Resources of Georgia v. J.R.*, 442 U.S. 584 (1979) (the procedures afforded to adolescents voluntarily admitted, however, were far less rigorous than those afforded to those subject to compulsory civil commitment).
[33] *Lessard v. Schmidt*, 349 F. Supp. 1078 (E.D. Wisc. 1972).
[34] *O'Connor v. Donaldson*, 422 U.S. 563 (1975); *Pennhurst State School and Hospital v. Halderman*, 451 U.S. 1 (1981).
[35] *Mills v. Rodgers*, 457 U.S. 291 (1982).
[36] *U.S. v. Palmer*, 369 F.Supp. 1030 (D.C. Cal. 1974); *U.S. v. Leazer*, 460 F.2d 864 (D.C. Cir. 1972).

that no treatment facilities were available.[37] Drug-dependent people saw treatment as a constitutional entitlement, whereas the government and courts saw it as discretionary.[38]

The Advent and Demise of Diversion from Criminal Justice

The rehabilitative principle of diversion from the criminal justice system reached its high-water mark in the decade beginning in the mid-1960s. The impetus for the wider use of rehabilitative diversion was provided by the President's Commission on Law Enforcement and Administration of Justice (1967). The commission observed that "in the century we have built our drug control policies around the twin judgements that drug abuse was an evil to be suppressed and that this could most effectively be done by the application of criminal enforcement and penal sanctions" (1967, 134, 222). The premise of these policies had been that the more certain and severe the punishment (typically, minimum mandatory sentences and ineligibility for suspension of sentence, probation, and parole) the greater the impact on drug use and crime. However, the commission found the effects of mandatory minimum sentences to be inconclusive, and probably harmful to the public health and safety. It recommended explicit policies for early identification of drug users and diversion to community resources for treatment. This could be accomplished through clearly stated criteria and procedures for diversion, greater prosecutorial and judicial discretion to opt for treatment, and a greatly expanded network of rehabilitative services.

The American Law Institute's Model Code of Pre-arraignment Procedure (para 320.5[d]) followed the commission's approach. Parties could

---

[37] *U.S. v. Butler*, 676 F. Supp. 88 (W.D. Pa. 1988). This issue even made it to the Supreme Court, which upheld the constitutionality of the Narcotic Rehabilitation Act (NARA) even though it excluded violent offenders from the opportunity for treatment. *Marshall v. U.S.*, 414 U.S. 417 (1974). Justice Marshall filed a dissent in which he said: "It simply makes no sense to deem an addict a 'hardened criminal' unworthy or unsuited for treatment simply because he has engaged in criminal activity." 414 U.S. at 437. Justice Marshall quotes a Congressman in the debate on NARA arguing that it is like "building a sanitorium to treat tuberculosis, and then refusing admittance to patients with a contagious disease." 112 Cong. Rec. 11812 (1976).

[38] *U.S. v. Butler*, 676 F.Supp. 88 (W.D. Pa. 1988); *People v. Victor*, 42 Cal. Rptr. 199, 398 P.2d 391 (1965); *U.S. v. Barrow*, 540 F.2d 204 (4th Cir. 1976).

agree to suspend prosecution for up to one year on condition that the defendant enter a rehabilitation program that may include treatment, counseling, training, or education. State statutes specifically authorizing diversion were almost uniformly held constitutional (Landis 1981).

Just as prosecutors began to reject the idea of civil commitment from the mid-1970s onward, so too did they turn against the rehabilitative ideal of diversion. Nelson Rockefeller's (1973) call for laws making punishment for drug users much more severe in order to "close all avenues for escaping the full force of this sentence" was symbolic of the change in heart. Only seven years earlier, Rockefeller (1966) had appeared before the U.S. Senate Committee on the Judiciary arguing for civil commitment as an alternative to punishment.

There followed a sustained effort by federal and state governments, reinforced through the Reagan years and up to the present, systematically to dismantle rehabilitation as a legitimate goal of criminal justice. This had the effect of virtually foreclosing opportunities for diversion for many drug law violators and other seriously drug-dependent persons. The so-called tough drug laws had two elements. First was the explicit prohibition or restriction on parole, probation, or suspension of sentence in cases of violent crimes (Smith 1980). The second required convicted drug offenders to be sentenced to a mandatory,[39] or a minimum,[40] prison term (Williams 1977). The courts uniformly upheld such statutes based upon the sovereign power of the state legislature to prescribe the penalty for commission of a crime.[41]

Even in some jurisdictions that did not formally adopt tough drug laws, prosecutors decided to exclude drug-law violators from diversion programs. One state supreme court upheld a district attorney's blanket policy of excluding all drug-law violators from diversion programs.[42]

---

[39] E.g., *U.S. v. Holmes*, 838 F.2d 1175 (11th Cir. 1988); *U.S. v. Brady*, 680 F.Supp. (W.D. Ky 1988); *State v. Pacheco*, 588 P.2d 830 (Ariz. 1978).
[40] E.g., *State v. Benitez*, 395 So. 2d 514 (Fla. 1981); *Draughn v. State*, 539 P.2d 1389 (Okla Crim. 1975). In a mandatory minimum sentence, the legislature prescribes a sentence without the possibility of parole until the person serves the minimum term. The legislature divests judges and probation officials of discretion to forego incarceration or suspend sentences (Glick 1979; Lambiotte 1987).
[41] E.g., *State v. Johnson*, 206 N.J. Super. 341, 502 A.2d 1149 (1985); *Scott v. State*, 479 So. 2d 1343 (Ala. App. 1985); *People v. Smith*, 414 N.E. 2d 1281 (Ill. 1980); see *Harmelin v. Michigan*, 1991 LEXIS 3816 (June 27, 1991).
[42] *State v. Greenlee*, 620 P.2d. 1132 (S.Ct. Kan. 1980).

The court based its decision on the "seriousness of the drug problem in society today, particularly its devastating effect upon young people."[43]

The tough drug laws make it legally difficult or impossible to use creative alternative sentencing such as to an inpatient or outpatient treatment facility. They also provide a marked disincentive for plea bargaining because the judge has little discretion in sentencing. This does not prevent imaginative prosecutors from finding ways around these legal constraints, for example, by informally staying the charge in exchange for a promise to receive treatment. However, such informal approaches depend upon the flexibility of prosecutors and the availability of alternative services. In a political climate where treatment is seen as "coddling" drug users, district attorneys (many of whom are elected) and their political bosses will not countenance use of rehabilitation in circumventing tough minimum sentencing laws (U.S. Office of National Drug Policy 1990a).

Singling out all drug offenders, including minor offenders, for harsh minimum prison terms treats them less favorably than other offenders and also precludes their rehabilitation. One dissenting judge in the supreme court of Kansas could not understand why a 22-year-old first offender convicted of unlawful delivery of 11 ounces of marijuana should receive a mandatory prison term, while the court maintained discretion to suspend the sentence of a person convicted of murder, armed robbery, or rape, even after a previous felony conviction.[44] Nor was it possible to provide treatment for the drug offender to help him overcome his dependency.

Although courts were prepared to uphold most draconian antidrug laws, one state legislature went too far. The supreme court of Michigan held that a state law providing a mandatory minimum prison sentence of 20 years for selling or giving away any quantity of marijuana was so excessive that it inflicted cruel and unusual punishment.[45]

Challenges to tough drug laws premised on the Eighth Amendment's proscription against cruel and unusual punishment took a major setback

---

[43] Id. at 1139.

[44] Id.

[45] *People v. Lorentzen*, 194 N.W. 2d 827 (Mich. S.Ct. 1972); *People v. Sinclair*, 194 N.W. 2d 878 (Mich. S.Ct. 1972) (overturning mandatory sentence for possession of two marijuana cigarettes). Still, most courts upheld statutes providing stiff penalties for simple possession of marijuana (Williams 1979).

with the Supreme Court's decision in *Harmelin v. Michigan*.[46] Harmelin was convicted of possessing more than 650 grams of cocaine and sentenced to a mandatory term of life in prison without the possibility of parole. Justice Scalia, delivering part of the opinion of the Court, rejected Harmelin's claim that his sentence is unconstitutional because of its mandatory nature, allowing no opportunity to consider "mitigating factors." Justice Scalia found no support in the text and history of the Eighth Amendment for the proposition that judges must maintain discretion in sentencing. Severe mandatory penalties may be cruel, but they are not unusual, having been employed throughout the nation's history.

Justice Kennedy, delivering another part of the Court's opinion, accepted a narrow proportionality principle in the Eighth Amendment — namely, that extreme sentences that are grossly disproportionate to the gravity of the offense are unconstitutional. Justice Kennedy recognized that a sentence of life imprisonment without parole is the second most severe penalty permitted by law. Nevertheless, the Court did not regard the sentence as disproportionate to Harmelin's crime of possessing more than 650 grams of cocaine. "His suggestion that the crime was nonviolent and victimless is false to the point of absurdity. Studies demonstrate the grave threat that illegal drugs, particularly cocaine, pose to society in terms of violence, crime, and social displacement."[47] The Court's decision suggests that it will grant "substantial deference" to state determinations imposing mandatory minimum sentences on drug offenders.

Justifications for Compulsory Treatment

The choice among the three most discussed options for a national drug strategy — criminal punishment, compulsory treatment, and legalization — should be based upon the method that would best achieve a reduction in morbidity and mortality caused by the drug epidemic and

---

[46] 1991 U.S. LEXIS 3816 (June 27, 1991).

[47] Justice Kennedy said a clear nexus between drug use and crime exists: (1) drug-induced changes in physiology may lead to criminal behavior; (2) drug users commit crime to obtain money to buy drugs; and (3) violent crimes occur as part of the drug business or culture. 1991 U.S. LEXIS 3816, 77.

the associated needleborne HIV epidemic (Gostin 1991a,b). The justification for compulsory treatment can be centered between the two extremes of legalization (Nadelmann 1989) and criminal punishment (Wilson 1990). Compulsory treatment, unlike the other two options, faces the public health dimensions of drug dependency head on by providing interventions that demonstrably lower drug use and its associated morbidity, mortality, and criminality. A public health approach to drug dependency emerges as critically important.

Avoiding the Harms of the Criminal Justice System

The declared policy of a "Drug Free America by 1995,"[48] supported by an ever-widening net of detection through drug screening and law enforcement, is a fruitless, impractical endeavor destined to overwhelm the criminal justice system. It becomes virtually impossible to present a credible law-enforcement program with an estimated 28-million people having used illicit drugs in 1988 alone (National Institute of Drug Abuse 1989). The 850,000 people arrested each year for drug offenses represent only a fraction of current drug users; more than three-quarters of these arrests are for simple possession, typically marijuana, and not for manufacturing, importing, or selling (Bureau of Justice Statistics 1989).

The Fiscal Year 1991 federal budget projected a total of just over $10.6 billion for the National Drug Control Strategy, more than 70 percent of which was designated for law enforcement and interdiction (U.S. Office of National Drug Policy 1990b). Federal monies devoted to drug law enforcement have quadrupled within the last five years (National Drug Enforcement Policy Board 1987; Shenon 1990). Nationally, arrests for drug law violations increased from 162,177 in 1968, or 112 per 100,000 people, to 850,034 in 1989, or about 450 per 100,000 people (Reinhold 1989).

The organs of the criminal justice system (law enforcement, the courts, and corrections), designed to provide swift, sure punishment, have become so clogged by the weight of cases that they cease to function, and require increasing resources to provide an effective deterrence and minimally humane conditions. Narcotic prosecutions in the federal

---

[48] Drug Free America by 1995 Authorization Act, P.L. 100-690, § 7603.

courts have risen 229 percent in the past decade, with drug law cases representing 40 to 65 percent of all criminal trials (Bureau of Justice Statistics 1988; Labaton 1990). Fifty-eight percent of all drug cases filed in federal district courts, moreover, were for sale or possession of marijuana (Bureau of Justice Statistics 1989). The result is that courts cannot manage the drug caseload, which results in inordinate delays in the prosecution of other criminal offenses. The impact of delays on civil and family cases is compounded because such cases have lower priorities than criminal cases.

The number of prisoners in federal or state corrections systems at the end of 1989 reached a record 710,054. The net increase in 1989 of 13 percent also set a new record, which translates into 1,600 new bed spaces per week. The growth in prison population in the 1980s was 115 percent. During this period, the per capita incarceration rate rose more than 97 percent from 139 per 100,000 to 274 per 100,000 residents. The federal prison system is currently operating at 63 percent above full capacity, while the state systems are, on average, between 7 and 27 percent above capacity (Bureau of Justice Statistics 1990). Nearly 40 states are operating under court orders as a result of overcrowding (Malcolm 1991).

Overall, a massive growth in the criminal justice system has emerged over the last 15 years to the point where 3.3 million individuals were under criminal justice supervision on the designated census days in 1987, compared with 1.3 million in 1976 (Institute of Medicine 1990, 113–14). In some poor, urban communities, one out of every ten black males is under criminal justice supervision, the majority of whom are either drug law violators or drug abusers.

Mandatory treatment would significantly ease the pressure on the organs of the criminal justice system by avoiding the heavy costs of prosecution, trial, and imprisonment. Treatment in lieu of prosecution would also allow government to shift resources currently placed into expanding law enforcement, the judiciary, and corrections into treatment expansion.

A Public Health Approach to Drug Dependency

Mandatory treatment, as a diversion from the criminal justice system, stands the best chance of reducing the morbidity, mortality, and criminality associated with the drug epidemic. Diversion programs provide an ideal opportunity to identify cases of seriously drug-dependent people; to provide treatment for those who otherwise would not attend public health intervention programs; and to require attendance for a period of time that maximizes the opportunities for success.

The criminal justice system provides a key forum for an effective public health program (Anglin and Hser 1991a). Because of the clandestine nature of their conditions, drug dependent persons are exceedingly hard to reach (Feldman and Biernacki 1988). This creates an obstacle to providing them with education on risk reduction, counseling, and treatment. Yet because police, prosecutors, and the courts have significant contact with the drug-dependent population, they constitute a valuable resource for providing services. Voluntary anonymous urine specimens from a sample of male arrestees in 22 cities reveal that at least 50 percent have recently used cocaine (Centers for Disease Control 1989). This figure, moreover, is an underestimate because the screening program limits the participation of persons who are arrested on charges of possession or sale of drugs. The finding that at least 20 percent of drug injectors in this study reported sharing needles indicates a continuing risk for spread of HIV and other bloodborne infections. Between 75 and 83 percent of incarcerated persons reported that they had used drugs in the past, and between one-third and two-fifths reported that they were under the influence of an illegal drug at the time of the offense (Bureau of Justice Statistics 1988; Office of Justice Programs 1989; Office of Technology Assessment 1990, 92–3).

Many prisoners even take drugs after they are incarcerated and often share injection equipment with other prisoners (Institute of Medicine 1990, 17). One rural prison system reported that 27 percent of the inmate samples tested positive for illicit drugs. Although the prison system was able to lower this rate to 9 percent with routine drug screening and punishments, it indicates that drug use among incarcerated inmates can be substantial (Vigdal and Stadler 1989).

Despite the large number of drug-dependent persons who come into contact with the criminal justice system, there are few comprehensive treatment programs. One national survey found that only 4 percent of state prison inmates received any treatment, and almost half of the nation's state prisons were not served by any identifiable drug abuse treatment program (Tims 1986). Some report slightly higher provision of correctional treatment (Bureau of Prisons 1990), but at least two-thirds of prison treatment involves nonintensive periodic group or individual talk sessions. This level of intervention is probably not intensive enough to effect any lasting behavioral changes (Institute of Medicine 1990, 119). For many in the criminal justice system, routine urine testing is the only "treatment" provided.

It makes little sense to process large numbers of drug-dependent persons, at exorbitant cost, through prosecution, trial, and imprisonment without systematic efforts to lessen their physical and psychological dependence on drugs. Drug-dependent persons are subject to the authority of the state. Yet many offenders are released early from overcrowded prisons, having learned nothing — except perhaps some criminal behaviors from other inmates (Malcolm 1991; Reinhold 1989). It is disturbing to observe that between one-half and three-fifths of those inmates who use major drugs did not do so until *after* their first arrest (Office of Justice Programs 1988).

"Treatment Works"

Criticism and calls for rejection of criminal diversion and correctional treatment programs peaked with a review article by Martinson (1974) concluding that treatment does not reduce drug use or recidivism and asking, "Does nothing work?" Five years later, Martinson (1979) renounced his position, stating that the benefits of treatment are "simply too overwhelming to ignore," but the severe retrenchment of treatment had already begun to occur.

Treatment outcome data, to be sure, are compromised by the lack of controlled clinical trials.[49] Much of the early research also focused on heroin rather than cocaine dependency. Despite the methodologic concerns, recent authoritative reviews of a large number of outcome studies conclude that treatment, including compulsory treatment, reduces the use of drugs, sharing of injection equipment, as well as criminal behavior (Institute of Medicine 1990; Office of Technology Assessment 1990; National Criminal Justice Association 1990; National Association of State Alcohol and Drug Abuse Directors 1990). Some studies have reported

---

[49] A wide array of factors complicates the assessment of treatment effectiveness: the chronic relapsing patterns of drug use, the heterogeneous composition of drug users, and the problem of patient self-selection of treatment and treatment modalities (Office of Technology Assessment 1990, 62–4).

similar levels of treatment efficacy for cocaine abuse (Simpson et al. 1986; Hubbard et al. 1989).

Much of the collective knowledge of treatment effectiveness derives from two large-scale, federally funded, longitudinal studies: Treatment Outcome Prospective Study (TOPS) (Hubbard et al. 1989) and the National Treatment System Based on the Drug Abuse Reporting Program (DARP) (Simpson and Sells 1990). A third large-scale national prospective study, the Drug Abuse Treatment Outcome Study (DATOS), is underway.

TOPS and DARP, together with numerous smaller studies (McLellan et al. 1982; National Institute on Drug Abuse 1983), demonstrated that each of the three primary treatment modalities were effective in causing significant and enduring declines in drug use and criminal behaviors — methadone maintenance, therapeutic communities (TCs), and outpatient drug-free (ODF) programs.

Methadone maintenance allows an "illicit short-acting opiate administered with needles to be replaced with a legal long-acting safe, and orally administered substance" (Zweben and Sorensen 1988). The Office of Technology Assessment (1990, 76) observes that the "consistency of the scientific literature regarding the safety, efficacy, and effectiveness of methadone is overwhelming, yet some still consider methadone a controversial treatment modality." In controlled clinical studies, heroin-dependent, heavily criminally involved populations who were randomly assigned to methadone or a control condition "demonstrated clinically important and statistically significant differences in favor of methadone on the gauges of drug use, criminality, and engagement in socially productive roles such as employment, education, or responsible child raising" (Institute of Medicine 1990, 143). Methadone has the highest retention rate of all treatment modalities, and lowers human immunodeficency virus (HIV) risk behavior by significantly reducing the number of injections and sharing of equipment (Cooper 1989). Although several pharmacotherapies such as buprenorphine are currently being evaluated (Mello et al. 1989; Office of Technology Assessment 1990, 78–9), the absence of any established efficacious agent is having dire consequences for cocaine-dependent persons and, if they are HIV infected, their sexual partners.

Therapeutic communities are "residential programs with expected stays of 9 to 12 months, phasing into independent residence" (Institute of Medicine 1990, 14). Therapeutic community clients end virtually all illicit drug taking and other criminal behavior while in residence and perform better than those not in treatment (in terms of reduced drug use and criminal activity and increased social productivity) after discharge (Institute of Medicine 1990, 188–9). Studies that evaluate progress upon completing the program report that 30 percent achieve absolute success (no drugs, no crime), with improvement rates ranging from 50 to 60 percent (Office of Technology Assessment 1990, 83). Retention rates, however, were poor, and success is directly related to length of time in treatment, with a minimum stay of three to nine months being desirable (Institute of Medicine 1990, 156–63).

Outpatient drug-free (ODF) programs display a great deal of heterogeneity, and range from one-time assessments and drop-in, or "rap," centers to virtual outpatient therapeutic communities with daily psychotherapy and counseling. The TOPS and DARP studies suggest similarly favorable outcomes for drug users attending outpatient drug-free programs. Yet evaluation is significantly hampered by the lack of uniformity in ODF programs and the small number of clients served.

The quality of evidence and the cost effectiveness of the three major modalities suggest a priority ranking of methadone maintenance, TCs, and ODF. Yet the Institute of Medicine (1990, 186) points out that the order of expenditures for these modalities is exactly the reverse of the order of knowledge about their effectiveness. Well-designed research on therapeutic communities, particularly ODFs, is essential.

Compulsory Versus Voluntary Treatment

A striking research consensus exists that the single greatest predictor of favorable treatment outcomes is the length of time in treatment (Cooper 1989; Hubbard et al. 1989). This bodes well for mandating programs that require minimum stays. The Institute of Medicine (1990, 119) aptly observed:

> Contrary to earlier fears among clinicians, criminal justice pressure does not necessarily vitiate treatment effectiveness and probably improves retention. Yet, the most important reason to consider . . . [compulsory treatment] is not that coercion may improve the results of treatment but that treatment may improve the rather dismal record of plain coercion — particularly imprisonment. . . .

The intuition that compulsory treatment will fail because drug-dependent people must be self-motivated in order to benefit (Schottenfeld 1989) simply is not borne out by the relevant data.[50] Indeed, state civil commitment programs died, not necessarily because of their lack of effectiveness, but because of a lack of political will to devote adequate resources to them.[51] In the California Civil Addict Program (CAP), which operated throughout the 1960s and early 1970s, daily narcotics use and property-related crime among program participants were reduced by 22 percent and 19 percent, respectively. This represented a threefold improvement in outcome measures over a comparison group of drug users who were admitted to the program but were discharged because of legal errors and who reduced their daily drug use and their criminal activities by only 7 percent (Anglin and Hser 1991a). Evaluations of clients in the federal and other civil commitment programs demonstrated that clients did as well as, or better than, those who volunteered for treatment (Anglin 1988; Anglin, Brecht, and Maddahian 1987; Leukfeld and Tims 1988). Legal coercion did not appear to interfere with treatment effectiveness in any modality ranging from methadone maintenance (Anglin, Brecht, and Maddahian 1987) to therapeutic communities (DeLeon 1988).

Extensive research has also been undertaken concerning the success of mandatory treatment in the criminal justice system — treatment as a condition of release on bail, probation, parole, or treatment while in prison. Both TOPS and DARP report benefits to individuals who were in treatment under the criminal justice system. The major model for treatment in the federal criminal justice system is the Treatment Alternatives to Street Crime (TASC) program. TASC was established as a small experimental program in 1972, and by 1988 it was operating in 18 states. The goals of TASC are to identify drug users who come into contact with the

---

[50] An annotated bibliography on compulsory treatment is published by the National Clearinghouse for Alcohol and Drug Information, Office of Substance Abuse and Prevention (18) 1290. See also the symposium issue on compulsory treatment in the *Journal of Drug Issues* 1988;18 (4): 503–661.

[51] James Inciardi (1988) concludes that New York's civil commitment program was doomed to failure because of mismanagement and misrepresentation; its treatment facilities were in former prisons whose environments were not conducive to behavioral change; facility directors were political appointees with little clinical experience; and its aftercare program was inadequate.

criminal justice system, to refer them to clinically appropriate treatment, to monitor their progress, and to return violators to the criminal justice system (Hubbard et al. 1989). TASC employs creative strategies, including deferred prosecution, community sentencing, diversion to the voluntary treatment system, and pretrial intervention to help funnel drug users into treatment. TASC also utilizes traditional strategies, such as probation and parole supervision, for probable and proven crimes.

More than 40 evaluations of TASC have concluded that it has intervened effectively to reduce drug abuse and criminal activity and that it has identified previously unrecognized drug-dependent persons (National Criminal Justice Association 1990). Indeed, researchers have concluded that criminal justice treatment clients favorably alter their behavior as much as or more than clients in other drug abuse treatment programs. Successes of compulsory treatment include significantly reduced drug use and criminal activity, and increased employment and social coping skills.

The most recent and influential models of treatment in the state criminal justice systems are Stay'n Out (a New York program based upon the social organization of a major therapeutic community, Phoenix House, and adapted to the prison setting) and Cornerstone (a modified therapeutic community program for state prisoners in the last year prior to parole eligibility, located in Oregon State Hospital in Salem). Studies of Stay'n Out (Speckart and Anglin 1986) and Cornerstone (Field 1989) show that program participants were convicted significantly less often than comparable released prisoners (Institute of Medicine 1990, 177–80).

Outcome evaluation of prison-based programs also shows "reductions in criminal recidivism rates and that time in treatment is positively related to increased time until arrest" (Bureau of Prisons 1990). A note of caution is sounded by researchers who have studied far less intensive (Besteman 1990) or traditional (e.g., "boot camp" or "shock incarceration"; Parent 1989) prison treatment programs and have shown little long-term effect on behavior.

The results of mandatory treatment programs are not unequivocal, but they are encouraging. The best programs produced marked, enduring changes in drug use and arrest rates. Criminal justice clients are "hard cases," but even a modest rate of success yields substantial social benefits. The reduction in arrest records produces benefits that can only be fully understood in reference to expert opinion that, for every arrest, criminally inclined individuals have generally committed hundreds of crimes (Speckart and Anglin 1986).

Cost-benefit studies (Hubbard et al. 1989; Tabbush 1986) suggest that every dollar spent on treatment will reap many more dollars because of reduced social costs stemming from fewer arrests, prosecutions, and incarcerations and because of reduced losses from theft and the economic benefits of an improved labor market and reduced medical costs (Institute of Medicine 1990, 102-4; Office of Technology Assessment 1990, 125-6). The Presidential Commission on the HIV Epidemic (1988) reported that the annual cost of keeping a person in prison is $14,500; as little as $3,000 is needed for drug treatment. The cost of treatment compares favorably with the estimated $50,000 lifetime cost of treating a person with AIDS (Fox 1990).

Compulsory treatment's demonstrated effectiveness may persuade even groups that are morally opposed to drug use to choose treatment over punitive measures. A mandatory treatment program could make a user's otherwise useless time in the criminal justice system productive. Because a clear nexus exists between duration and success, treatment in the criminal justice system could significantly increase the probability of positive outcomes. Despite the limits it places on personal autonomy, compulsory treatment promises a brighter future for drug-dependent persons than currently practiced punitive measures.

Mechanisms for Compulsory Treatment: A Proposal

The goals of compulsory treatment are to:

1. maximize the utility of treatment in order to reduce drug dependence and its associated criminal activity and dysfunctional behavior
2. reduce the costs of the criminal justice system
3. transfer resources to treatment programs

The mechanism of compulsory treatment best suited to meet these goals is a comprehensive pretrial diversion program. Linking compulsory treatment to the criminal justice system provides the best opportunity for identifying cases of individuals who are seriously drug dependent, criminally involved, and who could benefit from treatment. By emphasizing diversion before trial, the program would create an incentive to enter into treatment and avoid the inordinate costs of prosecution, trial, and incarceration. At the same time, the ability of prosecutors to continue the criminal process if compliance is not forthcoming provides a tool for enforcement.

These proposals do not preclude "pure" civil commitment outside the criminal justice system, but such a position would significantly widen the net of compulsion and incur civil liberties concerns. The proposals also do not preclude treatment in prison or as a condition of probation or parole. These treatment programs are essential, but do not have the advantage of easing the pressure on the criminal justice system.

Devising an effective mechanism for compulsory treatment requires the accommodation of two diverse perspectives:

1. *Justice.* The program must provide fair standards and procedures for individuals and be consistent with constitutional standards already set in the comparable area of mental health confinement.
2. *Societal benefit.* The program must achieve the goals for compulsory treatment stated above, including protection of the public.

These two perspectives can be accommodated by incorporating the following elements into the diversion program.

Client Agreement

The libertarian value of "justice" requires that programs respect individual autonomy as much as possible. Full respect for autonomy in a compulsory program is impossible to achieve. The person's consent is offered within the context of a coercive criminal system. Yet entry into many well-regarded treatment programs has been subject to negotiation or multilateral agreement and performance expectations. In effect, a social contract is formed, which requires the client, the treatment program, and criminal justice authorities to fulfill their respective obligations (Institute of Medicine 1990, 184–5). Client agreement to enter the program therefore should be a requirement. Past experience suggests that many persons prefer the option of compulsory treatment to the punitive sanctions of the criminal justice system.

The fact that client agreement is sought does not render the program "voluntary." The fact that the alternative to "agreement" is a potentially severe prison sentence introduces a sure element of coercion into the program.

The Right to Procedural Due Process

Compulsory treatment restricts liberty; therefore, it must be subject to the rules of procedural due process. Courts, in the context of both mental health[52] and juvenile[53] confinement, have recognized that even though the ostensible goal of the confinement is labeled therapeutic or beneficent, the person is still deprived of liberty. The client therefore is constitutionally entitled to a hearing with many of the elements of a criminal trial: notice, a hearing by a court or tribunal, and the right to be present, to confront and cross-examine witnesses, and to appeal. The fact that the person is already being processed under the criminal justice system does not justify the denial of rigorous procedures.[54]

Drug Dependence and Susceptibility to Treatment

Compulsory treatment programs should give priority to those for whom treatment would provide the greatest benefit—to themselves and to society. Accordingly, eligibility criteria should focus on persons who are seriously dependent upon drugs and susceptible to treatment. Dependence is the most extreme pattern of drug consumption, defined as the persistent seeking and consumption of drugs in excessive amounts, despite high costs to health and social functioning (Institute of Medicine 1990, 5). Scarce treatment beds should not be allocated to casual or even regular drug users, but rather to those who are unable to control their drug use. The National Institute on Drug Abuse (1987) argues that because it is not possible to treat everyone identified as a drug user, it is necessary to examine drug abuse careers and choose persons with chronic and serious drug problems. Indeed, drug dependence may well be regarded as a constitutional prerequisite for confinement in the same way that "mental illness" is required for civil commitment (Perlin 1989,

---

[52] *Lessard v. Schmidt*, 349 F. Supp. 1376 (E.D. Wis. 1974).
[53] *In re Gault*, 387 U.S. 1 (1967).
[54] *Baxtrom v. Herold*, 383 U.S. 107 (1966).

48–9). It might be argued that this leaves casual users without treatment. Nothing in the proposal prevents casual users from seeking treatment voluntarily. It serves no public purpose, however, to compel treatment of all users, at public expense, unless the need for treatment and the probable success of treatment are clearly established.

Dangerousness

Courts have concluded in mental health cases that the state's police powers can be exercised only where the person poses a significant danger based upon recent overt acts (Note 1977).[55] The police power cannot be invoked merely because the person is drug dependent or even because he or she is charged with an offense. Nor can the state rely on the statistical fact that some, even most, drug-dependent persons are criminally involved. The state must demonstrate that the specific individual has engaged in dangerous behavior.

The National Institute on Drug Abuse (1987) consensus meeting on compulsory treatment concluded that priority should be given to those who pose a serious public health danger, such as HIV-infected intravenous drug users or commercial sex workers who continue to share needles or have sexual intercourse.

Proportionality and Duration of Confinement

The Supreme Court in *Jackson v. Indiana* held, "At least, due process requires that the nature and duration of commitment bear some reasonable relation to the purpose for which the person is committed."[56] A person admitted for compulsory drug treatment should not be confined longer than necessary to reduce his dependence on drugs. Thus, the individual should have access to a periodic hearing, and should be released as soon as the criteria for the original admission are no longer met. The confinement, however, is not purely therapeutic but intertwined with the criminal process. To this end, the duration of confinement should be no longer than the person would have received had he or she been convicted of the offense. Once a person is released from drug treatment (whether because her dependence has been sufficiently

[55] *Lessard v. Schmidt*, 349 F. Supp. 1978, 1093 (E.D. Wis. 1972).
[56] 406 U.S. 715, 738 (1972).

ameliorated or because the maximum period of confinement is expired) the pending criminal charge should lapse. The time spent in drug treatment should be discounted from any criminal sentence in the event that she is tried and convicted on the original charge.

It could be argued that the public health goal served by treatment is not fully achieved if the drug user must be released from the program before he or she is ready. No doubt this is true, but a careful balance must be drawn for any policy between public health, public safety, and justice for the individual. Compulsory detention of individuals for a duration clearly disproportionate to the gravity of an offense needs a cogent justification, which goes beyond the carefully crafted proposal made in this article.

The Least Restrictive Alternative

Persons should receive compulsory treatment in the least restrictive setting necessary to serve the objective of client benefit and public safety. Thus, modern mandatory treatment programs should utilize the wide breadth of existing treatment modalities, ranging from inpatient drug-free to therapeutic communities and outpatient methadone maintenance and drug rehabilitation and counseling.

The Supreme Court developed the doctrine of the least restrictive alternative to prohibit the state from pursuing its goals by means that "broadly stifle fundamental personal liberties when the end can be more narrowly pursued."[57] The doctrine has been applied in mental health cases by placing the burden on the state to explore community-based alternatives to institutionalization.[58]

The Institute of Medicine (1990), Office of Technology Assessment (1990), and National Institute on Drug Abuse (1987) all urge the widest possible use of existing drug-treatment facilities in any compulsory program. Priority should be given to those facilities and modalities that have demonstrated successful outcomes through quality research.

The Right to Treatment

Persons who agree to enter compulsory treatment programs should have the right to receive high-quality, intensive treatment. In the 1970s,

---

[57] *Shelton v. Tucker*, 364 U.S. 479 (1960).
[58] *Lake v. Cameron*, 364 F.2d 657, 660 (D.C. Cir. 1966).

courts flirted with the idea that if the state had the power to detain a person for mental health treatment, then it had the constitutional obligation to provide minimally adequate treatment.[59] The Supreme Court never affirmed this doctrine, although it upheld a constitutional right of involuntary patients to adequate food, clothing, shelter, and medical care, as well as minimally adequate training to ensure safety and freedom from undue restraint.[60]

The legacy of compulsory treatment is that the state failed to provide adequate levels of service intensity, personnel quality and experience, and treatment capacity. The Institute of Medicine (1990, 230 et seq.) said that upgrading program performance, quality levels, and capacity should be the highest government priority in drug treatment. If individuals forgo their right to a criminal trial in exchange for the opportunity to enter treatment, then they should be entitled to minimally adequate levels of services appropriate to their needs. U.S. courts, of course, are reluctant to create treatment entitlements. The legislature could do so within compulsory drug-treatment statutes. Alternatively, federal or state governments could allocate adequate resources to ensure that program goals are met, benefitting both the individual and society through more enduring behavior change.

Conclusion

The idea of compulsory treatment is often roundly rejected by civil libertarians, government officials, and clinicians. However, their refusal to consider this idea is based largely on a misunderstanding of the goals of compulsory treatment and modern research findings. Civil libertarians are against any form of compulsion because they believe drug use is a voluntary behavior that, in itself, does not harm others. The proposal for compulsory treatment, to be sure, does not go as far as legalization. It does, however, respect a person's civil liberties more than the current punitive system. The compulsory treatment program proposed here would require the person's agreement, would not restrict freedom lon-

---

[59] *Wyatt v. Stickney*, 325 F. Supp. 781 (M.D. Ala. 1971), *aff'd sub nom, Wyatt v. Aderholt*, 503 f. 2d 1974; *New York State Ass'n for Retarded Children v. Rockefeller*, 357 F. Supp. 752 (E.D.N.Y. 1973).
[60] *Youngberg v. Romeo*, 451 U.S. 982 (1981).

ger than if the person were convicted, and would allow a less restrictive, more humane and effective alternative to incarceration. The distinct advantage of pretrial diversion is that it avoids the substantial erosion of civil liberties inherent in the criminal justice system (Glasser 1990). Civil libertarians also fear that compulsory treatment would widen the net of compulsion, but a program devised as an alternative disposition to imprisonment should become attractive to civil libertarians.

Government officials, particularly those on the political right, reject pretrial diversion because they see it as a soft option for drug users, and because it will not adequately protect public safety. Whether pure retribution for the act of ingesting drugs is ever justified is a matter for debate, but one can argue that compulsory treatment does have a punitive component because the person is denied his liberty. A more important goal is public safety. Here, outcome studies suggest that, in the long run, the public is better protected by treatment than by incarceration.

The most telling argument against compulsory treatment is put forward by clinicians. They argue that it is inherently wrong to provide compulsory treatment to persons accused of crimes, while many thousands of drug users who are actively and voluntarily seeking treatment must cope with long waiting lists. This essay does not suggest that persons eligible to receive compulsory treatment should have priority over those in the voluntary system. Compulsory treatment should not replace treatment capacity available to other clients. Compulsory treatment offers an opportunity to shift some of the huge investment in the criminal justice system in order to expand the treatment system. The empirical evidence demonstrating the efficacy of treatment, the philosophical arguments explaining its humanity, and the economic studies showing its cost benefit all militate toward a fundamental reevaluation of current policies favoring criminal punishment over public health interventions in combatting the drug epidemic.

References

Abromovsky A., and F.B. McCarthy. 1977. Civil Commitment of Noncriminal Narcotic Addicts: Parens Patriae: A Valid Exercise of a State's Police Power; or an Unconscionable Disregard of Individual Liberty. *University of Pittsburgh Law Review* 38:477–503.

American Jurisprudence 2d. 1990. Supp. *Deskbook* 124.

Anderson, S., and I. Keilitz. 1991. Involuntary Civil Commitment of

Drug Dependent Persons with Special Reference to Pregnant Women. *Mental and Physical Disability Law Reporter* 15:418–37.

Anglin, M.D. 1988. The Efficacy of Civil Commitment in Treating Narcotic Addiction. In *Compulsory Treatment of Drug Abuse: Research and Clinical Practice*, eds. C.G. Leukfeld and F.M. Tims. NIDA monograph 86. Rockville, Md.

Anglin, M.D., M.L. Brecht, and E. Maddahian. 1987. Pre-Treatment Characteristics and Treatment Performance of Legally Coerced versus Voluntary Methadone Maintenance Admissions. *Criminology* 27: 537–57.

Anglin, M.D., and Y. Hser. 1991a. Criminal Justice and the Drug Abusing Offender: Policy Issues of Coerced Treatment. *Behavioral Sciences and the Law* 9:243–67.

———. 1991b. Legal Coercion and Drug Abuse Treatment: Research Findings and Social Policy Implications. In *Handbook on Drug Control in the U.S.*, ed. J. Inciardi. Westport, Conn.: Greenwood Press.

Aronowitz, D.S. 1967. Civil Commitment of Narcotics Addicts. *Columbia Law Review* 67:405–29.

Besteman, K.J. 1990. Federal Leadership in Building the National Drug Treatment System. In *Treating Drug Abuse*, vol. 2, eds. D.R. Gerstein and H.J. Harwood. Washington: National Academy Press.

Brakel, S.J., J. Parry, and B.A. Weiner. 1985. *The Mentally Disabled and the Law*. Chicago: American Bar Foundation.

Brecher, E. 1989. Needles and the Conscience of a Nation. *Drug Policy Letter* 1:5–6.

Bureau of Justice Statistics. 1988. *Drug Law Violators, 1980–1986*. Washington: Department of Justice.

———. 1989. *Sourcebook of Criminal Justice Statistics*. Washington: Department of Justice.

———. 1990. *Prisoners in 1989*. Washington: Department of Justice.

Bureau of Prisons. *Proposal for the Evaluation of the Federal Bureau of Prisons Drug Abuse Treatment Program*. Washington: Department of Justice.

Centers for Disease Control. 1983. Introduction. In *Research in the Treatment of Narcotic Addiction State of the Art*. NIDA monograph ADM 87-1281. Rockville, Md.

———. 1989. Urine Testing for Drug Use Among Male Arrestees— United States. *Morbidity and Mortality Weekly Report* 38:780.

Cooper, J.R. 1989. Methadone Treatment and Acquired Immune Deficiency Syndrome. *Journal of the American Medical Association* 262:1664–68.

DeLeon, G. 1988. Legal Pressure in Therapeutic Communities. *Journal of Drug Issues* 18:625–40.

Feinberg, J. 1970. *Doing and Deserving: Essays in the Theory of Responsibility*. Princeton, N.J.: Princeton University Press.

Feldman, H.W., and P. Biernacki. 1988. The Ethnography of Needle Sharing Among Intra-Venous Drug Users and Implication for Public Policies and Intervention Strategies. In *Needle Sharing Among Intra-Venous Drug Abusers: National and International Perspectives*. NIDA monograph 80. Rockville, Md.

Field, G. 1989. The Effects of Intensive Treatment on Reducing the Criminal Recidivism of Addicted Offenders. *Federal Probation* 53:51–72.

Fox, D. 1990. The Cost of AIDS: Exaggeration, Entitlement, and Economics. In *AIDS and the Health Care System*, ed. L. Gostin, New Haven, Conn.: Yale University Press.

Ginnow, A.D. Ed. 1974. Drugs and Narcotics Supplement. *Corpus Juris Secundum* 28:paras 230–40.

Glasser, I. 1990. Now for a drug policy that doesn't do harm. *New York Times* (December 6).

Glick, H.R. 1979. Mandatory Sentencing: The Politics of the New Criminal Justice. *Federal Probation* 43:3.

Gostin, L. 1991a. An Alternative Public Health Vision for a National Drug Strategy: "Treatment Works." *Houston Law Review* 28:285–308.

———. 1991b. The Interconnected Epidemics of Drug Dependency and AIDS. *Harvard Civil Rights–Civil Liberties Law Review* 26:113–84.

Gulick, G.S., and R.T. Kimbrough. Eds. 1990. Drugs, Narcotics and Poisons. *American Jurisprudence 2d Supp.*, para. 74.

Hubbard, R., M. Marsden, J. Rachal, H. Harwood, E. Cavanaugh, and H. Ginzburg. 1989. *"Drug Abuse Treatment" A National Study of Effectiveness*. Chapel Hill: University of North Carolina Press.

Inciardi, J.A. 1988. Compulsory Treatment in New York: A Brief Narrative History of Misjudgment, Mismanagement, and Misrepresentation. *Journal of Drug Issues* 10:547–60.

Institute of Medicine. 1990. *Treating Drug Problems*, vol. 1. Washington: National Academy Press.

Labaton, S. 1990. New Tactics in the War on Drugs Tilts Scales of Justice off Balance: The Courts Overwhelmed. *New York Times* (December 29): 1.

Lambiotte, B.J. 1987. Retribution or Rehabilitation? The Addict Exception and Mandatory Sentencing After Grant v. U.S. and the District of Columbia Controlled Substances Amendment Act. *Catholic University Law Review* 37:733.

Landis, D.T. 1981. Pretrial Diversion: Statute or Court Rule Authorizing Suspension or Dismissal of Criminal Prosecution on Defendant's Consent to Non-criminal Alternative. *American Law Reports 4th* 4:147-82.

Leukfeld, C.G., and F.M. Tims. 1988. Compulsory Treatment: A Review of Findings. In *Compulsory Treatment of Drug Abuse: Research and Clinical Practice*, eds. C.G. Leukfeld and F.M. Tims. NIDA monograph 86. Rockville, Md.

Majority Staffs of the Senate Judiciary Committee and the International Narcotics Control Caucus. 1990. *Fighting Drug Abuse: A National Strategy.* Washington: U.S. Congress.

Malcolm, A.H. 1991. More Cells for More Prisoners, but What End? *New York Times* (January 18): 16.

Martinson, J. 1974. What Works? Questions and Answers About Prison Reform. *Public Interest* 35:48-62.

———. 1979. New Findings, New Views: A Note of Caution Regarding Sentencing Reform. *Hofstra Law Review* 7:252.

McLellan, A.T., L. Luborsky, C.P. O'Brien, et al. 1982. Is Treatment for Substance Abuse Effective? *Journal of the American Medical Association* 247:1423-28.

Mello, N.K., J.K. Mendelson, M.P. Bree, et al. 1989. Buprenorphine Suppresses Cocaine Administration by Rhesus Monkeys. *Science* 245:859-62.

Musto, D. 1989. The History of American Drug Control. *Update on Law-Related Education* 13:2-6, 47-56.

Myers, P.H. 1974. Determination of Duration of Commitment of Narcotic Addict Under the Provisions of Narcotic Rehabilitation Act of 1966 (18 USCS para 4253[a]) that Commitment Shall be for Indeterminate Period of Time Not to Exceed 10 Years, but in no Event in Excess of Maximum Sentence that Could Otherwise Have Been Imposed. *American Law Reports Federal* 18:854-63.

Nadelmann, E.A. 1989. Drug Prohibition in the United States: Costs, Consequences, and Alternatives. *Science* 245:939-47.

National Association of State Alcohol and Drug Abuse Directors. 1990. *Treatment Works: A Review of 15 Years of Research Findings on Alcohol and Other Drug Abuse Treatment Outcomes.* Washington.

National Criminal Justice Association. 1990. Treatment Options for Drug Dependent Offenders: A Review of the Literature for State and Local Decisionmakers. Washington: U.S. Department of Justice.

National Drug Enforcement Policy Board. 1987. *National and International Drug Law Enforcement Strategy.* Washington: Department of Justice.

National Institute on Drug Abuse. 1983. *Research on the Treatment of Narcotic Addiction: State of the Art.* NIDA monograph ADM 83-1281. Rockville, Md.

————. 1987. *Consensus Statement: Research Panel on Compulsory Treatment and Drug Abuse*, January 27. Rockville, Md.

————. 1988. *Compulsory Treatment of Drug Abuse: Research and Clinical Practice*, eds. C.G. Leukfeld and F.M. Tims. NIDA monograph 86. Washington: U.S. Department of Health and Human Services.

————. 1989. *National Household Survey on Drug Abuse: Population Estimate 1988*. Rockville, Md.

Note. 1975. Pre-Trial Diversion: The Threat of Expanding Social Control. *Harvard Civil Rights–Civil Liberties Law Review* 10:180.

————. 1977. Overt Dangerous Behavior as a Constitutional Requirement for Involuntary Civil Commitment of the Mentally Ill. *University of Chicago Law Review* 44:562.

Office of Justice Programs. 1988. *Drug Use and Crime*. Washington: Department of Justice.

————. 1989. *Drugs and Crime Facts*. Washington: U.S. Department of Justice.

Office of Technology Assessment, U.S. Congress. 1990. *The Effectiveness of Drug Abuse Treatment: Implications for Controlling AIDS/ HIV Infection*. AIDS-related issues background paper 6. Washington.

Parent, D.G. 1989. *Shock Incarceration: An Overview of Existing Programs*. Washington: National Institute of Justice.

Pear, R. 1990. Drug Policy Debate Turns to Feud Between Moynihan and Bennett. *New York Times* (June 18): A20.

Perlin, M.L. 1989. *Mental Disability Law: Civil and Criminal*. Charlottesville, Va.: Michie.

Presidential Commission on the Human Immunodeficiency Virus Epidemic. 1988. *Report*. Washington.

President's Commission on Law Enforcement and Administration of Justice. 1967. *The Challenge of Crime in a Free Society*. Washington.

Reinhold, R. 1989. Police, Hard Pressed in Drug War, are Turning to Preventive Efforts. *New York Times* (December 28):1.

Rockefeller, N.A. 1966. Statement of the Governor of New York. Hearings before the Subcommittee on Criminal Laws and Procedure of the Senate Committee on the Judiciary, 89th Cong., 2d Sess., 193, 195.

————. 1973. Governor's Annual Message. *McKinney's 1973 Session Laws of New York*: 2309, at 2318 et seq.

Schopler, E.H., A.M. Swarthout, and C.T. Dreschler. Eds. 1964. Validity and Construction of Statutes Providing for Civil Commitment of Arrested Narcotic Addicts. *American Law Reports, Annotated 2d* 98:726–32.

Schottenfeld, R.S. 1989. Involuntary Treatment of Substance Abuse Disorders—Impediments to Success. *Psychiatry* 52:164–76.

Shenon, P. 1990. The Score on Drugs: It Depends on How You See the Figures. *New York Times* (April 22): 6, 17.

Simpson, D.C., G.W. Joe, W.E.K. Lehman, and S.B. Sells. 1986. Addiction Careers: Etiology, Treatment, and 12-year Follow-up Outcomes. *Journal of Drug Issues* 16:107.

Simpson, D.D., and S.B. Sells. Eds. 1990. *Opioid Addiction and Treatment: A 12-Year Follow Up.* Melbourne, Fla.: Krieger Publishing.

Smith, J.E. 1980. Validity of Statues Prohibiting or Restricting Parole, Probation, or Suspension of Sentence in Cases of Violent Crimes. *American Law Reports 3d* 100:431–61.

Speckart, G.R., and M.D. Anglin. 1986. Narcotics and Crime: A Causal Modeling Approach. *Journal of Quantitative Criminology* 2:3–28.

Tabbush, V. 1986. The Effectiveness and Efficiency of Publicly Funded Drug Abuse Treatment Programs in California: A Benefit Cost Analysis. Los Angeles: University of California Press.

Tims, F. 1986. *Drug Abuse Treatment in Prisons.* Research report no. ADM 86-1149. Rockville, Md.: National Institute on Drug Abuse.

U.S. Office of National Drug Policy. 1990a. *National Drug Control Strategy.* Washington.

———. 1990b. *National Drug Control Strategy: Budget Summary.* Washington.

Vigdal, G.L., and D.W. Stadler. 1989. Controlling Inmate Drug Use Cut Consumption by Reducing Demand. *Corrections Today* (June):96.

Williams, J.C. 1977. Validity of State Statutes Imposing Mandatory Sentence or Prohibiting Granting Probation or Suspension of Sentence for Narcotics Offenses. *American Law Reports 3d* 81:1192–1205.

———. 1979. Constitutionality of State Legislation Imposing Criminal Penalties for Personal Possession or Use of Marijuana. *American Law Reports 3d* 96:225–51.

Wilson, J.Q. 1990. Against the Legalization of Drugs. *Commentary* (February 21):28.

Zweben, J.E., and J.L. Sorenson. 1988. Misunderstandings About Methadone. *Journal of Psychoactive Drugs* 20:275–81.

Acknowledgments: The research assistance of Renée Solomon and Ann Gamertsfelder, and the technical assistance of San Juanita Rangel are gratefully acknowledged.

Address correspondence to: Lawrence O. Gostin, J.D., Office of the Executive Director, American Society of Law & Medicine, 765 Commonwealth Avenue, 16th floor, Boston, MA 02215.

Helping Women Helping Children:
Drug Policy and Future Generations

PATRICIA A. KING

Georgetown University Law Center

We are born into families, and the first society we belong to, one that fits or misfits us for later ones, is the small society of parents (or some sort of child-attendants) and of children. (Baier 1987, 55)

A DRUG POLICY DEVELOPED FOR WOMEN MUST TAKE into account the implications of their drug use, not only for themselves as autonomous adults, but also for their biological and social roles as procreators and caregivers. Only women gestate. Furthermore, caregiving has been and continues to be the overwhelming responsibility of women. Although men may also be procreators and caregivers, these roles are not culturally perceived as significant aspects of their lives. Unfortunately, because drug policy discussions have historically focused on the behaviors and needs of male addicts, the individual and social significance of procreative and caregiving roles has been ignored.

A standard approach to analyzing social issues, including drug regulation, is to frame the problem in terms of sensible accommodation between rights-based liberalism emphasizing individual autonomy and choice, on the one hand, and communitarianism, which stresses group interests, on the other. Policy debates concerning drug abuse reflect this framework, with options arrayed along a continuum defined by two mutually exclusive policy positions: legalization—the general elimination of legal restrictions on possession and sale of drugs—versus vigorous enforcement of criminal laws.

This framework is not useful to a discussion of women's substance abuse because it does not adequately account for the significance of procreative and caregiving roles. Decisions to reproduce and caregiving activities involve establishing and maintaining relationships with special others, especially offspring. A libertarian focus on individual autonomy and choice, therefore, fails to capture important features of women's drug use, such as the harm it may bring to others in these relationships. For example, debating whether to legalize the use and possession of drugs fails to grapple with the significant fact that the fetus in utero is harmed by legal as well as illegal substances. Similarly, vigorous enforcement of criminal laws aimed at preventing individuals from using illegal drugs undoubtedly penalizes the user. Yet, such enforcement is not likely to prevent harm to fetuses or children. Moreover, because fetuses and children are physically and psychologically closely linked with their mother, punishing her may often adversely affect them as well.

The social response to the complex problem of women's drug abuse has been primarily legal, highly punitive in nature, and targeted at pregnant women. This response has taken account of the fact that a woman's drug use has implications for her reproductive role. Unfortunately, however, the response assumes that the interests of the pregnant woman and the fetus are necessarily in conflict. Thus, two dominant perceptions have emerged: the deviant and irresponsible woman and the vulnerable fetus.

The use of addictive substances or participation by pregnant women in activities that risk harming the fetuses contradicts prevailing social norms and expectations about motherhood. Although in the past pregnant women have used alcohol or illegal substances like heroin that interfere with fetal development, women's use of crack, a highly addictive and concentrated form of cocaine, has created and shaped contemporary popular images of substance-abusing pregnant women. The conduct of women addicted to crack is dramatically different from maternal behavior associated with other addictive substances. They often have multiple pregnancies and give birth to infants who have been exposed to crack, frequently just prior to delivery. They seem to exhibit no interest in their infants, often abandoning them in the hospitals where they delivered.

This perception of women who use illegal drugs, particularly crack, as irresponsible mothers is reinforced by the illegal character of their activities. Thus, it becomes easier to condemn their conduct as morally blameworthy. In addition, the profile of women who use illegal addictive substances is consistent with the public perception of addicts as being members of minority groups and predominantly lower class, a perception that has proved influential in gaining public acceptance of punitive drug policies.

The depiction of women who use addictive substances as deviant, irresponsible, and morally blameworthy stands in stark contrast to the perception of the fetus, which is perceived as innocent and especially vulnerable to the pregnant woman's activities, thus requiring protection. As a result, the maternal–fetal relationship is perceived as being an adversarial one. Although the needs of pregnant addicts have been largely neglected by society, it is not surprising, therefore, that when there is active social response to a pregnant woman's drug use, it is characterized primarily as punitive, with the rationalization that such measures are required to protect the fetus or newborn.

Arguments in favor of, or in opposition to, punitive approaches share a common methodological approach when analyzing the policy issues raised by women's substance abuse. Although these arguments vary in their assumptions about fetal status and their justifications for state intervention, they all proceed on the premise that the matter at issue is essentially maternal autonomy versus state intervention. One set of arguments, particularly when grounded in the assumption that fetuses are persons or potential human beings, sees the issue as one of competing individual interests — woman versus fetus — that must be resolved in favor of one interest. They assume that maternal interests and fetal interests can be equated and are necessarily adversarial. The arguments differ only in terms of which interest should have priority. If state intervention is warranted, it is because the fetus, never the mother, needs the state's protection or assistance.

A second set of arguments, especially those that do not accord the fetus equal status with the woman, views the issue as one of maternal autonomy versus costs to the community. For example, the state may have an interest in constraining maternal autonomy to reduce the costs of taking care of humans born with disabilities. Alternatively, the unintended effects of taking punitive measures against women, such as discouraging pregnant women from seeking prenatal care, may be so costly that state intervention is contraindicated. These arguments focus attention only on women, not on third parties and social institutions, and ask whether certain acts are properly within the realm of maternal autonomy.

A more compelling analytical structure for developing drug policies for women would make different assumptions about the nature of the relationship that exists between mother and fetus, parent and child. This approach would assume that humans do not exist in self-interested isolation from others. In particular, we rely on parents to make decisions that will be in the best interest of their offspring. Much of this belief stems from our personal knowledge of the nature of interactions in intimate interpersonal relationships, such as those that exist between parents and children. The reality of family life and the sacrifice and attention to important others that it demands are not easily reconciled with a philosophy that judges human activities to be driven solely by self-interest.

Unlike the underlying perceptions driving current drug policies, this alternative framework is not predicated on an adversarial relationship between the mother and her fetus or child. Rather, it assumes that maternal–fetal and mother–child relationships can only be understood in terms of interactions where the needs of one define the needs of both. This framework permits recognition of the fact that often what adversely affects a parent also harms a fetus or child. The obverse is also true: what helps women become more confident, integrated persons nurtures their children's growth and development. This framework also does not presume that maternal choices will be irresponsible and lead to higher social costs.

Although this focus on a woman's relationship with her fetus or child does not necessarily preclude punitive or coercive responses to the problem of women's substance abuse, it nonetheless broadens the range of strategies to be considered in designing drug policy for women. Moreover, it does raise significant questions about the effectiveness of punitive and coercive strategies. Finally, it suggests that state intervention in the form of nonpunitive and noncoercive strategies emphasizing education, treatment, and removal of conditions that lead women to abuse drugs in the first place offer the greatest long-term prospect of sparing women, their offspring, and their families the harm that flows from mothers' abuse of legal and illegal psychoactive drugs.

The Scope and Nature of Women's Drug Use

The most important lesson to draw from the medical and social data about maternal substance abuse is that addiction to both *legal* and *ille-*

gal substances and a woman's entire lifestyle have serious implications, not only for a woman's health and well-being, but also for the health and well-being of her offspring. Maternal substance abuse during pregnancy by almost any measure is a source of significant infant morbidity and mortality that presents serious concerns for our society. Moreover, the policy implications of maternal substance abuse cannot be fully understood by focusing merely on the harms it causes to fetuses and newborns. Policy discussions must also address the implications of maternal substance abuse for children and future generations. Finally, to prevent harm rather than be satisfied with repairing damage already done, drug policy for women must focus on the underlying causes of substance abuse by women.

Women's substance abuse is a problem of serious social dimensions whose impact potentially falls heaviest on poor and minority women. Although there are indications that *illicit* drug use of all kinds is declining (Kandel 1991), the number of women of childbearing age who abuse legal and illegal drugs remains high. A recent estimate is that five million women of childbearing age (ages 15 to 44) currently use illicit drugs, including one million who use cocaine and over three million who use marijuana (U.S. Congress 1990, 4). In addition, approximately six million American women are alcoholics or alcohol abusers. Although women's *illegal* drug usage is associated in the public mind with women of color and poor women, data confirming this association are not available. There are data indicating that African Americans are overrepresented in morbidity and mortality linked with illicit drug use (Kandel 1991). Over time, poor and minority women may indeed constitute the majority of women who abuse *illicit* drugs in ways that put them at great social and medical risk.

The social implications of women's substance abuse cannot be defined solely in terms of the effects of their addictive behavior. Women substance abusers must often cope with economic, health, and psychiatric problems that may be both the cause and the result of their addiction (Daghestani 1988; Regan, Ehrlich, and Finnegan 1987; Regier et al. 1990). Many substance-abusing women had chemically addicted parents. Often they were physically and sexually abused as children and, as a result, are prone to depression and low self-esteem. Female addicts often live with men who batter them and/or men who also abuse drugs. Typically, they do not have marketable skills. As a result, many turn to prostitution to support their drug habit. Women involved in intravenous drug use and/or prostitution have a high risk of contracting the human immunodeficiency virus (HIV), and, if infected, are capable of transmitting the infection to their sexual partners and fetuses. The severity of these economic, health, and psychiatric problems makes it difficult for women substance abusers to parent in ways that society deems responsible without social assistance. Yet, support of any kind is typically unavailable.

Without support and treatment, women substance abusers who become pregnant pose serious threats to fetal well-being. One estimate is that 375,000 babies born per year have been exposed to illicit substances of all kinds in utero, including cocaine (Chasnoff 1989; *Medical World News* 1990). In addition, abuse of legal substances has potentially severe repercussions for fetal development. For example, the adverse effects of alcohol on fetuses have been known for many years (Abel 1973, 1990; Jones et al. 1973; Weiner and Morse 1988). A female drug user's lifestyle also puts her fetus at risk of HIV infection. There were 2,116 reported cases of pediatric acquired immune deficiency syndrome (AIDS) in children under age 13 as of February 1990. In 80 percent of these reported cases, AIDS was attributed to maternal transmission of the virus. Of these cases of maternal transmission, 90 percent of the babies' mothers either used intravenous drugs or had heterosexual partners who were intravenous drug users (U.S. Congress 1990, 7).

Although it is clear that many legal and illegal substances are potentially harmful to fetuses, the precise causal relationship between the ingested substance and resulting harm to offspring is difficult to discern, especially when the amount and timing of drug ingestion are unknown. There are relatively few clinical studies of pregnant drug users (Daghestani 1988). Even when such studies exist, outcomes are difficult to assess because of polydrug use and other factors in the pregnant woman user's environment that influence fetal development (American College of Obstetricians and Gynecologists 1990). These factors include poor nutrition, lack of prenatal care, maternal psychopathology, and a drug-seeking lifestyle (Keith, MacGregor, and Sciarra 1988). Our inability to differentiate and weigh the relative effects of various factors on fetal development suggests that a broad range of policy approaches may be required to address adequately the problem of maternal substance abuse.

Children who live with substance-abusing parents are also at risk of physical and emotional harm (Chasnoff 1988; Deren 1986; Hassett

1985; Rosenbaum 1979). Although addicted parents do not necessarily abuse their children, many substance-abusing parents have impaired parenting skills because of their troubled childhoods and their drug-seeking lifestyles. As a result, substance abuse is frequently noted in cases of child abuse and neglect (Black and Mayer 1980; Burns and Burns 1988; Egan 1990; Mayer and Black 1977). Most children live with or are cared for by women. As a consequence, if children come into contact with a substance-abusing parent, it is likely to be their mothers. Although children, unlike fetuses, can be removed from their parents' custody if they are being abused, removal does not guarantee that the child will be protected from harm. Foster care is not realistically a vast improvement over life with an addicted parent, given the current inadequacies of our foster care system.

Being parented is also the primary preparation for becoming a parent. Patterns of dysfunctional parenting seen in substance-abusing families are thus passed from generation to generation (Burns and Burns 1988). The result is an ongoing cycle of abuse and neglect leading to depression and self-degradation that, in turn, puts individuals at risk both for substance abuse as a form of self-medication and of becoming another inadequate, hurtful parent (Regan, Ehrlich, and Finnegan 1987).

Although the number of women who use addictive substances is substantial, there are comparatively few programs that treat women, and the available slots are severely limited. Even female substance abusers who have access to some economic and social supports have had difficulty gaining access to effective treatment. Obviously, women who do not have employment that provides health care benefits or access to health care by other means are especially disadvantaged. Historically, drug treatment programs have been oriented to the needs of the male addict. As a result, even if a woman gains access to a drug treatment program, she cannot be assured that such programs will meet her needs (Chavkin 1990).

The problem of access and appropriately designed drug treatment programs for women is further accentuated when a substance abuser becomes pregnant. She encounters even greater obstacles to getting treatment. For example, of 78 drug treatment programs surveyed in New York City, 54 percent excluded all pregnant women; 67 percent would not accept pregnant women on Medicaid; and 87 percent did not accept pregnant crack-addicted women on Medicaid (Chavkin 1990; McNulty 1987–88). In addition, drug treatment programs for pregnant women, when they do exist, are not well integrated into other programs furnishing health services to them (Dans et al. 1990; National Academy Press 1988).

Women addicts, therefore, face multiple obstacles — medical, social, and economic — in trying to overcome their addiction and related lifestyle problems. Obviously, if women substance abusers are unsuccessful in controlling their addiction or changing their lifestyles, their ability to be productive members of society and to parent effectively is severely compromised.

The Social Response to Women's Substance Abuse: Focused on Pregnancy and Punitive in Character

What social response there has been to the problems posed by drug use among pregnant women has been largely punitive in nature, taking the form of criminal prosecutions or coerced treatment. More recently, there have been several proposals to limit the reproductive options of pregnant women who use drugs (see section below, "Limiting Women's Reproductive Options"). Conceivably, reliance on punitive approaches could be explained by the belief that *using* drugs is immoral as well as illegal. However, male users and female users who are not pregnant are being prosecuted for possessing or selling illicit drugs, not for using them. Something more seems to be at work in these prosecutions of pregnant women.

The conclusion is inescapable that these prosecutions are connected with the status of pregnancy (Paltrow, Goetz, and Shende 1990). This focus on pregnancy has been fostered by developments in science and medicine that have increased knowledge about uterine life and a simultaneous desire to protect the fetus from life-threatening or permanent injury. Concern about protecting fetal health, coupled with the legacy of the abortion debate, which has stressed an adversarial view of the maternal–fetal relationship and noninterference by the state in women's reproductive decisions, has led to reliance on punitive and coercive strategies to alter maternal behavior.

Vulnerable Fetuses and Preventing Harm

As a result of rapid developments in science and medicine, the fetus has emerged as a discrete entity from its heretofore hidden and inaccessible existence in the womb. These scientific and medical advances have helped to blur the distinction between fetuses and children because they make it possible to visualize and interact with the fetus to some extent throughout all phases of fetal development (Callahan 1986). In medicine, this outpouring of knowledge and information about the fetus has led to the recognition of the fetus as a second patient. In both criminal and civil law, fetal interests have increasingly come to be recognized as separate and distinct from those of mothers (McNulty 1987–88).

The emergence of the fetus as a discrete entity has been accompanied by rapidly accumulating information about its growth and development, which has revealed that almost everything a pregnant woman experiences — what she eats, what she drinks, her health status — can adversely affect fetal well-being. It is not surprising, therefore, that efforts would be initiated to protect the fetus from preventable injuries caused by maternal conduct.

The public's virtually exclusive preoccupation with hazards to fetuses associated with maternal conduct has served to minimize the fact that many risks to the fetus, such as fetal exposure to the rubella virus, are not of maternal origin. Other risks typically described as being maternally imposed are actually created by other parties. For example, risks to a fetus as a result of a pregnant woman working in a dangerous workplace could more appropriately be described as failure of the employer to provide a safe work environment.[1] A frustrated commentator asks, "How have we come to see women as the major threat to the health of newborns, and the womb as the most dangerous place a child will ever inhabit?" (Pollitt 1990, 409). The answer is linked to a view of pregnancy that assumes that the self-defined interests of pregnant women are at times in conflict with the well-being of fetuses. It is also tied to an emphasis on maternal autonomy and choice — a focus that tends to privatize responsibility for fetal well-being onto women. These assumptions are a legacy of the abortion debates.

The Legacy of the Abortion Debate

Although the eugenics movement was concerned about who should procreate, abortion was the first significant moral and policy issue to arise out of pregnancy itself. The question of whether a pregnancy could be

---

[1] *International Union v. Johnson Controls, Inc.* 1991. *Supreme Court Reporter* 111:1196–1217.

terminated was highly influenced by the legal context in which the matter was often discussed. The question was typically framed (although it need not have been) in terms of the woman's right to choose to terminate her pregnancy versus the fetus's right to live. As a consequence, pregnancy has been widely understood in terms of either the woman being a container for the fetus or the fetus being a part of a woman's body, which she was entitled to control. Thus, the abortion debate pitted woman against fetus and assumed that their relationship was inherently adversarial in nature. In this context, new knowledge about hazards to fetal well-being easily led to preoccupation with maternal conduct as a source of harm. This perspective, in turn, led to social concerns that a woman's self-defined interests might conflict with fetal interests.

When this adversarial perspective is applied to the situation where a mother has decided to carry her fetus to term, it frames the issue of maternal conduct in terms of whether a woman has the right to act in ways that carry risks of harm to a fetus. Because a fetus who will be carried to term more closely resembles a child, a woman who acts in disregard of potential risks to that fetus seems selfish and uncaring. In addition, a fetus injured in utero will have to bear the burden of injury throughout its life. Thus, fetal injuries resulting from maternal behavior are similar to other intentionally or negligently inflicted injuries that, when performed by others, are capable of legal redress. Injuries caused by maternal conduct that are preventable with little cost to her are particularly troublesome. As a result, once a woman intends to carry the fetus to term, its claim to be free from injury is likely to prevail. Although women's interests in their own health and well-being will not be completely ignored, there is a higher probability that they will be given short shrift.

Framing the abortion issues in terms of maternal choice also emphasized women's desire to be free of governmental intrusion into decision making about their own bodies. Although the focus on autonomy and freedom from governmental interference was understandable, it nonetheless served to deflect attention from state responsibility. Little thought was given to helping women have children or to help them terminate their pregnancies. Women were free to make reproductive decisions, and they were also free to bear all the burdens associated with these decisions alone (Williams forthcoming).

Many individuals, especially women, are reluctant to move away from arguments about the maternal–fetal relationship that rest on autonomy and rights-based strategies. Alternative approaches that assume women have obligations to their fetuses are reminiscent of earlier definitions of women's roles and responsibilities that served as ways of subjugating women to male domination (Okin 1989). Rights-based strategies were the means that women successfully employed to free themselves from this oppressed condition. Women particularly fear adoption of a view of pregnancy that undermines gains in their right to exercise autonomous reproductive choices.

Although rights-based arguments played a critical role in furthering the interests of women in the context of abortion, reliance on them in other reproductive contexts is questionable (Wikler 1986). Traditionally, pregnant women have been expected to and have, in fact, done everything possible to promote the well-being of fetuses they intended to carry to term (American Medical Association 1990). At a time when women remained in the home and little was known about the fetus, these requirements were not particularly onerous. With new knowledge about the fetus, however, the demands on pregnant women have become increasingly substantial and burdensome. Even so, women usually do meet these expectations. When women fail to meet social expectations about promoting fetal well-being, they are met with hostility rather than understanding.

The consequence of using rights-based arguments is to risk penalizing women for being pregnant. Such arguments tend to hold women solely responsible for pregnancy outcomes, while permitting men and the state to ignore their responsibilities to women, fetuses, and children. Consequently, arguments framed in terms of maternal choice and noninterference from others, on the one hand, and protection of fetuses from harm, on the other, are both likely to lead to state intervention in matters of reproduction to protect the fetus in ways that are detrimental to women.

"Deviant" Moms: Enforcing Maternal Responsibility During Pregnancy

Interventions designed to prevent harm to fetuses by altering maternal behavior to conform with social expectations of pregnant women have employed punitive and coercive approaches. These measures, particularly in the drug context, are either initiated too late to prevent harm or

are of doubtful efficacy and are not demonstrably better than efforts
based on voluntary treatment.

Attempts to alter maternal behavior to prevent harm to fetuses are
not unknown in medical settings. In those environments, health care
administrators and their institutions have petitioned courts to compel a
pregnant women to submit to bodily intrusion in order to prevent harm
to their fetuses. Most of these early legal cases involved a woman's objection to a cesarean section or a blood transfusion. With the notable exception of the decision in *In re A.C.*,[2] most courts have ordered women to
comply with medical advice to prevent harm to their fetuses. This judicial willingness to intervene and override maternal autonomy is viewed
by some as a significant change in the prevailing moral and constitutional
approach to reproduction that has emphasized maternal autonomy,
choice, and privacy (Bayer 1990). Thus, in light of these precedents, concerned parties, especially prosecutors, looked to the courts for solutions to
the problem of maternal drug abuse.

Pregnant women who abuse illegal substances, however, have presented more complicated problems for courts. Unlike cases involving coerced cesareans and transfusions, prosecutions for maternal substance
abuse have typically been initiated after the baby has been born, so judicial intervention has been too late to prevent or mitigate harm at the
fetal stage. Even incarcerating the woman during pregnancy may not
prevent harm to the fetus. The fetus may already have been exposed to
drugs before the woman encounters the criminal justice system. Moreover, because drugs are available in prisons, incarceration may not provide a drug-free environment. Worse, prisons rarely offer services such
as the special diet, exercise facilities, and medical care that pregnant
women require (Barry 1989; Churchville 1988).

Because incarceration is not likely to prevent harm to existing fetuses,
prosecutions of women after the birth of a child exposed to drugs in
utero have been initiated in the belief that criminal sanctions will deter
other pregnant women from using drugs. It is doubtful, however,
whether general deterrence can be achieved in these circumstances
(McGinnis 1990). Female addicts do not necessarily realize they are
pregnant in the early stages of pregnancy; therefore, they could not

---

[2] *In re A.C.* (1990). *Atlantic Rep.*, 2nd series 573:1235–69. U.S. Ct. of Appeals, D.C. Circuit.

know that they are harming their fetuses through substance abuse. Even if she knows that she is pregnant, a female addict may not be aware that psychoactive substances may harm her fetus. Moreover, these prosecutions of pregnant women seem to many to be unduly harsh in view of the fact that a pregnant addict's conduct is not truly voluntary. As a result, there has been increased advocacy of mandatory drug treatment as a means of altering maternal behavior during pregnancy.

Requiring pregnant substance abusers to go into drug treatment is appealing to many. If effective, mandated drug treatment seemingly solves many of the medical and social problems associated with women's drug addiction. The woman stops harming herself; thus, state intervention takes the form of rehabilitation rather than punishment. The woman does not continue to physically harm the fetus, and perhaps she will be a better parent. Ideally, then, if we could get all women substance abusers of childbearing age into treatment, we would go a long way toward resolving problems generated by women's drug use.

Mandatory treatment strategies fall into two broad categories (see Gostin, this volume, p. 258). First, treatment may be required as a result of involvement with the judicial system. Such involvement ranges from conviction for a criminal offense unrelated to drug use to civil child abuse proceedings, in which retention of child custody is conditioned upon enrollment in a treatment program. If one assumes that the treatment offered is effective, that it is permissible under the Constitution, and that the woman has committed some breach of criminal or civil law independent of drug use itself, thereby permitting the state to take some action against the individual, I have no principled objection to this approach. Rehabilitation is an appropriate goal for redressing wrongs in this society. In addition, mandatory treatment is preferable to incarceration without treatment for redress of wrongs in which substance abuse is implicated.

Second, treatment may be mandated through involuntary civil commitment procedures. Typically, civil commitment is used to isolate and treat individuals with mental health problems who are a danger to themselves or others. Civil commitment could be used generally with substance users by considering substance abuse as analogous to mental health problems. A more recent approach calls for pregnancy-specific commitment statutes. For example, the Minnesota Omnibus Crime Bill of 1989 contains a provision entitled "Prenatal Exposure to Certain Con·

trolled Substances," which creates a special exception to civil commitment procedures for pregnant substance abusers.[3] Under this provision a pregnant woman who habitually and excessively uses certain controlled substances and refuses or fails treatment can be determined to be chemically dependent and subject to involuntary commitment. (Normally, only substance abuse that renders an individual incapable of self-management or a danger to self or others is sufficient to justify involuntary commitment [Renshaw 1990, 143].)

Although there is evidence to indicate that coercion does not compromise the effectiveness of drug treatment (see Gostin, this volume), we cannot confidently assume that research findings on its long-term effectiveness with male inmates and parolees is applicable to women drug users, much less pregnant substance abusers (National Academy Press 1990, 198–9). We do know that women addicts, especially those who bear and rear children, have special needs. We do not have sufficient knowledge about what treatment is effective in meeting these needs. Although there is evidence to indicate that costs associated with fetal cocaine exposure are of sufficient magnitude to make education and treatment programs for pregnant women cost effective (Phibbs, Bateman, and Schwartz 1991), we do not have any information about the costs and benefits of alternative forms of treatment for women. It seems premature, therefore, to mandate drug treatment for female substance abusers, much less those who are pregnant.

Even if we assume that mandatory treatment works for women, problems remain. Although mandatory treatment is often viewed as an alternative to the punitive nature of the criminal justice system, in fact, it merely substitutes another form of coercion that also has punitive effects. Therefore, involuntary civil commitment may be as inappropriate as more explicitly punitive strategies. The Minnesota statute is a good illustration of this problem. Although it specifically avoids criminal prosecution and mandates that pregnant substance abusers receive drug treatment, health care professionals report that pregnant substance abusers are avoiding prenatal care and hospital delivery — precisely the same effect seen in states using criminal prosecution (Nyhus Johnson 1990, 522).

Although many argue that mandatory treatment interferes with a woman's autonomy, the real problem with mandatory treatment is that

---

[3] 1989 Minn. Laws, ch. 290, Art. 5.

it carries with it the same assumptions of deviant mom and vulnerable fetus that underlie more explicitly punitive approaches. It assumes that maternal responsibility must be mandated. However, the time, care, and attention that fetuses and children need in order to grow and thrive cannot be coerced. Therefore, these parenting practices are exceedingly difficult for the state to enforce and cannot be easily provided by other means such as foster care. Similarly, the time and effort needed to succeed in drug treatment are difficult for the state to enforce except through the criminal justice system. There is some reason to believe that pregnant women are uniquely motivated to enter treatment voluntarily out of concern for their offspring (Chavkin 1991). Consequently, voluntary treatment programs for pregnant women should be tried before resorting to more punitive and coercive measures. Unfortunately, the Minnesota statute requiring drug treatment for pregnant women did not allocate sufficient funds to treat voluntary patients, let alone women involuntarily committed (Nyhus Johnson 1990, 523). The problem of underfunding is not unique to Minnesota, however. In addition, most voluntary drug treatment facilities use a 90-day program that is probably inadequate to treat addiction, which is a disease that can never be cured, only managed with the help of long-term treatment and lifelong support systems.

Whether persuasion in some form by health professionals should be employed to get women into treatment is a more difficult problem to resolve. (The decision presumes that drug treatment is available and offered in an effective manner.) There is no reason to consider this strategy if the women involved are not pregnant. Indeed, it would be unfair to single women out on the assumption that they might become pregnant. Men also need access to treatment, especially if they are caregivers. When women are pregnant, however, and they intend to carry their fetuses to term, persuasion for purposes of getting women to agree to treatment seems permissible as long as the pregnant woman clearly understands that the final decision about entry into treatment is hers. More persuasive forms of counseling are justified under these circumstances because the fetus that will be carried to term is at risk of harm and the woman's health is also imperiled. Moreover, the effects of her addiction on her ability to assess her situation, which do not justify mandatory treatment, cannot be totally ignored. Finally, pressure exerted by the family or employer to enter treatment in a health care situation is of the sort that is viewed as permissible because the ultimate decision remains with the pregnant woman. It should be noted, however, that steering pregnant women into treatment programs is at best a measure of last resort. In order to help women and to prevent harm to their fetuses and children, treatment of addiction and attendant problems should be initiated before pregnancy occurs.

Limiting Women's Reproductive Options

Although the rhetoric of social and legal discussions centers on the role of punitive and coercive strategies in protecting children, the reality may be that these social responses are directed at keeping some women from reproducing. For example, in Ohio legislation has been introduced that would mandate sterilization of women unable to overcome their addiction (Berrien 1990). The 1990 approval of Norplant® (a long-term implantable contraceptive) by the Food and Drug Administration has already led to a spate of proposals to use it to reduce the number of childbirths to teenagers, women on welfare, and female drug abusers (Egan 1990; Lev 1991; *Philadelphia Inquirer* 1990).

My belief that such strategies are designed to prevent specific groups of women from procreating receives partial support from the popular association between drug abuse and a user population that is poor and composed of minorities. In addition, poor and minority women have been disproportionately prosecuted for illegal substance abuse when compared with the known incidence of illicit drug use by women of all races and classes. In a survey by the American Civil Liberties Union of criminal prosecutions, 80 percent involved women of color (Paltrow, Goetz, and Shende 1990). Indeed, one study indicates that black women who are substance abusers are ten times more likely to be reported to the authorities than white women (Chasnoff, Landress, and Barrett 1990). Finally, we have a history in this country of coercing reproductive choices of minority women. For example, poor and minority women are disproportionately forced into having cesarean sections (Kolder, Gallagher, and Parsons 1987).

Coercing reproductive decisions — whether to delay or prevent conception — as the primary solution to women's drug abuse squarely poses the question of what motivation really underlies the punitive approaches we have taken in current drug policies for women. For some people, drug-abusing women should not be permitted to parent because they will expose future children to serious physical and psychological harm. Preventing or delaying reproduction is, therefore, an especially effective way of preventing future child abuse (Coyle 1989). For other people, drug-abusing women do not deserve to be parents. Their past conduct is so egregious that they merit severe sanctions. Whatever label or motivation we attach to strategies that prevent or delay reproduction, the potential for unfairly burdening minority groups and the poor is so high that they must be resisted. Preventing or delaying reproduction also contradicts fundamental values of reproductive freedom. Nevertheless, there are frightening historical precedents suggesting that these values can be ignored in times of acute social crisis, such as the current "drug epidemic."

Although the prevailing liberal view in this society has been that individuals should have freedom of choice in reproductive matters (Bayer 1990), a darker reality has always hovered over the exercise of reproductive options by some individuals and groups. The belief that some individuals should not be permitted to be parents lies deep in our culture. This belief first received widespread social and legal support through the eugenics movement early in this century. Although historically eugenics focused primarily on preventing the transmission of deleterious genes, concern about parental competence—an expanded notion of unfitness—was always implicit. These concerns justified coerced sterilization of immigrants, the poor, and the institutionalized in the early decades of this century. These sterilizations were sanctioned by the U.S. Supreme Court in *Buck v. Bell*,[4] a case whose reasoning has been undermined, but never overruled. Even as late as the 1970s, poor and minority women believed to be unfit for parental responsibilities were being coerced into accepting sterilizations under the threat that their welfare benefits would be withdrawn.[5]

Contemporary concern about parental competence grows, in part, out of legitimate distress about the conditions in which children live and the physical, emotional, and cognitive problems that they may suffer as a result of parental inadequacies. There is an added fear that the state will have to bear the costs of rearing children whose parents are unable, for economic or other reasons, to carry out their responsibilities. This legitimate concern is also accompanied by a persistent, pervasive, and highly discriminatory preference for homogeneity in parenting styles.

---

[4] *Buck v. Bell* (1927). *U.S. Reports* 274:200–8.
[5] *Relf v. Weinberger* (1977). *Federal Reports*, 2nd series, 565:722–7. U.S. Ct. of Appeals, D.C. Circuit.

African-American women have been a special target of these historical and contemporary concerns about parental competence (Roberts
1991). Stereotypes of African Americans as likely to prefer welfare to
work, to be more violent, lazier, and less intelligent are pervasive and
enduring (*Washington Post* 1991). In addition, drugs, violence, and
perinatal transmission of HIV infection are associated in the public
mind with the African-American community (Garcia 1990). All of these
factors reinforce the popular view that African Americans are not competent parents. Consequently, it takes only a small leap to arrive at the
view that drug-abusing women, like women on welfare and women who
are HIV infected, should be encouraged, perhaps coerced, into forgoing
reproduction in order to spare their potential children and the state the
harms and costs resulting from their conduct.

The fact that certain women continue to reproduce despite the
knowledge that their substance abuse during pregnancy places their offspring at risk of potentially very serious deficits is a source of legitimate
concern for all. The legitimacy of this concern, however, cannot alone
justify limiting the rights of individuals to reproduce. Control over the
body and its reproductive aspects are essential ingredients in the development of individual self-identity as well as fundamental constitutional
rights and cannot lightly be ignored.[6] Moreover, enduring unfairness
and injustice in this society growing out of race, class, and gender bias
call for caution in pursuing policies that single out certain groups of individuals for repressive reproductive strategies. Less drastic alternatives
to accomplishing the goal of improving children's lives and reducing the
necessity for public support should be pursued before giving the state
the power to decide who can or cannot reproduce or even to determine
the timing of reproduction.

It is not only direct governmental control over reproductive choices
that must be avoided. Social welfare policies and programs can also
meaningfully restrict the reproductive options that individuals realistically can exercise (King, forthcoming). For example, offering money to
impoverished women on condition that they use a long-term contraceptive may have the same discriminatory effect as passing a law that
requires sterilization or long-term contraceptive use. Although such arrangements retain the veneer of voluntariness, the fact is that they re-

---

[6] *Skinner v. State.* 1941. *Pacific Rep.*, 2nd series 115:123 (Oklahoma). *Roe v.
Wade.* 1973. *U.S. Reports* 410:113.

quire women to choose between unacceptable alternatives — remaining in need or relinquishing reproductive freedom — solely because they are poor.

On the other hand, a woman's addiction to drugs does compromise her ability to make well-thought-out choices. This fact, coupled with the harm that drug abuse brings to her and her children, suggests that in some circumstances directive counseling about reproductive options, emphasizing delayed reproduction, is warranted. John Arras advocates a form of counseling that lies between directive and nondirective approaches. He argues that HIV-infected women should be counseled in a manner that "clarif[ies] the client's values and expand[s] her awareness of the moral dimensions of her choices through respectful exchanges" (Arras 1990, 374). In principle, I agree with his view, because I am not convinced that counseling is ever value free, and because I do not think that mere recital of the possible consequences of a woman's drug addiction for her fetus provides her with enough information to make an informed judgment. Seeing the effects of drugs on infants in a nursery caring for addicted babies may facilitate understanding of those consequences in a way that mere verbal disclosure cannot. Therefore, as I understand Arras's model, it might, at least theoretically, enhance choice rather than impose predetermined outcomes.

Nonetheless, I remain profoundly skeptical about whether even this modified form of directive counseling can be conducted in a manner that realistically permits women to select any reproductive alternative, particularly outcomes we are trying to discourage. I am also convinced that this type of counseling would disproportionately target poor and minority women who, after all, receive most of their care from public sources where our concern about the social cost of their decisions is highest. Again the present-day realities of class, race, gender, and ethnic discrimination urge caution before adopting such a strategy. Less drastic infringements on long-valued rights of reproductive freedom and autonomy should be tried before we resort to these very stringent policies. Otherwise modern reproductive policies will be indistinguishable in their *effect* from their eugenic forebears.

As long as society persists in viewing the maternal–fetal relationship as adversarial and women as solely responsible for fetal lives, punitive and coercive strategies in response to maternal substance abuse are inevitable. Furthermore, punitive and coercive approaches will remain easy to justify as long as we view mothers who are substance abusers as deviant and their fetuses as primarily vulnerable to maternally inflicted injuries. This adversarial view of the maternal–fetal relationship, however, is not inevitable or preordained. In fact, it is antithetical to our own experiences as pregnant women and parents. Moreover, what is often perceived as an adversarial stance may in reality reflect the fact that women may need help in meeting the responsibilities associated with pregnancy and caregiving. To develop truly effective drug policies for women, then, we need to begin with a different, more realistic view of the maternal–fetal relationship.

In the Body, of the Body: A Reformed Understanding of Pregnancy

A rights-based approach that pits woman against fetus fails to capture the essential biological and emotional reality of pregnancy. The fetus is in the woman's body and part of the woman's body (Purdy 1990, 273). It is simultaneously self and not-self. Most fundamentally, however, the maternal–fetal relationship is an interconnected and interactive *unit*.

In one sense the fetus and woman are one. The fetus exists in a body that shelters it, so their interests are the same. The fetus's continued existence is totally dependent, in a very unique way, on the body of the pregnant woman. Both the fetus and the woman are vulnerable to those forces that impact on the woman's body. It is also clear that, to the extent the woman's body is treated well, both the woman and the fetus benefit. In another important sense, however, the pregnant woman and the fetus are separate. A single act that may not harm the mother, such as exposure to rubella, may hurt the fetus. Alternatively, the fetus may have a developmental problem that needs surgical correction in utero, which of necessity requires the mother to subject herself to risks that will not benefit her personally.

Because of fetuses' total dependence, pregnant women must take enormous care to shield them from many potential sources of harm. At times mothers must choose not simply between their own self-interest and fetal interests. There are circumstances when other individuals' needs must also be weighed into the mother's decision, and these may also diverge from fetal interests. For example, a woman may have to work in order to support her existing children, but she may also be advised that several months of bed rest toward the end of her pregnancy are necessary to prevent harm to her fetus. As the primary decision-maker for the maternal–fetal unit, and often indeed for the family unit, the pregnant woman may make a decision that results in harm to the fetus. This decision may be self-interested, or it may reflect a careful weighing and balancing of the needs of all. To view the woman's decision as solely adversarial to fetal interests misses the complexity of the interactions involved in the maternal–fetal unit.

Adversarial rights-based analytical frameworks work best when characterizing the duties and obligations that flow from relationships between strangers. These approaches are incapable of capturing "the continual rendering of services, kindnesses, attentions, and concerns beyond what is obligatory between persons whose lives are intimately and enduringly connected" (O'Neill and Ruddick 1979, 7). As Buchanan notes, "Members of an intimate relationship are seen as elements of an affectively integrated whole, who promote each other's good spontaneously out of love or direct concern, rather than from instrumental calculations of self-interest" (1982, 36). When an intimate relationship is also one in which there is a dependent member, the inadequacy of rights-based frameworks is even more glaring. Surely women have rights of privacy and bodily integrity. Yet, the autonomy argument does not seem compelling in discussing a woman's gestational and caretaking roles because harm to her frequently results in simultaneously harming her fetus. Alternatively, although an assertion of fetal rights may result in protecting the fetus from maternal harm, it does little to promote fetal well-being in the sense of ensuring that the mother receives access to social resources needed by the fetus for normal development.

In short, treating a fetus as though it were in fact the equal of the woman, using "rights" terminology as a means of establishing its claims to protection or care, tells us nothing about what should be the moral relationship between the pregnant woman and the fetus (Baier 1987, 53). We also need to take special note that individuals in many important intimate relationships do not have equal power in those relationships. Understanding the maternal–fetal relationship as an intimate interactive unit, in which there is a severe discrepancy in power, better helps us define the nature of the moral relationship that exists between the pregnant woman and the fetus.

It is generally agreed that parents have moral obligations to their children that are derived from their decision to reproduce (Arras 1990; Buchanan 1982; O'Neill and Ruddick 1979). Extension of these obligations to the prenatal period in light of the information that we now possess about the uterine environment seems warranted once there has been a decision to continue pregnancy. Indeed, once a woman decides to carry a fetus to term, it is useful to think of the maternal–fetal relationship as analogous to the parent–child relationship (American Medical Association 1990).

The scope of the moral obligation that parents owe children, however, is not well defined (Blustein 1979). Although it is generally accepted that parents do have obligations of care and support and may not physically abuse or neglect their children, it is not clear how far parents are required to go in sacrificing their own interests for the sake of their children. As Blustein points out, "Child rearers cannot be completely defined by their role as child rearers. . . . If child rearers perceive the raising of their children as an overwhelming burden which makes it impossible to pursue these other desires and interests, child-rearing becomes intolerable. . . . Hence children too have an interest in their rearers being free to pursue other desires and interests" (Blustein 1979, 118–19). Moreover, the fact that philosophers have failed to focus on justifications for promoting another's good in the context of intimate relationships compounds our problem in analyzing moral responsibilities when we move from adult friendships and parent–child relationships to maternal–fetal relationships. Pregnancy, after all, is a unique condition in which two entities are physically joined. As a result, fundamental questions about moral responsibilities raised in the context of pregnancy have no obvious answers.

First, if we assume that decisions to procreate carry obligations to dependent others, the question that arises is whether circumstances in the lives of potential procreators morally require them not to reproduce or at least to delay reproduction. John Arras, for example, has taken an important and courageous step in exploring this issue (although I do not entirely agree with his reasoning) in the context of HIV-infected women and concludes that the risk of transmitting HIV infection is a "good reason," although not in every case a compelling reason, for not procreating (Arras 1990). If there is a moral obligation to refrain from or to delay procreation, would that obligation also justify, if not morally require, abortion in some circumstances?

A second fundamental question concerns the scope of the pregnant woman's obligation to promote the good of the fetus. How should we think about a woman's use of legal or illegal drugs during pregnancy? Is the pregnant woman inflicting harm on the fetus? Viewed in this way, the pregnant woman might have an obligation of nonmaleficence: to refrain from inflicting harm. Alternatively, would it make more sense to think of the pregnant woman's use of drugs as a failure to benefit another? From this perspective the pregnant woman's obligation is somewhat less obligatory because she is not acting, but rather failing to act in relation to another (Beauchamp and Childress 1989, 120–7). To be sure, whether we view the pregnant woman's actions as inflicting harm or as failing to promote the good of the fetus, the fetus will suffer the same harm. However, the way we define the scope of the pregnant woman's obligation has implications for how we morally regard her conduct and for the policies we develop in response to it.

The lack of attention given special intimate relationships by philosophers, especially relationships that are unequal in power, is reason to urge caution in statements about moral responsibility in specific circumstances like pregnancy. However, our lack of consensus on the scope of a pregnant woman's moral obligation to her fetus is not sufficient reason to reject the idea of moral obligation altogether. Certainly, great sensitivity would be required in developing models of responsibility and obligations to fetuses, but there are a number of philosophical and cultural values that we could rely on in this process. Fetuses are regarded as only potential persons in this society. As a consequence, a woman's moral obligation to her fetus should not be greater than it is to her child (Murray 1987; Purdy 1990). Because men are also parents, there would be some constraint on any undue tendency to burden women. There is no moral requirement that parents of either sex sacrifice their lives or health interests for their children after birth. In her role as parent, a woman should not be required to do so for the sake of the fetus.

Defining the maternal–fetal relationship in terms of an interactive unit is a vast improvement over the adversarial model because it more closely approximates our experience of pregnancy and relationships with special intimate others. This model of the maternal–fetal relationship posits that maternal and fetal interests are inextricably linked. Policies that promote women's interests enhance fetal well-being as well. Thus, women have an interest in providing nurturing and healthy environments for their fetuses because they simultaneously further their own interests. Looked at from this perspective, parental failure may not only have adverse implications for the fetus but perhaps represents defeat of the parents' own hopes for the future as well. The primary issue raised by substance-abusing pregnant women is thus transformed from what to do about deviant women—an approach that encourages use of coercive and punitive policies—to how to cope with the reality that all women are not equally situated with respect to their capacity to fulfill their moral obligations to their fetuses.

Strategies that emphasize education, treatment, and removal of the conditions that lead to a woman's addiction in the first place thus seem more compelling than those based on coercion and punishment. More importantly, understanding that maternal and fetal interests are linked has import for the structuring of such strategies. Existing programs are often focused exclusively on pregnancy, that is to say, on the child-to-be (Chavkin and St. Clair 1990), sometimes to the detriment of maternal health (Minkoff and Moreno 1990). Yet, meaningful reduction in maternal and infant mortality and morbidity requires intervention and assistance to women before and after pregnancy. Programs must target the social, economic, and medical needs of women of reproductive age. Women need and deserve help for themselves. They also need and deserve assistance to enable them to meet the needs of their children.

References

Abel, E.L. 1973. Recognition of the Fetal Alcohol Syndrome in Early Infancy. *Lancet* 2:999–1001.
———. 1990. *Fetal Alcohol Syndrome.* Oradell, N.J.: Medical Economics Books.
American Medical Association, Board of Trustees. 1990. Legal Interventions During Pregnancy. *Journal of the American Medical Association* 264:2663–70.
American College of Obstetricians and Gynecologists. 1990. Cocaine Abuse: Implications for Pregnancy. Committee opinion no. 81 (March). Washington, D.C.
Arras, J.D. 1990. AIDS and Reproductive Decisions: Having Children in Fear and Trembling. *Milbank Quarterly* 68:353–82.
Baier, A. 1987. The Need for More Justice. *Canadian Journal of Philosophy* 13(suppl.):41–56.
Barry, E. 1989. Pregnancy Prisoners. *Harvard Women's Law Journal* 12:189–205.
Bayer, R. 1990. AIDS and the Future of Reproductive Freedom. *Milbank Quarterly* 68(suppl. 2):179–204.

Beauchamp, T.L., and J.F. Childress. 1989. The Principle of Nonmalef-icence. The Principle of Beneficence. In *Principles of Biomedical Ethics*, 120–255. New York: Oxford University Press.

Berrien, J. 1990. Pregnancy and Drug Use: The Dangerous and Un-equal Use of Punitive Measures. *Yale Journal of Law and Feminism* 2:239–50.

Black, R., and J. Mayer. 1980. Parents with Special Problems: Alcohol-ism and Opiate Addiction. *International Journal of Child Abuse and Neglect* 4:45–54.

Blustein, J. 1979. Child Rearing and Family Interest. In *Having Chil-dren: Philosophical and Legal Reflections on Parenthood*, eds. O. O'Neill and W. Ruddick, 115–22. New York: Oxford University Press.

Buchanan, A.E. 1982. Philosophical Foundations of Beneficence. In *Be-neficence and Health Care*, ed. E.E. Sharp, 33–62. Boston: Reidel.

Burns, W.J., and K.A. Burns. 1988. Parenting Dysfunction in Chemi-cally Dependent Women. In *Drugs, Alcohol, Pregnancy and Parenting*, ed. I.J. Chasnoff, 159–71. Boston: Kluwer.

Callahan, D. 1986. How Technology Is Reframing the Abortion De-bate. *Hastings Center Report* (February):33–43.

Chasnoff, I.J. 1988. Introduction: The Interfaces of Perinatal Addic-tion. In *Drugs, Alcohol, Pregnancy and Parenting*, ed. I.J. Chas-noff, 1–16. Boston: Kluwer.

———. 1989. Drug Use and Women: Establishing a Standard of Care. *Annals of the New York Academy of Sciences* 562:208–10.

Chasnoff, I.J., H.J. Landress, and M.E. Barrett. 1990. The Prevalence of Illicit-Drug or Alcohol Use During Pregnancy and Discrepancies in Mandatory Reporting in Pinellas County, Florida. *New England Journal of Medicine* 322:1202–6.

Chavkin, W. 1990. Drug Addiction and Pregnancy: Policy Crossroads. *American Journal of Public Health* 80:483–7.

———. 1991. Mandatory Treatment for Drug Use During Pregnancy. *Journal of the American Medical Association* 226:1556–61.

Chavkin, W., and D. St. Clair. 1990. Beyond Prenatal Care: A Com-prehensive Vision of Reproductive Health. *Journal of the American Medical Women's Association* 45:45–57.

Churchville, V. 1988. D.C. Judge Jails Woman as Protection for Fetus. *Washington Post* (July 23):A1.

Coyle, C.M. 1989. Sterilization: A "Remedy for the Malady" of Child Abuse? *Journal of Contemporary Health Law and Policy* 5:245–62.

Daghestani, A.N. 1988. Psychosocial Characteristics of Pregnant Ad-dicts in Treatment. In *Drugs, Alcohol, Pregnancy and Parenting*, ed. I.J. Chasnoff, 7–16. Boston: Kluwer.

Dans, P.E., R.M. Matricciani, S.E. Otter, and D.S. Reyland. 1990. Intravenous Drug Use and One Academic Health Center. *Journal of the American Medical Association* 263:3173–6.

Deren, S. 1986. Children of Substance Abusers: A Review of the Literature. *Journal of Substance Abuse Treatment* 3:77–94.

Egan, T. 1990. Chief Judge Says Crack May Overwhelm Courts. *New York Times* (December 3):B3.

Garcia, S.A. 1990. Birth Penalty: Societal Responses to Perinatal Chemical Dependence. *Journal of Clinical Ethics* 1:135–46.

Hassett, D.G. 1985. Family Alcoholism and Child Abuse. *Focus on Family and Chemical Dependence* 8:14–15, 31.

Jones, K.L., D.W. Smith, C.N. Ulleland, and P. Streissguth. 1973. Pattern of Malformation in Offspring of Chronic Alcoholic Mothers. *Lancet* 1973:1267–71.

Kandel, D.B. 1991. The Social Demography of Drug Use. New York: Columbia University. (Unpublished manuscript)

Keith, L.G., S.N. MacGregor, and J.J. Sciarra. 1988. Drug Abuse in Pregnancy. In *Drugs, Alcohol, Pregnancy and Parenting*, ed. I.J. Chasnoff, 17–46. Boston: Kluwer.

King, P.A. Forthcoming. The Past as Prologue: Race, Class and Gene Discrimination. In *Using the Ethics and Law as Guides*, eds. G. Annas and S. Elias.

Kolder, V.E., J. Gallagher, and M.T. Parsons. 1987. Court-Ordered Obstetrical Interventions. *New England Journal of Medicine* 316: 1192–6.

Lev, M. 1991. Judge Is Firm on Forced Contraception, but Welcomes an Appeal. *New York Times* (January 11):A17.

Mayer, J., and R. Black. 1977. Child Abuse and Neglect in Families with an Alcohol and Opiate Addicted Parent. *International Journal of Child Abuse and Neglect* 1:88–98.

McGinnis, D.M. 1990. Prosecution of Mothers of Drug-Exposed Babies: Constitutional and Criminal Theory. *University of Pennsylvania Law Review* 139:505–39.

McNulty, M. 1987–88. Pregnancy Police: The Health Policy and Legal Implications of Punishing Pregnant Women for Harm to Their Fetuses. *Review of Law & Social Change* 16:277–319.

Medical World News. 1990. Drug Babies: An Ethical Quagmire for Doctors (February 12):39–56.

Minkoff, H., and J.D. Moreno. 1990. Drug Prophylaxis for Human Immunodeficiency Virus-Infected Pregnant Women: Ethical Considerations. *American Journal of Obstetrics and Gynecology* 163: 1111–14.

Murray, T. 1987. Moral Obligations to the Not-Yet-Born: The Fetus as Patient. *Clinical Perinatology* 14:329–43.

National Academy Press. 1988. *Prenatal Care: Reaching Mothers, Reaching Infants.* Washington.

————. 1990. *Treating Drug Problems.* Washington.

Nyhus Johnson, J.M. 1990. Minnesota's "Crack Baby" Law: Weapons of War or Link in a Chain? *Law and Equality* 8:485–531.

Okin, S.M. 1989. *Justice, Gender, and the Family.* New York: Basic Books.

O'Neill, O., and W. Ruddick. 1979. *Having Children: Philosophical and Legal Reflections on Parenthood.* New York: Oxford University Press.

Paltrow, L., E. Goetz, and S. Shende. 1990. Overview of ACLU National Survey of Criminal Prosecutions Brought against Pregnant Women: 80% Brought against Women of Color, October 3. New York: American Civil Liberties Union. (Memorandum)

Phibbs, C.S., D.A. Bateman, and R.M. Schwartz. 1991. The Neonatal Costs of Maternal Cocaine Use. *Journal of the American Medical Association* 266:1521–6.

Philadelphia Inquirer. 1990. Poverty and Norplant. (Editorial.) (December 12):18-A.

Pollitt, K. 1990. A New Assault on Feminism. *Nation* 26:409–18.

Purdy, L.M. 1990. Are Pregnant Women Fetal Containers? *Bioethics* 4:273–91.

Regan, D.O., S.M. Ehrlich, and L.P. Finnegan. 1987. Infants of Drug Addicts: At Risk for Child Abuse, Neglect, and Placement in Foster Care. *Neurotoxicology and Teratology* 9:315–19.

Regier, D.A., M.E. Farmer, D.S. Rae, et al. 1990. Comorbidity of Mental Disorders with Alcohol and Other Drug Use: Results from the Epidemiological Catchment Area (ECA) Study. *Journal of the American Medical Association* 264:2511–18.

Renshaw, K.K. 1990. A Civil Approach to a Controversial Issue: Minnesota's Attempt to Deal with Mothers of "Cocaine Babies." *Hamline Journal of Public Law and Policy* 11:137–50.

Roberts, D. 1991. Punishing Drug Addicts Who Have Babies: Women of Color, Equality, and the Right of Privacy. *Harvard Law Review* 104:1419–82.

Rosenbaum, M. 1979. Difficulties in Taking Care of Business: Women Addicts as Mothers. *American Journal of Drug and Alcohol Abuse* 6:431–46.

U.S. Congress. 1990. Getting Straight: Overcoming Treatment Barriers for Addicted Women and Their Children. Hearing before the U.S.

House of Representatives, Select Committee on Children, Youth and Families, April 23. Washington.

Washington Post. 1991. The Centrality of Race. (January 12):A20. (Editorial)

Weiner, L., and B.A. Morse. 1988. FAS: Clinical Perspectives and Prevention. In *Drugs, Alcohol, Pregnancy and Parenting*, ed. I.J. Chasnoff, 127–48. Boston: Kluwer.

Wikler, N.J. 1986. Society's Response to the New Reproductive Technologies: The Feminist Perspective. *Southern California Law Review* 59:1043–57.

Williams, J.C. 1992. Gender Wars: Selfless Women in the Republic of Choice. *New York University Law Review.* (forthcoming).

Acknowledgments: I wish to thank Professors Anita Allen, Gary Peller, and Gerry Spann and the known and unknown reviewers of this article for their many thoughtful comments. My special thanks to Zoe Ulshen, my research assistant, who researched, read, and edited many versions of this article.

Medicalization of Psychoactive Substance Use and the Doctor–Patient Relationship

ROBERT J. LEVINE

Yale University School of Medicine

UPPOSE THE UNITED STATES ADOPTED A POLICY OF medicalizing cocaine, heroin, marijuana, and other substances commonly called "psychoactive substances of abuse." Under such a policy these substances could be obtained on the prescription of a physician; when thus acquired, their possession or use would no longer be considered criminal offenses. What effect would such a new policy have on the practice of medicine? Are there features of the norms and traditions of medical practice that might thwart the implementation of such a policy? Are there reasons to believe that physicians or patients would or should either welcome or resist the medicalization of psychoactive substances of abuse? In this essay I will attempt to respond to these questions.

Let us first imagine a patient walking into a doctor's office today and making a straightforward request that the doctor supply him with heroin, cocaine, or marijuana. The doctor is entitled to respond by refusing this request without offering any explanation beyond a simple statement that it is against the law. A good doctor would, of course, go beyond this minimal requirement and would engage the patient in a conversation designed to explore at least the patient's reasons for making this request and what he intends to do if the doctor refuses to cooperate. She would then proceed to offer advice on alternative courses of action that are available to accomplish the patient's objectives. At the end of this conversation, however, the prudent doctor must refuse to cooperate or else risk being penalized by the criminal justice system, losing her license to practice medicine, and being censured by colleagues.

The situation is, to some extent, analogous to that presented in some of the United States in 1970 (before *Roe v. Wade*) by women who requested elective abortions, or in 1960 (before *Griswold v. Connecticut*) by patients who requested contraceptives. It is analogous to the extent that doctors were entitled to refuse such requests without offering any explanation beyond simply stating that they were against the law.

Some doctors, however, found ways to respond without violating the letter of the law. They advised patients of the availability of elective abortions in other countries or performed "therapeutic abortions" justified by highly tenuous "diagnoses." For example, as head of a hypertension clinic I was often asked to certify that a pregnant woman who had one isolated diastolic blood pressure measurement of 91–95 mm Hg required a therapeutic abortion in order to avoid a serious complication of pregnancy known as eclampsia, a condition characterized by convulsions and coma; all parties to the discussion knew the probability of developing this complication was very small. Some patients had uterine dilatation and curettage (D&C) performed, ostensibly for the diagnostic evaluation of menstrual irregularities. The gynecologists always feigned shock at finding that their patients were pregnant because "their" pregnancy tests had been negative; the gynecologists had advised these women to submit a sample of their husband's urine rather than their own for pregnancy testing. In the late 1950s, a bus service was provided from the city in which I did my residency to a neighboring state where doctors could lawfully prescribe contraceptives.

I do not mean to suggest that surreptitious violation of the law is generally acceptable ethically. Rather, I am committed to the position that professionals should conduct their practices according to socially established norms. In this regard, I affirm principle 3 of the American Medical Association's *Principles of Medical Ethics*: "A physician shall respect the law and also recognize a responsibility to seek changes in those requirements which are contrary to the best interests of the patient" (1982). Accordingly, doctors who feel a moral obligation to violate a law governing medical practice because it is contrary to patients' best interests assume a prima facie obligation to make their disobedience to the law a public act; covert violations do not accomplish the moral purposes of civil disobedience (Madden and Hare 1978).

My purpose in recalling earlier experiences with contraceptives and abortion is twofold. First, they remind us that simply because the law forbids something does not necessarily mean that no doctor will do it.

There are, for example, doctors who now prescribe narcotics for patients who are addicted to them primarily to prevent symptoms of withdrawal; such doctors typically pretend that the purpose of their prescriptions is to relieve pain.

Second, these experiences remind us that not all people and not all doctors believed before *Roe v. Wade* was decided that elective abortion was absolutely and invariably wrong any more than they later believed it to be absolutely and invariably right. I suggest that there may be the same diversity of perspectives on the moral legitimacy of doctors providing prescriptions for cocaine, heroin, marijuana, and other so-called psychoactive substances of abuse. Doctors holding various perspectives on this subject will differ in their reactions to medicalization of access to these substances.

The Purpose of Medicine

Under a medicalization policy, the only lawful mode of access to cocaine, heroin, marijuana, and other psychoactive substances of abuse would be on the prescription of a physician. Are there any reasons for a physician not to cooperate with requests for such prescriptions?

It can be argued — and it often is — that doctors should refuse to cooperate because these requests are either contrary to or disconnected from the purposes of medicine. The traditional purposes of medicine are, according to the distinguished medical historian Henry Sigerist, to promote health, prevent illness, restore health, and rehabilitate those whose functioning or well-being is impaired (1951, 7). In the twentieth century the focus of the medical profession has centered on diseases: on the treatment of patients with diseases with the aim of providing cure, remission, restoration of impaired function, or palliation, and on the prevention of diseases (R.J. Levine 1978). Professional encounters between doctors and patients are seen most securely as legitimate if their purpose is to treat or prevent disease.

This raises the question of whether the use or abuse of heroin, cocaine, marijuana, or other drugs with abuse potential can properly be seen as a disease. In the mainstream of Western medicine a condition is identified as a disease if its presence can be verified objectively (R.J. Levine 1978). The identification is established most securely if the requisite objective verification is accomplished using the devices of the

natural sciences, such as anatomy, chemistry, physiology; diseases relying on the behavioral or social sciences for their identification or diagnosis, or both, tend to be more problematic. It is unclear whether some
maladaptive deviations from "normal" behavior should be considered
sins, crimes, or diseases (Fox 1989, 28ff). Such is the ambiguity of some
of these classifications that deviant persons may be offered a choice between the sick role and the criminal role (Burt 1978; R.J. Levine 1978;
Murphy and Thomasma 1981).

What about the use of cocaine, marijuana, heroin, and other psychoactive drugs of abuse? The American Psychiatric Association (APA)
states:

> In our society, use of certain substances to modify mood or behavior
> under certain circumstances is generally regarded as normal and ap-
> propriate. Such use includes recreational drinking of alcohol, in
> which a majority of adult Americans participate, and uses of caffeine,
> in the form of coffee or tea, as a stimulant. On the other hand, there
> are wide cultural variations. In some groups even the recreational use
> of alcohol is frowned upon, whereas in other groups the use of var-
> ious illegal substances for mood-altering effects has become widely
> accepted. In addition, certain psychoactive substances are used medi-
> cally for the alleviation of pain, relief of tension, or to suppress appe-
> tite. (1980, 165)

The APA distinguishes "recreational" and "medical" uses from
"pathological" use, which is characterized by "symptoms and maladaptive
behavioral changes":

> [These] would be viewed as extremely undesirable in almost all cul-
> tures. Examples include continued use of the psychoactive substance
> despite the presence of a persistent or recurrent social, occupational,
> psychological, or physical problem that the person knows may be ex-
> acerbated by that use and the development of serious withdrawal
> symptoms following cessation or reduction in use of a psychoactive
> substance. These conditions are here conceptualized as mental disor-
> ders. . . . (1980, 165)

Thus the use of psychoactive substances in and of itself is not regarded as disease. Only when such use is associated with maladaptive
behavioral changes and persists for more than a month does it become
eligible for the diagnosis of "psychoactive substance abuse" (APA 1980,

169). A more advanced condition, "psychoactive substance dependence," is characterized by such attributes as loss of control over when and how much of the substance is to be used, partial or complete loss of important social, occupational, or recreational activities, and, with some substances, the development of withdrawal syndromes.

According to the American College of Physicians (ACP), "Chemical dependence is a medical illness requiring medical diagnosis and treatment" (ACP 1985). The Presidential Commission on the HIV Epidemic (1988) states: "Drug addiction is a disease of the whole person involving multiple areas of function."

At this point there appears to be a prima facie case against authorizing physicians to write prescriptions for recreational or pathological use of psychoactive substances. Recreational use appears at best to be foreign to the purpose of medicine and may lead to the development of a disease; pathological use is itself identified as a disease. Further light can be shed on this problem by considering another dimension of the purpose of the medical profession. The medical profession responds not only to disease but also to the sick role.

The Sick Role

Sickness is not merely a biological or behavioral condition or disturbance. It is a social role characterized by certain entitlements, obligations, and exemptions from social obligations; this social role is shaped by the society, groups, and cultural tradition to which the sick person belongs (Fox 1989, 21ff). Talcott Parsons (1951, 1972), in his highly influential description, identifies four aspects of the institutionalized expectation system regarding the sick role:

1. There is an "exemption from normal social role responsibilities, which . . . is relative to the nature and severity of the illness. This exemption requires legitimation . . . and the physician often serves as a court of appeal as well as a direct legitimatizing agent . . . being sick enough to avoid obligations cannot only be a right of the sick person but an obligation upon him. . . ."

2. "The sick person cannot be expected by 'pulling himself together' to get well by an act of decision or will. In this sense also he is exempted from responsibility—he is in a condition that must 'be taken care of' . . . . the process of recovery may be spontaneous

but while the illness lasts he can't 'help it.' This element in the definition . . . is crucial as a bridge to the acceptance of 'help.' "

3. "The state of being ill is itself undesirable with its obligation to want to 'get well.' The first two elements of legitimization of the sick role thus are conditional in a highly important sense. It is a relative legitimization as long as he is in this unfortunate state which both he and alter [authority] hope he can get out of as expeditiously as possible."

4. There is an obligation upon the sick person "to seek technically competent help, mainly, in the most usual sense, that of a physician and to *cooperate* with him in the process of trying to get well. It is here, of course, that the role of the sick person as patient becomes articulated with that of the physician in a complementary role structure."

To a large extent the social purpose of the medical profession is to respond to the needs of persons in the sick role. Persons in the sick role need "technically competent help" in dealing with their diseases. They also need "legitimation" of their exemptions from normal social role responsibilities. In general, this legitimation is completely dependent upon the diagnosis of a disease (R.J. Levine 1978, 1991; Siegler 1979).

Doctors and patients working together in relationships of the sort implied by Parsons's description of the sick role find themselves on familiar ground. Within these familiar relationships they can confidently appraise the behaviors of themselves and each other. The doctor, for example, may think that a patient is a "good patient" for wanting to get well as expeditiously as possible. Within this familiar social system, the good doctor finds support for her attempts to persuade or admonish the patient to lose weight, stop smoking, or take all of his pills. This familiarity and social support contribute to the successful conduct of medical practice — to the realization of the purposes of medicine. Doctors and patients understand and try to play their roles as "good doctor" and "good patient."

Recreational Use

Those who support making drugs like heroin, cocaine, and marijuana available by prescription for recreational use do so because it will, in their view, yield several important advantages over the current system (Nadelmann 1989). They anticipate that it would, for example, reduce the crime rate associated with drug abuse and reduce the health hazards to individual drug users.

Let us first consider briefly the prediction of a reduction in the crime rate associated with drug abuse. If recreational use of these drugs were decriminalized, persons who use them would cease to think of themselves as criminals. Currently, possession or use of these drugs is regarded as criminal behavior. Because users already perceive themselves as criminals, or at least as being so labeled, it is for them a relatively small step to engage in other activities considered criminal. Moreover, in order to secure supplies of drugs, they must encounter persons who are possibly more committed to the criminal role and more familiar with the range of activities available to those willing to assume the criminal role. Recreational drug users often find it necessary to engage in criminal behavior in order to pay the high prices charged for the drugs. The vendors are often able and willing to offer advice on how to become a prostitute, drug pusher, robber, and so on.

Parenthetically, it is often predicted that one of the benefits of medicalizing recreational drug use would be a decrease in the price of the drugs. This would have the advantage of reducing pressure on drug users to assume the criminal role. Musto (1990) provides historical evidence that we cannot confidently predict a medicalization policy to bring about a reduction in the retail price of drugs. He studied the price of illicit cocaine "on the streets" of New York during a period (1907–1914) when this drug was made available to all persons (regardless of diagnosis or lack thereof) on the prescriptions of doctors. When expressed as a multiple of the average industrial hourly wage, the street price was somewhat higher than it was from 1982 to 1989 when there was no legally authorized access.

Let us next consider the proposition that a medicalization policy would reduce the health hazards of recreational drug use. This salutary objective would be realized by standardizing the doses or concentrations of drugs and regulating their purity, thus avoiding the very severe and occasionally lethal adverse effects associated with inadvertent overdoses or reactions to mixtures represented as single agents. It would also reduce exposure to toxic agents such as paraquat sprayed on marijuana crops in an effort to destroy them (Nadelmann 1989). Moreover, medicalization would entail providing prescriptions for clean needles and other apparatus, which would reduce the likelihood both of contracting infections like bacterial endocarditis and of transmitting diseases like AIDS and hepatitis.

All of these advantages could be achieved at least as efficiently by adopting a policy of legalization rather than medicalization. Standardization of doses and purity of products could be reasonably assured by treating these drugs as the Food and Drug Administration (FDA) now regulates over-the-counter products available for purchase without a doctor's prescription. Clean needles and other apparatus could similarly be made available over the counter. The only reason that prescriptions are now required for needles and syringes is fear that they will be diverted to illicit use. The desired reduction in price of drugs could be accomplished more efficiently if one did not have to pay fees to doctors for writing prescriptions.

Other putative advantages of a medicalization policy—in contrast with those just mentioned—*are* dependent on the professional skills of physicians. As recreational drug users reported periodically to their physicians for refills of their prescriptions, they could be monitored for adverse effects of drug use. They could be queried about whether drug abuse was becoming involuntary (e.g., cocaine binges) and advised of strategies for maintaining control of their substance-using behaviors. They could, for example, be counseled about the hazards of smoking "crack" cocaine, which are disproportionately higher than snorting the more traditional preparation; cautioned against escalating from cannabis to narcotics; and monitored for adverse drug reactions or "complications" like hepatitis resulting from intravenously administered drugs.

Thus, a medicalization policy could provide advantages that would not be realized through a policy of legalization. To the extent that such a policy would draw upon the skills of health professionals to assist persons in their efforts to prevent or avoid diseases, it appears to be legitimate. However, if the reasoning that causes us to accept this as a legitimate activity for physicians is applied consistently, what else must we consider legitimate?

I can think of no true analogies in the current practice of medicine. No drugs intended for recreational use are available only on prescription by a physician. A truly analogous situation would obtain if a prescription were required for cigarettes and alcoholic beverages. Prescribing doctors could monitor their clients' recreational use of these products, offering counseling for their safer use and monitoring through repeated histories, physical examinations, and laboratory tests for early signs of emphysema, lung cancer, cirrhosis of the liver, and peripheral neuropathies, to cite some examples. As grotesque as this proposition might appear, there are good reasons to predict that it would be far more efficient in the early detection of remediable disease than a similar policy directed at marijuana, cocaine, heroin, and other psychoactive substances.

Let us now consider the reasons for rejection by physicians of any policy that would call upon them to write prescriptions for recreational drug use. As already noted, the fact that such prescription writing is not directed at the treatment or prevention of disease suggests that it lies outside the proper domain of the medical profession.

In writing prescriptions for recreational drugs, the doctor is responding to the nonmedical wants or desires of the person rather than to his medical needs. This does not necessarily disqualify such prescription writing from the proper domain of the doctor. Our society offers general social support for doctors to "treat" nondiseases like pregnancy by performing abortions, infertility by providing artificial insemination or in vitro fertilization, and fertility by prescribing contraceptive drugs and devices. Those who oppose these practices do so because they regard the actions themselves as immoral, whether performed by physicians or others. Those who view the actions as socially acceptable support the performance of these procedures by health professionals because they are the ones who exclusively have the skills necessary for performing them safely and effectively.

Certain other activities of physicians are generally accepted, although they are not directed at the treatment or prevention of disease. These include the prescription of minoxidil (Rogaine®) to combat male pattern baldness as well as many of the activities of cosmetic plastic surgeons. Opposition in such cases is concentrated on whether activities directed toward patients' wants and desires rather than their medically defined needs should be covered by third-party payors. Although some may consider the goals of such activities to be frivolous, the authority of well-informed adults to assume the risks entailed in their pursuit is generally affirmed. Furthermore, it is necessary for doctors to cooperate in the pursuit of these goals because no other profession has the requisite skills to perform the cosmetic surgery or to assure the safety of minoxidil administration.

Much more likely to be considered dubious are prescribing behaviors directed toward questionable goals when the prescribed drugs are perceived as having substantial risks. Examples include the use of anabolic steroids by athletes to increase strength and human growth hormone (hGH) to increase the height of smaller-than-average children (Walker et al. 1990; Werth 1991). Contributing to their negative image is the recognition that the purpose of such activities is to gain a competitive advantage by resorting to means not equally available to all contestants.

In sum, doctors' activities that are designed to assist patients in pursuing goals unrelated to treating or preventing disease are most likely to be approved socially if the goals are worthy (or at least neutral), if the risks are commensurate with the worth of the goals, and if their safe and effective pursuit requires the professional skills of a physician. The prescription of psychoactive drugs of abuse fails the first two of these tests because the goal is generally perceived as unworthy and the risks are seen as substantial. These activities only marginally pass the third test and probably not by so comfortable a margin as would the prescription of cigarettes and alcohol.

Primum non nocere is commonly said to be the first principle of medical ethics. Literally it means "first," or "above all, do no harm." This principle is not intended to be interpreted and applied literally (Jonsen 1978); to do so would preclude almost all therapeutic activity in which risks of harm are customarily justified by expectations that the benefits will be greater in probability or magnitude (preferably both) than the harms. The principle is intended to serve as a powerful barrier to doctors' activities that are likely to be harmful without expectation of benefit.

Because the recreational use of drugs is widely perceived as harmful and the benefits of such use are generally regarded as dubious (at best), writing prescriptions for them is likely to be viewed as violating the first principle of medical ethics. Doctors who were willing to cooperate in such prescription-writing activities might try to justify their behavior in terms of the expected benefits or by arguing that they were not introducing their clients to dangerous substances. Rather, they were cooperating with clients who had already chosen to use such substances. "If they get their drugs from me, it's safer than getting them in the street," thinks such a doctor. "Besides, if they don't get them from me they'll just get them from the doctor across the street." This is a familiar "justification" used, for example, by doctors who capitulate to their patients' insistence upon receiving antibiotics for febrile illnesses by prescribing penicillin for viral infections. It is easier to write a prescription than to educate the patient. Their colleagues regard such practices as undesirable but understandable.

Prescription-writing doctors might also respond to allegations of violation of the do-no-harm principle by asking, "What harm?" What is the harm of cannabis usage? It is not addicting. It may impair judgment but the order of magnitude is about the same as it is with alcohol. Most casual snorters of cocaine do not appear to develop any serious problems (Gawin and Ellinwood 1988).

Attempted medicalization of the recreational use of psychoactive drugs of abuse would encounter yet another formidable obstacle. Because there would be no sick role for the client to assume or to which the doctor could respond, there would be some of the same problems already noted in connection with the lack of a disease to treat or prevent.

In addition, both members of the doctor–client dyad would feel uncomfortable or awkward, as one does in unfamiliar social settings. Although each participant tries to understand and play his or her role as "good doctor" or "good patient," how can the recreational drug user "want to get well," or "cooperate with technically competent help"? How will these people know whether they are succeeding in their social roles, or at least making a praiseworthy effort?

Of further concern to some observers is the fact that in our social system the doctor is expected to perform as a legitimizer. She has the authority and the responsibility to decide, for example, whether any individual claim to the entitlement and exemptions of the sick role are legitimate. The medical profession's power to direct or endorse behavior is perceived by the public as very great indeed. "Doctor's orders," says the *New York Times*, are the reason that President Bush suspended his beloved jogging routine for over six weeks until another headline proclaimed, "Doctor Says He's Normal." The advertising industry capitalizes on this authoritative image. One product we are told repeatedly is "like a doctor's prescription." Journalists and the advertising industry reinforce many times daily the public's impression of the medical profession as a powerful and authoritative legitimizer. There is, therefore, good reason to be concerned that, if doctors write prescriptions for drugs for recreational use, such use will tend to be perceived as legitimate — "just what the doctor ordered."

Medical Use

Given the purpose of this article, there is little need for extensive discussion of medical use of psychoactive drugs. It is worth noting that it shares with other socially approved categories of medical therapy the goal of ameliorating the manifestations of diseases. The patients thus are considered legitimate claimants to the entitlements and exemptions of the sick role. Doctors and patients understand whether they are measuring up to good doctor or good patient standards.

These points notwithstanding, there are many manifestations of strong prejudice against certain of the drugs with the primary reputation of being illicit. The safe and effective use of amphetamine and methylphenidate (Ritalin®) for treating minimal brain dysfunction in grammar-school-aged children provoked a loud public outcry, hearings in Congress, and the appointment of a high-level panel to investigate the matter (Stoufe and Stewart 1973; U.S. Department of Health, Education, and Welfare 1981). Tetrahydrocannabinol, an alkaloid derived from marijuana, is generally regarded as the best safe and effective therapy for the highly pernicious and disabling nausea and vomiting associated with cancer chemotherapy; its distribution to patients in need of it is obstructed persistently by the federal Drug Enforcement Administration (Nadelmann 1989). Other examples of obstructing the development or distribution of agents such as heroin, cocaine, and psychedelic drugs have been reviewed recently by Nadelmann (1989).

Many physicians are extremely conservative in their writing of prescriptions for the use of narcotics like morphine and meperidine (Demerol®) for the relief of pain because of their concern about causing addiction. This attitude often works to the detriment of patients' legitimate interests. Oddly, such physicians may prescribe inadequate amounts of narcotics even for terminally ill patients for whom the development of addiction is a matter of no practical consequence.

Pathological Use

Should physicians provide prescriptions for psychoactive substances for persons having the attributes of psychoactive substance dependence? Let us consider first whether the physician should function as a mere supplier of such prescriptions for persons who do not intend to try to discontinue their use. The relevant considerations on this topic are, I believe, almost identical to those bearing on the question of physician prescribing for recreational use. The main difference is that in consideration of recreational use it was necessary to calculate or speculate on the probability that such use might lead to the development of disease. Now there is no need for speculation; the user already has a disease. Thus, I conclude once again that physicians should not cooperate as mere suppliers of psychoactive substances. Some of these persons may have symptoms or signs associated with their drug-taking behavior and may request the physician's services in dealing with those. Even though it would be compatible with the purpose of the medical profession for physicians to assume responsibility for taking care of such persons, to help them manage the manifestations of their disease, the physician still should not prescribe the psychoactive substances. Most of the important goals of legalizing access to psychoactive drugs of abuse can be accomplished without requiring doctors to serve as legitimizers or vectors of disease-causing agents.

In passing it is worth noticing that some physicians prescribe drugs for ostensibly legitimate indications knowing or suspecting that they will be used recreationally or pathologically. Among the drugs for which such prescriptions are said to be relatively common are diazepam (Valium®), barbiturates, narcotics, dextroamphetamine (Dexedrine®), and methylphenidate (Ritalin). These activities reflect the diversity of opinion that exists within the medical profession about the legitimacy of affording access to such drugs. Although I cannot estimate confidently the prevalence of such prescription writing, I believe this practice is less frequent than the earlier practice of offering of advice about obtaining what were at the time illegal contraceptives and abortions.

Finally, let us consider patients with one of the mental disorders categorized as psychoactive drug dependence who want to assume the sick role. If such patients seek out the services of a physician for technically competent help in coping with their diseases, should the physician provide access to psychoactive drugs? In contexts defined by four essential features I believe the answer should be yes:

1. The drug-dependent person must recognize his dependency as undesirable and must want to cooperate with the physician in a mutual effort to end the dependency or, if this is not feasible, to mitigate its destructive effects. In short, the patient must be willing to play the role of good patient as defined within the sick role.

2. There should be a reasonable expectation of success. That is to say, there should be satisfactory scientific evidence that, in most individuals having the same type of drug dependence, administration of the prescribed drug is likely to have the desired effect.
3. The role of the physician should surpass that of mere prescription writer. There should be a fully developed doctor–patient relationship in which the doctor offers the full range of professional services typical of such relationships appropriate to the requirements of particular patients. Otherwise, there is no need to involve the physician.
4. The physician must be qualified by virtue of her professional education (C. Levine and Novick 1990) and personal disposition to serve patients with psychoactive substance dependence. Many physicians have extremely negative attitudes about patients whom they consider self-abusive or self-destructive; they reflect these negative reactions by avoidance or punishment (Groves 1978; R.J. Levine 1991; Mizrahi 1986). As a consequence of highly negative attitudes toward drug addicts—attitudes that are already well established in third-year medical students (McGrory, McDowell, and Muskin 1990) and in medical residents (Mizrahi 1986)—few physicians have developed the professional competence necessary to provide appropriate care for addicted persons (C. Levine and Novick 1990). Consequently, the American Society of Addiction Medicine is examining the possibility of creating a specialty board in addiction medicine (Pinkney 1990).

Specification of these four essential features of appropriate context in which to write prescriptions for pathological users of psychoactive drugs is, in effect, requiring that this prescription writing conform to the norms of medical practice. Thus, the drug use thereby authorized would conform to the definition of medical rather than pathological use, even though the patients are pathological users.

The first of these essential features calls upon the patient to cooperate with the physician. This is not to be construed as an appeal for a return to the paternalistic or authoritarian model of the doctor–patient relationship. Rather, according to the shared decision-making model (President's Commission 1982), the doctor and patient negotiate agreements about their goals and the means they will employ to pursue them. The patient is expected to cooperate within the framework defined by these negotiated agreements.

The preferred goal is, in general, to end the dependency. For some patients this goal may be unattainable, either permanently or temporarily. In such cases the doctor and patient may reach an agreement to strive for mitigation of the destructive consequences of the chemical dependency. For some heroin addicts, for example, this might entail the use of methadone maintenance. Such treatment has been validated in appropriate scientific studies and calls upon the physician to assume responsibilities for much more than mere prescription writing in accord with features 2 and 3, respectively.

Methadone, of course, is not precisely the drug on which these heroin addicts became dependent. Although closely related, it has attributes that make it preferable to heroin for long-term-maintenance therapy. Would it make a difference if the drug prescribed by the doctor were precisely the one to which the patient had become addicted?

I believe that it would not, so long as the requirements of the four essential features were satisfied. A credible example of such a drug is nicotine polacrilex (Nicorette®) available by prescription only to cigarette smokers who are seeking to quit smoking "while participating in a behavioral modification program under medical or dental supervision" (Medical Economics Company 1991, 1299–1302). Nicotine, the actual drug to which these persons became addicted, is said to be as addictive as heroin (*Lancet* 1991; Nadelmann 1989, 944). Although it has all of the adverse drug affects that the smoker experiences from smoking cigarettes, it differs in that it does not cause cancer or chronic lung disease. Moreover, it is not intended for long-term use.

With regard to other pathologically used psychoactive substances, given the nature of cocaine dependency (Gawin and Ellinwood 1988), there seems to be no place for writing prescriptions for cocaine or any of its presently known congeners because success is not a reasonable expectation. Nor is there a rational basis to consider prescribing cannabis for those dependent on this drug. The American Psychiatric Association's manual of mental disorders (DSM-III-R) does not recognize dependence on such drugs as phencyclidine and related substances or hallucinogens (APA 1980).

Summary and Conclusions

If my assumptions and analysis are correct, any attempt to medicalize cocaine, heroin, marijuana, and other psychoactive substances of abuse in the United States is likely to encounter the strong opposition of many responsible physicians. Such opposition would be grounded in their perceptions that medicalization would be contrary to the two primary purposes of medical practice: (1) to prevent diseases or to treat persons with diseases with the aim of providing cure, remission, restoration of function or palliation, and (2) to respond to the needs of persons in the "sick role." Resistance would further reflect physicians' concerns about avoiding actions that could harm patients and refraining from creating the appearance of legitimizing the recreational or pathological use of substances of abuse.

Most, but not all, of the advantages anticipated by proponents of medicalization could be secured even more efficiently by adopting a policy of legalization. For various reasons, which are beyond the scope of this essay, I do not think it likely that the United States will adopt such a policy. I mention legalization only to show that the most weighty arguments supporting medicalization of cocaine, marijuana, and heroin apply at least as forcefully to tobacco and alcoholic beverages. Thus, to be consistent, those who use these arguments to support adoption of a medicalization policy for cocaine, heroin, and marijuana must also support making tobacco cigarettes and whiskey available only on a doctor's prescription.

I believe that most responsible physicians would resist medicalization of all recreational use of psychoactive substances. Many of them would, however, be willing to consider prescribing such substances for pathological users within the context of a fully developed doctor–patient relationship in which the patient recognized his dependency as undesirable and wanted to cooperate with the physician in a mutual effort either to end the dependency or, at the very least, to mitigate its destructive effects. In short, the patient must be willing to play the role of good patient as defined within the sick role. Under such conditions, physicians who are suitably qualified by virtue of their professional education would be willing to consider prescribing psychoactive substances when there was available satisfactory scientific evidence that their administration would be likely to have the desired therapeutic effect.

References

American College of Physicians, Health and Public Policy Committee. 1985. Chemical Dependence: Position Paper. *Annals of Internal Medicine* 102:405–8.

American Medical Association (AMA). 1982. Principles of Medical Ethics. In *Current Opinions of the Judicial Council of the American Medical Association*. Chicago.

American Psychiatric Association (APA). 1980. *Diagnostic and Statistical Manual of Mental Disorders*, rev. 3rd ed. Washington.

Burt, R.A. 1978. Informed Consent in Mental Health. In *Encyclopedia of Bioethics*, ed. W.T. Reich, 763–7. New York: Free Press.

Fox, R.C. 1989. *The Sociology of Medicine: A Participant Observer's View*. Englewood Cliffs, N.J.: Prentice-Hall.

Gawin, F.H., and E.H. Ellinwood. 1988. Cocaine and Other Stimulants: Actions, Abuse and Treatment. *New England Journal of Medicine* 318:1173–82.

Groves, J.E. 1978. Taking Care of the Hateful Patient. *New England Journal of Medicine* 298:883–7.

Jonsen, A.R. 1978. Do No Harm. *Annals of Internal Medicine* 88:827–32.

Lancet. 1991. Editorial. Nicotine Use after the Year 2000. *Lancet* 337:1191–2.

Levine, C., and D.M. Novick. 1990. Expanding the Role of Physicians in Drug Abuse Treatment: Problems, Perspectives. *Journal of Clinical Ethics* 1:152–6.

Levine, R.J. 1978. Biomedical Research. In *Encyclopedia of Bioethics*, ed. W.T. Reich, 1481–92. New York: Free Press.

———. 1991. AIDS and the Physician–Patient Relationship. In *AIDS and Ethics*, ed. F.G. Reamer, 188–214. New York: Columbia University Press.

McGrory, B.J., D.M. McDowell, and P.R. Muskin. 1990. Medical Students' Attitudes toward AIDS, Homosexual, and Intravenous Drug-Abusing Patients: A Reevaluation in New York City. *Psychosomatics* 31:426–33.

Madden, E.H., and P.H. Hare. 1978. Civil Disobedience in Health Services. In *Encyclopedia of Bioethics*, by W.T. Reich, 159–62. New York: Free Press.

Medical Economics Company. 1991. *Physicians' Desk Reference*. Oradell, N.J.

Mizrahi, T. 1986. *Getting Rid of Patients*. New Brunswick, N.J.: Rutgers University Press.

Murphy, W.D., and D.C. Thomasma. 1981. The Ethics of Research on Court-ordered Evaluation and Therapy for Exhibitionism. *IRB: A Review of Human Subjects Research* 3(9):1–4.

Musto, D.F. 1990. Illicit Price of Cocaine in Two Eras: 1908–14 and 1982–89. *Connecticut Medicine* 54:321–6.

Nadelmann, E.A. 1989. Drug Prohibition in the United States: Costs, Consequences, and Alternatives. *Science* 245:939–47.

Parsons, T. 1951. *The Social System.* New York: Free Press.

———. 1972. Definitions of Health and Illness in the Light of American Values and Social Structure. In *Patients, Physicians and Illness: A Sourcebook in Behavioral Science and Health,* ed. E.G. Jaco, 107–27. New York: Free Press.

Pinkney, D.S. 1990. Specialty Board in Addiction Medicine Eyed. *American Medical Association News* May:9–10 [cited in C. Levine and Novick (1990)].

Presidential Commission on the Human Immunodeficiency Virus Epidemic. 1988. *Report.* Washington.

President's Commission for the Study of Ethical Problems in Medicine and Biomedical Research. 1982. *Making Health Care Decisions: The Ethical and Legal Implications of Informed Consent in the Patient–Practitioner Relationship.* GPO report no. 040-000-00459-9. Washington.

Siegler, M. 1979. The Nature and Limits of Clinical Medicine. In *Changing Values in Medicine,* eds. E.J. Cassell and M. Siegler, 19–41. Bethesda, Md.: University Publications of America.

Sigerist, H.E. 1951. *A History of Medicine.* Vol. 1: *Primitive and Archaic Medicine.* Yale University, Department of the History of Medicine, pub. no. 27. New York: Oxford University Press.

Stoufe, L.A., and M.A. Stewart. 1973. Treating Problem Children with Stimulant Drugs. *New England Journal of Medicine* 189:407–13.

U.S. Department of Health, Education, and Welfare. 1971. *Report on the Conference on the Use of Stimulant Drugs in the Treatment of Behaviorally Disturbed Young School Children, January 11–12.* Sponsored by the Office of Child Development and the Office of the Assistant Secretary for Health and Scientific Affairs. Washington: Office of Child Development.

Walker, J.M., S.A. Bond, L.D. Voss, P.R. Betts, S.A. Wootton, and A.A. Jackson. 1990. Treatment of Short Normal Children with Growth Hormone — A Cautionary Tale. *Lancet* 336:1331–34.

Werth, B. 1991. How Short Is Too Short? *New York Times Magazine* (June 16): 14–17, 28–29, 47.

Legalizing Drugs:
Lessons from (and about) Economics

KENNETH E. WARNER

University of Michigan

THE MOST AUDIBLE PORTIONS OF THE DEBATE OVER drug policy in the United States are the polarized extremes: the conservative call for more aggressive (some would say draconian) law enforcement on the one end and the libertarian plea for policy shock therapy — drug legalization — on the other. Characterized by competing visions of a dismal future (should the opponent's position emerge victorious), the debate has engaged otherwise subdued policy analysts in published exchanges exhibiting an extraordinary emotional intensity and even vitriol (Scarlett et al. 1990; Wilson 1990).

Reading around and among the rhetorical flourishes, one discerns two distinct battlegrounds for the debate: a philosophy/morality terrain and an economic terrain. The former encompasses disparate concerns about the message that legalization would send to children, for example, and debate over the extent and legitimacy of the state's regulating the behavior of adults (Nadelmann 1989; Wilson 1990; Sterling 1990; Ostrowski 1990). The tone of this component of the debate is captured in stereotypical catchwords like "zero tolerance" and "just say no" and in emotive statements such as "The war on drugs [is making] our Bill of Rights into a shattered remnant of the vital shield it once was" (Sterling 1990).

On its surface, the economic battlefield is less emotive, but it is no less important. At the core of debate lie conflicting beliefs about the health effects of drugs and their economic ramifications, under various conditions of regulation and availability, as well as the health and economic implications of criminalizing drug sale and use. Jarvik (1990) recently concluded that "the principal argument for drug legalization is economic," an observation echoed explicitly, or implicitly, by interested parties from both extremes of the debate, as well as from its middle. The leading academic proponent of legalization has framed the policy issue largely in cost–benefit terms, albeit qualitatively (Nadelmann 1989). Furthermore, the arguments in recent writings advocating legalization are grounded in explicit cost–benefit calculations (Dennis 1990; Ostrowski 1990). To counter the legalization argument, opponents have also employed economic reasoning (Wilson 1990) and estimation (Kondracke 1988).

The frequency of the recent appeal to economic logic suggests the perceived utility and perhaps innate attraction of "the dismal science" to drug policy warriors of all political stripes. To many observers, cost–benefit analysis and other modalities of economic analysis connote rationality, dispassion (objectivity), comprehensiveness, and decisiveness (answers), all values to be sought in the emotional heat and confusion of the drug policy debate.

In practice and even in theory, however, the potential of economic analysis may fall far short of such expectations. To date, cost–benefit analysis has been applied in the drug policy arena as an advocacy tool with a clear prescriptive intent; the published literature reveals no unbiased positive science applications. The utility of future economic analysis will be essentially qualitative: given inherent limitations, at its best such analysis can and should serve to orient analysts' and policy makers' *thinking* about drug policy. An effective cost–benefit study, for example, should help to identify critical issues and to clarify which questions are most deserving of further investigation. It will not "determine" an optimal policy.

Further, much as we might wish it to do so, economic analysis will never resolve the "great unknowns" of the drug policy debate; but it may offer helpful insights. Preeminent among the "great unknowns" is the question of how much, if at all, legalization would increase drug consumption, and to what effect. Although not answering this critical question, analysis of the price elasticity of demand for drugs can narrow the range of plausible estimates and focus attention on the most important parameters. Research by economists has already offered assessments of the likely effects of drug interdiction efforts on street price (Reuter, Crawford, and Cave 1988). Early research on the relationship between drug prices and urban crime rates could serve as a model for more contemporary analysis (Brown and Silverman 1974). In the realm of the licit drugs, application of "price elasticity of demand" analysis to tobacco and alcohol consumption has made significant contributions to policy (Cook 1984; Warner 1986; Coate and Grossman 1988) and may shed light on changes in demand for the currently illicit drugs under a regime of legalized or decriminalized availability (Warner et al. 1990).

This article distills the essence of the economic argument employed in the drug policy debate, as it is embodied in the language of cost–benefit analysis. I will also discuss the insights generated by study of the price elasticity of demand for drugs. In both instances, my interest focuses on contributions found in the published literature and on the as-yet unrealized potential of analysis, with the purpose of examining the validity and utility of applying economic methods and thinking in the area of drug policy. The ensuing pages offer no answers to pressing questions in the drug policy debate. I will present no new empirical analysis, thus precluding the derivation of specific substantive conclusions. The objective, rather, is to develop appreciation of the potential and limits of one discipline's analytical armamentarium in grappling with a social and policy dilemma that knows no disciplinary boundaries.

To concentrate attention on issues of economic analysis, rather than differences in illicit drug types and policy approaches, I will consider a single policy model, legalization, without distinguishing drug types. The focus on legalization reflects the fact that it has been the principal model in which cost–benefit analysis has constituted a major component of the policy debate. Legalization can take many forms, ranging from an unfettered "supermarket" of freely available drugs to highly regulated conditions of sale and promotion, with restrictions on age, time, place, and conditions of use (Kleiman and Saiger 1990). Obviously, costs and benefits will vary widely depending on the characteristics of the specific policy under consideration (Moore 1977), as well as the drug in question. The costs and benefits of legalizing marijuana, for example, would be expected to differ, likely substantially, from those associated with legalizing crack cocaine (Kleiman and Saiger 1990).

Cost–Benefit Analysis

Cost–benefit analysis (CBA) and its close relatives, cost–effectiveness analysis (CEA) and cost–utility analysis (CUA), are nothing more, nor less, than a formal accounting and comparison of the negative and positive consequences of a policy decision, a paradigm for thinking about rational decision making (albeit one molded by the economist's perspective, and biases). Throughout this paper, the term "cost–benefit analysis" will be employed to refer generically to all three techniques. The techniques are discussed in detail by Warner and Luce (1982).

Cost–benefit analysis is both much maligned and effusively praised. A dispassionate appraisal of both the technique and its applications suggests that neither reaction is wholly warranted. The naive enthusiast tends to perceive CBA as imbued with some mystical ability to forge coherence from chaos, to objectify the diverse parameters of complicated decision problems, and thus to discern ultimate truths. A CBA, however, is no better than the analyst performing it and is subject to the analyst's errors of omission and commission and problems of bias.

Whereas the enthusiast exaggerates CBA's capabilities and usefulness, the technique's most vociferous detractors tend to exaggerate and decry its influence. They see it as a technocractic decision-making mechanism that, intentionally or otherwise, suppresses critical qualitative inputs, and thereby subverts decision making. However, given the technical limitations of CBA (discussed below and by Warner and Luce [1982]) and the dominance of political and bureaucratic factors in policy decision making, the principal role of CBA is, and ought to be, as a decision-*assisting* technique. That is, at its best, CBA should aid decision makers — not replace them — by providing insight into the objective dimensions of inherently subjective policy decisions (Warner and Luce 1982).

Examination of the published literature on the application of CBA to the issue of drug policy vividly illustrates both the limits of analysis and its potential to make a modest contribution to the ongoing policy debate.

Applications in the Published Literature on Drug Legalization

The spirit of cost–benefit analysis explicitly pervades much of the literature both supporting and criticizing a policy of drug legalization. Actual attempts at empirical CBA number only a handful, each subject to significant deficiencies.

The Conceptual Framework. The "godfather" of the cost–benefit argument favoring drug legalization is Milton Friedman, Nobel laureate in economics, known for his energetic and articulate defense of the free market. Two decades ago, following President Nixon's declaration of a war on drugs, Friedman (1972) advocated drug legalization as the policy likely to minimize the harms associated with drug abuse. Although not framing his argument in explicit cost–benefit terms, he derived his position from a qualitative assessment of the social costs of a policy of illegality (and hence the benefits of legalization), bolstered by a philosophical position concerning individual liberties.

In a prominent article published in *Science*, the leading academic proponent of legalization in the contemporary era, Ethan Nadelmann (1989), presents a reasonably comprehensive identification of the items of cost, benefit, and risk that would comprise a formal cost–benefit analysis, but he does not purport to perform a CBA and indeed does not refer to cost–benefit per se. Nevertheless, by virtue of enumerating so many of the positive and negative implications of both legalization and the law enforcement status quo, this article constitutes an initial blueprint from which one could begin to construct a CBA. At the heart of Nadelmann's analysis favoring legalization is the argument that the major costs associated with illegal drugs are created by the fact of their illegality. This is a theme that pervades the writings of proponents of legalization. Ostrowski (1990), for example, develops specific estimates of the mortality toll associated with illegal drugs, attributing the vast majority of it to the criminalization of drug use and sale, as noted below.

Building on Nadelmann's work, development of a CBA would benefit by consulting Nadelmann's critics as well (e.g., Kondracke 1988; Wilson 1990), both to identify additional categories of costs and benefits and to develop appreciation of the range of estimated values associated with each. An essential supplement is the recent work of Kleiman and Saiger (1990), who consider costs of legalization downplayed by Nadelmann and other supporters of legalization. More generally, an older paper by Moore (1977) concerning the legalization of heroin provides an unusually thorough and well-organized cataloging of the dimensions of the drug problem. Moore analyzes the arguments and evidence pertaining to four of these attributes in tables organized by alternative visions of predicted effects of legalization.

Among the papers making qualitative contributions to drug policy CBA, the work of Nadelmann, Kleiman and Saiger, and Moore likely represents state-of-the-art thinking at this early stage of CBA interest in drug policy. At the opposite end of the spectrum is another recent article published in *Science*. In a generally instructive review of evidence pertinent to the legalization issue, Goldstein and Kalant (1990) conclude that "from a cost–benefit analysis based on pharmacologic, toxicologic, sociologic, and historical facts, . . . [legalization] would be likely, on balance, to make matters worse rather than better." Despite the wealth of information presented by these authors, the article offers *no* explicit cost–benefit comparisons, quantitative *or* qualitative. This appears to be a dramatic illustration of using the cost–benefit label to confer "legitimacy" on a subjective conclusion.

Quantitative Analyses. The handful of quantitative cost–benefit comparisons in the published literature employs "hard" numbers to lend an aura of objectivity to the authors' political and philosophical positions on drug legalization. Despite their quantitative orientations, these analyses fall far short of the standards an economist would expect of a rigorous CBA. Nevertheless, these early applications of CBA to the issue of drug legalization are instructive for both the potential and pitfalls of formal quantitative analysis.

One of the most comprehensive evaluations of legalization published to date, that of Ostrowski (1990), includes a CBA as a component of a more expansive examination of the arguments supporting "The Moral and Practical Case for Drug Legalization." A similar economic argument is developed by Dennis (1990). Unabashedly presented as advocacy for legalization (of marijuana and noncrack cocaine in Dennis's case), these articles employ specific estimates of the potential increase in drug addiction under legalization and explicit estimates of economic costs and benefits of legalization.

In Dennis's article, the benefits of legalization include eliminating the cost of government prosecution of the drug war (this includes aggressive application of the domestic criminal justice system, from arrest to incarceration, and combatting efforts by the Colombian drug lords); tax revenues derived from sale of legalized drugs; and avoidance of specific social costs of drug use, including drug-related health care costs, productivity losses, and the value of stolen property associated with drug-related crime.

Ostrowski's economic evaluation includes similar variables, with a few important distinctions in categories of costs and in specific estimates, the former reflecting a greater economic sophistication. Notably, Ostrowski avoids a technical error committed by most proponents of legalization, including Dennis: valuing drug-related theft as the cost of stolen property. Such property does not cease to exist once stolen; rather, it is "transferred," or "redistributed," from its rightful owners to the thieves. As such, its value does not measure a social cost to be avoided (and hence to become a benefit) under legalization. Rather, the true cost of the criminal activity includes its psychosocial effects on the immediate victims and the value of their time devoted to replacing stolen items. There are also potentially profoundly important psychosocial costs for those who *fear* becoming victims. In the quantitative dimension, an associated cost of drug-related crime, ignored in many discussions of drug policy, is Americans' investments in home protection devices (burglar alarm systems, guns, etc.). All such costs—the true social costs of drug-related crime—are much more difficult to measure, much less to value, than the worth of stolen property. Although Ostrowski includes home protection costs in his cost–benefit arithmetic, neither he nor anyone else has tried to place a value on the psychosocial costs, despite the possibility that they constitute the single greatest aggregate drug-related burden imposed on society.

Despite Ostrowski's appreciation of the transfer issue, the single largest item in his assessment of the costs of prohibition is itself a transfer: the above-market expenditures on drugs paid by consumers, totaling some $70 billion by his estimate.

In a similar vein, the excise tax "benefits" associated with taxation of legalized drugs constitute a substantial item on almost all prolegalization lists of benefits, including that of Dennis. (Even many opponents of legalization acknowledge this "benefit.") However, the tax revenues represent transfers from drug dealers (when illegal) to governments (when legal) (or from consumers to the government, in the instance of people who would use drugs when legal but not when illegal). As such, from a true *social* perspective, the tax revenues constitute neither a cost nor a benefit. From the (narrower) perspective of revenue-seeking governmental units, they do represent a benefit.

In practice, another limitation of CBA concerns its difficulty in handling the distributional implications of differing drug policies. With the burden of drugs and their illegality experienced disproportionately in the urban ghetto, one might assume that policy costs and benefits experienced by ghetto residents should be weighted more heavily than those experienced by suburban dwellers, for example. Yet CBAs on a myriad of subjects have rarely differentiated cost and benefit measurements in this fashion, and to date none of the quantitative analysis of drug policy has addressed this issue.

Although the ghetto currently bears a disproportionate share of the social burden of the drug trade, it may also receive a disproportionate share of the economic rewards of the illicit industry. If legalization increased drug use and reduced the black market, the economic impact on the ghetto community, in terms of reduced income flow, could greatly exceed that experienced by surrounding areas, while the social burden of drug use conceivably could increase. In principle, CBA ought to be able to distinguish such differential impacts, but the track record of analysis in other areas does not offer much reason for optimism.

These examples illustrate the technical failings found in drug policy CBAs, many of which only an economist would notice. The most important limitation of CBA, both in principle and practice, relates to a different and inescapable problem: how to represent, in the quantitative calculus of CBA, the existence and importance of major consequences of drug policies that do not lend themselves neatly to quantification or valuation. Only if all of the important consequences of each policy could be quantified and valued could CBA be expected to produce "answers" to the evaluation question. Yet the outcomes of drug policies include many of great importance that defy meaningful quantification. Proponents of the law enforcement approach, for example, believe that the availability of psychoactive drugs, under a regime of drug legalization, would (further) erode the moral fabric of the society (Wilson 1990). How could one quantify, much less value, this consequence? Similarly, how could one quantify the libertarian's exasperation with a drug restriction law that prohibits adults from engaging knowingly in behaviors affecting only themselves (Sterling 1990; Ostrowski 1990)?

A design feature of the best CBAs involves structuring the analysis in a manner that will readily and clearly permit readers to juxtapose the formally valued consequences of a policy against these unquantified qualitative issues (here, the "philosophy/morality terrain") (Warner and Luce 1982). Kleiman and Saiger (1990) assert, however, that the "consequentialist" argument (roughly analogous to quantifiable impacts) and the debate about "liberty and virtue" are wholly irreconcilable. Like Kleiman and Saiger, Ostrowski (1990) devotes much of his comprehensive article to the ethical and philosophical issues, yet he makes no explicit attempt to integrate these dimensions with the economic. Having taken the reader through a lengthy assessment of quantifiable costs and benefits, he concludes his analysis with the statement that "utilitarian analysis breaks down and drug legalization unavoidably becomes a moral issue."

The juxtaposition that I propose here does not conflict with the basic point made by these writers. Rather than suggesting that quantifiable and qualitative considerations are directly comparable, the juxtaposition simply clarifies the drug policies' implied trade-offs between tangible health, crime, and economic outcomes and less tangible (but not necessarily less important) philosophical implications. Explicit acknowledgment of the trade-offs also reinforces mutual recognition by adversaries in the debate of both the quantifiable and philosophical dimensions of drug policy. No answers will emerge from such comparisons. Perhaps a modest incremental understanding will.

Finally, the problem of developing valid and reliable measures of policy consequences that are in principle quantifiable is at least equally important in limiting the contribution of formal analysis, if more prosaic than the difficulties inherent in grappling with distributional and philosophical issues. For example, both proponents and opponents of drug legalization concur that legalization per se could (opponents say "would") increase the size of the drug-consuming population. However, the two sides differ wildly in their estimates of the magnitude of the effect. Whereas Dennis (1990) considers an estimate of two million cocaine addicts a "worst case" scenario in a postlegalization world, Kondracke (1988) estimates the number at "somewhere between" 8.5 million and 42 million. A difference of this magnitude radically shifts conclusions in the cost–benefit calculus, much of which depends on the size of the drug-abusing population (for estimates of needed health care, social costs, etc.). Not surprisingly, Kondracke's calculations lead him to conclude that legalization would be a dismal economic failure, not to mention its implications for health and social disruption.

Dennis calculates that "almost a 100 percent increase in the number of addicts would be required before the net benefits of drug peace equaled zero. This would seem to be a worst-case scenario." This is considerably more conservative than Ostrowski, who sees *no* prospects of the "net benefits of drug peace" ever equaling zero. He concludes that "in order for legalized drug use to match the overall death toll of prohibition [which he estimates at roughly 8,000 deaths per year], use would have to increase more than thirteen-fold." In contrast, opponents of legalization estimate that, under their assumptions, the death toll could rise as high as 100,000 to 500,000, staggering figures comparable only to the toll of the legal drugs, tobacco and alcohol (McDonald and Du-Pont, as cited in Kondracke 1988).

Differences of this magnitude highlight the essential issue in the nonphilosophical debate over drug legalization: what would happen to consumption levels under legalization, and to what effect? Proponents and opponents of legalization diverge radically on both questions. Some "legalizers," for example, argue that a regime of legalized drugs, regulated drug dosage and purity, as well as circumstances of use, could decrease the health toll from drugs, despite increased use, with drug-related mortality falling from its current level of a few thousand per year (Nadelmann 1989). Ostrowski (1990) develops this argument with detailed calculations comparing the death toll directly caused by drug consumption per se (which he characterizes as small) with that produced by the illegality of use (relatively much larger). The latter reflects poisonings and overdoses caused by adulteration of drugs, variations in dosages, and dirty needles. It also includes murders associated with black market activity.

One theme underlying the legalization camp's expectation that the health cost of legalization would be modest, if not absent altogether, is the possibility of drug substitution. Most frequently mentioned is the prospect that, if legalized, marijuana might be substituted often for alcohol consumption, in which case society might witness a decrease in both the health and the economic burdens of drug consumption. Contemplating the legalization of cocaine, Ostrowski develops specific illustrative estimates of mortality benefits, concluding that an increase of ten million cocaine users would lead to a substantial net decrease in drug-related deaths if "a mere five percent of these users switched to cocaine from tobacco." Opponents of legalization have largely ignored the substitution issue, typically increasing health toll estimates proportionate to their estimates of consumption increases. To date, the extent of drug substitution, and its implications for health and social costs, remains exclusively a matter of conjecture.

Potential Contributions

Despite the limitations of drug policy CBA, careful identification of costs and benefits, regardless of how amenable each is to quantification or valuation, can improve the caliber of the drug policy debate. It can make interested parties aware of important consequences that may have escaped their attention (intentionally or inadvertently). It can force advocates to acknowledge and confront considerations that challenge their positions. It encourages a thoughtful weighing of negatives and positives. It may focus attention on the important unknowns. Careful cataloguing of the diverse cost and benefit categories may even encourage examination of the usefulness of alternative paradigms for dealing with "the" drug problem, be they the public health model (Jonas 1990; Mosher and Yanagisako 1991) or the criminal justice model (Office of National Drug Control Policy 1989; Sterling 1990), each of which arguably tends to undervalue the concerns of the other.

Clearly, addressing the quantitative dimensions of a policy question is CBA's long suit. The published literature offers notable examples of where CBA can offer useful perspective on the quantifiable implications of drug policies. A reasonable degree of agreement can be reached concerning the law enforcement costs associated with current policy, for example, and hence the potential savings associated with legalization. Kondracke (1988), a strong opponent of legalization, values the law enforcement costs associated with illegal drugs close to the figures employed by Ostrowski and Dennis. As such, differences in estimates of these costs could not explain the (opposite) "bottom line" appraisals of legalization.

In contrast, estimates of the health effects of legalization vary dramatically. Quantitative treatment of this "great unknown" may not reveal any bottom-line "truths," but it does demonstrate the use of sensitivity analysis. One of the critical design features of cost–benefit analysis, sensitivity analysis, entails varying the values of uncertain parameters to determine whether the uncertainty significantly affects the qualitative findings of analysis (e.g., whether or not one policy approach is clearly preferred to another). Both Ostrowski and Dennis illustrate the use of sensitivity analysis in their handling of possible increases in legal drug use and the associated health effects. Dennis calculates a "break-even" increase in the prevalence of use that he characterizes as a "worst-case" scenario; that is, he estimates the increase in drug use, under legalization, that would eliminate the cost–benefit attraction of legalization, and he considers this increase highly improbable (the "worst case"). Both "break-even" analysis and "worst-case" analysis are standard methods of sensitivity analysis (Warner and Luce 1982).

In developing estimates of the costs and benefits of legalization, opponents employ alternative sets of assumptions concerning the lethality of drug use per se, the nonfatal health effects of addiction, and other consequences of drug use. Comparison of opponents' approaches with those of the "legalizers" illuminates critical issues in developing refined (and hopefully less biased) estimates of the health effects of legalization. The disparity in estimates thus itself serves to refine the research agenda.

The emotionality of the drug policy issue, combined with the enormous discrepancies in the health consequences estimated by those favoring and opposing legalization, suggests an alternative approach for the use of CBA to enlighten the drug policy debate. Rather than strive for an objective study performed by unbiased analysts—the sine qua non of "proper" CBA—one might seek competing analyses prepared by proponents of each position, perhaps even establishing a forum for an adversarial proceeding featuring the competing analyses. This pragmatic approach would utilize the reality of the current environment of analysis of drug policy, and by making the analytical competition explicit, might produce new insights where they are sorely needed.

Analysis of Drug Price and Consumption

A Brief Primer on the Law of Demand and Its Relation to Drug Policy

Economics is blessed with a few universal laws. Preeminent among these is the law of demand, which states that there is an inverse relationship between the price of a commodity and the quantity of the good demanded by consumers. While few people would question the law's applicability to the demand for cars, for example, many believe it does not apply to addictive drugs. According to the conventional wisdom, addicts have a "fixed" demand for their drug, regardless of its price. In the instance of highly addictive drugs, this perspective suggests, demand will not comply with its famous "law."

In point of fact, however, addicts' demand for drugs complies fully with the law of demand, an observation deriving from such disparate sources as survey research and experimental evidence from laboratory research. This is true for both the licit and illicit drugs—for tobacco and alcohol, as well as for cocaine and heroin—and the law even holds across species: addicted laboratory animals demand less of their drugs when the "price" of obtaining them—for example, the number of times they must push a lever—is increased (Griffiths, Bigelow, and Henningfield 1980). Indeed, based on data reflected in graphs in Griffiths, Bigelow, and Henningfield (1980), I have calculated that the animals' "cost response" patterns are similar to those of humans consuming alcohol and tobacco.

The best evidence pertaining to drug users' price responsiveness is found in the literature on the price elasticity of humans' demand for alcohol and tobacco. A measure of demand's responsiveness to changes in price, price elasticity is defined as the percentage decrease in demand induced by a 1 percent increase in price. The larger the coefficient of elasticity (in absolute value), the more "elastic" is demand.

Comparison of the price elasticities of demand for alcohol and tobacco suggests (but does not prove) that addiction may *reduce*, but not eliminate, price response. An estimated 90 to 95 percent of smokers are addicted, compared with approximately 10 percent of drinkers. The demand for cigarettes is relatively inelastic, on the order of -0.25 to -0.45 in the United States (i.e., a given percentage increase in price will decrease demand by a quarter to almost half as much) (Chaloupka 1991; Lewit and Coate 1982; U.S. Department of Health and Human Services 1989). Estimates of the elasticity of demand for alcoholic beverages vary by product category, but generally exhibit greater elasticity than similar calculations for cigarettes. Reviewing the recent U.S. literature, Saffer and Chaloupka (1991) report mean estimates of a demand elasticity of -0.72 for distilled spirits, -0.68 for wine, and -0.47 for beer.

The implications of addiction for consumers' price responsiveness are the subject of increasing attention within the discipline of economics at present, driven primarily by the development of a "theory of rational addiction" by Becker and Murphy (1988). Unlike the conventional wisdom, which treats addictive consumption as irrational, or arational, this theory attempts to explain, in an economic model, how consumers can choose, rationally, to consume addictive products, aware of the implications for future consumption patterns. Empirical work fitting this model is cited by proponents as supporting the notion that consumers may behave rationally in consuming addictive substances (Chaloupka 1991; Becker, Grossman, and Murphy, 1991). It is difficult, however, to distinguish these findings from those appearing in studies that do not consider addiction as a special factor in consumption (U.S. Department of

Health and Human Services 1989). Critics of the rational addiction perspective point to its limited applicability, particularly when applied (as it has been) to cases like cigarette smoking (Chaloupka 1991). They contend that children—the population of new nicotine addicts—have no conception of addiction or its implications (Thomas Schelling, personal communication, August 16, 1991).

Effects of Drug Policies on Price and Consumption

How drug policies affect consumption through their effects on price has two separable components: (1) how policies influence prices and (2) how the prices of specific drugs affect their demand.

I have addressed the second component, but I have not offered quantitative estimates of the price elasticity of demand for illegal drugs. Clearly, drugs will vary in the demand elasticities that they exhibit. However, lacking good data on humans' patterns of drug consumption, as they relate to effective market prices, it will be exceedingly difficult to predict elasticities for a given drug with any sense of precision. Attempts can be made to employ government survey data on drug use, combined with estimates of market prices, to derive demand elasticities; but both consumption and price data are likely to be significantly flawed (Drug Policy Foundation 1991). There are virtually no studies of the price elasticity of demand for illegal drugs among humans. Years ago, Brown and Silverman (1974) published a relevant and intriguing analysis of the relationship between heroin price and crime rates. Acknowledging serious problems in both price and crime data, the authors provided tentative estimates of the price elasticity of each of several major crime categories in New York City. In general, they found increases in rates in most crime categories as heroin prices increased, with all of the elasticities less than 1.0. Unfortunately, it is not possible to extrapolate directly from this analysis to estimation of price elasticity of demand for heroin per se. Nevertheless, this type of analysis is relevant to estimating the crime costs associated with the high prices of heroin's illegality.

As an alternative strategy to contemplating demand elasticities for illicit drugs, one can draw on analyses of humans' price elasticity of demand for the principal legal drugs, and estimates of price elasticity from data on lab animals' behavior, to develop a range of estimates of likely price responsiveness for the now illegal drugs. Although neither method promises any precision, both hold significant potential for producing "ball park" estimates that will realistically delimit the likely effects of price changes on drug consumption. Kleiman (1989) illustrates the analytical thought process in an evaluation of the price elasticity of demand for marijuana that relies, in part, on analysis of the price elasticity of demand for cigarettes.

The first component of the policy–price–consumption question can be addressed both qualitatively and quantitatively. Qualitatively, for example, we can observe that current policy — the aggressive law enforcement model — should increase monetary drug prices by reducing supplies. In addition, intensified apprehension, prosecution, and penalizing of drug users may increase users' perception of the *effective* price of acquiring drugs (Becker 1968). At the opposite end of the policy spectrum, legalization would almost certainly decrease drug price — both monetary and psychological — possibly quite substantially.

The critical point here is that the relevant or true price affecting decision making about consumption is the price as it is perceived by the drug user (Reuter and Kleiman 1986). Perceived price consists of monetary outlay plus fear of apprehension and punishment, as well as time and hassle costs of acquiring drugs. Legalization would entail a clear decrease in the psychic costs of buying drugs because the fear element is removed. Note, however, that availability per se need not increase. The availability of legal drugs could be limited by place, time, and other restrictions that could increase effective price. (Some observers suggest that the thrill of engaging in illicit behavior may entice more people to use drugs than the fear of illegality discourages from use. If this were true, whereas legalization would still decrease the component of perceived price of drug use associated with fear of illegality, it would decrease a "benefit" of use, the thrill, even more.)

Critics of legalization point to the fact that, under legalization, the monetary component of effective price would have to be decreased enough to remove the incentive for illegal, or black market, trade (Kleiman and Saiger 1990). This, in turn, would increase demand (subject to the above caveats concerning the nonmonetary components of effective price). To minimize price-related increases in demand, the optimal price under legalization theoretically would be the highest price that could be sustained without inducing significant illicit trade or criminal activity on the part of the consumer. Some observers believe that this price would not be able to exceed production cost by much, that small increments over cost would induce black market activity (Drug Policy Foundation 1991). The evidence points to the contrary, however. Alcohol and tobacco retail prices greatly exceed production cost and there is no evidence of significant illegal trade in these commodities. Illegal trade itself entails significant costs that have to be incorporated into the black market price. Drug price in a regime of legal drugs could exceed production cost substantially, the major difference presumably reflecting government-levied taxes (or their equivalent in a regime of government-controlled sale). Still, legal drug prices would fall far short of those found under conditions of illegality. Former "Drug Czar" William Bennett estimated that the free-market price of cocaine (devoid of taxes) would run about one-twentieth of the current black market price (Office of National Drug Control Policy 1989).

The potential "width" of the gap between production costs and retail prices is indicated by international data on cigarette prices. In the United States, tax constitutes only 27 percent of the average retail price of cigarettes ($1.82 per pack), while it exceeds 50 percent in at least a dozen industrialized nations, where price per pack ranges up to $8.74 (in New Zealand)(Action on Smoking and Health 1991). None of these countries reports serious problems with illegal activity, with the recent exception of Canada, which has a unique situation: the difference between Canadian and U.S. prices is dramatic, and much of the border is unpatrolled. Within the United States, interstate price differences have at times prompted some interstate cigarette smuggling ("buttlegging"), although the extent of this phenomenon is believed to be quite small (Advisory Commission on Intergovernmental Relations 1985).

Quantitatively, economic analysis can be employed to assess the effects of selected policies on drug price. The best example to date is the work of Reuter, Crawford, and Cave (1988), who analyzed the effects on domestic drug consumption of increased governmental interdiction prior to the arrival of drugs at the U.S. border. Because smuggling costs comprise such a small share of total drug distribution costs (about 10 percent in the case of cocaine), the authors concluded that even substantial success with interdiction efforts would have only very modest effects on domestic drug price, availability, and consumption. Through careful modeling and judicious use of sensitivity analysis, the authors were able to explore a variety of quantitative assumptions in determining that their principal conclusion was quite robust, despite uncertainties about specific parameter values. This study is not the last word on the subject—ongoing research may challenge the conclusion (Mark Moore, personal communication, October 7, 1991)—but it indicates the potential power and usefulness of economic analysis in this arena.

Although economic analysis holds the potential to develop important new insights concerning the relationship between drug policy and consumption, as mediated by price, no one should underestimate the complexities of this undertaking. Estimating the change in perceived price is exceedingly difficult, given the myriad of factors that affect it; and implementation of major new policies would alter other aspects of the social environment as well. For example, with revenues from drug taxes, government could mount a large and sustained drug education campaign that could decrease demand, quite independent of price. A contemporary example is California's recent multimillion-dollar antitobacco media campaign, financed by the state's increase in 1989 of the excise tax on cigarettes by 25 cents per pack. More generally, antismoking publicity campaigns nationwide have been credited with significantly decreasing the rate of smoking since the mid-1960s (Warner 1989). Some of the most aggressive antismoking publicity has occurred at the same time as states were increasing their cigarette excise taxes at unprecedented rates (Warner 1981).

Conclusion

Reliance on the existing drug policy literature to assess the utility of economic analysis would be unfair. Clearly, the state of the art is primitive. In addition, data problems exceed those associated with virtually all legal consumption activities. The intangible consequences of drug policy, the ethical and philosophical dimensions, play a substantial role in the "big picture."

Still, the optimist can read this review as suggesting an opportunity for ambitious analysts. Drawing on qualitative discussions of the categories of drug policy costs and benefits, analysts could identify and structure the major consequences, distinguish those that are in principle quantifiable from those that are not, and further identify those amenable to monetary valuation. Then would come the drudgery of cost-benefit analysis, and in many ways the most challenging task: finding data, deriving ranges of reasonable estimates of parameter values, and carrying out the assessment of costs and benefits. Creative use of price elasticity estimates could produce new estimates of such critical variables as the consumption impact of legalization, and the crime costs of the price differential between regimes of legal and illegal drugs.

An obvious lesson of this review is that such an analysis could not hope to produce a clear-cut conclusion about the desirability of drug legalization (or an alternative policy). However, it could offer a new perspective on the relative importance of selected variables and insight into the analytical significance of the various "great unknowns" that I alluded to at the beginning of this article.

Another lesson from this review pertains to the "turf" of economic analysis. Grounded in empiricism and the pretense (if not always reality) of objectivity, traditional economic analysis offers a delimited ability to incorporate the full range of costs and benefits that characterize any complicated policy question. Economists may be able to identify the moral and philosophical consequences of a given policy that warrant attention; however, economists are no better equipped than the average citizen to evaluate their relative importance. As such, at best the optimal cost–benefit analysis can help to frame the policy debate, to place the moral and philosophical issues explicitly in a context in which they can be compared and contrasted with the more prosaic economic implications. This contribution would be useful, even essential, to a well-informed debate. It would also be more modest than that envisioned by the current practitioners of analysis in the drug policy debate.

Even absent its technical limitations, economic analysis cannot negate the ultimate need for reliance on a political and bureaucratic decision-making process to deal with the challenging ethical, social, legal, and political issues that pervade the problem of drugs in America. Economists will never captain the ship of drug policy, but they might help to chart the course.

References

Action on Smoking and Health. 1991. Taxes Paid by Cigarette Smokers. *ASH Review* (July/August):5.

Advisory Commission on Intergovernmental Relations. 1985. *Cigarette Tax Evasion: A Second Look.* Washington.

Becker, G.S. 1968. Crime and Punishment: An Economic Approach. *Journal of Political Economy* 76:169–217.

Becker, G.S., M. Grossman, and K.M. Murphy. 1991. Rational Addiction and the Effect of Price on Consumption. *American Economic Review* 81:237–41.

Becker, G.S., and K.M. Murphy. 1988. A Theory of Rational Addiction. *Journal of Political Economy* 96:675–700.

Brown, G.F., Jr., and L.P. Silverman. 1974. The Retail Price of Heroin: Estimation and Applications. *Journal of the American Statistical Association* 347:595–606.

Chaloupka, F.J. 1991. Rational Addictive Behavior and Cigarette Smoking. *Journal of Political Economy* 99:722–42.

Coate, D., and M. Grossman. 1988. Effects of Alcoholic Beverage Prices and Legal Drinking Ages on Youth Alcohol Use. *Journal of Law & Economics* 31:145–71.

Cook, P.J. 1984. The Economics of Alcohol Consumption and Abuse. In *Alcoholism and Related Problems: Issues for the American Public*, ed. L.J. West, 56–77. Englewood Cliffs, N.J.: Prentice-Hall.

Dennis, R.J. 1990. The Economics of Legalizing Drugs. *Atlantic Monthly* (November):126–32.

Drug Policy Foundation. 1991. The Dollars and Sense of the War on Drugs: Keeping Score on Drug Control. Washington. (Draft)

Friedman, M. 1972. Prohibition and Drugs. *Newsweek* (May 1):104.

Goldstein, A., and H. Kalant. 1990. Drug Policy: Striking the Right Balance. *Science* 249:1513–21.

Griffiths, R.R., G.E. Bigelow, and J.E. Henningfield. 1980. Similarities in Animal and Human Drug-Taking Behavior. In *Advances in Substance Abuse*, ed. N.K. Mello, 1–90. Greenwich, Conn.: JAI Press.

Jarvik, M.E. 1990. The Drug Dilemma: Manipulating the Demand. *Science* 250:387–92.

Jonas, S. 1990. Solving the Drug Problem: A Public Health Approach to the Reduction of the Use and Abuse of Both Legal and Illegal Recreational Drugs. *Hofstra Law Review* 18:751–93.

Kleiman, M.A.R. 1989. *Marijuana: Costs of Abuse, Costs of Control*, Chapter 6. Greenwich, Conn.: Greenwood Press.

Kleiman, M.A.R., and A.J. Saiger. 1990. Drug Legalization: The Importance of Asking the Right Question. *Hofstra Law Review* 18:527–65.

Kondracke, M.M. 1988. Don't Legalize Drugs. *New Republic* 198(26):16–19.

Lewit, E.M., and D. Coate, 1982. The Potential for Using Excise Taxes to Reduce Smoking. *Journal of Health Economics* 1:121–45.

Moore, M.H. 1977. An Analysis of the Decision to "Legalize" Heroin. John F. Kennedy School of Government, Harvard University, Cambridge, Mass. (Unpublished manuscript)

Mosher, J., and K. Yanagisako. 1991. Public Health, Not Social Warfare: A Public Health Approach to Illegal Drug Policy. *Journal of Public Health Policy* 12:278–323.

Nadelmann, E.A. 1989. Drug Prohibition in the United States: Costs, Consequences, and Alternatives. *Science* 245:939–47.

Office of National Drug Control Policy. 1989. *National Drug Control Strategy.* Washington: Executive Office of the President.

Ostrowski, J. 1990. The Moral and Practical Case for Drug Legalization. *Hofstra Law Review* 18:607–702.

Reuter, P., G. Crawford, and J. Cave. 1988. *Sealing the Borders: The Effects of Increased Military Participation in Drug Interdiction.* R-3594-USDP. Santa Monica, Calif.: Rand.

Reuter, P., and M.A.R. Kleiman. 1986. Risks and Prices: An Economic Analysis of Drug Enforcement. In *Crime and Justice: An Annual Review of Research*, eds. M. Tonry and N. Morris, 289–340. Chicago: University of Chicago Press.

Saffer, J., and F. Chaloupka. 1991. Alcohol Tax Equalization and Social Costs. New York: National Bureau of Economic Research. (Working paper)

Scarlett, L., K.B. Zeese, S. Neustadter, et al. 1990. On the Legalization of Drugs (letters from readers). *Commentary* (May): 4–12.

Sterling, E.E. 1990. Is the Bill of Rights a Casualty of the War on Drugs? Presented at the 92nd annual convention of the Colorado Bar Association, Aspen, September 14 (revised November 5).

U.S. Department of Health and Human Services. 1989. *Reducing the Health Consequences of Smoking: 25 Years of Progress. A Report of the Surgeon General.* DHHS pub. No. (CDC) 89-8411. Washington.

Warner, K.E. 1981. State Legislation on Smoking and Health: A Comparison of Two Policies. *Policy Sciences* 13:139–52.

———. 1986. Smoking and Health Implications of a Change in the Federal Cigarette Excise Tax. *Journal of the American Medical Association* 255:1028–32.

———. 1989. Effects of the Antismoking Campaign: An Update. *American Journal of Public Health* 79:144–51.

Warner, K.E., T. Citrin, G. Pickett, B.G. Rabe, A. Wagenaar, and J. Stryker. 1990. Licit and Illicit Drug Policies: A Typology. *British Journal of Addiction* 85:255–62.

Warner, K.E., and B.R. Luce. 1982. *Cost-Benefit Analysis and Cost-Ef-*

fectiveness Analysis in Health Care: Principles, Practice, and Potential. Ann Arbor, Mich.: Health Administration Press.

Wilson, J.Q. 1990. Against the Legalization of Drugs. *Commentary* (February):21–8.

Acknowledgments: I am grateful to Clifford Allo, Toby Citrin, Mark Moore, Ethan Nadelmann, and two anonymous reviewers for helpful comments on earlier drafts.

Notes on Contributors

Ronald Bayer is a professor at the Columbia University School of Public Health. He has been interested in the relationship between ethics and politics in the making of public health policy. Mr. Bayer is author of *Private Acts, Social Consequences: AIDS and the Politics of Public Health.*

Avram Goldstein is professor of pharmacology, emeritus, at Stanford University and former director of the Addiction Research Foundation at Palo Alto.

Lawrence O. Gostin is executive director of the American Society of Law and Medicine and adjunct professor of health law at the Harvard University School of Public Health. He has devoted his attention to the study of law and health policy, AIDS and human rights, and ethics in health care. Mr. Gostin is the Editor of *AIDS and the Health Care System.*

Harold Kalant is professor of pharmacology at the University of Toronto and formerly associate research director of the Addiction Research Foundation of Ontario.

Denise B. Kandel is professor of public health in psychiatry at Columbia University. She has been especially concerned with the epidemiology and natural history of substance use, as well as with the risks and consequences of such behavior. She is the co-author of "Friendship Networks, Intimacy, and Illicit Drug Use in Young Adulthood: A Comparison of Two Competing Theories," which appeared in *Criminology* (1991).

Patricia A. King is professor of law at the Georgetown University Law Center. Her fields of interest are law, bioethics, and public policy. Ms.

King has been particularly interested in the implications of race, ethnicity, and gender for policy in the area of human reproduction. She is the author of "The Past as Prologue: Race, Class and Gene Discrimination," to be published in *Using Ethics and Law as Guides*, edited by George Annas and Sherman Elias.

William Kornblum is professor of sociology and director of the Center for Social Research at the Graduate Center, City University of New York. His fields of interest include urban anthropology and youth and social problems. He is the co-editor of *In the Field: Readings in the Field Work Experience*.

Harry G. Levine is associate professor of sociology at Queens College and at the Graduate Center, City University of New York. He has published widely on the history and sociology of alcohol and drugs. He is currently completing a major study on the history of the alcohol question in America and Europe to be published by Basic Books.

Robert J. Levine is a professor of medicine and lecturer in pharmacology at the Yale University School of Medicine. His work has focused on the doctor–patient relationship and the ethics of research involving human subjects. He is the author of "Medical Ethics and Personal Doctors: Conflicts Between What We Teach and What We Want," which appeared in the *Journal of Clinical Ethics* in 1990.

Mark H. Moore is a professor at the John F. Kennedy School of Government at Harvard University. He has spent the past two decades examining drug and crime control policy. He is the co-author of *Beyond 911: A New Era for Policing*.

Gerald M. Oppenheimer is associate professor in the Department of Health and Nutrition Sciences at Brooklyn College, City University of New York. He has been interested in the history of medicine and especially in the history of the HIV epidemic. He is the co-author of "AIDS and the Crisis of Health Insurance," which appeared in *AIDS and Ethics*.

Craig Reinarman is associate professor of sociology at the University of California, Santa Cruz. His field of interest is drug law and policy and the social construction of drug problems. He is co-author of *Cocaine Changes*.

Kenneth E. Warner is professor and chair of the Department of Public Health, University of Michigan. His research has focused on tobacco policy and the economics of health promotion and disease prevention. His "Tobacco Industry Science Advisor: Serving Society or Selling Cigarettes?" appeared in the *American Journal of Public Health* in 1991.

Charles Winick is professor of sociology at the Graduate Center, City University of New York. He has been a student of drug dependence, deviant behavior, and mass communications.

Index